# 3D Studio MAX

for Windows® NT

# f/x

Creating
Hollywood-Style
Special Effects

NIMR

Jon A. Bell

Foreword by Tom Hudson,
3D Studio MAX co-developer

VENTANA

**3D Studio MAX f/x: Creating Hollywood-Style Special Effects**
Copyright ©1996 by Jon A. Bell

**Library of Congress Catalog Card Number: 96-060945**

First Edition  9  8  7  6  5  4  3  2  1

Printed in the United States of America

Ventana Communications Group, Inc.
P.O. Box 13964
Research Triangle Park, NC 27709-3964
919.544.9404
FAX 919.544.9472
http://www.vmedia.com

**Limits of Liability and Disclaimer of Warranty**
The author and publisher of this book have used their best efforts in preparing the book and the programs contained in it. These efforts include the development, research, and testing of the theories and programs to determine their effectiveness. The author and publisher make no warranty of any kind, expressed or implied, with regard to these programs or the documentation contained in this book.

The author and publisher shall not be liable in the event of incidental or consequential damages in connection with, or arising out of, the furnishing, performance or use of the programs, associated instructions and/or claims of productivity gains.

**Trademarks**
Trademarked names appear throughout this book, and on the accompanying compact disk. Rather than list the names and entities that own the trademarks or insert a trademark symbol with each mention of the trademarked name, the publisher states that it is using the names only for editorial purposes and to the benefit of the trademark owner with no intention of infringing upon that trademark.

**President/CEO**
Josef Woodman

**Vice President of Content Development**
Karen A. Bluestein

**Managing Editor**
Lois J. Principe

**Production Manager**
John Cotterman

**Technology Operations Manager**
Kerry L. B. Foster

**Product Marketing Manager**
Jamie Jaeger

**Creative Services Manager**
Diane Lennox

**Art Director**
Marcia Webb

**Acquisitions Editor**
Neweleen A. Trebnik

**Project Editor**
Jennifer Rowe

**Copy Editor**
Susan Christophersen

**Assistant Editor**
Paul Cory

**Technical Director**
Dan Brown

**Technical Editor**
Andrew Reese

**Desktop Publisher**
Jaimie Livingston

**Proofreader**
Meredith Morovati

**Indexer**
Rachel Rice

**Cover Illustrator**
Jon A. Bell

**Cover Designer**
Laura Stalzer

## About the Author

Jon A. Bell is a freelance 3D computer graphics artist and writer. After working 10 years as an editor and writer in the computer magazine industry, Jon changed careers to concentrate full time on producing 3D computer graphics and animation for television, films, computer games, multimedia, and print. He provided animation for the films *Exorcist III: Legion*, *Terminator 2: Judgment Day*, *Honey, I Blew Up the Kid*, and several AutoDesk promotional videotapes. His game industry work includes model designs and animation for LucasArts Entertainments' *X-Wing* and *Rebel Assault*, Sega of America's *Jurassic Park* and *Wild Woody* CD-ROM games, and Gametek's *Robotech*. Jon has worked with 3D Studio since Version 1, and from October 1995 to April 1996 was one of the Yost Group's primary 3D Studio MAX beta testers. You can reach him on CompuServe at 74124,276.

# Acknowledgments

I've long dreamed of writing a book. However, in my fantasies, it's either the standard Great American, Pulitzer-prize-winning, society-altering novel, or else a Hugo Award-winning science fiction book to rival, say, *Dune* or *Childhood's End*.

On the other hand, writing a book on creating special effects (a lifelong love of mine) using Kinetix's 3D Studio MAX (written by good friends of mine) is pretty cool, too. The notion of adding what weird ideas I've developed over the last five years to the general pool of 3DS knowledge was fun. Of course, the paparazzi-drenched, Robert Redford-like fame, and the vast, Sultan of Brunei-like fortune promised me by the project was compelling, as well.

Therefore, when my friends suggested that I turn my 3D Studio and special effects interests into a profitable how-to work, Great Art took a back seat to Great Fun. From that decision comes this book and this unorthodox opening to it. I hope you enjoy reading it as much I, of necessity, had to make myself enjoy writing it.

And, since I fail to subscribe to the French auteur theory, acknowledgments and thanks are due to the many supporting players behind *3D Studio MAX f/x* and my 3D career in general. So, thanks are due to the following:

- My agent Matt Wagner at Waterside Productions; Neweleen Trebnik, Jennifer Rowe, Amy Moyers, Paul Cory, Wendy Bernhardt, and Jaimie Livingston at Ventana.

- Gametek's Tom Reuterdahl, Mimi Doggett, Clifford and Wendy Lau, Ken Cope, and James Green for giving me the moral, software, hardware (and financial!) support to finish this book, and Scot Tumlin, a good friend and CGI artist who wanted to be mentioned here and get an autographed copy (so here you go).

- My developmental editors Andy and Stephanie Reese; their friendship, hard-nosed editing suggestions (and legal advice!) were invaluable.

- Industrial Light and Magic Effects Supervisors John Knoll and Bill George, Model Shop Supervisor John Goodson, and *Star Trek* modelmaker Ed Miarecki, who've provided expert advice to me over the years on both CGI and traditional cinematic effects; Daren Dochterman, Hollywood's Storyboard Artist to the Stars; Michael Spaw, contributor of the "bug ship" on the CD-ROM.
- 3D Studio/DOS and 3D Studio MAX developers Gary Yost, Jack Powell, Dan Silva, Don Brittain, Rolf Berteig and, of course, Tom Hudson.
- My parents, Jim and Bonnie Thomas, back in good ol' Springfield, Missouri; see, I *told* you that my interest in all this weird stuff would pay off.
- A big thank you to Harlean Moraweitz of Typing Aid, Redwood City, California; there's no way I could have written this book without her excellent transcription skills.

Finally, I'd like to thank my beautiful and patient wife Joan Gale Frank, who gave me her encouragement, support, and (occasionally, when I needed it) a swift boot in the buns to make me continue with this project. She had to live with it, and me, every day of its creation, and her contribution to this book, although seemingly hidden, is present on every page.

## Dedication

This book is dedicated to my grandfather, Thomas Milburn Roberts, 1910-1994. You encouraged my creativity throughout my life.

# Contents

# Part II: Optical Effects

# Part III: Modeling Effects

# Part IV: Underwater Effects

# Foreword

**A**s a programmer, one of the most gratifying things you can experience is to see all the varied applications people find for your software. This is particularly true for an application such as 3D Studio MAX, which unlike a word processor or spreadsheet, allows a user to express *visually* just about any concept he or she can dream up. From still-image ad art and TV station "flying logos" to accident reconstructions and 3D cartoons, 3D Studio users have done a tremendous amount of work that allows others to be informed or entertained.

Personally, one of the areas I've been most interested in seeing developed with 3D Studio is special effects work in motion pictures. Until recently, this work has been reserved for dedicated special-effects houses using physical models, blue-screen photography, and expensive optical printers, or millions of dollars worth of extremely powerful computers capable of dealing with the high-resolution imagery required for feature film work.

This is no longer the case. 3D Studio for DOS and 3D Studio MAX have been used to create special effects sequences for several major motion pictures. It's no longer necessary to spend thousands of man-hours building actual models that must be set up on a stage, painstakingly lit, filmed, and composited onto film. One person with an ordinary personal computer can now produce realistic special effects indistinguishable from the real thing, and which in some cases would be impractical—or nearly impossible—to create using physical models.

This was the goal when co-developer Gary Yost and I, way back in 1985, set out on the path that eventually led to 3D Studio MAX—to give ordinary people the ability to create photorealistic images with a personal computer. It's taken almost eleven years to get to this point, but it's been worth it. Just about every day, there are new examples of fabulous animations created with 3D Studio MAX available via the Internet and other online services. And perhaps the most exciting thing about all this is that many of these animations are the work of Jon Bell, author of this book and one of my best friends for more than twenty years.

In high school, Jon and I talked about how great it would be to get into the world of special effects and create our own *Star Wars* or *Close Encounters of the Third Kind*. At the time, it seemed like an impossible dream. Now, Jon's doing just that every day with 3D Studio MAX. In this book, he shares the knowledge and experience he's gained over the years to help others do the same.

Making dreams come true. In the world of software development, it doesn't get much better than that.

Tom Hudson
3D Studio/DOS and 3D Studio MAX Co-developer
Port Washington, WI
May 26, 1996

# Introduction

The other day, as I was working on a 3D Studio MAX scene of a deep-space vista, my wife, Joan, smiled and said to me, "You know, what's most unusual about you, Jon, is that you're not interested in what *is*. You're mostly interested in what *isn't*."

What my wife said was true. Ever since I was a little kid, I've been captivated by the imaginary worlds, mythical creatures, and wondrous vehicles that have been depicted on film through the magic of special visual effects.

Pardon me as I whip you through 30 years of history in a couple of pages. Way back in 1966, when I was five years old, I would sit on the floor of my grandparents' house, munch Cap'n Crunch cereal, and gaze, mesmerized, at the exotic goings-on that unreeled on their old black-and-white Philco television. I watched as the crew of the original "Star Trek" fired their phasers at lizardy Gorns and beamed up from alien planets in what looked like to me at the time a spray of water droplets glistening in the sun.

I gaped as Captain Crane, Admiral Nelson, and the crew of the mighty Seaview did battle with underwater dangers in "Voyage to the Bottom of the Sea." I marveled at Tony and Doug, tumbling end-over-end through shimmering time (or, at least, through a bunch of 20th Century Fox stock footage) in "The Time Tunnel." Each show possessed enough cool gadgets, spaceships, submarines, monsters, and robots to hold me in its spell...and make me completely oblivious to how the orange corn-and-sugar cereal chunks were shredding my upper palate.

Jump forward almost a decade to 1975, as my best high-school friend Tom Hudson (you may know the name) and I watched the premiere of a syndicated British show called "Space: 1999." In it, so many cool spacecrafts fired laser beams and blew up in showers of glittering sparks that I not only ignored cereal-induced soft tissue damage, I forgot about other minor things, such as, oh, dating girls and making perfunctory stabs at completing high school homework.

In the summer of 1977, *Star Wars* hit the theaters, and its rapid-fire presentation of far-off vistas, alien beings, and space battles blew me right out of my Qiana shirt and polyester pants. (Hey, it was 1977, remember!) For the next two years, Tom and I worked on creating our own bizarre worlds via a Super-8 science fiction spoof called "Buck Cosmo, Space Ranger." This proposed half-hour film (never completed, alas) was to feature almost 100 special-effects shots ranging from laser beams to planets and asteroid storms. We built miniature sets, double-exposed starfields and spaceships, painted planet artwork, and built rear-projection screens. We even constructed an entire spaceship cockpit in Tom's basement; cheap wood paneling, glass marbles, and Christmas tree bulbs led our way to the stars.

Fast-forward five years to 1982, and Tom (as chief programmer) and I (as managing editor) were working in Massachusetts at *A.N.A.L.O.G. Computing*, a magazine devoted to Atari 400 and 800 computers, and, later, to the Atari ST series. I began playing with rudimentary computer graphics programs on these machines; Tom began honing his considerable programming skills developing 2D paint and 3D modeling and animation routines. In our spare time, we built conventional models and experimented with special effects photography, both computer-generated and cinematic-style, as Chapter 2, "Saucer Attack," describes. We even shot wireframe graphics off an Atari monitor, clicking off Super-8 frames one at a time in our attempt to simulate the graphics in *Alien*, *Tron*, and *2010*.

In the intervening decade from 1985 to 1995, I left *A.N.A.L.O.G.*, moved to San Francisco, worked on various computer magazines, and played around with increasingly powerful and exciting computer graphics programs. I eventually left the publishing industry for the computer games industry; the career switch enabled me to concentrate full time on computer graphics and animation. (I also got around to dating and even got married to the lovely, aforementioned Joan. Computer graphics and science fiction don't completely destroy your ability to get a life, but they help, if that's the term.)

During that same period, Tom Hudson became an independent software developer. He wrote the number-one-selling paint program for the Atari ST, DEGAS, and began casting around for other projects. (He also diversified into other interests, such as getting married and doing massive house restoration, but that's another story.) In 1985, Tom met up with Gary Yost, founder of Antic Software, and they developed CAD 3-D, Cyber Studio, CyberSculpt, and a bunch of 3D plug-ins for the Atari ST.

After the success of these projects, Gary was approached by Autodesk, which wanted to market the next generation of 3D software for IBM PC compatibles. Subsequently, Tom became one of the primary developers for a program that we're all fans of: Autodesk's 3D Studio, and its newest incarnation: Kinetix 3D Studio MAX. 3D Studio has enabled thousands of people to visualize what heretofore was possible only in their imaginations, or from artists working for multimillion-dollar special-effects houses. This kind of power has enabled artists and architects, dabblers and dreamers to create their own realities, both ordinary or supernatural, right on their desktops.

As my wife pointed out, I've always seemed to be interested not in what is, but in what *isn't*. And when she made her comment the other day, I looked up from my Video Post settings, which displayed layers of stars, spacecraft, nebula, and other optical effects to composite, and I thought for a moment. Then I said, "You know, you're right. But what's important now is that I can not only imagine that place or thing that isn't, but I can go to it—or make it come to me. I can make it real." Then I went back to thinking up the most spectacular way to blow up a spaceship in the scene.

That's the real power of CGI (computer generated imagery) and especially 3D Studio MAX—they can make the unreal tangible, and take the average—and not-so-average—computer user to whatever place he or she can imagine.

Thanks to Gary Yost, Jack Powell, Dan Silva, Don Brittain, Rolf Berteig, and Gus Grubba, but thanks most especially to my good friend Tom Hudson. Thanks for giving me—and thousands of other people—not just the ability to *imagine* these fantastic worlds, but to *create* them.

Jon A. Bell
San Francisco, CA
May 26, 1996

# Part I

# An Introduction to Special Effects

# 1

# The Resurgence of Special Effects

If you were lucky enough (or old enough!) to have seen *Star Wars* in the theaters during its original run, then you'll probably never forget the opening shot, as the Imperial Star Destroyer chases down Princess Leia's rebel cruiser and cripples it with a fusillade of laser bolts. (In February of 1997, you can see it again in theaters, as LucasFilm Ltd. re-releases the film with THX sound and digitally enhanced visual effects.) From the TIE fighter attacks to the final assault on the Deathstar, the high quality and sheer range of the special effects in that movie—more than 350 shots in all—set a standard that hadn't been seen since 1968, when *2001: A Space Odyssey* premiered.

Six months after *Star Wars*, in December of 1977, *Close Encounters of the Third Kind* opened and the depictions of glowing UFOs wowed audiences all over the world. I still remember the collective gasp that went up from the audience as the Mothership, in a blaze of color and light, turned over in front of Devil's Tower.

The phenomenal box-office success of *Star Wars* and *Close Encounters* paved the way for more films that offered effects-laden spectacle and adventure. Indeed, of the top 10 highest-grossing films of all time, only one—*Home Alone*—doesn't use elaborate optical effects to help create the "world" portrayed in the film.

To refresh everyone's memory, here's the list of the top ten highest-grossing films as of May 1996. (Note that this list represents U.S. gross ticket receipts in millions and has been adjusted for inflation. In terms of gross dollar amount, *Jurassic Park* is acknowledged as the number one worldwide box office champ.)

| Rank | Gross (millions) | Movie | Year Released |
|------|------------------|-------|---------------|
| 1. | $407 | E.T. | 1982 |
| 2. | $357 | Jurassic Park | 1993 |
| 3. | $327 | Forrest Gump | 1994 |
| 4. | $323 | Star Wars | 1977 |
| 5. | $313 | The Lion King | 1994 |
| 6. | $285 | Home Alone | 1990 |
| 7. | $264 | Return of the Jedi | 1983 |
| 8. | $260 | Jaws | 1975 |
| 9. | $251 | Batman | 1989 |
| 10. | $242 | Raiders of the Lost Ark | 1981 |

As you can see, most of these films showcase complex (and in some cases, revolutionary) special effects. (Even the cel-animated *Lion King* used computer graphics imagery (CGI) to create the wildebeest stampede sequence.) More important, though, many films have relied increasingly on CGI to realize their out-of-this world visions, with certain films pioneering groundbreaking digital techniques.

*Young Sherlock Holmes* (1986), produced by Stephen Spielberg, marked the first use of a computer-generated character in a film (the hallucination sequence featuring a knight made from stained glass). The George Lucas production of *Willow* (1987) marked the first use of morphing in a motion picture. (Morphing is the effect of an object transforming smoothly into another. Personal computer users can now duplicate this effect by using software that costs less than $500.)

The pseudopod in *The Abyss* (1989) and the murderous chrome T-1000 in *Terminator 2* (1991) upped the ante, with the former featuring a photorealistic fantasy being made of water and the latter taking morphing to its extreme.

Without question, the next watershed was Spielberg's 1993 blockbuster *Jurassic Park*. Effects artisans at Industrial Light and Magic, armed with more than 200 Silicon Graphics workstations, Softimage, Alias, and numerous proprietary software routines, created 65 awesome CGI shots of dinosaurs interacting with humans. All were produced with breathtaking realism.

More recent films have showcased digital effects ranging from disquieting, erasing actor Gary Sinise's legs in 1994's *Forrest Gump*, to creating a stampede of jungle animals in *Jumanji* (1995), and on to the outrageous cartoon antics of *The Mask* (1994) and *Casper* (1995).

On the television front, producers have found that CGI enables them to produce spectacular yet cost-effective imagery on a weekly basis. Television shows such as "Babylon 5," "Star Trek: Deep Space Nine," and "Star Trek: Voyager" have used networks of relatively low-cost personal computers and off-the-shelf software to expand dramatically the scope of their series.

No reason exists, of course, to prevent us from attempting to duplicate (or even surpass) the efforts listed previously. All it takes is the right hardware, such as a well-equipped Pentium PC; the right software, such as 3D Studio MAX; and a smattering of imagination and inspiration. This book, I hope, will serve as your catalyst.

So . . . let's get started. Let's take our computers where they haven't gone before.

## About the Book

The intent of *3D Studio MAX f/x* is to introduce readers to creating Hollywood-style special visual effects using Kinetix 3D Studio MAX itself—additional plug-ins aren't required (unless you want to incorporate them into your effects). This book discusses how you can duplicate the effects you've seen in various Hollywood movies and TV shows, such as *Star Wars*, the *Star Trek* films and TV series, and "Babylon 5."

Therefore, this book is geared primarily to those 3D Studio MAX users who have an interest in special visual effects, particularly the unusual and otherworldly. It is *not* intended as an exhaustive tutorial on every capability found in 3D Studio MAX (the tutorials bundled with the software already do a pretty good job of that). Nor is it intended specifically for architects, forensic animators, or those users who need to duplicate reality in a precise way, although certain techniques discussed here may be useful in augmenting their work.

*3D Studio MAX f/x* is designed for seasoned 3D Studio Release 4 for DOS users, and those people wishing to "translate" their 3D Studio/DOS experience into the MAX realm. (*Some* of the techniques described here may also be created in the DOS versions of 3D Studio, although you may have to do some creative workarounds to produce the same effects.)

To get the most from this book, you need to have completed the tutorials included with 3D Studio MAX. In addition, having solid experience with 3D Studio/DOS is helpful, as well as experience with some of its more common plug-ins, such as The Yost Group's Disks 1-7, especially the VAPOR and FLAME routines, and Digimation's LenZFX and Inferno.

The effects discussed here range from creating believable outer space and underwater  environments to manipulating the elements therein. The chapters cover a wide range of optical effects, such as laser beams, nebulas, force fields, explosions, solar flares, and so on. The book discusses how you can use 3D Studio MAX's powerful Object Modifiers to build complex shapes quickly. It also covers 3D Studio MAX's new rendering features, such as environmental mapping, volumetric fog and lighting, and advanced texture-mapping techniques using the powerful new 3D Studio MAX Material Editor.

To present these effects, *3D Studio MAX f/x* is divided into four sections, covering deep space and underwater effects. In each section, a series of rendered scenes illustrates the effects. Each major element in the sequences, such as the laser beams in the space battle scenes, is explained in its own chapter, along with suggestions to the reader for customizing the effects.

Accompanying this book is a standard ISO 9660-format CD-ROM, located in a sleeve on the inside back cover. This CD-ROM contains all of the example animations and images contained in the book, as well as models, scenes, materials, material libraries, and Video Post .VPX files used to create the effects described here. The CD-ROM also includes more than 300 megabytes of original texture maps, distributed royalty-free and immediately available for your personal use. Finally, the CD-ROM also contains a free 3D Studio MAX plug-in: Rolf Berteig's Combustion.

My intention is to present a series of interesting, yet relatively easy-to-create effects from which 3D Studio users can learn, and that also serve as inspiration for your own experimentation. Have fun!

## Getting the Most From 3D Studio MAX f/x

All of the special effects techniques in this book require only 3D Studio MAX itself and the plug-ins on the *3D Studio MAX f/x CD-ROM*; you do not have to buy additional plug-ins. Most of the techniques discussed here involve creating the effects with 3D Studio MAX's core feature set "in-camera"—creating elaborate opticals without the use of third-party plug-ins or extensive image processing in Video Post.

To get the most out of this book, however, having a few other programs in your 3D toolbox is helpful. For instance, virtually every 3D animator today owns a paint and/or image compositing program (many people have several different types) that produces

24-bit images with an added alpha channel. Such programs as Autodesk Animator Studio, Adobe Photoshop, and/or Hi-res QFX are absolutely necessary for creating and retouching texture maps and in manipulating final rendered 3D scenes. The layering features of these 24-bit programs are invaluable in compositing pre-rendered 3D imagery, especially for print. Although you can use 8-bit programs such as Autodesk Animator Pro to create simple maps, for photorealistic textures, 24-bit images are the way to go.

Even Animator Pro still has many uses, such as creating flic files for animated materials, grayscale masks, bump, shininess, and opacity maps. It's also fun to take a flic file, change its palette to 256 levels of gray, and then force a bizarrely colored palette to it. This can produce effects ranging from liquid crystal photography to thermographs and *Predator*-style alien vision.

On the hardware side, because you're running 3D Studio MAX, you should also have the most powerful PC you can afford. Kinetix recommends that you have a Pentium (or Pentium-equivalent) PC with at least 32 megabytes of RAM, a 1-gigabyte hard disk drive or larger, a CD-ROM drive, and a 24-bit video display card (preferably one with 2-4 megabytes of onboard video memory).

Unlike its 3D Studio DOS ancestor, however, 3D Studio MAX running under Windows NT takes advantage of symmetric multi-processing (SMP) via multi-threading; that is, it can use multiple CPUs to perform its tasks. If you can afford a dual-CPU computer or motherboard (either a Pentium or Pentium Pro), you'll notice a large increase in both final rendering speed and screen redraws in the user interface.

And, speaking of screen redraws, another nifty piece of hardware that 3D Studio MAX can use is a graphics accelerator card. Such cards as the 3Demon from Omnicomp Graphics Corporation, the Sapphire from Fujitsu, and other cards based on the GLint chip technology can increase the interactivity of your PC to rival that of a Silicon Graphics workstation. See Appendix D, "3D Studio MAX Resources," for more information.

## Other Visual Effects References

Besides 3D Studio MAX's reference manuals, other books exist to help you produce better animations. Being a good computer animator means that you should also be a good filmmaker in general. Too often, computer animators get seduced by the near-instant gratification of being able to create their own desktop movies. They then go on to create animations that ignore the cinematic language that filmmakers have developed over the last 100 years.

Consequently, a good place to start is in the film, theatre, and video reference section of a good bookstore or your local library. Books on classical animation techniques, set design, cinematography, direction, lighting, and editing are all useful for 3D animators. (And, of course, nothing prevents you from checking out the latest in computer graphics books, too.) The manuals for your existing 3D and 2D software tools are useful, as are "how-to" software books in the computer section of your local bookstore.

Although it was written for 3D Studio/DOS, *Inside 3D Studio Version 4* from New Riders Publishing is not just an exhaustive manual on 3D Studio/DOS, but it also covers general 3D techniques, lighting, and materials editing as well. Other 3D Studio/ DOS books include CD-ROMs with numerous texture maps that you can easily employ in your 3D Studio MAX animations.

An increasing number of magazines are devoted to computer graphics in film and video production; some of the magazines feature extensive coverage of 3D Studio/DOS (and will cover 3D Studio MAX as well). Such magazines as *Computer Graphics World* (CGW), *3D Artist*, *AV/Video*, *Digital Video*, *Computer Artist*, *Morph's Outpost*, and *Digital Imaging* all cover CGI; *Planet Studio* covers 3D Studio exclusively. You can find these magazines at a good newsstand or perhaps at your local library. All of them also offer subscriptions, some of them free to qualified individuals. (If you attend the annual SIGGRAPH computer graphics trade show, you can often find booths where subscriptions to these magazines are free of charge.)

Several good publications cater to filmmakers with an interest in special effects techniques. Magazines such as *Cinefex*, *Cinefantastique*, and *American Cinematographer* offer behind-the-scenes looks at films that have special visual effects. The in-depth coverage in *Cinefex*, for example, is absolutely invaluable to special-effects artists.

For more information, check out Appendix D, "3D Studio MAX Resources," and Appendix D, "Special Effects, Animation & Filmmaking Resources," at the end of this book.

## 3D Studio MAX Forums Online

Another excellent place to get first-hand information on 3D Studio MAX is by using online services. Several newsgroups are on the Internet that discuss computer graphics and animation; you can also find newsgroups, such as comp.graphics.packages.3dstudio, and Web pages devoted specifically to 3D Studio/DOS and 3D Studio MAX. (For more information, use the Search features of your newsreader software or your Net browser. Just type **3D STUDIO** and see what's out there.) The newsgroups feature ongoing discussion and debate about their particular topics, and are also a good resource if you have questions about 3D Studio/DOS, 3D Studio MAX, or related software and hardware.

Probably the best source for 3D Studio information is the Kinetix Forum on the CompuServe Information Service. Technical support personnel from Autodesk's Kinetix subsidiary frequent the forum regularly and are available to answer questions. In addition, third-party vendors who provide supplemental tools for 3D Studio also have a strong presence on the forum. Programmers, animators, and hardware experts are always available to help you with your 3D Studio needs.

To find the forum, just type **GO KINETIX** at any CompuServe prompt.

## On the *3D Studio MAX f/x* CD-ROM

In the back of this book is a CD-ROM that contains the .MAX scene files, texture maps, and meshes used to create all of the special effects described here. The CD-ROM contains animation files in 24-bit .AVI format for the demonstration animations. The files for the particular effects are in separate directories on the CD-ROM.

You do not need to install the .MAX files from the *3D Studio MAX f/x CD-ROM* onto your hard drive. If you load the .MAX files directly into 3D Studio MAX, the program will add the proper CD-ROM directories to the 3D Studio MAX Map Paths list automatically. Due to the size of the demo animation files, however, you will probably want to copy them into your 3DSMAX\IMAGES directory and play them back from your hard drive to get better playback speed.

Also on the *3D Studio MAX f/x CD-ROM* is a large assortment of still and animated texture maps from my personal collection. Some of these maps are featured on the various models used in this book. Of course many of them started life as scanned photos of real-world industrial textures, which I then manipulated in Adobe Photoshop. Many of the textures have been created with an eye toward the industrial; they can serve to decorate your own highly detailed spaceship skins, futuristic factory walls, robot bodies, and the like (even though the source material often originated from photos of dumpsters and earth-moving equipment).

The majority of the textures are 24-bit color Targa files at 640 x 480 pixel resolution; the textures span a wide variety of colors. These images are designed to serve as a kit that you can alter and manipulate endlessly to create new materials. (For instance, if you wish to place a wide red stripe down the body of a spaceship, you might select a strip of the red CLEMBOX1.TGA material, which you then paste across ALUMINM6.TGA.) Other textures, including 8-bit flics and .AVIs, .GIF images, and .CELs have been included at varying resolutions and with varying color palettes, including grayscale. You can use many of these textures as bump, shininess, opacity, alpha, and reflection maps.

The texture maps are all found in the \MAPS directory; many of them are found in the respective CD-ROM chapter directories as well. (Although you can use the textures in your own projects, you may not resell or distribute them.)

A sampling of some of the maps is shown in the Color Gallery section in the middle of this book.

## 3D Studio MAX f/x Online Updates

The inescapable truth about the Internet is that it changes constantly. I've tried to make this book as up-to-date as possible concerning online resources for 3D Studio MAX. However, new Internet sites will certainly appear (and some may disappear) between the time of this writing and the time of this book's publication. Ventana provides an excellent way to combat this problem and keep the information in this book constantly updated—The 3D Studio MAX f/x Online Updates. Access this resource at Ventana's World Wide Web site, and you'll find updated material relevent to this book. This includes WWW sites of companies and individuals offering hardware, plug-in software, and services supporting 3D Studio MAX users. In addition, the 3D Studio MAX f/x Online Updates will feature additional texture maps, Material Library Settings, and model files for you to play with.

To get to the Online Updater, aim your browser at http:// www.vmedia.com/updates.html.

## Getting Started

The tutorials in *3D Studio MAX f/x* are divided into four major sections.

Part I, "An Introduction to Special Effects," gives a brief history of special visual effects. It then presents a look at how 3D Studio MAX co-creator Tom Hudson and I created a flying saucer effects still using conventional techniques, and how you can duplicate this shot using 3D Studio MAX. Finally, it discusses how I developed the space battle sequences that illustrate much of the book's effects. In Chapter 3, "Setting Up Your Scene," I discuss how I created the space battle scenes, from outline, script, and storyboards to the final rendering.

Part II, "Optical Effects," begins the coverage of the space effects and discusses starfields, nebula effects, suns, warp drive, tachyon torpedoes, and laser beams.

Part III, "Modeling Effects," continues the space effects discussion and covers planets, asteroids, and asteroid fields.

Finally, Part IV, "Underwater Effects," shows you how to create an underwater scene from start to finish. The effects include hydro-dynamic haze (murkiness, in other words), rippling underwater surfaces, caustic light patterns, volumetric light rays, plankton, bubbles, and even a swimming shark. It culminates with a look at all of these effects combined in a scene that features the Diving Bell from the 1960s TV series "Voyage to the Bottom of the Sea."

Each section covers a series of shots that illustrate the variety of effects described. The demonstration animations are included on the CD-ROM as .AVI files; all of them are rendered at 320 x 240 resolution. In addition, numerous frames from the sequences, as well as still images, are included as 24-bit, 640 x 480 TGA files. As you follow along with the instructions in each chapter, you will be either viewing or loading pertinent images, mesh, and/or scene files from the CD-ROM.

## The CD-ROM & Its Directories

The CD-ROM contains the following directories:

\CHAP_02 through \CHAP_27

These directories correspond to the tutorials presented in Chapters 2 through 27. They contain not only the scene files and textures required for each chapter's tutorial, but the figure renderings as well.

| | |
|---|---|
| \COMBUSTN | \MESHES |
| \DIVEBELL | \SCENES |
| \MAPS | \SPACEBTL |
| \MATLIBS | |

In addition, the texture maps presented in the various Chapter directories are also duplicated in the \MAPS directory. You can use 3D Studio MAX's File/Configure Paths option to let 3D Studio MAX load any maps you need from the correct directories of the *3D Studio MAX f/x CD-ROM*.

*Note: All of the maps you need for the tutorials are contained in their respective \CHAPTER directories, as well as in the \MAPS directory of your 3D Studio MAX f/x CD-ROM. To make sure you have access to all the maps on the CD-ROM, load 3D Studio MAX, select File/Configure Paths, and manually add the 3D Studio MAX f/x CD-ROM \MAPS directory to your map paths.*

*Note: All the tutorials and screen shots presented in 3D Studio MAX f/x use the 3D Studio MAX defaults present when you first install the program. If you have altered your keyboard hotkey assignments or other user-customizable features of the user interface (such as the viewport and grid colors, or the Modifiers section of the Modify Command Panel), you may find that some of the instructions presented here do not correspond precisely with your 3D Studio MAX desktop layout. If you wish, you can change most of your default screen settings back by using the File/Preferences Panel. Please see your 3D Studio MAX manuals for further information on configuring your program layout.*

## Moving On

In the next chapter, you'll take a look at how 3D Studio MAX co-creator Tom Hudson and I created a simple "flying saucer" special-effects shot using conventional photographic techniques. Then, in the second half of the chapter, you'll dip your toes in your first 3D Studio MAX tutorial and see how to recreate the flying saucer shot in the digital realm.

# 2

# Saucer Attack

**B**efore you delve into the major tutorial sections, take a quick look at an old-style special effects technique that I bring up-to-date in 3D Studio MAX. This discussion of old-style optical effects is designed to whet your appetite and show you how knowledge of conventional visual effects can help you in planning and executing your own modern CGI effects.

## The Fakery Is Out There

In the spring of 1984, 3D Studio MAX co-creator Tom Hudson and I decided to create a "faked UFO" photograph for our own amusement (and as gifts for strange friends). To start the project, I went out and shot 35mm color slides of open grassy fields in western Massachusetts. For the best results, I waited until the sun was directly overhead because I wanted a distinct shadow on the ground beneath the "saucer." This would help sell the idea that the saucer was actually hovering over the field. I then developed the pictures and got to work.

To create our UFO, we modified a Monogram plastic model kit of the flying saucer that appeared in the 1967–69 TV series "The Invaders." The modifications consisted of carefully cutting out the window and landing light areas, backing them with colored plastic, and putting tiny "grain-of-wheat" bulbs in the model. (These provided the on-board, or "practical" lighting.) The power connector for the lights protruded from the back of the saucer. We then went to a hardware store, bought a few odds and ends, and in one weekend assembled the setup and did the photography of the effect.

Even though the effects techniques that we used seem primitive by today's standards, the setup was inexpensive and easy to create. More important, however, it illustrates several concepts that reveal not only how traditional cinematic effects have been done for decades, but how these time-tested concepts can lend themselves to "creative problem-solving" when wrestling with 3D computer imagery.

## Setting Up the Shot

The illustration in Figure 2-1 shows the simple rear-screen setup for the final effects shot shown in Figure 2-2. The setup consisted of a sheet of window glass with the "Invaders" saucer model attached to a plastic mount hidden behind the craft; this was epoxied to the glass. A piece of frosted acetate film swung down from the back of the glass and served as a rear-projection screen. A 35mm slide projector approximately 10 feet behind the screen held various landscape slides that we had shot a few weeks earlier; we had composed the images to allow for the saucer's inclusion. Finally, a soft oval of black India ink airbrushed onto the glass served as the saucer's shadow. When backlit by the slide projector, the landscape image bled through the shadow ink somewhat, causing it to appear slightly translucent and thus heightening the effect.

Figure 2-1: *A simplified version of the setup for the original flying saucer effects shot.*

The shot called for three different exposures on the same piece of film to produce the final effect. The camera used was a 35mm Minolta SLR equipped with a standard 49mm lens; the stock was Kodak Kodachrome ASA 25 color slide film. We followed these steps:

1. We shut off all room lights and saucer practical (onboard) lighting, swung the rear screen down, and projected a slide of a grassy field onto the acetate. We then exposed one frame of film. During this pass, the unlit saucer appeared only as a silhouette—a hold-out matte for the beauty pass, next. (This matte was the analog equivalent of today's CGI alpha channel. I talk more about that in a later chapter.)

2. We swung the acetate out of the way (revealing black cloth far behind the glass setup), turned off the projector, and turned on two movie lights above the saucer. However, when we looked through the camera viewfinder, we were surprised by the

results. We had planned for the saucer to be a very bright object in the scene. Because the skin of the saucer was a shiny chrome silver, the movie lights showed up simply as two hot spots, although they were only a foot or so away. The rest of the saucer was dark, even though it was supposed to be hovering in an open field in broad daylight.

The problem was that the actual surroundings of the ship model *were* dark—the ship was simply reflecting the black cloth hung around the setup. Reflectivity is, of course, a quality. Even though we may tend to think of chrome objects as bright, they don't have a high ambient value as brightly colored or self-illuminated objects would.

After thinking about the problem for a few minutes, we hit upon the solution. To produce the illusion that the saucer was reflecting the sky shown in the background slide, we had to duplicate the environment into which we were placing the ship.

To fix the problem, we placed a piece of blue acetate above the saucer (off-camera), with frosted acetate cut-outs representing vague cloud shapes. The movie lights illuminated this artificial sky, which the saucer then reflected, causing it to appear bright in the scene. A polarizing filter on the camera lens helped kill unwanted reflections from the glass.

After we had approved the look through the camera viewfinder, we were back in business. We then did the second exposure, or beauty pass, which filled in the black hold-out matte described previously.

3. For the final exposure, we shut off all lights in the scene and attached a wire to the power connector in the back of the saucer, opposite of camera view. This illuminated a set of "practical" lights onboard the saucer, such as the green strip lights on top and the red and blue landing lights on the bottom. These lights, the only illumination in this pass, helped to "burn in" the colors but did not reveal any other details, such as the power wire running from out of scene to the ship. The final effect is shown in Figure 2-2.

Figure 2-2: *The finished 35mm composite.*

Although the effect achieved in Figure 2-2 is relatively convincing, note the graininess of the background due to the rephotography of the 35mm rear-projection. Also, note the circular drop-off in background illumination around the edges of the image. This was caused by both the rear projector and the light-gathering properties of the 49mm SLR camera lens used to photograph the scene.

## Historic Techniques

Although the techniques that we used were surprisingly simple, Hollywood effects personnel have used variations of these techniques since the earliest days of cinema. All the components are here: multiple exposures and mattes that build up layers of imagery on the same piece of film. Even in the original version of *Star*

*Wars*, the basic techniques of optical mattes and compositing were the same; they were simply augmented with computer-controlled, motor-driven cameras capable of precise, repeatable movements.

This shot and technique does have drawbacks, of course. In this image, a fair amount of light drops off around the edges of the image, due both to the conical beam of the rear projection, and the distance and focal length of the lens used to rephotograph the scene. (We used a standard 49mm lens from a distance of about 8 feet. Later experiments showed that a longer lens, such as an 85mm, shot from a greater distance helped mitigate the drop-off.)

In addition, we faced the problem with which everyone using rear-screen projection has dealt: rephotographing an existing image (such as the background "plate") adds graininess and contrast to the background. Because we were controlling the exposures, we lessened this somewhat by using the slowest-speed, finest-grain 35mm film available at the time. Ideally, the background plate should always be shot on higher-resolution film than the stock used to rephotograph the scene.

## In the Digital Domain

With today's computer graphics, you can eliminate the analog effects problems that Tom and I encountered a dozen years ago. (You wouldn't necessarily even have to use a 3D program to create a UFO shot as I described. For a still image, you could take photographed elements, such as the background and the saucer image, digitize them, and then composite them using Adobe Photoshop.)

However, with 3D programs such as 3D Studio MAX, you have greater flexibility in composing your shot, and you can create animations, of course. In the 3D realm, you can rerender and rephotograph digitally-created "rear-screens" as many times as you want, with absolutely no loss in quality. You can assign reflectivity and other textural qualities to your objects, and determine how much and what type of backgrounds will be reflected.

The camera in your 3D scene doesn't have to be stationary; as a digital motion control camera, you can run it through your scene as many times as you like, photographing whatever elements are present, and the camera viewpoint and physical position can remain in perfect registration, as shown in Figure 2-3. Objects in your 3D scene either need no mattes at all or can be generated automatically if you use alpha channels. You can load digitized video plates in the background of your scene and then do a "matched move" on the background with your 3D camera, synching up the foreground 3D objects with the "real" background. Finally, you can add as many layers of objects as you want via Video Post compositing techniques—the ultimate optical printer—as shown in Figure 2-4.

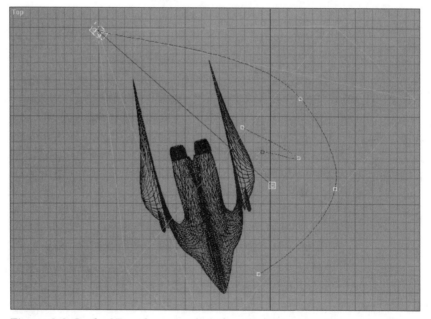

Figure 2-3: *In the 3D realm, your digital camera can move along any path as many times as necessary for you to create your effect.*

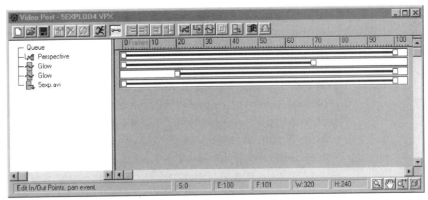

Figure 2-4: *3D Studio MAX's Video Post feature acts as a digital compositor for your 3D elements.*

Sounds easy? Well, it is—with 3D Studio MAX. You can recreate this effect, but this time, in the digital realm.

## "The Invaders" MAX Style

Now you'll duplicate the effects that I just discussed, but you'll create them in 3D Studio MAX. By using MAX's advanced texture mapping, materials editing, and rendering capabilities, you can duplicate the "Invaders" shot in the digital realm on your desktop. You can also take advantage of capabilities present in 3D Studio MAX that 3D Studio/DOS lacked, such as the capability to force shadows onto matte objects.

The following steps will get you started.

1. Load 3D Studio MAX. If necessary, you may need to reset it to the factory defaults to correspond to the images shown in Figures 2-5 through 2-12.

2. From the \CHAP_02 directory of your *3D Studio MAX f/x CD-ROM*, load SAUCER_1.MAX. After the file loads, your screen should look something like Figure 2-5.

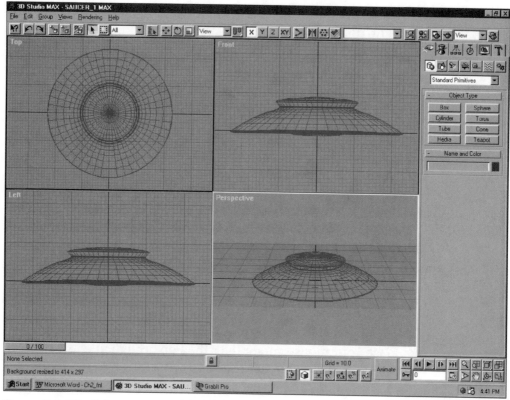

Figure 2-5: *The flying saucer model loaded into 3D Studio MAX.*

For copyright reasons, I'm not using a duplicate of the 1967 "Invaders" flying saucer, but a simplified original design for your updated shot. (Presumably, the Invaders have traded up for a sportier model.)

## Background Check

The first thing that you need to do is load the background that you're going to use for this flying saucer shot, as accomplished in the following steps:

1. Select Environment from the Rendering menu. In the Environment dialog, click on the Assign button to the right of Environment Map. The Material/Map Browser dialog appears.

2. Under Browse From, select New. In the list window to the right, double-click on Bitmap, and the Environment dialog reappears.

3. In the Environment dialog is the notation Map #1 (Bitmap). Click on this button. In the resulting dialog, click on Slot #2, then on OK. This will now assign the background texture map to Slot #2 in the Material Editor. Click the Window Close [X] button.

*Although you've set up your scene to load a background image, you first want to see what it will look like in your Perspective viewport. 3D Studio MAX lets you view a still image or a single frame of an animated sequence in the background of your viewports. By loading and viewing a pre-rendered background in your 3D scene, you can more easily tie your foreground objects and animations to the action present in the background imagery. This capability—called* rotoscoping—*lets 3D Studio MAX users tie 3D animation to match exactly the movement present in a digitized, real-world background.*

4. Place your mouse cursor over the Perspective title in the viewport and right-click. Turn on Show Background in the dialog and turn off Show Grid, so that you can see the background more clearly in this viewport.

5. Select Background Image from the Views menu. Then, under Background Source, click on Files. From the \CHAP_02 directory of your *3D Studio MAX f/x CD-ROM*, load FIELD640.TGA.

   Since you are going to be rendering your test image at 640 x 480 pixel resolution and the background image is already at 640 x 480 pixel resolution, you can leave the background Aspect Ratio settings as they are. However, make sure Display Background is checked, then click on OK. The FIELD640.TGA image appears in the background of your Perspective viewport, as shown in Figure 2-6.

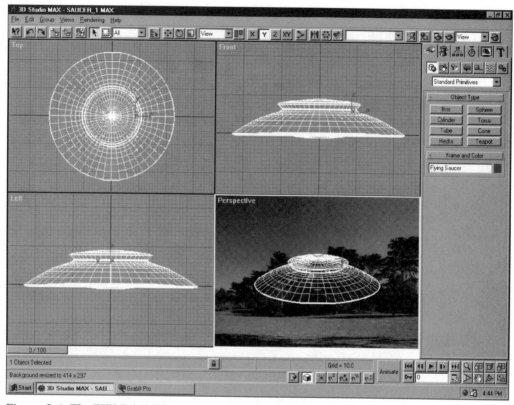

Figure 2-6: *The FIELD640.TGA image loaded as a visible background in the Perspective viewport.*

Note that, in this image, the flying saucer is positioned incorrectly in the scene. You'll fix that in a moment.

6. Click on the Material Editor icon to bring up the Material Editor. Notice that, in the Material Editor Slot #2, the sample sphere is black.

7. Click on Slot #2 to make it the active material. In the rollout menu at the bottom of the Material Editor screen is the Bitmap Parameters rollout for Map #2. You'll want to load the same FIELD640.TGA that you're displaying in the background of

your Perspective window as your Environmental background. (Simply displaying a particular background image in a viewport is not the same as loading it as an Environmental background; you must do the latter if you want to have the bitmap appear in the background of your rendered scene.)

8. First, take a look at the texture filtering. The default is Pyramidal. For the best antialiasing quality in your final output, use Summed Area texture filtering. For instructional purposes, however, you can leave this set at Pyramidal.

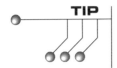

**TIP** For more information on texture filtering, see section 24-26, "Choosing Filtering for Bitmaps," *3D Studio MAX User's Guide, Volume 2.*

9. Now, double-click on the Bitmap name button to bring up the Texture Image File menu, and load FIELD640.TGA from the \CHAP_02 directory of your *3D Studio MAX f/x CD-ROM.*

10. When you return to the Material Editor, the file is loaded on the sample sphere in Slot #2. However, the file may look somewhat strange because the texture coordinates being used for the Environmental map default to Spherical mapping. You want to change this to Screen—a flat background image—because you're simply going to render a still image with no camera movement.

11. Move your mouse cursor until you see the small hand cursor, then drag the Bitmap Parameters rollout down (if necessary) until you see the rollout under the Coordinates menu. To change the Environmental Mapping from Spherical environment to Screen, click on the Down arrow to the right of Spherical Environment, scroll down to Screen, and click on it to replace Spherical Environment in the Mapping Coordinates box. When you do so, you will see the FIELD640.TGA image appear flat on the sample sphere in Slot #2. This texture map now appears properly as the background for the final rendered image.

## After Much Reflection . . .

Now you'll want to alter the material on your flying saucer to reflect its surroundings. To do this, you need to create a material, adjust its parameters so that it appears to reflect the FIELD640.TGA image, and apply it to the saucer. The following steps take you through that process.

1. Click on the sample sphere in Material Editor Slot #1 to make the default Material #1 active. You'll want to assign Material #1 to the flying saucer and adjust it to make it a reflective saucer-like material.

2. In any viewport, click on the flying saucer to select it.

3. In the Material Editor, under the Basic Parameters rollout, click on the Down arrow to the right of Shading: Phong. A list of shading types appears, including: Constant (a flat material), Phong, and Metal. Because you want the most realistic reflective finish for your saucer, scroll down until you see Metal and pick it to replace Phong with the Metal shader. You want your saucer to render at its chromium best. (The Specular map is disabled when the Metal shader is selected. However, you do want to increase the shininess value of this material, which you'll do in a moment.)

4. Now, click on the Ambient label and adjust the RGB settings for Ambient to 64, 64, 128. These settings turn the saucer a dark blue-gray.

5. Click on the Diffuse label and change the Diffuse RGB settings to 128, 128, 255. This imparts a brighter blue specular highlight to the metallic saucer material.

### Creating Better Materials in 3D Studio MAX

If you want to avoid the "plastic" look in your 3D materials, use this simple trick from Gary Yost, the 3D Studio/DOS and 3D Studio MAX Development Team leader.

When you're creating a material, don't lock the Ambient color to the Diffuse color. Keep them separate and make sure that the color settings are not identical. (For some special-case materials, the Ambient and Diffuse color settings make little or no difference in the final material appearance.)

Beginning animators often make this mistake of mixing the Ambient and Diffuse colors. When the Ambient and Diffuse colors are the same, you must depend completely on the *lighting* in your scene to create a color range between the Diffuse and Ambient components. No matter how well you light your scene, that range often won't be large enough to provide the dynamics necessary to make an image look deep.

Use the following two techniques for setting your Ambient and Diffuse lights to produce better results:

1. Make the Ambient color a much darker version of the Diffuse color. Use the same Hue and Saturation—just a different Luminance value.

2. Make the Ambient color a complimentary color of the Diffuse color. This is the "Maxfield Parrish" effect, and can produce some stunning results.

6. In the Basic Parameters rollout, set Shininess to 50 and Shininess Strength to 85. As you can see, in the Material Editor, the material is now a very shiny, metallic blue-gray.

   Now you're going to apply a reflection map to the object to correspond to the open field environment in which your flying saucer will be appearing.

7. In the Material Editor, open the Maps rollout and click on the check box to the left of Reflection. Because you don't want the flying saucer to look completely reflective, bring the Reflection map percentage down to 50 percent. This lets some of the Diffuse and Ambient colors come through. In this case, because the sky above the saucer is blue, doing this tints the saucer a faint blue.

8. Click on the Map button to the right of the Reflection label to bring up the Material/Map Browser. Again, under the Browse From choice of selections, make sure that New is selected and then double-click on Bitmap.

   When you return to the Material Editor, click on the Bitmap button under Bitmap Parameters. This brings up the Texture Image File browser.

9. From the *3D Studio MAX f/x CD-ROM*, load FIELDREF.TGA from the \CHAP_03 directory; it appears on the sample sphere in Material Slot #1.

   The FIELDREF.TGA image is a 960 x 480, 24-bit image adapted from the original FIELD640.TGA image. I loaded the FIELD640.TGA image into Adobe Photoshop, duplicated and mirrored it, and then made it seamless along the top and bottom edges so that it would wrap cleanly around the saucer. Finally, I reduced it to 960 x 480 from its original 1260 x 480 proportions (so that it could serve better as a spherical texture map). For your purposes, it's the perfect reflection map for the FIELD640.TGA background.

10. Under Coordinates, click on Texture rather than Environment. (The flying saucer already has its Generate Mapping Coordinates active; leaving the setting at Environment will produce undesirable results.) Then click on the Go To Parent icon to return to the standard Material Editor settings for Material Slot #1. Now place this material in the scene.

11. Click on the Assign Material to Selection icon to assign Material #1 to the flying saucer and then click on OK to replace Material #1.

12. Right-click in the Perspective viewport to activate it. You're going to do a quick test rendering. (Don't worry about the saucer height and angle right now; you'll fix that in a moment.)

13. From the Menu bar at the top of the screen, click on Rendering/Render. Leave the image resolution at 640 x 480 pixels and then click on Render. If you have the Virtual Frame Buffer (VFB) active the rendered image appears after a few moments, as shown in Figure 2-7.

**TIP** Whenever you want to render an image, you can select Render from the Rendering menu, click on the Render icon in the top right of your 3D Studio MAX toolbar, or use the keyboard alternate command Alt+R to bring up the Render dialog.

Figure 2-7: *The flying saucer model sitting above the ground of the open field.*

As you saw in the previous chapter, when Tom Hudson and I had to create the illusion that our analog model saucer was reflecting its surroundings, we had to simulate the surroundings present in the background rear-projected slide. I used the FIELDREF.TGA image (a modification of the FIELD640.TGA background) as a reflection map to the foreground saucer object for the same reason.

14. Close the Material Editor.

## Out of Alignment

Now it's time to align the flying saucer properly in your 3D scene. You'll want to move the flying saucer model up in the viewports to make it appear to be hovering at an appropriate altitude, relative to the background.

1. Choose Select and Move in the tool bar and limit movement to the Y axis. Right-click in the Left viewport to activate it.

2. Drag the flying saucer model up along the Y axis to approximately 150 units and then release the mouse button.

## The Shadow Knows

Now you're going to create an object to represent the ground plane. You will use this object to create the shadow underneath the flying saucer. This will make it look as if the saucer itself is casting a shadow on the open field in the background image.

1. Right-click in the Top viewport to make it active, and then click on the Min/Max Toggle button to enlarge the Top viewport to full screen. (Alternatively, you can press the W key to enlarge an active viewport to full screen.)

   To zoom out from the flying saucer model, you can click on the Zoom icon at the bottom of your screen, but pressing the Z key to zoom in, or Shift+Z to zoom out, is easier.

2. Press and hold down the Shift key and press Z several times until the flying saucer is approximately 1/16th the width of the viewport.

3. In the Create panel, select Geometry. Underneath the list of Geometry options, click the Down arrow to the right of Standard Primitives and scroll down until you see Patch Grids, then click on it. The Object Type menu appears. Click on Quad Patch; the Parameters rollout appears. Leave the settings as they are. Click on the 2D Snap toggle button at the bottom of your MAX desktop (or, press the S key to activate the 2D Snap toggle).

4. Move your mouse cursor in the Top viewport up to approximate coordinates of X -800 and Y 800. Click and drag diagonally downward to the right to approximate coordinates of X 800 and Y -800. Then release the mouse button to create the grid. In the Parameters window, the length and width should both be 1600 units. Leave the length segments and width segments at 1. Rename the object from QuadPatch01 to Ground Plane.

   Your screen should now look something like Figure 2-8.

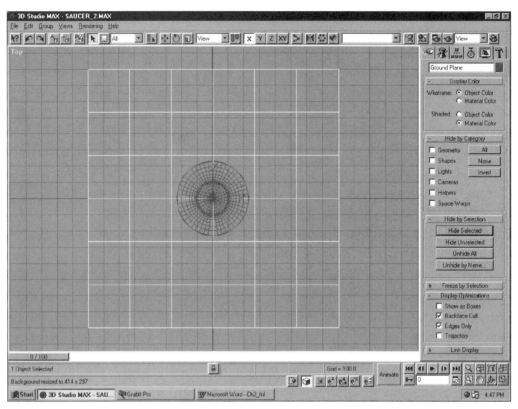

Figure 2-8: *The flying saucer model with the 2D Quad Patch Ground Plane object.*

This patch object will serve as the ground plane.

5. Click on the Min/Max Toggle button to return to the four viewports (or press the W key again). Press the S key to turn off the 2D Snap Toggle and then click on the Zoom Extents All button to center the Ground Plane and the flying saucer in each viewport.

Now you'll place a camera in the scene.

6. Right-click in the Left viewport to activate it; then create a target camera at approximate coordinates of X 0, Y -500 and Z 50. Left-click to place the camera and then drag the camera target to the center of the flying saucer. When you're finished, right-click in the Perspective viewport to activate it and press the C key to change the viewport to the Camera01 view.

7. Because the FIELD640.TGA background image that you're using for this shot was taken with a 35mm camera equipped with a 28mm wide-angle lens, you need to change the focal length of your 3D camera to match. Camera01 is still active, so you can change its lens type in the Create panel. Under Stock Lenses, click on 28mm. The focal length of the camera changes and you can see the saucer model aspect also change in the Camera01 viewport. Now click in the Show Horizon check box, just below Stock Lenses. This shows the camera horizon (a black line) in the Camera01 viewport. (It may be difficult to see, so you have to look closely.)

Your desktop after a few moments should look like Figure 2-9.

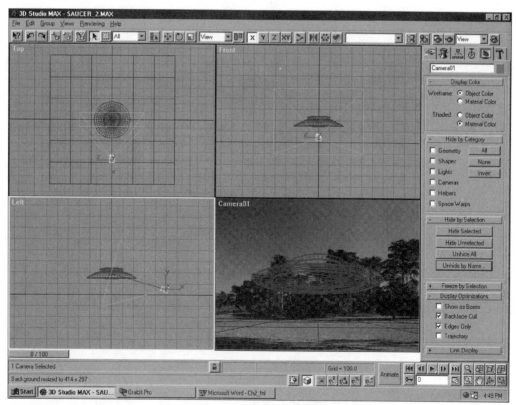

Figure 2-9: *The preliminary setup for the flying saucer still image.*

## Lights! Cameras!

Take a closer look at your background image. As the background in the Camera01 viewport indicates, you're looking at an open grassy field. I took this shot in Golden Gate Park, San Francisco, at approximately 10:00 a.m. on a sunny day in February 1996.

At the angle at which this photo was taken, the sun was off to the right. You therefore want to place a directional light, which will simulate the sunlight in your scene, above the flying saucer and slightly to the right.

Use the following steps to do so.

1. Right-click in the Top viewport to activate it and then press W to maximize it. In the Command Panel, click on Create/Lights and, under Object Type, click on Directional. The General Parameters rollout appears. First, increase the intensity of the light from the default values. Under General Parameters/ Color, change the light's RGB values from 180, 180, 180 to 255, 255, 255—or pure white. Under Directional Parameters, change Hotspot to 300, make sure that Show Cone is active, and, under Shadow Parameters, click on Cast Shadows.

2. In the Top viewport, move your mouse cursor to approximate coordinates X 300, Y 0. Click to place the Directional light. Press the W key to return to your four viewports; then click on the Zoom Extents All button to center your 3D objects in each viewport.

3. Right-click in your Front viewport to activate it and then click on the Select and Move button. Drag the Directional light up to approximate coordinates X 0, Y 700, Z 0. Then click on the Select and Rotate button, restrict rotation to the Z axis, and turn on the Angle Snap. Rotate the Directional light to Z -25.
   Your desktop should look something like Figure 2-10.

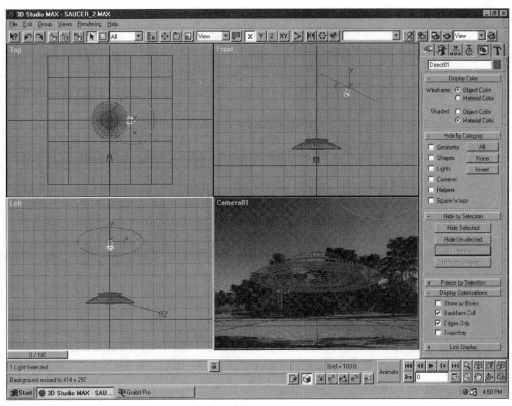

Figure 2-10: *The Directional light placed over the flying saucer model to simulate the sunlight present in the background scene.*

Now you have the rudiments of the scene; however, you need to line up the 3D flying saucer object in the scene to correspond to the angle at which the background photo was originally taken. To do this, you need to align the Camera01 viewport and the Ground Plane object to correspond to the horizon angle of the field background horizon.

4. Click on the Select and Move icon and then, in the Left viewport, move the Camera01 target on the Y axis until the Camera Horizon line roughly corresponds with the base of the trees present in the background image. Watch the grass at the left side of the background in the Camera01 viewport as you

slowly adjust the location of the target. In addition, you may have to click on the Camera01 body itself to move it either in the Y or the Z axes to get a good composition of the flying saucer hovering over the open field.

## Shadow Me

Now it's time to create a material for the Ground Plane object. You want to place a shadow-receiving Matte/Shadow material onto the object. This is another area in which 3D Studio MAX differs from 3D Studio/DOS. In 3D Studio Release 4, matte objects—objects that reveal whatever background is present in your 3D scene—are created by modifying the attributes of the particular objects themselves.

3D Studio MAX, however, lets you create Matte/Shadow *materials*; in addition, matte objects in 3D Studio MAX can both cast and receive shadows. Therefore, by applying a shadow-receiving Matte/Shadow *material* to an object in your scene that corresponds in location to a part of your background image, you can create the illusion that a 3D object in the foreground is casting a shadow on the background image.

This is what you're going to do: apply a matte material to the Ground Plane so that the flying saucer looks as if it's casting a shadow on the real digitized field background.

The following steps show you how to create the material.

1. Click on the Select by Name icon (or press the H key to bring up this dialog box), choose Ground Plane from the list, and click on Select. The Ground Plane quad patch turns white, indicating that it's now selected.

2. Bring up the Material Editor and then click on the sample sphere in Material Slot #3. You'll change this material type from a Standard material to a Matte/Shadow material.

3. Next to the word "Type," click on the Standard button. The Material/Map Browser appears. Under Browse From, click on New and then double-click on Matte/Shadow. The Matte/Shadow material appears in Material Slot #3.

As you can see, the Material #3 slot is now a flat green. This is the default appearance for a Matte/Shadow material in the Material Editor.

Take a look at the Matte/Shadow parameters. Because you're not going to worry about creating an alpha channel or atmospheric effects, you can leave the Matte Opaque Alpha and Atmosphere settings at their defaults.

4. You do want to check Receive Shadows under the Shadow option. Click on Receive Shadows to activate it. Leave Shadow Brightness at 0.5. Click on the Assign Material to Selection button to assign this Matte material to the Ground Plane object.

5. Activate the Camera01 viewport and render another test image.

   It should look like Figure 2-11.

Figure 2-11: *A test rendering of the flying saucer with a ground shadow. Note the low density of the shadow appearing on the ground below the saucer.*

As you can see, both on your own computer screen and in Figure 2-11, you have the beginnings of a reasonable UFO photograph. You can do some things to the scene, however, to improve the realism. If you take a look at the shadows appearing below the trees in the background image, you will notice that they are darker than the shadow appearing under the 3D flying saucer model. You'll want to adjust the flying saucer's shadow density to more closely match that of the background tree shadows. You can do this in the Material Editor.

6. Go back to Material Slot #3, the Matte/Shadow material. You want to adjust the Shadow Brightness. The default setting for Shadow Brightness is 0.5. Drag the spinner down to 0.15, or click and drag in the Numerical Entry window to highlight it and then type **0.15**. Press Enter to accept these values.

7. Render another test image; it should look like Figure 2-12.

Figure 2-12: *The flying saucer image with the revised shadow density parameters. Note how changing the shadow density to match that of the trees in the real digitized open field background makes the shadow of the flying saucer appear more realistic.*

## Varying the Techniques

You can vary these techniques in many ways, of course. You can, for example, adjust the spotlight parameters by increasing the diameter of the falloff circle. This makes the edges of the shadow appear softer.

In addition, by changing the map bias, or the size of the shadow map, you can adjust the smoothness of the edges of the visible shadow map. If you want to make the shadow follow the contours of an irregularly shaped background, you can apply a Displace modifier to your 2D plane, or you can sculpt geometry to better match the rolling hills and/or geometric shapes, such as buildings, that are visible in your digitized 3D background.

Finally, if you are rendering your 3D scene with atmospheric effects using 3D Studio MAX's Environment/Fog effects, you may want to activate the Apply Atmosphere attribute of the Matte/Shadow material. Doing so enables the matte object to show the effects of fog and attenuated or volumetric fog in the 3D scene.

*Note: You must apply the atmosphere effects to a matte object very carefully. If you select Apply Atmosphere at Object Depth and you are rendering a matte object to correspond to digitized real-world imagery in a background, the fog may either contaminate the matte object or reveal its edges. You must also be very careful about the matte object edge placement in relationship to the background if you are going to apply atmosphere to a 3D Studio MAX matte object.*

By loading a sequence of digitized "real-world" images into the background of your 3D Studio MAX scene, and carefully adjusting your 3D camera to match the perspective, angle, and focal length of the camera used to film the backgrounds, you can, for example, simulate a 3D flying saucer zooming down a real city street. If you set up matte objects in the scene, such as a 2D planar shape to correspond to a roadway or a parking lot, you could render a sequence of the flying saucer hovering over a parking lot. You could even move your "virtual" 3D Studio MAX camera viewpoint to correspond with that of the camera used to film the background plate of the original scene as it pans along with a moving 3D flying saucer.

When you are finished experimenting with this scene, you can save the materials used in the scene in your own Material Library; you should also save the scene itself in your \3DSMAX\SCENES directory as SAUCER_2.

The texture maps, and the MAX scene files SAUCER-1.MAX and SAUCER-2.MAX are in the \CHAP_02 directory of your *3D Studio MAX f/x CD-ROM*.

## Moving On

The next chapter shows how to create a special effects sequence from scratch. By starting with a simple outline, you progress to a shooting script, storyboards, and then rendered scenes. Then, Part II, "Optical Effects," begins the dissection of outer space optical techniques.

# 3

# Setting Up Your Scene

**I**t's time to proceed to something more complicated. In the next ten chapters, you're going to see how to design an entire special effects sequence, from concept to final rendering.

Although it's hard to tell from looking at some of the latest Hollywood offerings, every film or TV show starts with a script. Whether you're rendering a single shot or a series of shots to be inserted into another production, you may want to begin by writing out the action that occurs. Depending on your preferences (or those of your client), you might write your scene in either paragraph (outline) form or standard script format.

## The Space Battle in Outline Format

For the outer space scenes that you're about to examine, I conceptualized the action by first writing it down in paragraph form, as follows:

...We begin with a slow pan across deep space. A few errant asteroids tumble by from a nearby asteroid belt. In the distance is a large planet (perhaps a gas giant with a moon orbiting it) and a glowing yellow sun; surrounding everything is a colorful nebula. As we follow the asteroids, there's a flash of light and a "warp drive" tunnel appears with an enormous space cruiser roaring out of it. We track along with the cruiser as it emerges from the asteroid belt.

Suddenly, multiple flashes of light appear as fighter craft emerge from hyperspace and converge on the cruiser. The fighters begin to fire upon the cruiser with tachyon torpedoes; the cruiser raises laser cannons and returns fire, tracking with the ships. Fighters swoop and strafe; some are blasted by the cruiser and explode. However, the fighters get the upper hand and blow the cruiser's forcefield; they then target the cruiser's engines, which detonate. A giant fireball erupts and the cruiser explodes, blowing hundreds of pieces throughout space. As giant fragments of the ship tumble dangerously through space, the fighters beat a hasty retreat.

## The Space Battle in Script Format

After you've outlined the action that occurs in your sequence, you will probably want to break it down into a series of clearly delineated shots. The best form for this, of course, is the script.

If you were to render this sequence in standard motion picture script format, it would look something like this:

FADE IN:

SCENE 1-EXT. DEEP SPACE-THE V'OLTONE NEBULA-(FX)

WE ARE IN DEEP SPACE, a vista filled with thousands of BRILLIANT
STARS and COLORFUL NEBULA. As we PAN SLOWLY RIGHT, a few errant
ASTEROIDS tumble by from a nearby ASTEROID BELT. As we CONTINUE
PANNING, we see off in the distance a LARGE PLANET, a gas giant
like Jupiter, perhaps, with a SMALL MOON orbiting it.

As we follow the asteroids, there's a BRIGHT FLASH and a WARP
DRIVE TUNNEL appears; streaks of colorful light radiate down to
a vanishing point. Out of the tunnel comes an enormous SPACE
BATTLECRUISER, roaring directly at us. As it approaches the
CAMERA, we PAN LEFT with it as it heads through the asteroid
field.

SCENE 2-EXT. ASTEROID FIELD-FAVORING BATTLECRUISER-(FX)

We're looking down relative to the battlecruiser as it enters the
dense asteroid field. HOLD ON the cruiser as FLASHES OF LIGHT
appear on its FORCEFIELD, or shield, which is intermittently
visible like a soap bubble caught in a strobe light. The flashes
are caused by several impinging asteroids but the forcefield
holds; the ship BARRELS THROUGH the asteroids, which are nudged
out of the way.

SCENE 3-EXT. ASTEROID FIELD-FURTHER AWAY FROM CRUISER-(FX)

Another BRIGHT FLASH occurs above the asteroid field and the
cruiser; a second and third flash follow shortly thereafter.
It's another WARP DRIVE EFFECT heralding the appearance of three
ENEMY FIGHTER SHIPS, diving straight for the cruiser.

SCENE 4-EXT. SPACE-ANGLE ON FIGHTER SHIP-(FX)

We track with the first fighter as it plunges headlong toward
the cruiser. TACHYON TORPEDOES begin firing from the fighter's
wings; we see the sparkling balls of light impact on the
cruiser's shields. In the background, we see the other two
fighters begin their strafing run.

SCENE 5-EXT. CRUISER-ANGLE ON THE SIDE OF THE SHIP-(FX)

We track quickly alongside the flank of the cruiser as the first
fighter ship screams by. Its companions are beginning their
attack in the background, torpedoes firing from their wings.

SCENE 6-EXT. CRUISER-CLOSE ON GUN TURRET OF SHIP-(FX)

From the CONNING TOWER-LIKE GUN TURRETS on the cruiser's wings,
LASER BOLTS BEGIN FIRING back at the fighters.

SCENE 7-EXT. SPACE-FAVORING ONE OF THE FIGHTERS-(FX)

The second fighter is beginning a tight turn after having com-
pleted its strafing run when laser bolts RIP THROUGH the scene.
The laser bolts flash by, tracking with the fighter. The fighter
makes a tight turn, desperately trying to avoid the lasers, when
THEY SUDDENLY HIT THE FIGHTER DEAD-ON, raking across its wings.
There are SPARKS as the beams tear through the hull; then, with a
BRILLIANT FLASH, the fighter ship EXPLODES.

SCENE 8-EXT. SPACE-THE REMAINING FIGHTERS AND CRUISER-(FX)

In the background, we see the dying glow of the explosion as the
two remaining fighters regroup and make another pass at the
cruiser. Their torpedoes impact on the cruiser's shields, which
are flashing--

SCENE 9-CLOSE ON CRUISER LASER CANNONS-(FX)

The cruiser responds with a barrage of laser bolts--

SCENE 10-ANGLE ON THE TWO FIGHTERS-(FX)

The two fighters are diving down again at the cruiser when the left one is HIT and EXPLODES. However, the fighter on the right continues firing torpedoes; there's a tremendous FLASH as the cruiser's shields WHITE OUT and DISAPPEAR.

The last fighter releases a final torpedo at one of the cruiser's engine nacelles--

SCENE 11-CLOSE ON CRUISER ENGINE-(FX)

With a TREMENDOUS FLASH of light and sparks, the torpedo blasts into the engine nacelle, blowing pieces of the cruiser apart--

SCENE 12-TRACKING WITH FIGHTER-(FX)

We're tracking with the fighter ship as it pulls quickly away from the mortally wounded cruiser, drifting through the asteroid field. Lightning bolts are arcing across the cruiser's surface; they grow in frequency and then, with an ENORMOUS FIREBALL, the cruiser explodes. Pieces of the ship, still crackling with lightning, come flying by the camera as the fighter beats a hasty retreat.

*Note: For more information on film and TV script formats, see Appendix D: "Special Effects, Animation & Filmmaking Resources."*

Although not always required, a written description of your scene may help you sell your sequence to a prospective client. After your script has been approved, you should then proceed to the next step: the storyboard.

# Setting Up Your Scene: The Storyboard

Storyboards have become an integral part of today's filmmaking process. Ordinarily, storyboards are black-and-white illustrations that indicate the action to occur in a series of shots. (A comic book is, essentially, a short movie or TV show told in storyboard form.) During the preproduction phase of a film, the director, art director, production illustrators, and special effects artists go over the script and begin breaking it down into discrete sequences.

Sequences that are especially complex, with fancy camera moves, fast action, and elaborate effects, are the ones most likely to have storyboards. The storyboard enables a film or TV show's production managers to determine the optimum way of conveying the action. The storyboard is also an indispensable budgeting tool. If the sequences are carefully preplanned, the filmmakers need not engage in costly reshoots (ideally, that is). Some directors storyboard virtually all the scenes in their films, to be thoroughly prepared for every day of shooting. (Alfred Hitchcock was an early pioneer of this approach. Indeed, when he arrived on the set to shoot, he complained that he had already "made the picture" via storyboarding, and that shooting the actual footage was anticlimactic.)

As modern films rely more heavily on visual effects to tell their stories, so must they rely on storyboards to plan out how those elaborate shots will be accomplished. For my purposes here, I've taken the script excerpt that you've just read and had it rendered into storyboard format, as shown on the following pages.

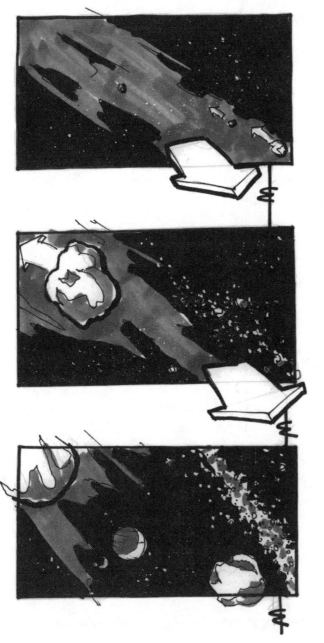

*Start on nebula*

*Asteroids drift by—*
*Pulling back and down*

*To asteroid field—*
*Planet and moon*

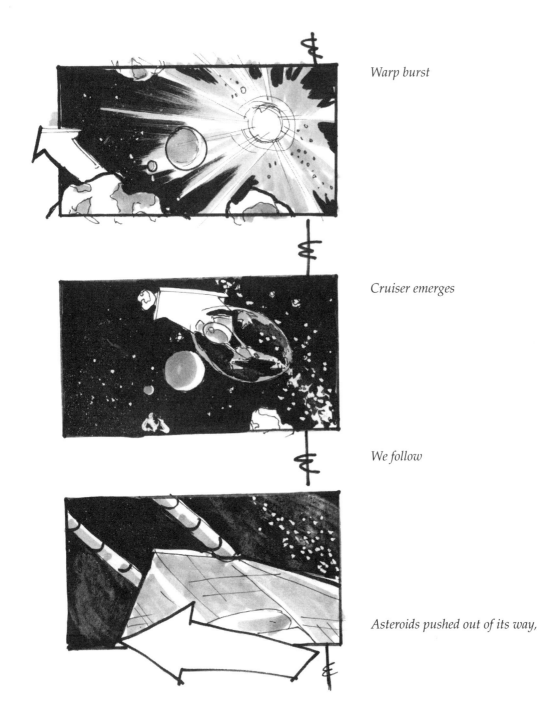

*Warp burst*

*Cruiser emerges*

*We follow*

*Asteroids pushed out of its way,*

*Some asteroids impact*

*Cruiser moves toward us—*

*Asteroids pushed out of its way*

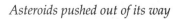

*Cruiser goes by underneath us—*

*Two warp bursts occur behind it,*

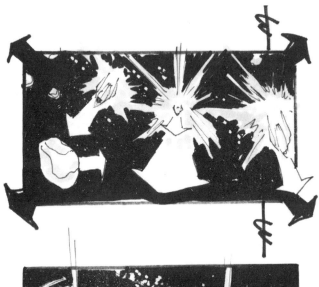

*Then a third*

*Fighters zoom toward us—*

*Fire torpedoes*

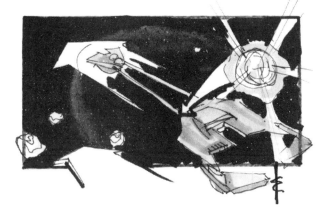

*Torpedoes enter frame (Moving with cruiser)*

*Fighter follows as torpedoes impact on shields*

*Fighter pulls up—*

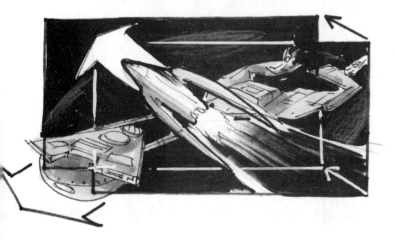

*Move with fighter in front of cruiser*

*Two other fighters start attack*

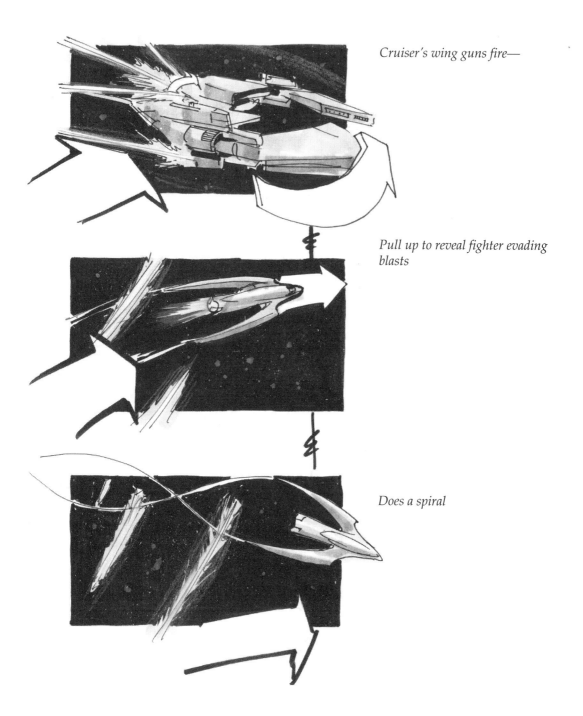

Cruiser's wing guns fire—

Pull up to reveal fighter evading blasts

Does a spiral

*Moving in on cruiser*

*Another fighter zooms in, fires—*

*Torpedoes impact on shields*

*Camera move—tracking with fighter*

*As it evades blasts*

*Then is hit…*

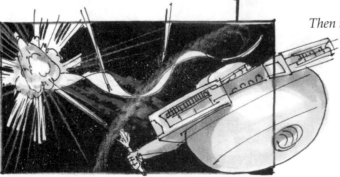

*Other fighters regroup*

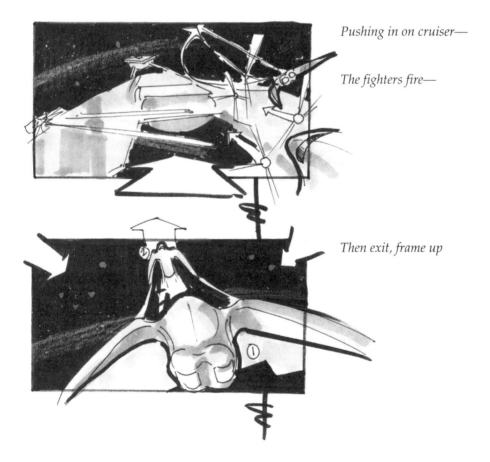

*Pushing in on cruiser—*

*The fighters fire—*

*Then exit, frame up*

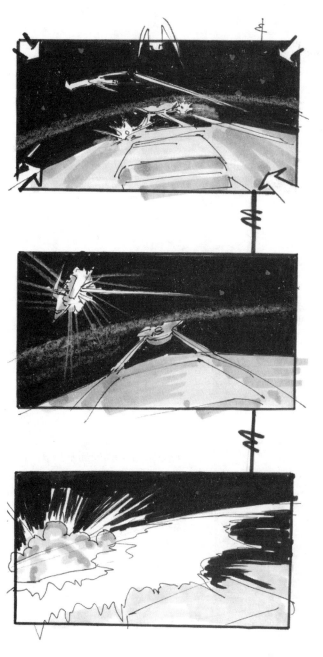

*Other fighter zooms left*

*But is hit—*

*And deflected to impact on shields*

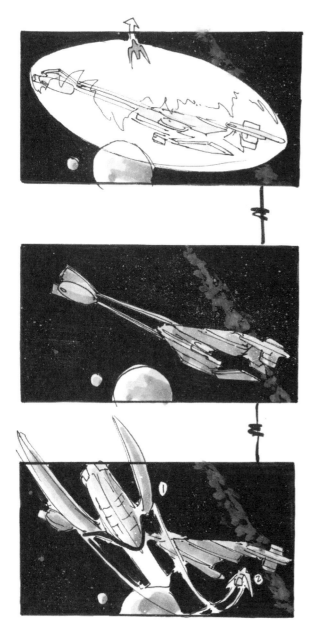

Shields white out—

Other fighter zooms up, loops—

Shields out—

Last fighter completes loop and enters frame

Heading for engine—

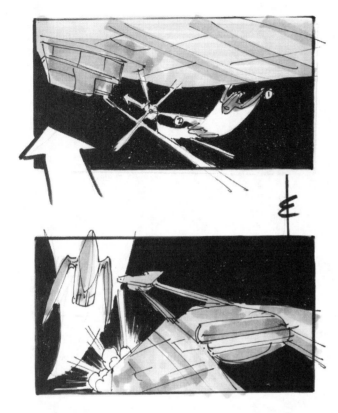

*Fires, and avoids blasts*

*Move up following fighter*

*A hit!*

*Cruiser starts to explode*

*Boom!*

*Fighter enters frame—*

*Explosion in background*

*Fighter heads toward us—*

*Then zooms away*

These storyboards were drawn by Daren Dochterman, a Hollywood production illustrator, storyboard artist, and composer. Daren's credits include *The Abyss*; *Honey, I Blew Up The Kid*; *Star Trek, Voyager*; and *Ace Ventura: When Nature Calls*.

As you can see, the 36 boards indicate the number of shots in the planned sequence, along with camera directions and angles, and motion dynamics. (Daren drew the boards in the standard wide screen 1.85:1 motion picture aspect ratio.) Regardless of whether you're shooting live action or traditional effects or rendering CGI, storyboards are an excellent tool to help you previsualize your scene.

## From Storyboards to Final Rendering

Now you'll take a look at how the scripted action, black-and-white art, and camera directions translate into some of the rendered sequences in the individual stills shown here (Figures 3-1 through 3-7). Although the final renderings do not follow the storyboards precisely, the boards still serve to indicate object motion, speed, camera movements, and overall scene dynamics.

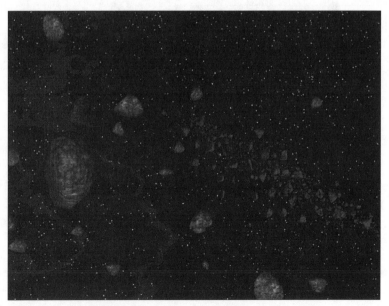

Figure 3-1: *An asteroid field somewhere in deep space.*

The space battle opening appears in Figure 3-1. The elements included in this shot consist of starfield and nebula artwork mapped onto a sphere encompassing the scene, multiplane aster- oid artwork, and 3D mesh asteroid models. The asteroid artwork was opacity-mapped to 2D Quad Patch objects in the scene, creating the illusion of a dense asteroid field.

Figure 3-2: *A bright flash heralds the appearance of a battlecruiser out of warp drive.*

The warp drive effect is shown in Figure 3-2. I created the warp drive imagery by mapping a series of prerendered bitmaps onto simple 3D meshes. (See Chapter 11, "Warp Speed!") The imagery was created with Digimation's 3D Studio/DOS LenZFX Plug-in, using custom gradient .GIF images to produce the radial spokes of light. The effect was rendered as two different sets of 400 x 400 pixel, 24-bit .TGA images, each 30 frames in length. These images were then planar-mapped onto counter-rotating conical shapes, which are hidden until necessary. The rapid increase in size is due to the shapes morphing from very small to large objects.

*Note: At press time, LenZFX was not yet available for 3D Studio MAX; it should, however, be available by the time you read this.*

Figure 3-3: *The battlecruiser is protected by a forcefield.*

Figure 3-3 shows the battlecruiser, protected by its forcefield. The forcefield is a spherical mesh textured as a shiny, virtually transparent object. The shimmering reflections playing across its surface are created by using a prerendered, looping flic created with James Gleick's CHAOS: The Software from Autodesk. (This flic is on the *3D Studio MAX f/x CD-ROM* in the \MAPS directory. Unfortunately, the software itself is no longer available.)

Figure 3-4: *Enemy fighter ships appear out of hyperspace and fire on the cruiser.*

In Figure 3-4, the fighter ships appear out of hyperspace and unleash a barrage of tachyon torpedoes. Like the warp burst effect, the torpedo imagery was created using LenZFX, with the gradient color settings ranging from white to yellow to red, and applied to opacity-mapped 2D Quad Patches.

Figure 3-5: *The fighters' torpedoes impact on the cruiser's shields.*

In Figure 3-5, the visible impacts on the battlecruiser's shields were created by placing 36-segment spheres on the shield surface and then binding Bomb Space Warps to each sphere. At the point at which the torpedoes hit, the spheres unhide (using Visibility keys set in Track View) and then detonate. A Glow filter applied in Video Post creates the illusion of a giant fireball.

Figure 3-6: *The battlecruiser shoots back at the attacking fighters.*

In Figure 3-6, the battlecruiser begins firing its laser weapons at the attacking fighters. The laser beams consist of an Autodesk Animator Pro flic file mapped onto elongated 2D Quad Patches. These planar shapes are then animated as "in-camera" objects. The initial flak burst at the origin of the beam is a variation of the tachyon torpedo effect, again mapped onto 2D shapes.

Figure 3-7: *An unlucky fighter takes a direct hit.*

One of the fighters takes a direct hit and explodes, as shown in Figure 3-7. The fireball explosion is created by attaching a Bomb Space Warp to a complex sphere; the sphere has a self-illuminated material applied to it. A Combustion Plug-in apparatus (included on the *3D Studio MAX f/x CD-ROM*) provides a fireball that engulfs the fighter ship.

## The Space Battle: Selected Scenes

It's time to take a look at the first 3D sequence. You'll preview five shots from the space battle sequence that is discussed in this chapter. Each shot shows off examples of the space effects that are covered in this book: from asteroid fields and nebulas to tachyon torpedoes and laser beams.

1. Make sure that the *3D Studio MAX f/x CD-ROM* is loaded into your PC's CD-ROM drive and that the drive is active.

   For the fastest playback, you may want to copy the .AVI files from the CD-ROM to your hard drive. Depending on how much RAM your computer contains, viewing the files directly from the CD-ROM may make them play back very slowly.

   If necessary, go to either the File Manager or the Explorer of Windows NT 3.51 or 4.0 and copy the .AVI files to your \3DSMAX\IMAGES subdirectory. If your hard drive space is at a premium, you may want to copy, preview, and then delete each .AVI file from your hard drive before proceeding to the next one.

2. Load 3D Studio MAX. Select File/View File and, from the \CHAP_03 directory of your *3D Studio MAX f/x CD-ROM*, click on the file SPACEBT1.AVI to load it. When the Media Player appears, click on the Play button to play the file.

   This 320 x 240 resolution, 350-frame-long shot is the opening scene from the space battle sequence. As the camera tilts through space, you see distant stars and the faint colors of a nebula. Asteroids are tumbling slowly by the camera. In the distance is an asteroid field; these asteroids consist of 2D textures applied to five Quad Patch objects using Diffuse and Opacity maps. As the camera tilts down, a flash of light occurs; this signifies the battlecruiser coming out of warp drive. As it roars by, you pan with it and see that it's protected by a glassy forcefield bubble.

3. When you're finished previewing this file, stop the animation playback. Click on File\Open in the Media Player and load the file SPACEBT2.AVI from the \CHAP_03 directory. When the animation appears, click on the Play button to play it.

   This is the second shot in the battle sequence. As the cruiser passes beneath you, you tilt up to see three more warp bursts and three fighter ships appearing out of hyperdrive. As they come roaring towards you, the lead fighter fires off two tachyon torpedoes.

4. When you're finished previewing this shot, stop the animation, load the file SPACEBT3.AVI from your \CHAP_03 directory, and play it.

   This is the third shot in the space battle sequence. It's a fast cut to a reverse angle of the torpedoes as they enter the frame and impact on the cruiser's shields. The shields absorb the brunt of the impact as the fighters go roaring by on their first strafing run.

5. Load the file SPACEBT4.AVI from your \CHAP_03 directory and play it. SPACEBT4.AVI represents scene #6 of the sequence as the cruiser begins to return fire with its laser cannons.

6. Load the file SPACEBT5.AVI from your \CHAP_03 directory and play it. SPACEBT5.AVI represents scene #7 of the script as a laser beam catches one of the fighters dead-on and destroys it.

7. When you're finished playing the animations, close the Media Player.

 All the models, scene files, and texture maps used to create these sequences are contained on your *3D Studio MAX f/x CD-ROM*. The scene files for SPACEBT1-SPACEBT5.MAX are in the \CHAP_21 and \SPACEBTL directories.

## Moving On

Periodically throughout the tutorials to come, you may want to refer back to various elements in the five shots that you just previewed. Again, you may want to watch the sequences several times through to get a feel for the motion and dynamics present. By the time you finish each tutorial, you'll be well on your way to being able to choreograph and render the entire space battle sequence as storyboarded (if you want). In addition, you'll have plenty of 3D ammunition that you can bring to your own outer space action scenes.

So, stay tuned!

.

# Part II

# Optical Effects

# 4

# Starlight, Starbright, Part I

If you're creating a deep-space environment in 3D, then your first effects consideration is your starfield background. Luckily, this is also one of the easiest effects to create in any 3D package. For most 3D space renderings, stars appear simply as grayscale or subtly colored pixels against a black backdrop.

3D Studio MAX gives you several ways to place stars in the backgrounds of your space scenes. To start with, you can load rendered starfield bitmaps or Noise textures into the background as Environmental maps. You can also take these textures and map them onto a large 3D mesh object, such as a giant sphere, that surrounds your entire space scene. If you then attach that sphere to the same path as the camera, you can produce distant starfield backdrops that move properly with respect to your camera.

By using this technique, you can create the dynamic camera movements that you want for your space scenes, yet your stars' appearance will always remain (theoretically) at infinity. You therefore won't run the risk of having the camera get too close to the inner sphere surface, making the stars look like glowing blobs.

(In Chapter 8, "Nebulas on the Move," you see how to link a nebula and/or starfield sphere object to your camera path for the proper effect.)

*Note: If you want to create motion-blurred starfield backgrounds using this technique, you must assign scene and/or object motion blur using the Video Post options.*

Finally, you can produce starfield backdrops in your space scenes by using a procedural Starfield filter, loaded into your Video Post queue. Although 3D Studio/DOS came with the STARS.IXP IPAS routine included for creating motion-blurred stars, at the time of this writing, a procedural Starfield generator was not yet available for 3D Studio MAX. However, by the time you read this, at least one (and possibly more) 3D Studio MAX Starfield plug-ins should be available, both as freeware and as commercial products.

To find out the latest news of 3D Studio MAX plug-ins, check out the various online services, such as the Kinetix forum on CompuServe (GO KINETIX), the Kinetix Web site (http://www.ktx.com), or the Ventana Web site (http://www.vmedia.com). When a freeware Starfield plug-in is available, you'll find it on these forums, ready for download and incorporation into your copy of 3D Studio MAX. In addition, check out Appendix C, "3D Studio MAX Resources," for more information about 3D Studio MAX software and hardware support.

## Creating Starfields With Environmental Mapping & Bitmaps

Now you'll take a look at how to create starfields, both for animations and still images, with 3D Studio MAX's powerful Environmental mapping feature. In this section, you'll see how you can load starfield bitmaps into spherical Environmental backgrounds to produce deep-space vistas.

First, examine 3D StudioMAX's Environmental Mapping feature. Unlike the flat bitmap, gradient, or solid-color Background options in 3D Studio/DOS, 3D Studio MAX's Environmental Mapping feature lets you set up many different ways to create backgrounds for your 3D scenes. In 3D Studio/DOS, a background is loaded simply as a flat image or series of images behind your existing 3D scene. Unless the background images that you load contain an animation sequence that corresponds exactly to the camera movement of your foreground 3D scene, the foreground objects don't move in synchronization with the background. The background remains fixed.

However, by using 3D Studio MAX's Environmental Mapping, you can set up backgrounds that behave as 3D backdrops encompassing your foreground scene—and the background even moves in relation to the foreground Camera.

Follow these steps to take a look at this feature.

1. In 3D Studio MAX, select Environment from the Rendering menu. The Environment dialog box appears. In the Background section, click on the Assign button; the Material/Map Browser dialog box appears. Under Browse From, click on New and then double-click on Bitmap.

2. Back in the Environment dialog box, click on the main map button, which should now read Map #1 (Bitmap), and the Put to Material Editor dialog box appears; the default is Slot #1. It now contains Material #1. Click on OK or press Enter to approve the choice; then, close the Environment dialog box.

3. Click on the Material Editor button in the toolbar to bring up the Material Editor.

   As you can see, the sample sphere in Slot #1 is black; you haven't loaded a bitmap or other texture yet. You need to load a starfield bitmap from the *3D Studio MAX f/x CD-ROM* to use as your background.

4. In the Bitmap Parameters rollout, double-click on the Bitmap button. The Select Texture Image File dialog box appears. From the \CHAP_02 directory of your *3D Studio MAX f/x CD-ROM*, select the file STAR1024.TGA and then click on View to view the image.

   The STAR1024.TGA image is a 1024 x 512 pixel image of a deep-space starfield created in Autodesk Animator Pro and Adobe Photoshop. At this high resolution, it allows a large number of stars to appear in the scene. In addition, with its 2:1 width/height ratio, it's well-suited for use both as a Spherical Environment map and applied to geometry using Spherical UVW mapping coordinates.

5. When you've finished viewing the image, click on OK to return to the Material Editor. When you do so, the STAR1024.TGA image appears on the Sample sphere in Slot #1.

   As mentioned earlier, 3D Studio MAX's Background options using the Environment feature are much more extensive than 3D Studio/ DOS. Under the Coordinates section of the Material Editor rollup, take a look at the mapping field. In the main field you see that Spherical Environment is active.

6. Click on the Down arrow to the right of Spherical Environment; another list of options appears. These are Spherical Environment (the default), followed by Cylindrical Environment, Shrink-wrap, and Screen.

   The first two options, Spherical Environment and Cylindrical Environment, apply spherical or cylindrical mapping coordinates to an imaginary sphere or cylinder encompassing your 3D scene. Shrink-wrap Environment trims the corners of your bitmap image and then wraps the image around the imaginary sphere; consequently, no seams are visible in your bitmap image.

The final option, Screen, works the same way as the old Background option in 3D Studio/DOS. Screen simply loads a bitmap (or series of bitmaps) as a flat background image. (For more information on mapping types, see "Choosing Environment Mapping, 35-5, *3D Studio MAX User's Guide, Volume 2.*)

7. You'll want to keep the Spherical Environment setting, so make sure that it's active and then minimize the Material Editor.

8. Right-click in the Perspective viewport to activate it; then, either click on Rendering/Render or press Alt+R. When the Render Scene dialog box appears, press Enter to render a 640 x 480 still image. After a few moments, the Spherical Environmental texture appears, and it should look like Figure 4-1.

Figure 4-1: *The STAR1024.TGA material applied as a Spherical Environmental map.*

As Figure 4-1 shows, you now have softly glowing stars appearing in the background of your 3D scene. However, the stars appear quite large; they look more like glowing spheres, stretched somewhat by the spherical mapping coordinates, than pinpoint stars. Although they might be suitable for a low-resolution video game, you should scale them down so that they will look better in your 640 x 480 still renderings.

## A Zillion Points of Light

You can make your stars appear more numerous in the background rendering and also make them smaller by changing the Tiling options in the Material Editor.

1. Close your Virtual Frame Buffer (VFB) rendering window and then click on the Material Editor Restore button to return to the Material Editor.

   When the Material Editor appears, look under the Coordinates section of the rollup and examine the Tiling section. The STAR1024.TGA texture map has simply been wrapped once around the background sphere in both the U and V directions. You need to increase the tiling.

2. Under the U section of Tiling, change both the U and V tiling from 1.0 to 3.0. When you do, the number and size of the stars changes on the sample sphere in Slot #1. (They may become so small that they don't appear any more on the sample sphere; don't worry about this.)

3. Right-click in your Perspective viewport to activate it; then, render another test image. After a moment, the rendering appears. It should look something like Figure 4-2.

Figure 4-2: *The new Spherical Environment starfield background with UV tiling increased from 1.0 to 3.0.*

As Figure 4-2 shows, you now have a much more realistic starfield. The number of stars visible is increased dramatically. The stars' size has also decreased, creating much more realistic pinpoints of light in your scene.

4. When you've finished viewing the file, close your Virtual Frame Buffer window.

If you want, return to the Material Editor and save this environmental mapping texture to your Materials Library as Star1024 Background. This material is also saved in the 3DSMAXFX.MAT Material Library on your *3D Studio MAX f/x CD-ROM.*

## Creating Starfields With Environmental Mapping & Noise

Now that you've seen how to create starfield backdrops using the 3D Studio MAX Environmental mapping options and starfield bitmaps, explore how to use the 3D Studio MAX procedural Noise texture to create starfields for still renderings.

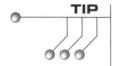

**TIP**   You can use a Noise texture as an Environment map to create *still images only*. Because the Noise texture is reapplied randomly on every frame, the starfield backgrounds that are produced flicker unacceptably during the course of an animation sequence. This might work for some sort of strange space effect, but it's not useful for creating simple starfields.

1. Bring up the Material Editor. Slot #1 should still contain your STAR1024 Background material. You need to change this material type from a Bitmap to a Noise procedural texture.

2. Click on the Type button to bring up the Material/Map Browser. Make sure that New is selected under Browse From; then, from the list window to the right, double-click on Noise to load it. When the Replace Map dialog box appears, click on OK to discard your old texture map.

   As the Noise procedural loads in the Material Type slot, the sample sphere in Slot #1 turns a mottled gray. In the Coordinates rollout, XYZ is highlighted and XYZ Tiling is set to 1.0. You will want to change the Noise parameters to create procedural stars.

3. In the Noise Parameter rollout, reduce the size of the Noise function from 25 to 0.01 and then press Enter.

   The sample sphere in Slot #1 changes from a default gray to a speckled gray; it looks something like gray granite.

4. Change the Noise Threshold Low value to 0.5, leave the High setting at 1.0, and press Enter.

   As the sample sphere in Slot #1 indicates, most of the intermediate grays disappear and you're left with a black background speckled with intermittent white and gray dots. At this point, you're starting to get something resembling a starfield, so it's time to do another test rendering and check it out.

5. Right-click in your Perspective viewport to activate it and then render a test image. After a moment, the image appears; it should look like Figure 4-3.

Figure 4-3: *The procedural Noise function used to create an extremely dense starfield.*

Although this effect is interesting, it's definitely not the realistic starfield you were probably hoping for. The size and number of stars are much too uniform, and there is not enough shading differentiation between the individual stars. Unless your scene takes place, say, in the center of the universe about five minutes after The Big Bang, there's far too much cosmic debris sitting on your screen.

You can fix this, however, by changing a few more parameters in your Material Editor.

6. Close the Perspective VFB and return to the Material Editor. Under Noise Threshold, change Low from 0.5 to 0.65. Then, under Noise Size, change this from 0.01 to 0.1.

7. Right-click in your Perspective viewport again and render another test image. After a few moments, the new settings for the starfield appear on your screen.

Take a moment to examine this image. As you see, the number of stars has diminished considerably. However, the starfield itself is somewhat dim. Instead of looking like a deep-space scene filled with thousands of bright stars, the effect looks more like a nighttime scene on the Earth's surface. (This in itself might be a useful effect for some nighttime scenes. This material is included in your 3DSMAXFX.MAT Material Library as Stars Noise Night.) However, if you adjust these settings just a little bit more, you can create a more realistic outer space starfield.

8. Close your Perspective VFB and return to the Material Editor. Under Noise Parameters, change Noise Type from Regular to Fractal. This changes the appearance of the stars, as indicated on the sample sphere in Slot #1. There's now more of a range in size and color.

9. Right-click in your Perspective viewport and render another test image. After a moment, the new image appears; it should look like Figure 4-4.

Figure 4-4: *A Fractal noise texture used to create a deep-space starfield.*

As Figure 4-4 indicates, you now have a fairly decent range between bright stars of sufficient size with more dense stars in the background. This may be all you need to create a realistic deep-space image for your outer-space still images. You might also render a still image of this background to use as a bitmap texture on another piece of geometry, as you'll see in the next chapter.

Again, please remember that you cannot use a Noise texture on a Spherical Environmental map for animated sequences; the Noise texture is randomized every frame and will produce undesirable results.

If you want to experiment further, return to the Material Editor and play with the Noise parameters. You may want to save your various Noise textures renderings to your own 3D Studio MAX Material Library.

The material you've just created is included in the 3DSMAXFX.MAT Material Library as Star Noise Fractal.

## Moving On

In the next chapter, you'll explore how to create starfields by using 3D geometry, the Noise texture, and high-resolution bitmaps. In subsequent chapters, you'll see how you can fill all that star-filled space with everything from glowing nebulas to burning suns.

# 5

# Starlight, Starbright, Part II

**W**ith 3D Studio Release 4 for DOS, situations often occur in which, to create a background image that moves properly with your "foreground" camera, you have to take a background image bitmap and map it onto a *cyclorama* object. (A cyclorama in theater or movie nomenclature is a curved piece of material, perhaps wood or canvas, on which a background image has been applied. Cycloramas can give the impression of a distant background out the windows of a stage or movie set.)

In 3D Studio/DOS and 3D Studio MAX, a cyclorama object can be a 2D shape or Quad Patch object, the inner faces of cylinder, a hemisphere, or a sphere. This object then encompasses your 3D foreground scene and provides the illusion of a distant background. Using this technique, you can move your camera within the foreground set and the background image stays in synchronization with the foreground objects.

This technique has drawbacks, of course. If your camera gets too close to the cyclorama object, the bitmap applied to the cyclorama may become too fuzzy and "soft," betraying its 2D nature.

You would then realize that, instead of being on the horizon line (theoretically at infinity), the background image is mapped onto 3D mesh geometry surrounding your foreground scene. (You can mitigate or correct this by increasing the resolution of your background image and by using judicious camera movements.)

Sometimes, however, you might want to use this effect to create a starfield in a 3D Studio MAX space scene. For example, you might actually want to cause an area of space to "distort" (creating a *Star Trek*-style anomaly, for instance). To create this distorted effect, you could apply a Space Warp modifier to part or all of the cyclorama geometry that you're using to create your starfield. Adjust a few parameters, and zap!—you've got a rippling starfield, perhaps heralding the appearance of a decloaking ship. (Although this book doesn't cover that specific effect, it would be very interesting for you to try...)

## Creating Starfields With Geometry & Images

Creating starfields as 3D cyclorama objects is pretty easy. The techniques explored in the previous chapter of using the STAR1024.TGA image and the procedural Noise textures loaded as Environmental map backgrounds can just as easily be used to create starfields as combinations of geometry and images.

If you want to use a bitmap as your background, you can start by taking starfield imagery created with a paint program such as Autodesk Animator Pro, Autodesk Animator Studio, or Adobe Photoshop, and mapping that imagery onto a large 3D sphere—one big enough to hold the elements in your space scene. You can also take digitized images from NASA archives or retouched astronomical photos and use those as your textures.

Also, as you saw in the previous chapter, you can use 3D Studio MAX's procedural Noise textures to create the textures for your star sphere. Again, occasions may come up when you want to create your optical effects "in-camera" and combine starfields with other optical, lighting, or object modifier manipulation effects. Using bitmap images or procedural textures mapped onto 3D geometry surrounding your scene makes doing this easier.

*Note: One advantage of applying a Noise starfield texture onto a cyclo-rama object is that, unlike Environmental Mapping, the Noise starfield texture isn't reapplied randomly on every frame of your animation. Therefore, the Noise starfield texture won't produce undesirable results during the course of your animated sequences. (Of course, if you want, you can animate your Noise starfield texture to produce unusual effects. You can try this on your own.)*

The following steps show you how to create a sphere and apply a starfield bitmap to it; later, you'll modify the material to produce a Noise starfield texture.

1. If you have not reset 3D Studio MAX, save your current work; then select File/Reset to change your 3D Studio MAX desktop to its default settings. You need to create a high-resolution sphere.

2. From the Command Panel, select Create/Geometry if it is not already selected. Under Object Type, click on Sphere. The Sphere Parameters rollout appears.

3. Leave Creation Method rather than Edge as the default of Center. In your Top viewport, place your mouse cursor in the center of your construction grid crosshairs. Click and drag to create a sphere with a radius of approximately 200, as indicated under the Parameters section of the Sphere rollout. When you're finished, release the mouse button to create the sphere. If you want, you can select and highlight the number field in radius and type **200** to create a sphere exactly 200 units in radius.

    You now want to increase the Segments number to bring up the complexity of the sphere and to make the surface of it smoother.

4. Return to the Create Panel. Under Segments, change the number from 16 to 36 and press Enter. In your viewports, you'll see the sphere change from a 16-sided sphere to a much smoother, 36-sided sphere. Now go up to the name field, highlight Sphere01, and rename it Star Sphere. Your screen should look like Figure 5-1.

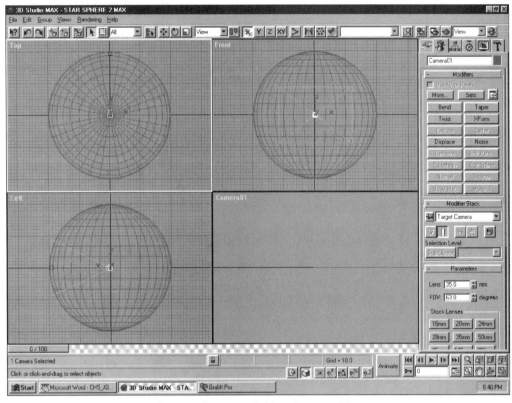

Figure 5-1: *A 36-segment sphere used as a starfield cyclorama object.*

5. In the Create Panel, click on Generate Mapping Coordinates to activate it. This eliminates the need to apply a separate UVW map for this tutorial.

6. Click on the Zoom Extents All button to center the Star Sphere object in all four of your viewports.

7. Return to the Create Panel and click on the Cameras button rather than Geometry. Under Object Type, click on Target; the Parameters rollout for a targeted camera appears.

8. Go back to the Top viewport (which should still be active) and move your cursor to the center of the Star Sphere object. Click and drag to place a targeted camera in the center of the sphere.

Drag the target of the camera along the Y axis until the target touches the top edge of the sphere at approximately the 12 o'clock position in the Top viewport. Release your mouse button to create the camera.

9. Now change your lens parameters from a 50mm lens to a 35mm lens. Under the Stock Lenses section of the Camera01 rollout, click on 35mm.

10. Move your mouse cursor to the Perspective viewport, right-click to make that viewport active, and press the C key to change the Perspective viewport to the Camera01 viewport.

    Now you'll create a variation of your Stars 1024 Background material from the previous chapter and apply it to the sphere.

11. Click on the Star Sphere object to select it and then click on the Material Editor icon to bring up the Material Editor. When it appears, click on the sample sphere in Slot #1 to make it active. You'll change the parameters of this material to create a new Star Sphere material.

12. Change the Ambient and Diffuse colors of Material #1 to pure black, or RGB 0, 0, 0. Change both Shininess and Shininess Strength to 0. Under Self-illumination, change this to 100. You want to make this a completely self-illuminating material.

13. At the bottom of the Material Editor dialog box, open the Map rollout. Load the STAR1024.TGA bitmap from the \CHAP_05 directory of the *3D Studio MAX f/x CD-ROM*.

14. Click in the check box to the right of Diffuse to activate it and then, under Map in the Diffuse name field, double-click on None to open the Material/Map Browser. When it appears, make sure that New is selected from the List of Options, and double-click on Bitmap to return to the Material Editor.

15. In the Bitmap Name field, double-click to bring up the Select Texture Image File browser and, from the \CHAP_05 directory of your *3D Studio MAX f/x CD-ROM*, load the file STAR1024.TGA. It appears on the sample sphere in Slot #1 of the Material Editor. Click on the Go to Parent button to return to the main Material Editor rollout for Material #1.

16. In the Maps parameter rollout, click and drag the Texture #2 (Bitmap) STAR1024.TGA file from the Diffuse slot down to the Self-illumination map slot, and release. The Copy (Instance) Map dialog box appears. Because you're not going to change any of the parameters for the Self-illumination Bitmap texture, under Method, click on Instance rather than Copy, and then click on OK.

17. Now, click and drag the STAR1024.TGA bitmap from the Self-illumination map slot to the Opacity slot. Again, when the Copy (Instance) Map dialog box appears, click on Instance and then click on OK.

    You've now created a new STAR1024 material that you can apply to your Star Sphere object. As you noticed when you dragged the STAR1024.TGA bitmap to the Opacity mapping slot, because the Bitmap is predominantly black with white pinpoint stars, the sample sphere in Slot #1 changes: the material becomes largely transparent but with a scattering of white and grayscale stars.

18. Now that you have created your new starfield material, highlight the Material #1 name and change it to Stars 1024 Sphere. Press Enter to accept the changes.

    If you want, you may place this material in your own Material Library; note that this material is also in the 3DSMAXFX.MAT Material Library.

19. Now apply this material to the Star Sphere geometry. Make sure that the Star Sphere object is selected and, in the Material Editor, click on the Assign Material to Selection icon. When you do, you'll see small white triangles appear in the corner of the selected Slot #1 to indicate that this is now a "hot" material in your scene.

## Inverting the Face Normals

At this point, if you were to render the Star Sphere geometry from the Camera01 view, you would quickly notice that no stars appear in your scene. This is because the camera is inside the Star Sphere, the sphere's face normals are pointing outward, and your Stars 1024 Sphere material is a one-sided material. Therefore, the material appears only on the face normals that are visible in a camera view.

To see the Stars 1024 Sphere material on the inside of the object, you can either make the material two-sided, force a two-sided rendering when you create a test image, or invert the face normals of the sphere.

The first option is easy. In the Material Editor, simply click on the Two-sided option to make the Stars 1024 Sphere material a two-sided material. Because this is a "hot" material in the scene, it makes the material two-sided automatically on your Star Sphere geometry; that is, it's applied both to the inner and outer face normals of the object.

However, to speed up rendering time, you can do something slightly more complicated. You can apply a Normal Object Modifier to your Star Sphere object and use it to invert the face normals.

The following steps show you how to do that.

1. From the Command Panel, click on the Modify tab if it's not already active. Under Modifiers, select Normal. (If you've changed your Modifier settings, or if Normal doesn't appear in your default list, click on the More button to bring up the Normal Object Modifier.) When you select Normal, the Normals rollout appears. Under Parameters, click on the check box next to Flip Normals. As you do so, you'll see the face normals appear in your Camera01 viewport, as shown in Figure 5-2.

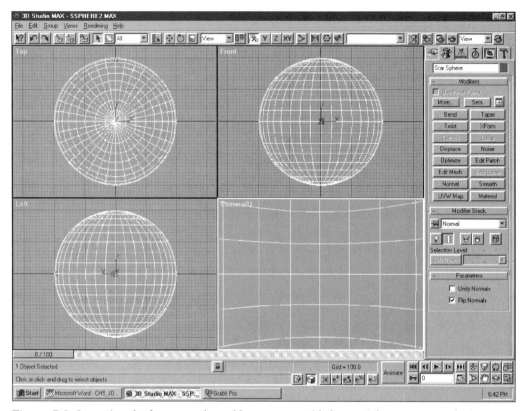

Figure 5-2: *Inverting the face normals enables your one-sided material to appear on the inner faces of the Star Sphere object.*

2. Now you can render a test image of your Star Sphere. Make sure that your Camera01 viewport is active and then press Alt+R and Enter to render a single 640 x 480 image. After a few moments, the image appears on your screen, as shown in Figure 5-3.

Figure 5-3: *The STAR1024 material mapped onto the inside of the sphere. Note the relatively large size of the stars and the sparseness of the number of stars.*

As you saw previously, when you rendered the starfield image as an Environment map, you may need to increase the tiling on the STAR1024.TGA texture map to increase the number of stars.

3. Return to the Material Editor and use the hand cursor to scroll the rollout up to the Maps section. Because you placed the STAR1024.TGA image in the Diffuse slot first and the Self-illumination and Opacity slots are instances of the Diffuse slot, you need to change only the Map parameters for Diffuse. (The Diffuse changes will be applied automatically to Self-illumination and Opacity.) In the Diffuse map section, double-click on the STAR1024.TGA map to open the Bitmap Parameters rollout.

4. Go to the Coordinates section. Under UV Tiling, change both U and V from 1.0 to 3.0; then press Enter. Click on the Go to Parent icon to return to the main Material Editor, right-click again in the Camera01 viewport to activate it, and then render another test image. After a few moments, the revised texture appears.

Now the stars have increased greatly in number and have diminished in size to a more appropriate size and intensity for 640 x 480 resolution space scenes.

If you were to use this Star Sphere object to create your background stars for an animation, you would need to make sure that your Camera didn't get too close to the inner surface of the sphere. Otherwise, you would see that the stars aren't at infinity, but are simply mapped onto a piece of geometry.

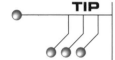

**TIP**

To create the best results for a moving starfield background using a cyclorama object, you want to attach the Star Sphere object to the same path that your camera is traversing during an animation. After you do that, you can tilt, roll, and pan the camera through the scene and the stars will wheel in motion relative to the camera. Because the Star Sphere object remains a fixed distance from the Camera01 body, however, the stars will always present the proper image to the Camera01 lens. For a demonstration of this technique, take a look at the "Moving Nebulas: Adjusting Parallax" and "Converting the Trajectory to a Spline" sections of Chapter 8, "Nebulas On The Move."

Unlike a procedural starfield Video Post filter, to get proper motion blurring of the stars appearing on your Star Sphere object, you must render your animation from Video Post, with Scene Motion Blur active. With the proper settings, your bitmapped star images will streak properly during fast camera moves.

5. When you are finished looking at the rendering, close your Camera01 VFB window.

If you want, you can save the Stars 1024 Sphere material to your Material Library; don't reset 3D Studio MAX, however, because you're going to use this Star Sphere object to understand the procedural Noise starfield texture.

CD-ROM    Your current scene is in the \CHAP_05 directory of your *3D Studio MAX f/x CD-ROM* as SSPHERE1.MAX.

## Creating Starfields with Geometry & the Noise Texture

To create a dense starfield using the procedural Noise texture, you need to change only a few of the parameters that you had set previously in the Material Editor using the STAR1024.TGA image.
The following steps show you how to do it.

1. Return to the Material Editor and scroll down to the Maps rollout under the Stars 1024 Sphere material. Because Diffuse contains the controlling map for the other textures in the Self-Illumination and Opacity map slots, all you need to do is change the parameters for Diffuse. Double-click on the STAR1024.TGA Bitmap in the Diffuse Maps section. This takes you to the Diffuse Bitmap Parameters rollout, where you see the STAR1024.TGA image loaded. You'll change this to the Noise Texture.

2. To the right of Type, double-click on the word Bitmap to bring up the Material/Map Browser. Under the Browse From section, click on New if it is not already selected and then double-click on Noise. When the Replace Map dialog box appears, click on OK to discard your old texture map. When you return to the Material Editor, you'll see that the material on the sample sphere in Slot #1 has changed to a mottled gray.

3. Under the Noise Parameters section of the rollout, change the following parameters: Under Size, change it from 25.0 to 0.1; under Noise Type, change it from Regular to Fractal; under Noise Threshold: Low, change the amount from 0.0 to 0.5. Press Enter to accept these settings. When you're finished, click on the Go to Parent icon to return to the main Material Editor rollout.

4. Highlight the Stars 1024 Sphere material name and change it to Stars Noise. Again, you may save this material to your own 3DSMAX.MAT Material Library, although it is already saved in the 3DSMAXFX.MAT Material Library.

Because this material is active on the Star Sphere object, the changes that you've made to the material are applied automatically to the object. Therefore, you don't need to select the object and reassign the new material. If you look under Maps, you'll see that, because you loaded the Noise texture into the Diffuse slot, the texture has also loaded into the Self-illumination and Opacity slots because they are instances of the Diffuse Bitmap slot.

5. Right-click again in the Camera01 viewport to activate it and render another test image. After a few moments, the procedural Star Noise texture appears on the Star Sphere object, as shown in Figure 5-4.

Figure 5-4: *The procedural Noise starfield texture used on the inside of the Star Sphere.*

Again, note that this material may be appropriate not just for a deep space scene but perhaps a nighttime earthly scene. Properly applied, you could create the illusion of a star-filled night sky showing the faint dusting of stars across the Milky Way.

When you are finished experimenting with this scene, you may want to save it to your local 3DSMAX\SCENES directory. This scene is also in the \CHAP_05 directory of your *3D Studio MAX f/x CD-ROM* as SSPHERE2.MAX.

## Moving On

Now that you've finished creating distant stars, you'll focus your attention a little closer. In the next two chapters, you'll explore how you can create the illusion of a burning sun, using volumetric lights, 3D geometry and the Noise procedural texture.

# 6

# Nebulas Made Simple, Part I

**I**n the last two chapters, you examined how to create starfield effects in a variety of ways. By using combinations of 3D Studio MAX's Environmental Mapping, 3D geometry, procedural Noise and bitmap textures, you can create the illusion of a cosmos filled with billions and billions of stars. (Carl Sagan would be proud.)

In this chapter and the next two, you will see how you can use variations of the starfield techniques to create colorful nebula effects. In addition, you will see how to set up your animation so that your nebula moves properly against your starfield backgrounds.

## Nebulas: Astronomical Wonders or Just a Bunch of Gas?

Although creating star-filled backgrounds in 3D Studio MAX is easy, populating your deep-space vistas with nebulas is also quite interesting. Astronomically speaking, a nebula is simply a cloud of gas, often made up of primitive compounds such as methane, ammonia, and the like. Different gases produce different colors, which usually include purple, magenta, and red shades. (You've probably seen images from NASA of the Crab and Horseshoe Nebulas, for example, showing these tones to good effect.) Nebulas add color and definition to your space scene, and break the monotony of black space and white stars. (They also look pretty nifty.)

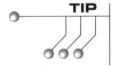

**TIP** For a realistic deep-space look, you should generally use a harsh, single-source light and little or no fill light. A colorful gas cloud helps silhouette spaceship contours and other foreground objects such as planets, moons, and asteroids. For a brighter fantasy effect, the presence of nebulas can also provide a rationale for a particular color of ambient or shadow-casting fill light.

The basic principles used to place a nebula in your space scene are the same as those used to create starfields: Environmental maps and/or applying texture maps to geometry in your 3D Studio MAX scene. In the case of the latter, you can take an image—either painted, scanned or computer-generated—and use Texture, Self-illumination, and Opacity maps to place it on geometry in your 3D scene. The geometry itself can be a 2D shape, or it can be a 3D mesh surrounding your scene.

Finally, you can create nebula images by using transparent yet shiny geometry, and placing tinted lights inside. The specular highlights kicked up by the lights can produce interesting, subtle effects.

The following sections take a look at how you can create all of these effects.

## Creating a Nebula with Environmental Mapping & Noise

In Chapter 4, "Starlight, Starbright, Part I," you saw how you could use 3D Studio MAX's Environmental mapping to place starfields in your outer space scenes. Now you'll see how you can use a variation of this technique to create starfields and nebula effects through the use of bitmaps and the procedural Noise texture.

1. First, reset 3D Studio MAX. If you have not saved your scene settings from the previous chapter, please do so before you select Reset.

2. Open the Material Editor. You are going to create a new procedural starfield material and combine it with a procedural Noise texture to create a simple nebula. In the Material Editor, Material Slot #1 should be active. Ignore the settings under the Basic Parameter section of the rollout because altering these will have no appreciable effect on this Environment map.

3. Click on the small map button to the right of the Diffuse swatch to bring up the Material/Map Browser. Under Browse From, select New; then, from the list window, double-click on Mix to return you to the Material Editor with the Mix Parameters rollout open.

    A Mix material type lets you mix combinations of bitmaps, procedural textures, or other types of textures in a single material. You'll want to load a combination of textures into the Color #1 and Color #2 slots.

4. Do Color #1 first. Under the Maps section, click on the map name button (that now reads None) to bring up the Material/Map Browser again. Make sure that New is selected in the Browse From section; then, double-click on Bitmap. You are returned to the Material Editor with the Bitmap Parameters rollout open.

5. Click on the Bitmap name button to bring up the Select Texture Image file Browser. From the \CHAP_06 directory of your *3D Studio MAX f/x CD-ROM*, load the file STAR1024.TGA. The bitmap appears on the sample sphere in Slot #1.

CD-ROM

6. Under the Coordinates section of the rollout, click on Environment to change from Texture to the default Spherical Environment map. Then, change Tiling for both U and V from 1.0 to 3.0. (Doing so will make the starfield appear more dense in your test rendering.) When finished, click on the Go to Parent icon to return to the Mix Parameters rollout. You'll see that next to Color #1, the STAR1024.TGA bitmap is listed under Maps.

7. Click on the map name button next to Color #2 to bring up the Material/Map Browser again. This time, instead of selecting Bitmap in the list window, select Noise. You are returned to the Material Editor with the Noise Parameters rollout open.

8. Now you'll change the settings. Change Noise Type to Fractal. Leave Size at 25; then, click on the White color swatch of Color #2 to bring up the Color Selector. Change this color to RGB settings 64, 0, 128, or a dark purple; then, dismiss the Color Selector.

9. Click on the Go to Parent icon to return to the Mix Parameter Screen. Change Mix Amount to 0.5; then, press Enter to accept these settings.

10. From the Menu Bar, select Rendering/Environment. The Environment Map dialog box appears. Under Background, click on Use Map; then, under Environment Map, click on Assign. The Material/Map Browser appears.

11. Under Browse From, select Material Editor. At the top of the list is the word None; directly below are the settings for the Slot #1 material that you just modified. Double-click on Texture #1 (Mix). This loads your new Texture #1 into the Environment Map slot. Then, dismiss the Environment dialog box.

12. Now you'll do a test rendering of this texture. Activate your Perspective viewport and then press Alt+R and Enter to render a 640 x 480 still image. After a few moments your image appears; it should look like Figure 6-1.

Figure 6-1: *The STAR1024.TGA bitmap combined with a Noise texture using a Mix material.*

Notice that, on your screen, the dark-purplish Noise texture in the Color #2 slot of the Mix material has resulted in a soft, shaded wash of color in your outer space scene. Again, because this is a procedural texture applied as an Environment map, the purplish color completely covers the background, no matter which direction you point your camera.

Although this effect is useful for still images, you may want to adjust the Noise settings to change the appearance of the nebula gas clouds in your scene. In addition, by varying the Mix amount, you can increase the preponderance of the STAR1024 imagery and make it override the Noise texture in the Color #2 slot.

The material you just created is in the 3DSMAXFX.MAT Material Library as Stars/Nebula Mix 1. You can also rename Material #1 to Stars/Nebula Mix 1 and save it to your local Material Library before proceeding to the next step.

## The Art of Noise: Layering the Textures

Now that you've created a nice stars-and-nebula Mix material, you can improve it. 3D Studio MAX's Material Editor lets you build up as many layers of textures as you need. So, continue to layer your Stars/Nebula Mix 1 material.

1. In the Material Editor, locate the Mix parameters rollout. Click on the button labeled Tex #3 (Noise) to bring up the Noise rollout. Under Noise parameters, the deep-purple color is in the Color #2 slot; Color #1 is still black. Now you'll add another color layer, using another Noise map, on top of the initial dark-purple Noise in Color #2 slot.

2. Click on the Names button next to the Color #2 swatch (it now reads None). In the Material/Map Browser, make sure that New is selected; then, double-click on Noise. Another Noise Parameters rollout appears.

   You now have a secondary layer of Noise on top of your first dark-purple Noise layer. You can see some of the changes in the Material Sample Slot #1.

3. Under Noise Parameters, change the size to 15 and change Noise Type to Turbulence. Then, click on the white Color #2 color swatch to bring up the Color Selector. Change the RGB settings to 200, 0, 32 (dark red); then, close the Color Selector.

4. Click on the Go to Parent button to return to the previous Noise parameters rollout; then, click on Go to Parent again to return to the main texture level. Because this is a "hot" or active texture in your scene, the changes you made are reflected immediately in the Environment map.

5. Now you'll render another test image. Activate the Perspective viewport; then, press Alt+R and Enter to see the effect of your new Noise settings on the background. After a moment the image appears on your screen.

Notice how combining and layering the noise textures has resulted in the purple and deep-red colors blending together.

As mentioned earlier, 3D Studio MAX lets you create very complex textures—and very subtle effects, too—by layering combinations of material types, whether procedural or bitmap.

Naturally, you don't need to limit this effect to creating Environment maps; you should apply these textures to geometry in your scene and experiment. Try different levels of colors, Noise parameter settings, and bitmap images to get the effect you want.

## Creating a Nebula Using Environmental Mapping & Bitmaps

As you've just seen, when you use the layering features of 3D Studio MAX's Material Editor, you can build up complex textures to be loaded into your Environment Map backgrounds.

Of course, there's no reason that you can't use a prerendered, high-resolution bitmap that combines a nebula texture with a starfield. If you want, you can use a Mix material and combine a starfield background with a nebula image; you can also use a single nebula and starfield bitmap.

Now, examine the latter, very simple effect:

1. Save your previous work if you have not already done so; then, select File/Reset. Make sure that your Perspective viewport is active, then select Rendering/Environment. The Environment Editor appears. Under Background, click on Use Map; then, click on Assign. The Material/Map Browser appears.

2. Under Browse From, select New; then, double-click on Bitmap. When the Environment dialog box reappears, you can see that Map #1 (Bitmap) has been loaded in the Environment Map slot; click on it. The Put to Material Editor dialog box appears, and Slot #1 should be active as the default. Click on OK; then, close the Environment dialog box and open the Material Editor.

3. In the Material Editor, Slot #1 is empty. You want to load a prerendered starfield and nebula image; therefore, in the Bitmap Parameters rollout, click on the Bitmap name button. The Select Texture Image file dialog box appears.

4. From the \CHAP_06 directory of your *3D Studio MAX f/x* CD-ROM, highlight the file STARNEB1.TGA and click on View. This is a very high-resolution image (2048 x 1024 pixels) created in several different programs. I created the initial grayscale starfield by using the Spray feature of Autodesk

Animator Pro, with color cycling turned on. The Nebula image was created by using the Yost Group Vapor IPAS routine, running in 3D Studio/DOS. After changing the colors from fiery reds, golds, and yellows to blues and purples, I rendered a high-resolution still image. I then took both the starfield and the vapor images and composited them in Adobe Photoshop.

When you're finished viewing the image, close the view window and double-click on the filename to load it.

5. When you return to the Material Editor, you should see the STARNEB1.TGA image appear on the material sample sphere in Slot #1.

6. Activate your Perspective viewport and render a test image. After a moment the image appears; it looks like Figure 6-2.

Figure 6-2: *A starfield and nebula bitmap loaded as a spherical Environment background.*

Yuck. This isn't really what you want—even at 2048 x 1024 resolution the stars appear as out-of-focus blobs and the nebula is nowhere to be seen. You can fix this by bumping up the UV tiling of the image.

7. Return to the Material Editor, and under the Coordinates section, change the Tiling for both U and V from 1.0 to 4.0. Then, activate your Perspective viewport and render another test image, as shown in Figure 6-3.

Figure 6-3: *The increased UV tiling results in a denser starfield with a better-looking nebula background.*

## Dissecting the Effect

At this point, I need to do a "good news, bad news" dissection of this effect. The good news is that you now have a proper-looking starfield and nebula background for 640 x 480 resolution renderings. And, unless your camera target moves drastically throughout a long animation sequence, you probably won't notice that the nebula image and star patterns repeat.

The bad news is that, even with a high-resolution texture map, you still have to increase the bitmap tiling—which might be noticeable, depending on the camera movement in your final animation. And, of course, loading a single giant texture into your Environment map may take up more RAM than you can spare. So, how can you duplicate this effect without loading a gigantic bitmap?

Actually, you should already have the knowledge you need to address this problem. The \MAPS\TGA directory of your *3D Studio MAX f/x* CD-ROM has several starfield backgrounds, such as the 640 x 480 STARS640.TGA image, as well as several stand-alone NEBULA images. By using a Mix material, you can load a low-resolution starfield background (even 320 x 240), increase its tiling, and use it as Texture #1. Then, by loading a lower-resolution, stand-alone Nebula texture and tiling it (or not) to suit your needs, you can create the same effect without having to use a giant, memory-gobbling bitmap. (And, depending on your camera placement and how the nebula is placed in your scene, you may not notice that a low-resolution starfield is tiling.)

**CD-ROM**

Although this technique is not covered explicitly in this book, at this point you should feel comfortable enough with the Mix material and 3D Studio MAX's layering abilities to explore this technique on your own.

## Moving On

Coming up in the next two chapters: how to create nebulas using Geometry, Omni lights and/or bitmaps, and how to get them to move properly against your starfield backgrounds. It's amazing what you can do with a simple sphere and a couple of Omni lights.

# 7

# Nebulas Made Simple, Part II

**I**n the last chapter, you saw how you could create nebula effects by using Mix materials, loaded as backgrounds using 3D Studio MAX's Environment feature. In this chapter, you will see how you can create nebulas by applying different textures on 3D geometry in your scenes. You will also see how you can use a combination of geometry and Omni lights to create nebula effects.

## Creating Nebulas Using Geometry & Omni Lights

Okay, now that you've explored how you can use bitmaps and other textures to create nebula effects, here's another interesting way to create nebulas as combinations of 3D geometry, lights, and custom materials in your 3D space scenes.

1. Save your current work; then, reset 3D Studio MAX. You want to create a sphere that will serve as a physical nebula object.

2. In the Create Command Panel, select Geometry/Sphere. In the Top viewport, click your cursor in the center of the grid and drag outward to create a sphere with a radius of approximately

200. After you have created it, you can make it exactly 200 units in radius by typing **200** in the Radius number field and pressing Enter.

3. Change Segments from 16 to 36 and press Enter. You'll want a fairly complex sphere for this effect. Then, highlight the name Sphere01 and change it to Nebula01.

4. Select File/Preferences, and when the Preferences dialog box appears, toggle off Cast Shadows and Receive Shadows on the Nebula01 object.

Now, modify the topology of this Nebula01 sphere. If you were working in 3D Studio/DOS, you might distort the surface of this sphere by selecting vertices by hand and moving them, or by using IPAS Plug-ins such as Displace, Crumple, or Fractalize. Then, by applying various amounts of tessellation, you could modify the sphere so that it resembled a smooth, yet uneven, perhaps rocky surface.

However, in 3D Studio MAX, you don't have to move vertices by hand unless you want to. Instead, you can distort your Nebula01 object by applying various Object Modifiers to it. (You'll explore this in greater depth in a later chapter, when you create your own asteroids.)

## Adding Modifiers for Fun & Profit

Now you'll add some object modifiers to the Nebula.

1. Click on the Zoom Extents All icon. This will center the Nebula01 object in all four of your viewports so that you can see the Modifier effects more clearly. Make sure that the Nebula01 object is selected. Then, from the Command Panel, click on the Modify tab to bring up the Modify Panel.

    The first Modifier that you want to apply is Noise. Noise applies a procedural topology distortion effect to selected 3D geometry in your scene.

2. If Noise is not already a part of your Modifier set, click on the More button to bring up the Modifier list; then, click on Noise. When you pick Noise, an orange box will appear around your

Nebula01 object. This is the Noise Modifier Gizmo. In the Modify Panel, you should also see the Noise modifier appear in the Modifier Stack.

3. Scroll the Modify Panel until you can see the Noise Strength and Animation options under Parameters. Under Noise, click on Fractal to activate it. Change Roughness from 0.0 to 1.0. Leave Iterations at its default setting of 6.0. Under Strength X, enter **10**; under Y, enter **15**; under Z, enter **25**. Then, press Enter to accept all these changes.

The Noise modifier has applied a fair amount of distortion to the surface of your Nebula01 object, as shown on your screen and in Figure 7-1.

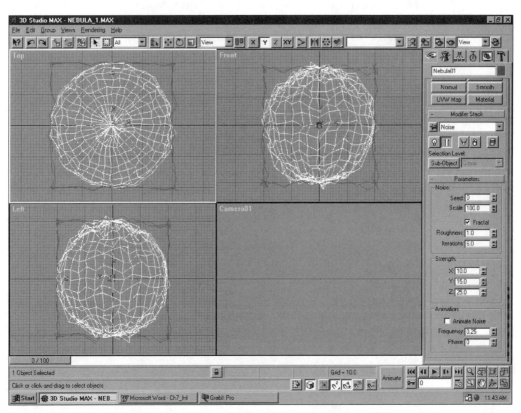

Figure 7-1: *The Nebula01 sphere object with the Noise Edit Mesh modifier applied.*

Although this is an interesting effect, you need to smooth the surface of this object to create a better nebula.

4. From the Modifiers Command Panel, click on Edit Mesh from the Modifiers list; this modifier is added to the top of the Modifier Stack.

At this point, you are at the Sub-Object selection level. The default is Vertex, so the object's vertices are visible as Vertex Ticks. You'll want to select all the faces of the Nebula01 object because you're going to tessellate it to smooth its surface.

5. Under Selection Level: Sub-Object, click on the Down arrow and select Face rather than Vertex. The vertical ticks disappear and you see the rollout change beneath the Selection Level.

6. Click on the Select Object icon. Then, in any of your viewports, drag a bounding box around the entire Nebula01 object to select all of its faces. As you do so, you'll see the faces turn red on your screen, indicating that they're selected.

7. Return to the Modify Panel and scroll the rollout up until you see the Tessellate section. Click on the Tessellate button. You see the number of faces on the Nebula01 sphere increase, and the edges of the Nebula01 object become smoother, as shown in Figure 7-2.

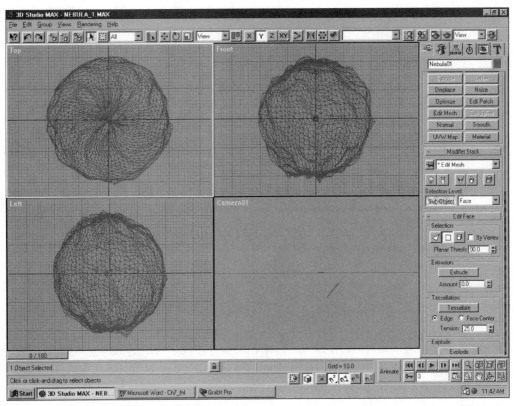

Figure 7-2: *The Nebula01 object with a Noise modifier and an Edit Mesh: Tessellate modifier applied.*

Although the result of tessellating an object in 3D Studio MAX resembles the same effect as that achieved in 3D Studio/DOS, you can remove the modifiers (as you can with virtually all of 3D Studio MAX's Object modifiers) and restore your object to its original, unmodified state.

Now, because you'll place a camera inside the Nebula01 object and apply a one-sided material to the object (to speed rendering), you need to flip the Nebula01's face normals.

8. Return to the Modify Command Panel and click on Normal from the Modifiers rollout (or from the list of additional modifiers). This applies a Normal modifier to the Nebula01 modifier stack. Under Parameters, click on Flip Normals. This inverts the face normals of the Nebula01 object so that they now face inward rather than outward. A one-sided material applied to this object will now appear to a camera placed inside the object.

## On That Note...

...You will now create a camera and an Omni light, and put them inside the Nebula.

1. Click on the Create tab of the Command Panel; then, click on the Camera button. Under Object Type, pick Target.

2. Move your cursor to the center of your Top viewport; then, click and drag vertically upward until you create a targeted camera sitting directly in the center of your Nebula01 object. (If you check the status line at the bottom of your screen, you should drag the Camera01 target to approximately Y 170.) Release your mouse button to create the camera.

   Now, you'll change the focal length of the camera to create a wide-angle view.

3. Under the Stock Lenses section of the Create Panel, click on 28mm. Then, right-click in the Perspective viewport to activate it and press the C key on your keyboard. This changes your Perspective viewport to the Camera01 viewport; the interior faces of the Nebula01 object appear.

4. Return to the Create Panel and click on the Lights icon. Under Object Type, click on Omni. Under General Parameters, change the color of the Omni light to the following RGB settings: 32, 0, 180. Move your cursor to the Top viewport, activate it, and place your mouse cursor to approximate XY coordinates X 70, Y 150. Left-click to place the Omni light, making sure that the Omni light is inside the boundaries of the Nebula01 object.

   Your screen should look like Figure 7-3.

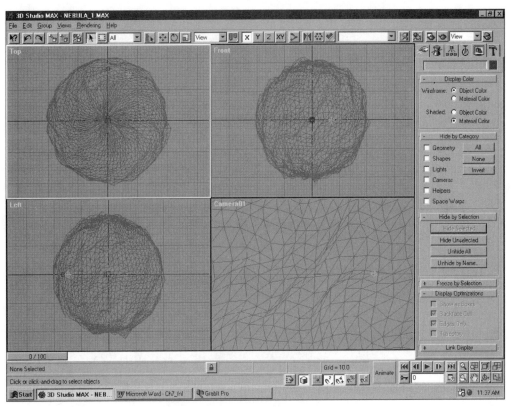

Figure 7-3: *A 28mm camera and Omni light placed inside a tessellated sphere.*

## Living in a Material World

Now it's time to create a simple material and apply it to your Nebula01 object.

1. Select the Nebula01 object (either click on it or press the H key to bring up the Select by Name dialog box, and select it.) The object turns white.

    Because you won't be applying a specific bitmap as a texture, you don't need to activate the Nebula01's Generate Mapping Coordinates or apply a UVW Mapping modifier to the sphere.

    Now you'll create a shiny but completely transparent material to apply to the Nebula01 object.

2. Click on the Material Editor icon to bring up the Material Editor. You'll make the changes to Material #1 and then apply it to the Nebula01 sphere. Under Basic Parameters, change both Ambient and Diffuse to solid black, or RGB 0, 0, 0. Change Specular to pure white, or RGB 255, 255, 255.

3. Change the Shininess value to 25 and Shininess Strength to 100. Then, change Opacity from 100 to 0 (right-click on the spinner to reduce it to 0 quickly). As the Material #1 sample sphere indicates, you now have a shiny but completely transparent material (like clear glass). Because you inverted the face normals of the Nebula01 object, you don't need to make Material #1 a two-sided material. Now, change the Material #1 name to Nebula Glass 1.

   If you want, you may put this material in your own 3DSMAX.MAT Material Library, but—you guessed it—it's also saved in the 3DSMAXFX.MAT Material Library.

4. Click on the Assign Material to Selection icon to assign Nebula Glass 1 to the selected Nebula01 object.

   You have one more thing to do before you do a test rendering: load a starfield background to properly show off the new nebula effect.

5. Select Rendering/Environment from the Menu Bar. The Environment dialog box appears. Under Background, click on Use Map to activate it; then, click on Assign to bring up the Material/Map Browser. Under Browse From, click on New and then double-click on Bitmap. This action loads the Bitmap parameters into the Environment Map.

6. Under Environment Map, click on the Name button. When the Put to Material Editor dialog box appears, click on Slot #2 to place this material in Slot #2 of the Material Editor. Then, click on OK to dismiss this menu. Close the Environment dialog box.

   Now return to the Material Editor and in Slot #2, you'll see a black sample sphere.

7. Click on Slot #2 to make it active; the Bitmap Parameters rollout appears. Click on the Bitmap name button to bring up the Select Texture Image file Browser. From your *3D Studio MAX f/x CD-ROM*, go to the \CHAP_07 directory and load the file STARS640.TGA.

When you return to the Material Editor, you should see very little change on the sample sphere in Slot #2. That's because you haven't yet changed the default Spherical Environment mapping coordinates for the background.

8. Under the Coordinates section of the rollout, click on the Down arrow to the right of Spherical Environment and change it to Screen. You now see that the stars appear properly in Slot #2.

9. Now, activate the Camera01 viewport, press Alt+R, and press Enter to render a 640 x 480 test image.

After a few moments the image will appear and should look something like Figure 7-4. Naturally, its appearance will vary, depending, of course, on how the Noise modifier affected the Nebula01 object.

Figure 7-4: *An Omni light inside the Nebula01 object picks out specular highlights on the object, creating the appearance of nebulous-looking gas clouds.*

Take a few moments to examine the effect on your screen. Although it's simple to produce, it's surprisingly effective. The Omni light picks out the specular highlights on the Nebula01 object, resulting in soft washes of color, but the Nebula01 object itself is totally invisible. The specular highlights appear more as an optical effect than as an attribute of solid 3D geometry.

## Varying the Effect

You can vary this technique of using Omni lights inside distorted geometry to create soft gas clouds and nebula effects for your outer space scenes in many ways. For instance, you can adjust the Noise and Tessellation parameters of your Edit Mesh modifiers to change the topology of your initial Sphere01 object, or apply other modifiers, such as a Displace modifier.

You can also adjust this effect by manipulating the Omni light (or lights) in the Nebula01 object. Depending on the Omni lights' positions, you can produce interesting effects as the lights pick out specular highlights running along creases and ridges of the Nebula object.

Another thing to try is to create multiple, nested nebula objects, each with its own assigned lighting and geometry modifiers, to produce variegated color effects. Remember to use the Edit/ Properties command and change the Shadow Casting and Shadow Receiving attributes on the Nebula objects to Off to avoid any unwanted shadows.

You may also want to confine the color effects to specific areas. To do this, you can select the particular Omni lights that you want to adjust, turn Attenuation On, and adjust the ranges of the lights.

Finally, you might also change the material attributes of the Nebula01 object. For a softer, more translucent gas effect, you could lower the Shininess and Shininess Strength values. For a harder, sharper glow, you would simply increase those values. The current Nebula Glass 1 material has Shininess and Shininess Strength set to 25 and 100, respectively. If you change the Shininess Strength to 50, then the specular highlight will be more translucent than it is with a setting of 100.

## Adding Lights to Blend Colors

Now that you've seen how to create nebula effects with a combination of transparent, shiny geometry and an Omni light, you can go on to vary this effect further. Now you'll create a second Omni light (with a different color from the first one) to see the effect of blended specular highlight colors.

1. Click on the Select by Name button (or press H on your keyboard) to bring up the Select by Name dialog box. Click on Omni01, then, press Enter to select the light.

2. Now, click on the Select and Move icon, go to the Top viewport, and holding down the Shift key, drag the Omni light to the left to the approximate coordinate X -110. When you release the mouse button, the Copy Options dialog box appears. Click on OK or press Enter to make a copy of the Omni light, called Omni02.

3. Right-click in the Left viewport to activate it. Because you're still in Select and Move mode, move the Omni02 light up to the approximate coordinate Y 45.

4. With this light still selected, click on the Modify tab of the Command Panel. Under General Parameters, change the RGB color settings for the Omni02 light to 196, 0, 32; then, press Enter. You've now created a reddish-magenta light.

5. Activate your Camera01 viewport and do a test rendering. After a few moments, the image appears.

Do you see how the specular highlight colors blend together on your screen? (For the purposes of this tutorial, I've deliberately set the Omni light colors to be somewhat bright so that you can more clearly see the effect. For added realism in your outer space scenes, you may want to bring down the intensity of the colors.)

## Isolating the Effect

As mentioned earlier, if you want to limit the range of the light effect, you can do this easily by activating the Ranges and Attenuation of the Omni lights in the scene.

1. Close the Camera01 Virtual Frame Buffer window and then return to the Modify Panel.

   Now you'll restrict the influence that the Omni02 light has on the Nebula01 object. The Omni02 light should still be selected.

2. In the Modify Panel, drag the rollout up until you see the Attenuation section at the bottom. Under Attenuation, click on Use and Show to activate them. When you do so, the Start range and End range icons appear around the Omni02 light.

   These spheres show the default hotspot and falloff ranges for the Omni02 light. The defaults are a Start Range of 80 and an End range of 320. Because these are fairly large for your scene, you should reduce them.

3. Select Start Range and change it from 80 to 50. Then, select End Range and change it from 320 to 100. Press Enter to accept these settings.

4. Now click on the Omni01 light to select it and return to the Modify Panel. Go down to Attenuation and click on Use and Show to activate the Attenuation icons for the Omni01 light. Set the Start range to 50 and the End range to 150. Press Enter to accept these settings.

   When you're finished, activate your Camera01 viewport and render another test image, as shown in Figure 7-5.

Figure 7-5: *The attenuation and ranges set on the two Omni lights restrict the specular highlight on the Nebula01 object to a relatively small area.*

5. Close the Camera01 VFB window.

Again, note how in this rendering the ranges and attenuation settings have resulted in the specular highlight effect being restricted to a relatively small area on the Nebula01 object.

## Ooh, Shiny Object

Now you'll explore some other ways that you can change the appearance of your nebula simply by altering the shininess values of the Nebula Glass 1 material.

1. With the Omni01 light still selected, return to the Modify Panel and turn off Use and Show Attenuation. Select the Omni02 light and do the same.

2. Click on the Material Editor icon to bring up the Material Editor. You'll modify the Nebula Glass 1 material parameters. Change Shininess to 15 and set Shininess Strength to 75. This creates a softer, more translucent glow; it also makes the nebula colors less intense. (If you want, you may also click on Soften to further soften the highlight.)

At this point, if you want to check on the effect, activate your Camera01 viewport and re-render a new test image. (I'll wait.)

Now you'll continue adjusting this effect.

3. In the Material Editor, open the Maps rollout and click on the Maps name button next to Shininess. When the Material/Map Browser appears, click on New; then, click on Noise to load as a Shininess map. When you return to the Material Editor, change Noise Type from Regular to Fractal. Change Size from 25.0 to 5 and press Enter to accept these settings.

4. Activate your Camera01 viewport and render another test image, as shown in Figure 7-6.

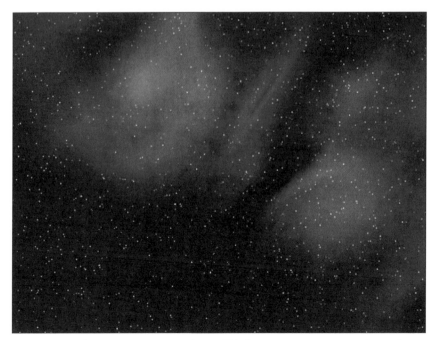

Figure 7-6: *The Noise texture used as a Shininess map creates a variegated specular highlight on the Nebula01 object.*

As you examine the rendering on your screen, notice how the Noise Shininess map has broken up the specular highlight into a dappled pattern. In addition, it produces a mix of the reddish-magenta and bluish highlights from the Omni lights, resulting in an altogether more interesting effect.

## Crossing the Threshold

Okay, what other wackiness can you do? Why don't you see what happens when you change the Noise Size and Noise Threshold level?

1. Close the Camera01 VFB and return to the Material Editor. Under Noise Parameters, change Size to 10. Under Noise Threshold, change Low from 0.0 to 0.5 and press Enter to accept these settings. This effectively clamps the Noise function to a narrower range.

2. Okay, you know the drill. Activate your Camera01 viewport and render another test image.

    As you examine this test rendering, you see that raising the Low Threshold setting has caused a more random blotchy pattern to appear in the specular highlight of the magenta and red Omni lights.

3. When you're finished, close the Camera01 viewport.

 You may want to save these material settings to your own Material Library, but, again, the three settings that you've just experimented with have been included as Nebula Glass 1, Nebula Glass 2, and Nebula Glass 3 in the 3DSMAXFX.MAT Material Library.

What other things can you try to change the appearance of your nebula? Well, you can try animating the Noise parameters of the Shininess map to create the illusion of a swimming series of gas clouds. In addition, you can animate the Noise parameters of the Nebula01 object, the colors of the Omni lights, their positions in the scene during your animation, and even their attenuation and ranges.

Finally, you don't even have to be restricted to creating nebulas with only geometry and Omni lights. If you want, you could remove the Object Modifiers from the Nebula01 sphere, turn on its Mapping Coordinates, and apply a nebula bitmap or Noise texture to it, using Diffuse and Opacity maps. The possibilities are almost endless.

When you have finished experimenting with the nebula object, you may want to save it to your 3DSMAX\SCENES directory as NEBULA_1.MAX because you'll be using it in the next chapter. A version of this file is also in the \CHAP_07 directory of the *3D Studio MAX f/x CD-ROM*.

**CD-ROM**

## Moving On

In the next chapter, you'll see how you can get your nebula to move properly in relationship to a starfield background. By using 3D Studio MAX's Trajectories and Spline Paths options, you can link your nebula object to the camera—and wherever the camera goes, the nebula will follow.

# Nebulas On The Move

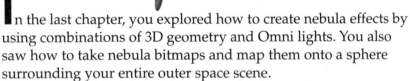

**I**n the last chapter, you explored how to create nebula effects by using combinations of 3D geometry and Omni lights. You also saw how to take nebula bitmaps and map them onto a sphere surrounding your entire outer space scene.

That technique has several advantages over using a Spherical Environmental background. For one thing, using 3D geometry and textures is more versatile. For example, you can create concentric, nested nebula objects (each fitting inside the other like a Russian *matrioska* doll) and produce interesting layered effects. By using combinations of diffuse and opacity-mapped textures, shininess maps, and tinted lights, you can produce nebulas of considerable depth. It's also easier to create animated effects by varying the materials, the geometry, the lights, or all three during the course of your scene.

Using a nebula sphere to encompass all the elements of your 3D outer space scene has a drawback, however. The problem? No matter how large your nebula sphere object is in your scene, it will still appear to be closer than your background starfield. As your camera moves and pans inside the nebula object, you encounter a phenomenon known as *parallax*.

## Parallax: A Definition

*Webster's New Collegiate Dictionary* defines *parallax* as "the appearance of displacement or the difference in appearance of direction of an object as seen from two different points not on a straight line with the object." In other words, objects such as your nebula that are closer to you—or your 3D camera—appear to be moving more quickly relative to you and your position than do objects that are further away, such as the horizon—or your starfield. And, of course, your starfield backdrop, relative to you, is at infinity.

There are a few ways to fix this. First, depending on how complex your camera move is, the effect may not be particularly noticeable. If the camera inside your nebula sphere simply pans and tilts but doesn't move much in relation to the sphere, then you won't see the nebula image "sliding" over the stars. Unfortunately, this lack of movement lends itself to quite static-appearing compositions and is not particularly exciting.

Are there other workarounds? Sure—if you map both a starfield texture and a nebula texture on the same sphere, then these elements are automatically at the same distance. Finally, in some cases, you may actually *want* the nebula effect to appear to be much closer than the distant stars—as if your spaceships and other elements are present inside it.

What if you're keeping all your foreground elements—planets, moons, suns, asteroids, and battling spaceships—inside a giant nebula sphere, though, and you don't want your nebula image to slip and slide over your Video Post Starfield? In that case, you need to make sure that the nebula object maintains its position relative to the camera no matter what outrageous camera move you may be plotting.

The following section explains how to do it.

## Moving Nebulas: Adjusting Parallax

Unlike 3D Studio/DOS, 3D Studio MAX lets you link virtually any object in your 3D scene to another. This includes the ability to link objects to cameras or to the paths on which the cameras are traveling.

Now, if it were as easy as simply plotting out your camera move, centering your Nebula01 object over the camera on frame 0, and linking the nebula to the camera, you would be all set. Unfortunately, that's only half the battle.

If you link the Nebula01 object to the body of the camera, even though the nebula object will always stay at a fixed distance relative to the camera body, you can't roll the camera without the nebula imagery also rolling with the camera body. Of course, that defeats the purpose: as the camera body rolls, the nebula imagery stays fixed in relation to the camera but it will be sliding and rolling with the camera body against the distant starfield.

Rather than link the Nebula01 object to the camera itself, you link it to a spline path extracted from the camera's path. You can examine this effect by using the Nebula01 object that you created in the previous chapter.

*Note: This tutorial requires the Nebula01 object that you created in the last chapter. If you don't have a copy of that object, you can load and use the scene file NEBULA_1.MAX from the \CHAP_08 directory of your 3D Studio MAX f/x CD-ROM.*

## Linking the Lights

It's time to get started.

1. Load 3D Studio MAX. If you still have the Nebula01 object loaded from the previous tutorial, keep it; you use it in this chapter.

2. If you don't have your Nebula01 object and lights currently loaded, save your current work and select File/Reset to reset your 3D Studio MAX. Then, from the \CHAP_08 directory of your *3D Studio MAX f/x CD-ROM*, load the file NEBULA_1.MAX.

The first thing to do is link the Omni01 and Omni02 lights to your Nebula01 object.

3. Activate the Top viewport. Then, press the H key on your keyboard to bring up the Select by Name dialog box. Hold down the Ctrl key and click on Omni01 and Omni02 from the list. Release the Ctrl key and press Enter (or click on the Select button) to select both of these lights.

4. Now click on the Select and Link icon in the menu bar and move your cursor back into the Top viewport. When your mouse cursor moves over either of the selected Omni lights, the crosshair cursor changes to the Select and Link cursor. As it changes to Select and Link, click and drag down diagonally to the right. As you do, you'll see two dotted lines stretching from the Select and Link cursor back to the selected Omni lights.

5. Drag the Select and Link cursor around the screen over the Nebula01 object and then release your mouse button. The Nebula01 object briefly flashes white, indicating that it's now the parent of the two selected Omni lights. They are now linked to this object and will follow the object wherever it goes.

*Note: Another way to do this is to simply select both the Nebula01 object and the Omni lights and Group them. Making the Omni lights children of the Nebula01 parent object, however, gives you greater flexibility in adjusting the nebula effect during the course of your animation. If necessary, it's easier to impart secondary movement to linked Omni lights than to Grouped objects. You may have to Open the Group, select and move the objects, and then close the Group.*

Now you'll hide the Nebula01 object for a moment. This will make it easier to both move your camera and see its trajectory.

6. Click on the Select Objects button to get out of Select and Link mode, and click on the Nebula01 object to select it. From the Command Panel, click on the Display tab, and in the Hide by Selection rollout, click on Hide Selected. This makes the Nebula01 object (but not its linked Omni lights) disappear.

## Animating the Camera

Okay, you see what the subhead above says. Now you'll animate the camera.

1. Make sure that the Time Slider indicating the number of frames at the bottom of your Screen is set at 0/100, indicating that you are at frame 0 of the 100 frames for this test animation. Click on the Animate button. The button turns red.

   3D Studio MAX is now in animation mode. Virtually any activity you perform on any element in your 3D Studio MAX scene when you are not at frame 0 will be keyframed and become part of an animation.

2. Drag the Time Slider to frame 50. Click on the Select and Move icon, activate your Top viewport, and drag the Camera01 body to approximate XYZ coordinates X 120, Y 80, and Z 0. (To make it easier to place your camera at these coordinates, you may want to press the S key on your keyboard to activate 2D Snap.)

3. Activate the Left viewport and drag the Camera01 body up to approximate XYZ coordinates X 0, Y 120, and Z 0.

4. Now, drag the Time Slider all the way to frame 100. With Select and Move mode still active, go back to the Left viewport and drag the Camera01 body down to the left to approximate XYZ coordinates X -250, Y -125, and Z 0.

5. With the Left viewport still active, drag the Camera01 Target down to XYZ coordinates X -170, Y -100, and Z 0.

6. Finally, move back to the Top viewport and drag the Camera01 Target to coordinates X -100, Y 100, and Z 0. Click on the Animate button again to toggle animation mode off.

# Checking Out the Animation

Now take a look at the animation that you just created.

1. With the Time Slider at frame 100, click on the Zoom Extents All icon to center Camera01 and the Omni lights in each of your viewports and then click on the Camera01 body to select it. Now, drag the Time Slider back and forth from frame 0 to frame 100.

   You should see the camera rotating counterclockwise around the Omni lights and the camera target moving down and to the left in the Top viewport.

2. If you want, activate the Camera01 viewport and click on the Play Animation button to see the camera movement. Then, drag the Time Slider back to frame 0 or click on the Go to Start button.

   When you drag the Time Slider back to frame 0, you should notice a white bounding box appearing around Camera01. This indicates that you've set a key at this frame. If you drag the Time Slider to frame 50, you'll see the box appear again, indicating the second key you set. Finally, if you drag it to the end, or frame 100, you'll see the final key you set.

   Now take a look at the camera path that you created when you set those keys.

3. Make sure that Camera01 is selected. Then, from the Command Panel, click on the Motion tab. Under Selection Level, Parameters should be selected. Click on the Trajectories button. When you do, you'll see the Camera01 path appear as a series of small dots on a multicolored line, with key frames indicated as small white boxes along the camera path. To see this path more clearly in all the viewports, you may want to click again on the Zoom Extents All button. Your screen should resemble Figure 8-1.

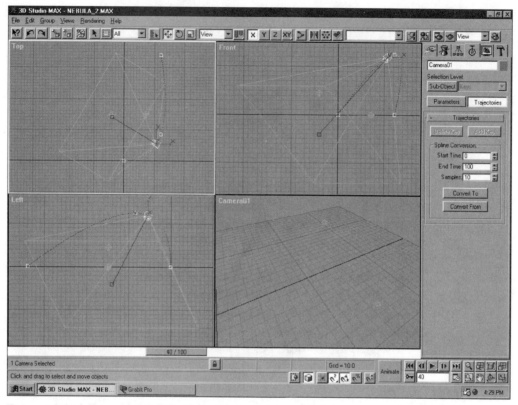

Figure 8-1: *The Camera01 animation path shown as a visible trajectory at frame 40 of the animation.*

## Converting the Trajectory to a Spline

Now you'll create a spline path for your Nebula01 object to follow. You do this by deriving the spline path from your existing Camera01 animation path so that it will exactly match the camera's movement. Here's how to do it:

1. With the Camera01 body still selected, activate the Top view and click on the Convert To button under the Trajectories section of the Motion rollout. When you do so, you should see another path overlaid on top of the original Camera01 path.

This is a spline object derived from the Camera01 path. (For very complex camera movements, you may want to increase the Sample number. For your purposes here, you can leave it at 10.)

2. Click on the Camera01 path; you should see the new spline object appear (it turns white, indicating that it's selected). Press the H key on your keyboard to bring up the Select by Name dialog. When it appears, you'll see Shape01—the new spline—selected. This is the path that your Nebula object will follow.

3. Click on the Display tab of the Command Panel. Under Hide by Selection, click on Unhide All. This unhides your Nebula01 object.

   Now you need to link the Nebula01 object to the new Shape01 spline so that it will exactly match the Camera01 path.

4. Select the Nebula01 object, then Click on the Motion tab again. Click on Parameters (which toggles Trajectories off). The Parameters rollout appears. Open the Assign Controller rollout. When you do, you'll see the various controllers that are currently assigned to Position: Bezier Position, Rotation=TCB (Tension/Continuity/Bias) Rotation, and Scale (Bezier Scale).

5. Click on Position: Bezier Position to highlight it, and click on the Position/Rotation/Scale button just under the Assign Controller title to assign a new controller to the position of Nebula01. When the Replace Position Controller dialog box appears, pick Path. Then, click on Okay.

6. Under Path Parameters, the Current Path Object should be None. Click on Pick Path. Then, in any of your viewports, click on the Shape01 path. When you do, you'll see that the Current Path Object now reads Shape01; the Nebula01 object will now travel linearly along this spline object.

*Note: Under Path Options, do* not *click on Follow and/or Bank. If you do so, the Nebula01 object will pivot and bank to follow the contours of the Shape01 path. This will destroy the illusion that the nebula imagery is the same distance from the camera as the background stars (and it defeats the entire purpose of this tutorial!).*

7. Now, drag the Time Slider bar back and forth from frame 0 to frame 100 to preview the animation.

    In all your viewports, you should see the Nebula01 object follow the same motion path as the camera, as shown in Figure 8-2.

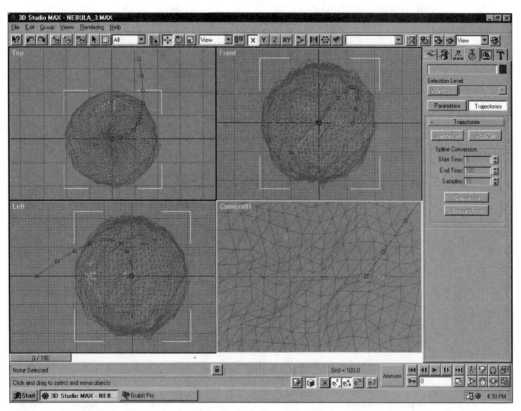

Figure 8-2: *The Nebula01 object and its linked Omni lights now follow the same path as the camera.*

8. Click on the Zoom Extents All button to center the geometry in your viewports, and scratch through the animation again by dragging the Time Slider.

Congratulations! You now have a nebula object that follows the exact path of your camera. However, the nebula imagery will move relative to the camera body but not to the camera target. Thus, the nebula will always appear at a fixed distance from the camera. Consequently, if you've set up your foreground nebula imagery to provide the desired look against your starfield backdrop, the nebula will always stay fixed to the starfield coordinates. This effect works well whether you're using a Spherical Environment starfield bitmap or (better yet) a Starfield Video Post plug-in to generate your stars. With this technique, you can set up the camera movements in your space scene to be as frenetic as you want, and the nebula imagery will stay right on track.

9. To see an example of the effect that you just completed, select File/View File, and from the \CHAP_08 directory of your *3D Studio MAX f/x CD-ROM*, select the file NEBULA_3.AVI. When the Media Player appears, click on the Play button to preview the animation.

As you see, the nebula imagery remains fixed to the background stars. (For this animation, the background has been changed to a Spherical Environment rather than Screen; the background image is the STAR1024.TGA bitmap.)

10. When you've finished viewing the animation, close the Media Player.

This technique is not confined just to outer-space scenes, of course; you can also use it for terrestrial landscapes. For example, you can map a high-resolution horizon and/or sky image to a cylindrical or hemispherical object and place your foreground 3D objects (buildings, city streets) inside. By linking the background object to the camera path, you can pan, tilt, and roll your camera any way you want, but the horizon will always stay at the same distance relative to the camera.

*Note:* Camera01 and the Nebula object are actually on two different paths. Remember, you placed the Nebula on a spline path extracted from the existing Camera01 path. If you make changes to the Camera01 path, you have to convert it to a new spline path and reassign the Nebula object to the new path.

 The examples used in this tutorial (the linked Nebula01 and Omni lights, and the Nebula01 linked to the camera path) are in the \CHAP_08 directory of your *3D Studio MAX f/x* CD-ROM as NEBULA_2.MAX and NEBULA_3.MAX.

## Moving On

In the next two chapters, you'll see how to create burning suns with volume lights, 3D geometry, and my favorite procedural texture. It's going to be a very "noisy" time!

# Here Comes the Sun, Part I

In many outer-space films, we are treated to scenes of spaceships flying through the void, with the ships very brightly—and unrealistically—illuminated. Not only is the primary lighting quite intense, but a large amount of fill light brings out detail that should have been hidden in shadow. In these cases there is often no rationale for the bright lighting; all you have are thousands of distant stars and no nearby light source, such as a sun (or multiple suns).

The scenes in the space battle shots from the *3D Studio MAX f/x CD-ROM* are very brightly lit. An off-screen sun provides the rationale for all the lighting in the scene. If you'll be using a glowing sun effect in your outer-space special-effects scenes, there are many different ways to do it.

The easiest way is to use 3D Studio MAX's volumetric light functions. The name derives from the concept that a light source actually illuminates a "volume" present in your 3D scene, creating a glow. The glow could be present because of atmospheric haze and dust, fog, or underwater murkiness. Of course, space has no real atmospheric volume, but you can still use a volumetric light to produce the illusion of a brightly glowing sun. The soft glow created by the volume light effect suggests a lens flare, but without the (now overused) lens elements.

When you apply a volumetric environment effect to an Omni light in 3D Studio MAX, you can get an excellent approximation of a nearby glowing sun. You can even apply noise effects to it to "fuzz" up the edges and create the illusion of solar flares.

## A Healthy Glow

Now you'll set up a 3D Studio MAX scene, using a volumetric Omni light to create a simple glowing sun effect. Here's how to do it:

1. Save your current work in 3D Studio MAX and reset it.

2. From the Command Panel, select Create/Lights; under Object Type, click on Omni. Now you'll alter the light settings. On the General Parameters rollout, change the light's color to pure white, or RGB setting 255, 255, 255. On the Attenuation rollout, click on Use and Show to activate the Attenuation Range icons. Leave the Attenuation Start and End Ranges at their defaults. Finally, change the name of the Omni01 light to Sun.

3. Move your cursor to the center of the grid in the Top, Front, or Left viewports, and click once to place the Sun Omni light.

4. Now, select Rendering/Environment; the Environment dialog box appears.
   As long as you're here, you should first set up a starfield background before you apply the Environment volumetric lighting to the Omni light.

5. Under Background, click on Assign to bring up the Material/ Map browser. Under Browse From, make sure New is selected; then double-click on Bitmap. When you return to the Environment dialog box, you'll see that the Bitmap texture type is loaded in the Environment Map slot; it should be called Map #1.

6. Click on the Map #1 (Bitmap) button; the Put to Material Editor dialog box appears. You can leave this at the default Slot #1, so click on OK to dismiss this dialog box and return to the Environment dialog box. (In a moment, you'll go to the Material Editor and finish loading your starfield background.)

7. Under Atmosphere Effects, click on Add to bring up the Add Atmospheric Effects dialog box. Click on Volume Light; then, click on OK. The Volume Light Parameters rollout appears.

8. Under Lights: Pick Light, click on Pick Light. In any viewport where the Sun light is visible, click on it. When you do so, the Sun light appears in the name field under Volume Light Parameters.

    Take a look at the volume settings. For this tutorial, keep them as they are. The Fog Color is pure white, Density is 5.0, the Max Light Percentage is 90, and the Minimum Light Percentage is 0. (For more information on what these settings do, see "Using Volumetric Light and Shadow," 35-18, *3D Studio MAX User's Guide, Volume 2.*)

9. Close the Environment dialog box and click on the Material Editor button to bring up the Material Editor. The Material Editor appears, and you can see that the Map #1 slot is active. You haven't loaded a bitmap image, however, you'll do so now.

10. Under Bitmap Parameters, click on the Bitmap name button to bring up the Select Texture Image file dialog box. From the \CHAP_09 directory of your *3D Studio MAX CD-ROM*, load the file STARS640.TGA. In the Coordinates rollout, change Spherical Environment to Screen and close the Material Editor.
    Now you'll do a test rendering.

11. Click on the Zoom Extents All button to center the attenuated volumetric Sun light in all viewports.

12. Activate your Perspective viewport and then render a test image. After a moment, you'll see the volumetric lighting effect appear on your screen, as shown in Figure 9-1.

Figure 9-1: *The environmental volumetric lighting effect applied to the Omni01 light with the default parameters.*

Figure 9-1 shows the default settings for a volumetric light. As you can see, the light has a brilliant white core with a soft diffused glow emanating from it.

3D Studio MAX's volumetric lighting effects are extremely powerful and can be used in many different ways. Obviously, you can use the lighting effects to create a simple effect such as this glowing sun. You can also use variations of this effect to create glowing car headlights, street lamps, or other optical effects. In addition, you can create volumetric spotlights, producing the effect of a beam of light cutting through atmospheric haze, dust, fog, or underwater murkiness. And finally, with volumetric spotlights you can load bitmaps or procedural textures, such as Noise, into projector volumetric spotlights and have the projected texture actually affect the volumetric light casting or volumetric beam. (You'll take a look at the latter effects in Part IV, "Underwater Effects.")

## Changing the Sun Settings

Now you'll adjust the attenuation and density settings of the volumetric light to alter the effects.

1. Click again on Rendering/Environment to bring up the Environment Map. Under Atmosphere: Effects, click on Volume Light to bring up the Volume Light parameters rollout.
   You're going to change a few of these parameters.

2. Under Fog Color, click on the color swatch to bring up the Color Selector and change the RGB color settings to 255, 255, 128. This produces a pale yellow glow, somewhat like the color of our own sun. Close the Color Selector when you've finished.

3. Return to the Environment dialog box. Click on the name of the light in the Effects list window to bring up the Volume Light Parameters rollout. Then, in the Attenuation section, change Start Percentage from 100 to 5 and press Enter to accept these settings.

4. Activate your Perspective viewport again and do another test rendering. After a moment, the revised volumetric light settings appear in the rendering, as shown in Figure 9-2.

Figure 9-2: *The modified Attenuation settings and color has resulted in a slightly smaller sun core object and a larger Corona emanating from the body of the sun.*

You can use the Attenuation settings in the Environment Map to change the overall size of the core light object plus the halo that emerges from it. Let's alter these settings one more time.

5. Return to the Environment dialog box; change Attenuation Start Percentage to 0. Then, change Attenuation End Percentage to 25 and press Enter to accept these settings.

6. Activate your Perspective viewport again and do another test rendering; it should look much like Figure 9-3.

Figure 9-3: *The drastically reduced Attenuation setting has resulted in a much smaller sun object without a visible hot core.*

Notice how the sun-like object itself is much smaller; in addition, it consists mainly of a corona—there is no hot core in the center of the sun. You should also notice that because you brought the Attenuation Size down and set the Starting Attenuation to 0, the light is translucent. You can see the background stars through the volumetric lighting effect.

Now you'll change these settings again to bring back the corona.

7. Return to the Environment dialog box. Under Attenuation Percentage, change Start to 5 and change End Percentage to 50. This brings down the overall size of the sun effect. Under the Volume section, change Density from 5.0 to 25. Then, change the Max Light percentage from 90 percent to 50 and press Enter.

8. Activate your Perspective viewport and render another test image, as shown in Figure 9-4.

Figure 9-4: *Note how changing the Attenuation density and maximum percentage settings has changed the appearance of the Omni light Sun.*

Figure 9-4 shows how these settings have drastically altered the appearance of your sun effect. When you altered the density of the sun, you increased the apparent size of its core; you also made it translucent. You should also note, however, that the halo is now extremely small in proportion to the overall size of the sun core, and the light is now extremely dim. By bringing down the maximum light percentage from 90 to 50, the sun now looks like a flat, slightly glowing disk through which the stars are visible.

## Using Noise with Volumetric Lights

Now you'll modify the volumetric light with my favorite procedural effect: the Noise parameter. As you've seen in previous chapters, 3D Studio MAX's Noise procedurals—whether used as Material Editor textures to create geometric displacements (coming up in our Asteroids chapters) or as volumetric light effects—are incredibly useful. When used properly, procedural textures such as Noise can produce fascinating organic textures, both still and animated.

Return to the Rendering/Environment editor to adjust the volumetric light effects. This time, you'll apply Noise to the volumetric Sun Omni light; you'll also see what happens when you animate the Noise procedural.

1. Return to the Environment dialog box. Click on the color swatch under Volume Fog Color to bring up the Color Selector. You'll change your sun from a pale yellow to an orange, so change the RGB settings to 255, 128, 0 and then dismiss the Color Selector.

2. Change Density back to 5.0; change Max Light Percentage, back to 90. Now go back to the Attenuation section and change Start Percentage and End Percentage each to 100.

3. Go down to the Noise section of the rollout. Click in the Noise On check box to activate it and then change the Amount from 0.0 to 0.5. Change Uniformity to 0.5; leave Size at 20. Finally, change Phase to 25.0, change Wind Strength to 25.0, and leave Wind at the Front.

4. When you're finished, activate your Perspective viewport again and render another test image. After a moment, the rendering appears as shown in Figure 9-5.

Figure 9-5: *The Noise settings applied to the volumetric sun light.*

Take a look at your rendering. As you can see, adding Noise to the volumetric light has produced a mottled or dappled effect in the corona of the sun object. Notice how the noise effect has also altered the core of your volumetric sun object. The edges of the sun core are no longer perfectly round, but are broken up by the noise texture.

## A Hunka-Hunka Burning Gas

One nifty effect that you can try is to animate the Noise parameters of your volumetric sun object. By turning on the Animate button and adjusting the uniformity, size, phase, percentage, and/or wind strength parameters at a nonzero frame, you can create the illusion of waves of gas radiating from the core of your volumetric sun. This will enable you to produce an effect resembling the photosphere of the sun—the sun's "atmosphere."

You don't even need to animate all of these parameters to produce this effect, however. By animating just one Noise parameter—the Phase parameter—you can produce the effect of burning gases emanating from the sun's core. (The Phase parameter controls the speed of the Wind setting.)

Take a look at a demonstration .AVI file of this effect.

1. Select File/View File, and from the \CHAP_09 directory of your *3D Studio MAX f/x CD-ROM*, click on the file SUNNOIS1.AVI to load it. When the Media Player appears, click the Play button to play the animation.

   This is a 100-frame, 320 x 240 .AVI file of your animated sun. The only Noise parameter that has changed is the Phase setting. On frame 0, Phase is set to 25; but on Frame 100, I turned on the Animate button and changed Phase to 50. This simple change, combined with the Wind Strength at 25 and Wind from the Front, results in the effect of an animated border on the sun, suggesting radiating waves of gas or plasma emanating from its edges.

2. When you have finished previewing the file, dismiss the Media Player and the SUNNOIS1.AVI.

   The file used to create this effect, SUNNOIS1.MAX, is also in the \CHAP_09 directory of your *3D Studio MAX f/x CD-ROM*. Load it and experiment with your own animated sun effects!

## Moving On

In the next chapter, you'll see how you can create a burning sun effect by using 3D geometry and a procedural Noise texture. In addition, you'll see how you can augment this 3D sun object with the volumetric light effects that this chapter covered.

# Here Comes the Sun, Part II

**I**n the last chapter, you saw how to can create a simple glowing sun effect by using 3D Studio MAX's volumetric lights and Noise. This effect can work well for suns depicted in distant and medium shots.

In some of your outer space scenes, however, you may want to depict a bright sun as close up as opposed to a volumetric glowing light off in the distance. If, for example, you have a sequence of a spaceship approaching dangerously close to the sun and you want to show the boiling, gaseous activity on the sun's surface, you might want to create the sun as a physical object with an animated texture. This is quite easy to do using self-illuminated Noise textures in 3D Studio MAX.

The following sections explain how to do it.

## Creating a Sun with Geometry & Noise Materials

Okay, you've read the preceding subhead. You've gotta build some simple geometry, so...

1. If you have been working in 3D Studio MAX, reset it; then, go to the Create Panel and select Geometry/Standard Primitives. Under Object Type, click on Sphere. Press the S key to activate 2D Snap. In your Top viewport, place your mouse cursor in the center of the viewport and click and drag until you've created a (large) sphere approximately 300 units in radius. You may find it easier to hit this value exactly by creating a sphere of any radius and then editing its Radius value in the Parameters rollout to 300. Rename the Sphere01 object as Sun.

2. You're going to increase the complexity of your Sun Object, so return to the Create Panel and increase the Segments value in the Parameters rollout from 16 to 60. This creates a reasonably high-resolution Sun object. When you're finished, click on the Zoom Extents All button.

   For your test renderings, you'll want to see your Sun object sitting in space, so you should load the standard STARS640.TGA background as a Screen Environment background. You should already be familiar with how to do this from the last tutorial. If not, go back to the previous chapter and in the section "A Healthy Glow," follow the instructions on loading a bitmap Screen background for your scene. Place it in Slot #1 of the Material Editor.

   A copy of the STARS640.TGA image is included in the \CHAP_10 directory of your *3D Studio MAX f/x CD-ROM*. You can load the image either from that directory or from the \MAPS directory of the CD-ROM.

3. When you've finished loading the starfield background, go to the Material Editor. Slot #1 should have the STARS640.TGA background image loaded. So, use Material #2 for your Sun surface material.

4. Click on Material Slot #2 to activate it; then, click on the Assign Material to Selection icon. Because this is now a "hot" material in the scene, any changes that you make update automatically on your Sun object. Now you'll turn this into a glowing sun. For your purposes, you don't need to adjust the Ambient or Diffuse color settings. Under Basic Parameters, reduce Shininess and Shininess Strength both to 0 and increase Self-Illumination from 0 to 100. Leave Opacity at 100.

5. Open the Maps rollout and click on the Diffuse name button to bring up the Material/Map Browser. Under Browse From, make sure that New is selected; then, click on Noise. The default Noise texture (a mottled gray) loads in the Material #2 slot and appears on the sample sphere.

6. Now you'll change the Noise size and color settings. Under Noise Parameters, change Size from 25 to 10. Then, click on the Noise Color #1 color swatch to bring up the Color Selector. Change the RGB settings to pure red, or 255, 0, 0. Now click on the Color #2 color swatch to make it active, and change its RGB settings to 255, 255, 0, or a bright yellow. When you've finished, close the Color Selector and change the name of Material #2 to Sun Noise 1.

   We now have a basic Sun Noise texture, so it's time to do a test rendering.

7. Activate your Perspective viewport and render a still image. After a few moments, the image appears, and it should resemble Figure 10-1.

Figure 10-1: *A basic Noise texture applied to a Sun sphere.*

Notice how, in this image, the procedural Noise texture creates a cloud-like yet fiery pattern on the surface of your Sun object. Of course, because this is a procedural texture, you don't need to activate mapping coordinates on the Sun object, nor do you have to apply UVW mapping to it. As you've seen in previous chapters, however, you can produce organic-looking patterns by animating the Noise texture. Later in this tutorial, you'll set up an animation to create a roiling, burning sun surface.

## Hey, Keep Down That Noise!

Okay, this is a neat effect but it doesn't yet look much like a big burning ball of gas. You'll work on that, but first you'll change your Noise parameters and see the effects.

1. Return to the Material Editor. Under Noise Parameters, change the Noise Size from 10 to 15 and then change the Noise type from Regular to Fractal. Notice that the Sun Noise 1 material

on the sample sphere in Slot #2 is slightly different from before; it has become grainier.

2. Activate your Perspective viewport and render another image; the Sun object with its modified Noise settings appears in Figure 10-2.

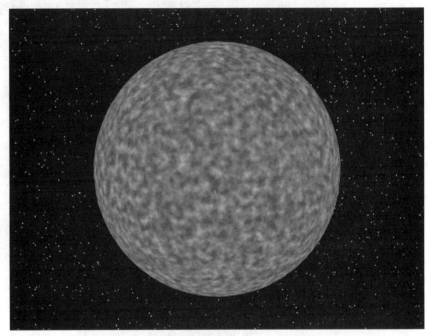

Figure 10-2: *The Sun object with a Fractal noise texture applied to it.*

Notice how changing the Noise Type from Regular to Fractal creates a more granular, "layered" effect for the surface of your Sun object. The Fractal Noise type makes it look as if multiple layers of color iterations are appearing within the basic fiery "orange peel" texture on your Sun.

Now you'll change the Noise Type again.

3. Click in the Material Editor to activate it and change the Noise type from Fractal to Turbulence. This will dramatically change the appearance of the Sun Noise 1 material on the sample sphere.

4. Activate your Perspective viewport and render another test image. It should look something like Figure 10-3.

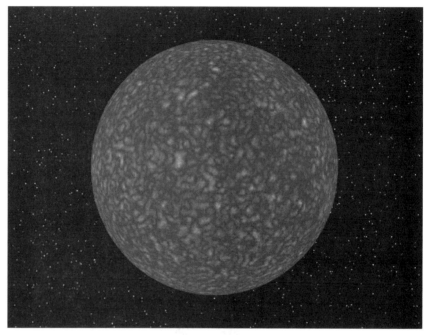

Figure 10-3: *The Sun object with a Turbulence Noise material applied to it.*

The Turbulence Noise Type provides a very interesting effect for your Sun object. The texture surface is broken up even further and the reddish-orange color predominates. In addition, the Noise itself displays more of a procedural "ropi-ness." Thus, it appears more organic looking than either the Regular or Fractal Noise Types. (Actually, it looks somewhat like microphotography of someone's intestinal cells, but it seems to make a nifty sun texture, too. Hmm…)

Okay, let's make one more alteration to this basic Noise texture.

5. In the Material Editor, change Noise Type back from Intestinal—er, Turbulence—to Fractal. You should also change the Noise Threshold settings to "clamp" the range of color gradations in

this texture. Change Noise Threshold: High from 1.0 to 0.75; change Low from 0.0 to 0.25. Press Enter to accept these settings.

6. Activate your Perspective viewport again and render another test image, as shown in Figure 10-4.

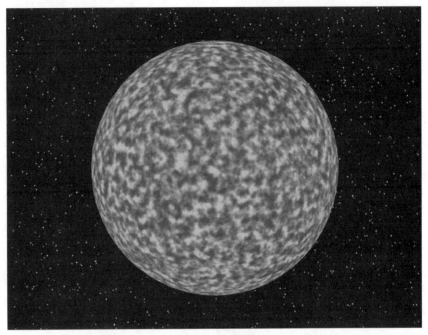

Figure 10-4: *The Fractal Noise texture with the Noise Threshold settings brought closer to the mid-range of colors.*

Notice how changing the Noise Threshold settings affects your rendering. You have effectively clamped the range of gradations available between the bright red and bright yellow textures. The patches of yellow on the surface of the sun are now much more distinct, and the contrast overall between the colors has increased greatly. In addition, note how this creates the illusion of several layers of Noise texture going down more toward the center of the Sun object. The large, high-contrast yellow patches look as if they are closer to the surface of the Sun object than the smaller, softer orange patterns.

Playing with the Noise Threshold parameter can yield some very interesting results. In Chapter 18, "Planets & Other Heavenly Bodies," you see how you can use Noise and specific Threshold settings to create procedural clouds. In addition, by animating the UVW or XYZ tiling, the Levels and/or Phase of the Noise texture, you can create the illusion that clouds are actually moving, growing, and dissipating over a planet's surface. (So, stick around.)

## Doctoring Your Sun

Although you can use Noise textures to create the illusion of a burning sun surface, the effect isn't really complete until you make the Sun object glow. There are two ways you can do this.

First, you can assign an Effects Channel in the Material Editor to your Sun Noise 1 Material and then apply a Glow filter as an Image Filter Event to this material in Video Post. (For more information on using Video Post's Filters, see "Using Video Post: Image Filter Events," 36-14, *3D Studio MAX User's Guide, Volume 2*.) Don't worry about Glow, for the moment—I cover it in a later chapter when I discuss how to create laser beams.

The emphasis of this book is to create many of your effects "in-camera," so you're going to see how you can create a glow around your 3D Sun object by applying what you learned in the last chapter. By using a combination of your 3D Sun object and a volumetric Omni light, you can make your 3D Sun appear to glow with a bright halo.

Now you'll explore how to create these effects.

1. Close your Perspective VFB if it's still open, and return to the Material Editor. Change Noise Type from Fractal back to Turbulence. Change Size to 15. Then, change the Noise Threshold back to the default settings—High should be 1.0 rather than 0.75; Low should be 0.0 rather than 0.25.

2. Click on the Color #1 swatch to bring up the Color Selector. Change the RGB settings to 255, 128, 0—a bright orange. Leave Color #2 as a bright yellow. When you've finished, close the Color Selector.

   Now it's time to create another Omni light and apply volumetric effects to it.

3. From the Create Panel, click on Create\Lights, and under Object Type, pick Omni light. Change the color to pure white, or RGB 255, 255, 255. Under Attenuation, click on Use and Show; set the Start Range at 10 and the End Range at 400. Change the name of the light to Omni Sun. Then, in the Top viewport, place your cursor directly in the center of the viewport (and the Sun object) and click to place the Omni Sun light.

4. From the menu bar, select Rendering/Environment. When the Environment editor appears, under Atmosphere, click on Add... and pick Volume Light. Under Volume Light Parameters: Lights, click on Pick Light. Then, in any of your viewports, click on the Omni Sun light.

5. In the Environment editor, click on the Fog Color swatch and change its RGB settings to 255, 255, 128, or a pale yellow. Close the Color Selector.

6. Activate your Perspective viewport, then render a still image. After a moment, the image will appear as shown in Figure 10-5.

Figure 10-5: *A volumetric Omni light provides a soft glowing halo around the Sun object.*

By combining a volumetric Omni light with 3D geometry, you can get the "best of both worlds," as it were, for a physical sun object. The volumetric light provides a soft glow or halo around the Sun object. In addition, you can animate the Sun's Noise texture to create a roiling surface.

## Sun & Light: Noisy Neighbors

Now you'll make one final change to this object. You'll add Noise to your volumetric Omni lighting.

1. Return to the Environment editor. Under Attenuation, keep the Start Percentage at 100 but change End to 105 percent.

2. Now, under the Noise section of the rollout, click in the Noise On checkbox to activate it. As you saw in the last chapter, if you apply Noise to a volumetric Omni light, you can create the effect that the glow effect is radiating energy. Under Amount, change 0.0 to 0.5. Change Uniformity to 0.75 but keep Size and Phase at 20. Finally, change Wind Strength to 25 and keep Wind from the Front.

3. When you're finished, activate your Perspective viewport and render another still image. (Because you're using a procedural Noise texture on both the Sun object and the volume light, at 640 x 480 resolution, this image may take a few minutes to render on your computer.) When it appears, the image should look something like Figure 10-6.

Figure 10-6: *A glowing Sun with a procedural Noise texture applied both to the Sun object and the volumetric light.*

Take a look at the new sun image on your screen. By adding Noise to the volumetric Omni Sun light inside the Sun sphere, you've varied the glowing halo surrounding the Sun object. Again, as you explored in the last chapter, by animating various Noise parameters such as Phase, you can make the halo appear to radiate waves of energy around the Sun's periphery.

To see an example of this effect, take a look at a demonstration animation.

4. Select File/View File, and from the \CHAP_10 directory of your *3D Studio MAX f/x CD-ROM*, pick the file SUNNOIS2.AVI. When the Media Player appears, click the Play button to play the animation.

This is a 100-frame, 320 x 240 animation of your Sun and Omni Sun effect. The animated Noise effect on the Sun object and Omni light is produced by animating the Phase parameters of both items. In the case of the Sun Noise 1 material, the Phase increases from 0.0 on frame 0 to 1.0 on frame 100; for the Omni light, the Phase changes from 0.0 on frame 0 to 10 on frame 100.

5. When you've finished viewing the file, close the Media Player.

 Note that the Sun Noise material (and its variations) that you created are in the 3DSMAXFX.MAT Material Library. In addition, the various .MAX files that you created are in the \CHAP_10 directory as SUNNOIS2.MAX and SUNNOIS3.MAX.

At this point, you may want to go back and tweak your light and material settings, render the scene, and examine the effects. You may also want to try applying a subtle Glow effect to the Sun Noise 1 material in Video Post, just to see how much high-powered sizzle you can add to your sun.

## Moving On

This chapter concludes the sun effects. In the next chapter, you'll take a look at how to create a "warp drive" effect by using a combination of simple geometry and imagery created with Digimation's LenZFX plug-in for 3D Studio/DOS.

 You don't have a copy of LenZFX for either 3D Studio/DOS or 3D Studio MAX? Don't worry—the *3D Studio MAX f/x CD-ROM* contains two prerendered LenZFX warp drive bitmap sequences. In just a few moments you'll be creating portals into hyperspace— and all from the comfort and safety of your own home.

# 11

# Warp Speed!

**W**hen you previewed the space battle scenes in Chapter 3, "Setting Up Your Scene," you probably noticed how the battlecruiser comes out of warp drive in a flash with colored streaks of light. This effect was created with a combination of 3D geometry and Diffuse and Opacity-mapped texture maps applied to the objects.

I created the original texture maps for the objects by using Digimation's LenZFX 2.0 program, running in 3D Studio/DOS. LenZFX is a 3D Studio/DOS and 3D Studio MAX plug-in that works in Video Post. At its core, LenZFX provides photorealistic lens flares, Z axis blurring, glows, and aura effects for 3D Studio. LenZFX enables you to change the lens flare, blur, and glow settings to provide an almost infinite variety of customizable and animatable optical effects.

In this chapter, I discuss how you can use LenZFX-created imagery to produce optical effects such as the warp drive burst that you saw at the beginning of the space battle sequence. Later you'll see how you can use LenZFX imagery to create effects such as a *Star Trek*-style photon torpedo.

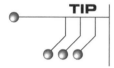

*Note: At the time this book went to press, a final version of Digimation's LenZFX for 3D Studio MAX plug-in was not yet available. If you have a copy of it for either 3D Studio/DOS or 3D Studio MAX, however, you may already be able to duplicate the look of the warp drive and torpedo effects that I discuss here. (If you don't have a copy of LenZFX for either 3D Studio/DOS or 3D Studio MAX, don't worry. All the LenZFX texture maps that you need for this tutorial are included on the* 3D Studio MAX f/x CD-ROM *in the* \CHAP_11 *and* \MAPS *directories. For further information on Digimation's products, see Appendix C, "3D Studio MAX Resources.")*

The warp drive effects filenames are WARPA000.TGA through WARPA030.TGA and WARPB000.TGA through WARPB030.TGA. Each sequence consists of a series of sequentially numbered, 24-bit, 400 x 400 resolution .TGA files. In addition, the \CHAP_11 directory contains the .IFLs, or Image File Lists, to create animated, looping materials based on these files.

**TIP**

If you are trying to create a new .IFL file from an image sequence on the *3D Studio MAX f/x CD-ROM*, you must copy the sequence images to your local hard drive before you create the .IFL file. 3D Studio MAX creates an .IFL file in the same directory as the image files and cannot write on a read-only device, such as a CD-ROM.

## Let's Do the Space Warp Again

The tutorial that follows has you do something a bit different. Rather than create a warp drive effect from scratch, in this tutorial, you'll load a demonstration warp drive file and then deconstruct it, piece by piece, to see how the effect was done.

First, though, I should go over a little background. Science fiction films and TV series such as "Star Trek" and "Babylon 5" often depict spacecraft emerging from or going into warp drive (or hyperspace, depending on your religion). A typical way of presenting this effect is to have a "tunnel of light" materialize; this tunnel serves as the entrance and/or exit point for the spacecraft. In many instances, the warp drive optical effect appears abruptly in the middle of normal space and holds as the ship emerges or departs; then, the warp effect closes down just as quickly.

The warp drive effect that I present in this chapter follows these conventions. Later in this chapter, as you examine the key settings in the Track View, notice how I've set up the keys to present this specific, multistage effect.

1. In 3D Studio MAX, select File/Open (or press Control-O). Go to the \CHAP_11 directory of your *3D Studio MAX f/x CD-ROM* and load the file WARPDRIV.MAX.

    You should see a simple 3D Studio MAX desktop consisting of a targeted camera, an Omni light and some very small geometry. The geometry provides the basis for your warp drive tunnel effect.

    Now you'll take a look at this effect.

2. Move your mouse cursor down to the Time Slider and then drag the Slider back and forth, from frames 0 to 100 and back.

    As you "scratch" through the animation, you should see two conical objects, a blue one and a green one, appear. They grow outward from their end points toward the camera; the blue cone first, followed by the green code. As the green cone attains its maximum length, the blue cone recedes; shortly thereafter the green cone recedes also, until both objects return to their original sizes. In addition, as you drag the Time Slider back and forth, you can see that the cones are rotating. The green cone is rotating counterclockwise, the blue cone clockwise.

3. Drag the Time Slider to frame 50 and stop. You'll see that both the blue and the green cones representing the warp drive effect are at their full extension, and your screen should look like Figure 11-1.

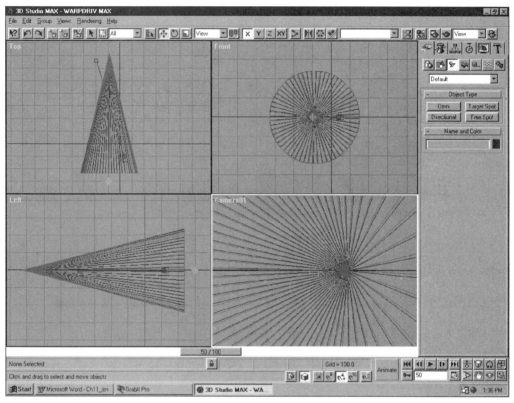

Figure 11-1: *The warp drive cone effects at their full extension.*

I created these conical shapes in 3D Studio MAX very easily. First, I created a single, 60-sided cone primitive. I then applied an Edit Mesh/Faces modifier to the flat end of the cone, selected the faces there, and deleted them. Next, I applied a Normal modifier to the cone and inverted the faces so that the normals would point inward, toward the camera. Then I applied a UVW map using Planar mapping coordinates applied to the open end of the cone. Finally, I modified the cone's Object Properties to turn off Cast Shadows and Receive Shadows. When finished, I created a duplicate of the first cone and named the cones Warp 1 Small and Warp 2 Small.

I created this warp drive effect not just with two conical objects, however, but with four. After I created both cones, I selected the vertices of their open ends—the mouth of the cones—and Shift-scaled them outward from the ends to create two much larger cones, called Warp 1 Large and Warp 2 Large. These large conical objects then became morph targets for the final warp drive effect.

By counter-rotating the initial two Warp 1 and 2 Small objects and morphing them at varying intervals into the two Warp 1 and 2 Large cones, I create the illusion that a warp drive tunnel suddenly materializes, holds for a moment, and then disappears just as quickly.

4. To see how this effect works, make sure that your Camera01 viewport is active and then click on the Play Animation button. You should see the blue cone materialize and expand rapidly from a small cone in the center of the screen; then, after it expands, the green cone expands and the blue cone recedes, and finally, the green cone recedes again to a pinpoint. When you've finished viewing the wireframe animation, click on the Play button again to stop playback.

## A Warped Perspective

Now take a look at the warp drive bitmaps that are mapped on to the cones.

1. Select File/View File, and from the \CHAP_11 directory of your *3D Studio MAX f/x CD-ROM*, select the file WARPA000.TGA. When the image appears, it should look like Figure 11-2.

Figure 11-2: *The first frame of the WARPA.TGA image sequence.*

2. Select File/View File, and from the \CHAP_11 directory, select the file WARPB000.TGA and view it. Notice how, in Figure 11-3, it differs in appearance from the WARPA000.TGA image.

Figure 11-3: *The first frame of the WARPB.TGA image sequence.*

I created both starbursts in LenZFX 2.0 for 3D Studio/DOS. The core is a brilliant white with reddish diffraction rings surrounding it. A bluish-purple glow also emanates from the core, as well as bright blue, magenta, and purple shafts of light radiating out from the center. The WARPB bitmaps have a smaller white core and have several diffraction rings surrounding it, ranging from dark blue, to magenta, to red, and then magenta again. If you view some of the other images in both sequences, you'll see that the number of light shafts for the WARPB bitmaps is reduced from that of the WARPA bitmaps.

By adjusting and varying the Gradient and Linear color ramp settings in LenZFX and by using different UV gradients to provide the radial shafts of light, I created two warp drive bitmap effects that appear different. For each of these sequences, I turned off both the Rays and Lens Element options of LenZFX, so that the result is simply a multicolored starburst effect.

Now take a look at a test rendering of this effect.

3. Drag the Time Slider back to frame 50. Make sure that your Camera01 viewport is active; then, press Alt+R and Enter to render a still image of frame 50. After a few moments the image appears, as shown in Figure 11-4.

Figure 11-4: *A test rendering of frame 50 of the warp drive sequence.*

In Figure 11-4, you see the warp drive effect against a starfield backdrop. Notice how both the camera angle and the planar mapping of the cones has resulted in the WARPA and WARPB textures stretching down the length of the cones.

Now take a look at the Material Editor settings for these warp drive materials.

4. Close your Camera01 VFB window and bring up the Material Editor. When the Material Editor appears, you see the two different warp drive materials in Slots #1 and #2, as well as the STARS640.TGA background image in Slot #3.

   Slot #1 contains the Warp 1 material. Take a look at the settings for this. The Ambient and Diffuse colors are black, and Shininess and Shininess Strength are both set to 0. To make the effect as bright as possible, however, Self-Illumination is set to 100.

5. If you open the Extended Parameters rollout, you'll see that Opacity Falloff has been set to Out and Opacity Type has been set to Additive. Again, the reason for these settings is to make the warp drive texture maps created with LenZFX appear as bright as possible. (In the WARPDRIV test scene, I've also placed a pure white Omni light to better bring out the colors of this effect.)

6. Go down to the Maps section of the rollout and open it. You see the WARPA000.IFL (Image File List) loaded in the Diffuse and Opacity map slots. This simple text file lists all 30 of the WARPA .TGA bitmaps. If you examine the settings for the Warp 2 material, you'll see that its parameters are identical to those of Warp 1, except for using WARPB000.IFL for the Diffuse and Opacity maps, of course.

Notice that when you place these random bitmap sequences on counter-rotating geometry, such as the Warp cones, you get a sparkling or spinning lens flare effect. The effect is reminiscent of the Enterprise warp drive effect used in the 1979 film *Star Trek: The Motion Picture*.

7. Click the Close button to dismiss the Material Editor.

## Making Tracks

Now that you've seen the materials used for the warp drive effect, you'll examine the morph settings used in this animation.

1. Click on the Track View button in the toolbar to bring up the Track View dialog box, and click on the Maximize button to enlarge it to full screen.

2. From the list of items in your 3D Studio MAX World, click on the square + button to open Objects. The following items appear: Camera01.Target, Camera01, Warp 1 Small, Warp 2 Small, and Omni01. Open the Warp 1 Small and Warp 2 Small object tracks. When you do, you'll see track listings appear for Visibility, Transform, Object (Morph; this contains the tree for the Warp 1 and 2 Small and Warp 1 and 2 Large objects), and Warp 1 and Warp 2 (the materials applied to the two objects).

3. Open the Transform and Object (Morph) tracks for both the Warp 1 Small and Warp 2 Small objects. When you do so, your screen should look something like Figure 11-5.

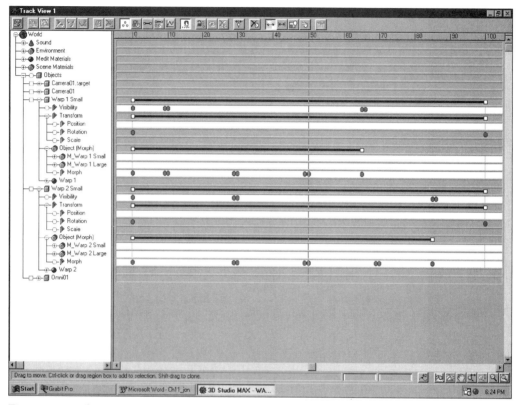

Figure 11-5: *The Track Viewport open to show the Warp 1 and Warp 2 objects and their visibility and morph keys.*

To better see the settings in Track View, you may want to click on the Zoom Horizontal Events button at the bottom of your screen. Now examine the Track View settings for the Warp 1 Small and Warp 2 Small objects.

4. Look at the Visibility track for the Warp 1 Small object. There are keys set at frames 0, 9, 10, 65, and 66. Highlight, then right-click on the key set at frame 0 of the Warp 1 Small Visibility track. This brings up the Key Info dialog box for this track. (If necessary, drag it down in your viewport so that you can see the Visibility track of the Warp 1 Small object more easily.) You see that the Value for this key is set to 0. This indicates that the Warp 1 Small object is actually hidden on frame 0 of this rendering.

5. In the Key Info dialog box, click on the forward (or Right) arrow to the left of 1 to move to the second key at frame 9. It turns white to indicate that it is the active key. Again, the Value at this key is 0, indicating that the Warp 1 Small object is still hidden in the rendering.

6. Click again on the Right arrow to move to key 3 (frame 10). Now, if you look at this key's Properties, you'll see that the value has changed from 0.0 to 1.0. This indicates that the Warp 1 Small object appears suddenly on frame 10. (Visibility is binary; that is, an object can be either visible or not only when a visibility key is set for it. If the value of the key is less than or equal to 0, the object is invisible; if it is greater than 0, the object is visible.)

7. Click again on the Right arrow to move to key 4 (frame 65). The Value is still 1.0; the Warp 1 Small object is still visible. Finally, if you move forward one more key (key 5 on frame 66), you see the Value return to 0 again. The Warp 1 Small object disappears; it's visible only from frames 10 through frames 65. When finished, close the Key Info dialog box.

8. Take a look at the Warp 1 Small and Warp 2 Small Rotation keys. Only two keys are set: one at frame 0 and one at frame 100 for both objects. Both objects are rotating about their local Z axes, but in opposite directions. From the Camera01 view-point, the Warp 1 Small object rotates clockwise; the Warp 2 Small object rotates counterclockwise.

9. Look at the morph keys for the Warp 1 Small object. If you look under the hierarchy tree under Object (Morph), you'll see a compound morph object created from the two Warp 1 Small and Warp 1 Large cones. On the Morph track, you'll see keys placed on frames 0, 9, 10, 29, 30, 49, 50, and 65.

   Notice how the Visibility keys set for the Warp 1 Small object also coincide partially with the object's entire morphing cycle. The Warp 1 Small object is hidden on frames 0 to 9. Then, on frame 10, it appears, holds until frame 65, and disappears completely on frame 66.

10. Now examine the Morph track for the Warp 1 Small object. The Warp 1 Small object keeps its initial size on frames 0 through frames 9 and 10. Then, starting at frame 10, the Warp 1 Small object morphs into the Warp 1 Large object and attains its final size on frame 29 (where the fourth morph key was set.) It holds at this size from frames 30 to frames 49. Then, starting on frame 50, it morphs back to the original Warp 1 Small object, culminating in the end of the morph on frame 65. (It then disappears entirely on frame 66, as shown in Figure 11-5.)

11. At this point, take a look at the Visibility and Morph keys set for the Warp 2 Small object and compare them with the Warp 1 Small object. Notice how the keys are offset approximately 20 frames from the corresponding keys set for the Warp 1 Small cone.

    The Warp 2 Small object is hidden on frames 0 through 29; it then appears on frame 30. It stays visible until frame 85 and then disappears on 86. If you look at the Morph keys for the Warp 2 Small object, you'll see that keys are set for frames 0, 29, 30, 49, 50, 69, 70, and 85. From frames 0 to 29 the Warp 2 Small object remains at its original size. The key at frame 30 is a duplicate of the first two keys on frames 0 and 29.

    The morph sequence starts on frame 30, however. From frames 30 to 49, the Warp 2 Small object morphs into the Warp 2 Large object. It holds at this size from frames 50 to frame 69; then, starting on frame 70, the Warp 2 Large object morphs back into the Warp 2 Small object by frame 85.

    Again, as I stated earlier, I created the WARPDRIV.MAX file to provide a specific demonstration of an admittedly esoteric effect. Although the geometric and textural elements used to create this effect are fairly simple, in this instance, "timing is everything"—the warp drive effect depends on its elements appearing in a certain way with a specific duration. You may want to merge this .MAX file into your own space effects scenes and then adjust the textures, geometry sizes, and overall key timings to suit your needs.

12. When you have finished examining these settings, close the Track View menu to return to your 3D Studio MAX desktop.

## We Have Second-Stage Ignition

Now that you've thoroughly examined these warp drive morph settings, take a look at a demonstration .AVI file of your WARPDRIV.MAX scene.

1. Select File/View File, and from the \CHAP_11 directory of your *3D Studio MAX f/x CD-ROM*, load WARPDRIV.AVI. When the Media Player appears, play the animation.

   As you can see, the Warp 1 object appears first. After it attains its full size, the Warp 2 object materializes. When the Warp 2 object reaches its full size, the Warp 1 object recedes and disappears, followed shortly thereafter by the Warp 2 object. This gives the impression of a two-stage warp burst and is a little more interesting visually.

2. When you've finished viewing the file, close the Media Player.

As you may recall from the opening of the space battle, the warp drive effect simply pops on into the 3D scene. This creates the effect of glowing streaks of light (the WARPA and WARPB bitmaps) suddenly appearing and streaking outward past the camera, with the battlecruiser following. The warp drive effect holds, spinning for a few moments, and then recedes as the cruiser emerges. It's as if the warp drive tunnel effect appears momentarily to allow the battlecruiser to come out of hyperspace; as the cruiser emerges into normal space, the warp drive effect quickly dissipates and disappears.

Again, as I mentioned earlier, to make this effect more striking I applied the 400 x 400-pixel WARPA and WARPB.TGA files across the wide-open ends of the cones, using planar mapping. Therefore, the streaks of light present in the bitmaps become even more pronounced as they stretch down the length of the cone.

## I'll Take Slot Gags for $20, Alex

In this chapter, I've thrown out a lot of explanations and answers. Now it's time to pose a question (albeit a rhetorical one, since I'm going to answer it myself, again.)

Why are the cones counter-rotating (or rotating at all, since the Warp 1 and Warp 2 textures feature randomly-spinning starbursts)?

Here's the answer. Even though both warp drive bitmap sequences feature spinning starburst images, each sequence contains only 30 looping frames. During the course of any given animation, you may choose to have the warp drive effect stay on the screen for longer than 30 frames. By counter-rotating Warp 1 Small and Warp 2 Small, you create the illusion that the warp drive effect is actually longer than the bitmap sequences comprising it. Because the combined, rotating bitmap textures appear in different positions on any given frame, the overall pattern produced by the two sequences attains greater randomness. (Sounds like something a mystic would strive for—a life of "greater randomness.") Anyway, with this effect, you will not see the warp drive effect loop and repeat during a long animation.

This use of counter-rotating or moving objects, each mapped with its own separate texture, creates what is known in Hollywood special effects jargon as a *slot gag*. A slot gag is simply a moving moiré pattern. By taking two sets of patterns, each with very similar or even identical imagery, offsetting one of them, and then rotating or moving one pattern relative to the other, you can create moving interference patterns.

This can be very useful for creating certain types of effects. For instance, in many animated films, the illusion of sunlight sparkling on the surface of a body of water is created with slot gags. These effects are often produced by taking backlit artwork consisting of thin lines or random dots and then moving that artwork against a similar or identical pattern. (You can also create this effect in 3D Studio MAX by taking similar or identical bitmaps or procedural textures and loading them into offset, counter-rotating projector spotlights.)

Another reason that you might want to use a slot gag technique is to mitigate or eliminate the need for an animated texture consisting of a large number of bitmaps. For some effects, you may be able to use a single bitmap per 3D object. By offsetting your 3D meshes, moving and/or counter-rotating them relative to one another, you may be able to create the illusion that the artwork itself is animated. It's not—it's simply a desirable by-product of the moiré effect.

## Moving On

Now it's time to continue your exploration of applying LenZFX imagery to 3D geometry. In the next chapter, you'll begin to delve into creating science-fiction weaponry such as *Star Trek*-style photon torpedoes. Again, you don't need LenZFX for 3D Studio/ DOS or for 3D Studio MAX to do this effect; everything you need is included on the *3D Studio MAX f/x CD-ROM*.

Soon you'll be able to create an antimatter weapon that'll strike fear into the hearts of men, Klingons, or Vorlons (whoops— different show).

# 12

# Tachyon Torpedoes Away

In the last chapter, you examined how you can use a combination of prerendered LenZFX bitmaps and simple geometry to produce a striking warp-drive optical effect.

In this and the next three chapters, you'll explore various ways to create science fiction weaponry such as antimatter torpedoes and laser beams, using techniques similar to those covered in Chapter 11, "Warp Speed." Again, my intention is to show you how to create as many of these effects "in-camera" as possible, although you'll also look at how you can use the Glow filter in Video Post to augment the look of your futuristic firepower.

## From Photons to Tachyons

If you've seen any of the *Star Trek* films or the various incarnations of the *Star Trek* TV shows, you've probably seen the effect of photon torpedoes. In the context of *Star Trek*, a photon torpedo is an antimatter projectile with a very characteristic appearance. In both *Star Trek* films and the later TV series (starting with "The

Next Generation"), a photon torpedo typically appears as a brilliant pinpoint of light with shafts of light radiating from it. The shafts of light wax and wane quickly as the photon torpedo is fired from a starship to its target.

The first appearance of this type of photon torpedo appeared in *Star Trek: The Motion Picture* (1979). It was created by artists at Apogee, the special-effects company formed by John Dykstra, who won an Academy Award for *Star Wars*. To produce their photon torpedoes, the effects artists took a chunk of glass crystal and attached it to the end of a clear Lucite rod. The Lucite rod was then placed in a black room filled with smoke. By firing a real laser up through the Lucite rod and then rotating the rod, they produced the effect of a bright spark of light with shafts of light flying from it. They then took this imagery and optically composited it into the footage of the Klingon starships and, later, the Enterprise.

In the TV series *Star Trek: The Next Generation*, the photon torpedoes were created as video effects using the high-end Quantel Harry video paint system. (Today, many of Harry's video manipulation and special-effects features have been duplicated by lower-cost desktop computers running off-the-shelf software.) In the later *Star Trek* films such as *Star Trek II: The Wrath of Khan* up until *Star Trek VI: The Undiscovered Country*, the photon torpedoes were created using traditional rotoscoped artwork.

However, for *Star Trek: Generations*, Industrial Light and Magic special effects supervisor John Knoll decided to create the look of the photon torpedoes using computer graphics. Knoll, who is also the co-developer of Adobe Photoshop, used a variation of his Photoshop Lens Flare filter to create the torpedoes. (Knoll originally designed the Photoshop Lens Flare filter for Stephen Spielberg's movie, *Hook*. Since then, Knoll has commented, half-jokingly, that due to the overuse of this effect in television and movie CGI sequences, he should have patented his Lens Flare code.)

## Load Torpedo Tubes!

Even if you don't yet own a lens flare plug-in for 3D Studio MAX, you can still create the illusion of an energy torpedo using planar geometry and prerendered images produced with Digimation's LenZFX plug-in for 3D Studio/DOS or for 3D Studio MAX.

For this chapter, you'll create your own version of a projectile energy weapon—a tachyon torpedo. (*Tachyons* are faster-than-light particles, much-debated by quantum physicists.) Like the new "Invaders" flying saucer that you saw in Chapter 2, "Saucer Attack," your tachyon torpedo will be vastly different from its televised predecessor. Whereas *Star Trek's* photon torpedo is powered by antimatter, your tachyon torpedo will use, um, "maxi-phasic anti-phlogiston"—designed to fend off both evil aliens and attacks from Paramount Pictures' legal department.

Here's how you create this weapon.

1. In 3D Studio MAX, activate the Front viewport and then press the W key on your keyboard to expand the viewport to full screen. From the Command Panel, select Create\Geometry\Standard Primitives. Under the Standard Primitives options, click on the Down arrow and change from Standard Primitives to Patch Grids. Under Object Type, select Quad Patch.

2. Press the S key on your keyboard to activate the 2D Snap toggle. Then, looking at the status bar at the bottom of your screen, move your crosshair cursor to approximate XYZ coordinates X -50, Y 0, and Z 50. Click and drag the Quad Patch down diagonally to the right until you are at approximate XYZ coordinates X 50, Y 0, and Z -50. Release to create the QuadPatch01 object.

   From the Command Panel, you should see the Length and Width of the Quad Patch object set to 100. The Length and Width Segments should both be at 1.

3. Click on the Modify tab of the Command Panel. From the Modifiers Set, select UVW Map. (If this is not part of your default Modifier button set, click the More button and pick

UVW Map from the list of modifiers.) An orange planar mapping icon appears, fitted to the QuadPatch01 object. (Leave these settings as they are for the moment.)

4. Select Edit/Properties, toggle off Cast Shadows and Receive Shadows on the QuadPatch01 object, and then close the Properties dialog box. (You can also reach the Object Properties dialog box by placing the cursor over the object, right-clicking, and then selecting Properties from the menu.)

    You'll want to make two copies of your QuadPatch01 object. You'll create these copies by using 3D Studio MAX's Shift-cloning feature.

5. Click on the Angle Snap Toggle button. This makes rotating and cloning the Quad Patch objects in five-degree increments easier. You'll want to snap the objects along the Y and X axis to 90 degrees.

6. Click on the Select and Rotate button; then, click on the Re-strict to Y button. You'll want to restrict your initial Shift-clone-rotation of the Quad Patch objects to the Y axis. In the Front viewport, the Y axis is pointing directly up.

7. Move the Select and Rotate cursor over the selected QuadPatch01 object; then, holding down the Shift key, click and drag the mouse until the QuadPatch01 object has rotated –90 degrees on the Y axis. When you finish Shift-rotating the object, the Clone Options dialog box appears. Under Object, click on Instance rather than Copy. Then, click on OK or press Enter to create a copy of the Quad Patch object.

8. Click on the Restrict to Z button and then move your cursor down to the center of your Front viewport until the Select and Rotate cursor appears again. You'll want to Shift-clone and rotate the new QuadPatch02 object.

9. Hold down the Shift key and, with the Select and Rotate cursor visible, click and drag the mouse until the QuadPatch02 object has rotated on the Z axis -90. When you've finished, create another Instance object called QuadPatch03 and close the Clone Options dialog box.

10. Click on the Min/Max Toggle button (or press W on your keyboard) to return to the default four viewports; then, click on the Zoom Extents All button.

11. Right-click in the Perspective viewport to activate it and click on the Arc Rotate icon (or press Control+R). When the Arc Rotate arcball appears, move your cursor inside the arcball and adjust the view until you're looking down on the three Quad Patch objects at approximately a 45-degree angle, as shown in Figure 12-1.

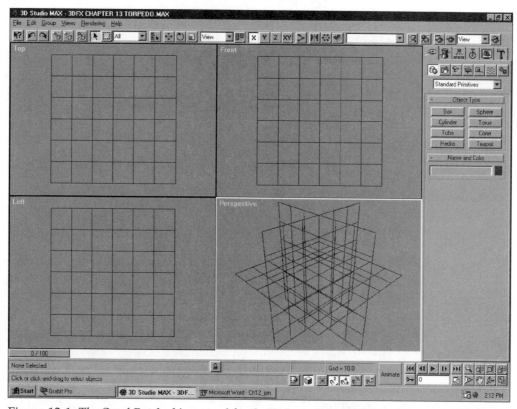

Figure 12-1: *The Quad Patch objects used for the Tachyon Torpedo Effect. (Note that in this figure the grid has been turned off in all four viewports so that you may more easily see the Quad Patch objects.)*

12. When you've finished, right-click to dismiss the Arc Rotate option and then left-click in any of your viewports outside the selected Quad Patch objects to deselect them.

## Fried Green Torpedoes

Now it's time to map the Quad Patch objects with your Tachyon Torpedo texture. But first, you'll place your torpedo effect in a proper environment by loading the familiar STARS640.TGA texture as a background.

1. Select Rendering/Environment, and when the Environment dialog box appears, click on Assign in the Background section. The Material/Map browser appears. Select New and double-click on Bitmap. Map #1 (Bitmap) loads in the Environment Map name field. Click on this name field to bring up the Put to Material Editor dialog box. Under Select Slot, change from Slot 1 to Slot 2; then, click on OK and dismiss the Environment dialog box.

   Now you'll apply your torpedo texture to your Quad Patch tachyon torpedo objects and set up your star background.

2. Bring up the Material Editor and click on Slot #2 (the background bitmap) to make it the active material. Under Coordinates, change the Environment background type from Spherical Environment to Screen. Then, under Bitmap Parameters, click on the Bitmap Name field, and from the \CHAP_12 directory of your *3D Studio MAX f/x CD-ROM*, load the STARS640.TGA bitmap.

   When you return to the Material Editor, click on Slot #1 to activate it. As with the warp drive effects discussed in the previous chapter, you'll want to load a series of images to map onto the Quad Patch objects to produce your tachyon torpedo effect.

   Now you'll create this material.

3. Under Basic Parameters, click on 2-sided. Because you're mapping this material onto 2D planar shapes, you'll want to make sure that the material shows up regardless of whether you are facing the front or the back of the face normals of these Quad Patches. Change the Ambient and Diffuse colors to pure black (RGB 0, 0, 0). Now, change Shininess and Shininess Strength to 0. You don't want any specular highlights appearing on this material. Finally, change Self-Illumination to 100. You'll want your material to be completely self-illuminated to simulate a bright optical effect.

4. Open the Extended Parameters rollout. Change Opacity Falloff to Out rather than In, and change the Type to Additive. This will make the torpedo material brighter on the object.

5. Open the Maps rollout and click on the Diffuse Map Name Field. When the Material/Map browser appears, make sure that New is selected and double-click on Bitmap. Then, click on the Bitmap name field, and from the \CHAP_12 directory of your *3D Studio MAX f/x CD-ROM*, scroll down until you see the files TORPG000.TGA through TORPG0030.TGA (green torpedo bitmaps), and TORPR000.TGA through TORPRO30.TGA (red torpedo bitmaps). Click on the TORPR000.TGA image once to highlight it; then, click on the View button to view this image.

Like the warp drive textures in the previous chapter, I created the 400 x 400 resolution torpedo bitmaps using Digimation's LenZFX plug-in program for 3D Studio/DOS. I created the effect by using a grayscale .GIF image as a UV gradient; this created the shafts of light radiating out from the center. In addition, I turned the Rays and Lens Element options off and set up custom color ramps to create the effect of a hot, white core that trails off into yellow, orange, and red.

Finally, I rendered 30 frames of this torpedo imagery in 3D Studio/DOS. As with the warp drive textures, each frame presents a different number of light rays emanating from the core; the light rays also vary in intensity. Therefore, during the course of an animation, these 30 frames create the illusion of a sparkling, fiery ball of light. It's perfect for your tachyon torpedo effect.

6. When you've finished viewing this file (or subsequent images), close the View File window. Now, instead of loading one of the TORPR000.TGA images, load the TORPR000.IFL file from the \CHAP_12 directory. As you do, you'll see the first frame of the red torpedo sequence appear on the sample sphere in Slot #1. (An .IFL for the TORPG000.TGA bitmaps is also included in this directory.)

7. Click on the Go to Parent icon in the Material Editor and go down to the Maps section. Click and drag the TORPR000.IFL from the Diffuse slot down to the Opacity slot. Click on Instance rather than Copy and then click on OK.

   As you copy this image file sequence from the Diffuse map section down to Opacity, you'll see the material settings change on the sample sphere in Slot #1. The combination of these material and map settings produces a brightly glowing tachyon torpedo effect.

8. Change the material name to Torpedo Red.

At this point, you may want to save this material to your local 3DSMAX.MAT Material Library. (This material is also saved in the 3DSMAXFX.MAT Material Library, along with a Torpedo Green material, using TORPG000.IFL.)

## A 2D Texture in a 3D World

Now you'll assign your Torpedo Red material to the Quad Patches and group them together to make a torpedo object.

1. Click on the Select by Name button (or press the H key on your keyboard) to bring up the Select Objects browser. Click on the All button at the bottom of the dialog box to select all three Quad Patch objects; then, click on Select. The three objects all turn white, indicating that they're selected.

2. Return to the Material Editor and, with the Torpedo Red material active, click on the Assign Material to Selection button. This assigns your new Torpedo Red texture to the Quad Patch objects.

   Now you'll do a test rendering.

3. Activate your Perspective viewport to activate it, and press Alt+R and Enter to render a single 640 x 480 frame of your test torpedo object. After a few moments, the image appears. It should look something like Figure 12-2.

Figure 12-2: *The Torpedo Red texture applied to the three Quad Patch 2D planar objects.*

Take a look at this rendering, and you'll see an irregularly shaped ball of light with shafts of light radiating from it. By mapping an image sequence onto these 2D Quad Patches, you've created what resembles a three-dimensional optical effect.

4. When you've finished looking at this effect, close the Perspective VFB window and Material Editor.

The Quad Patch objects that you've just created, both with and without the Torpedo Red textures, are saved in the \CHAP_12 directory of your *3D Studio MAX f/x CD-ROM* as TORPEDO1.MAX and TORPEDO2.MAX. (In an upcoming chapter, you'll use this grouped Torpedo mesh object to create a "muzzle flash" for the emanation point of a laser beam.)

## I'm With the Dummy

Now you'll do a test to see how this effect holds up during the course of an animation. You'll first group your Quad Patches into a single torpedo object and then animate it in your scene.

1. The three Quad Patch objects should still be selected, so from the 3D Studio MAX menu bar, select Group/Group. For Group Name, type **Torpedo**, then press Enter or click on OK. You have now grouped your three Quad Patch objects into a single Torpedo object.

   At this point, you could set up a camera in your scene and then animate the Torpedo object to see the effect of this 3D optical. However, another way to demonstrate this is to merge an existing animation file consisting of an animated dummy object and a camera.

2. Select File/Merge, and from the \CHAP_12 directory of your *3D Studio MAX f/x CD-ROM*, click on the file TORPPATH.MAX. When the Merge dialog box appears, click on All to merge both the Camera01 and the Dummy01 objects into the scene and then click on OK. As you do so, you see a targeted camera appear in your viewports.

3. Click on the Zoom Extents All icon. You now see your Torpedo object, the targeted camera, and the Dummy01 object in all your viewports. The Dummy01 object already has an animation path applied to it. If you click on the Play button or drag your Time Slider, you'll see the Dummy travel from right to left, in a gentle arc in front of the camera. Return to frame 0.

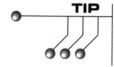

**TIP** If you want to see a visible motion path for the Dummy01 object, select the Dummy and then click on the Motion panel. Under Selection Level, click on Trajectories. The Dummy01 motion path appears. This shows the slightly curving path of the Dummy01 object across the 100-frame animation sequence. As the Dummy01 object flies by the camera, the camera pans with it to keep it in the frame.

4. Activate your Top viewport; then, press the W key to enlarge it to full screen. You'll want to center your Torpedo object on the Dummy object and then link it to the Dummy so that it travels along the Dummy's preset animation path.

5. Press the S key on your keyboard to turn off the 2D Snap toggle. Click on the Restrict to XY button. Then, click on the Select and Move button and drag the Torpedo object over to the Dummy01 object. Check the status bar at the bottom of your screen, and drag the Torpedo object to approximate XYZ coordinates X 840, Y 260, and Z 0.

6. When you have the Torpedo object centered on the Dummy01, click on the Select and Link button and press the H key on your keyboard to bring up the Select by Name dialog box. Because you are in Select and Link mode, the Select Parent dialog box appears. Click on Dummy01 to select it; then, click on Link. The Torpedo object is now linked to Dummy01 and will inherit its motion.

7. Press the W key on your keyboard to return to your four viewports; then, click on the Zoom Extents All button. Your viewports should now look like Figure 12-3.

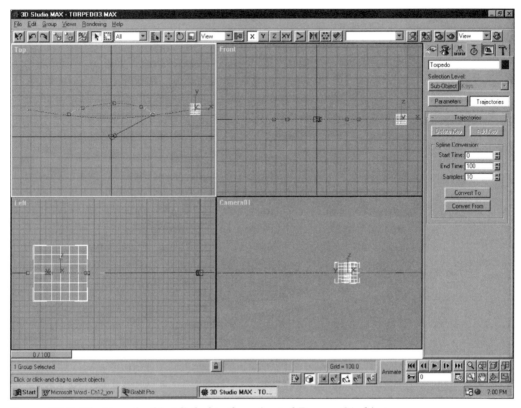

Figure 12-3: *The Torpedo object linked to the animated Dummy01 object.*

8. Activate your Perspective viewport and press the C key on your keyboard to switch to the Camera01 view. Then, click on the Play Animation button.

   As you can see, the Torpedo object is linked to the Dummy01 object and travels with it from right to left across your scene. The camera pans to follow and track with the objects.

9. Click again on the Stop Animation button to stop the animation.

## Whirling Dervishly

At this point, if you were to load a spherical starfield background into your scene and render it, you would get a reasonable animation of your tachyon torpedo flying through space. And, because you've applied a two-sided texture to these XYZ-rotated and cloned Quad Patches, they present enough surface area perpendicular to the camera so that the Torpedo Red texture always looks like a fully-3D effect.

Of course, you can improve this technique by increasing the apparent randomness of the 30-frame texture sequence. One way to do this is to apply an extreme XYZ rotation on your torpedo object during the course of an animation. By doing so, you change the apparent appearance of the three identical textures applied to the Quad Patch object, relative to the camera viewpoint.

1. Drag the Time Slider at the bottom of your screen all the way over to frame 100; or, click on the Go to End icon button. Now, click on the Animate button. It turns red, indicating that you are now in animation mode.

2. Click on the Select and Rotate button and then on the Restrict to XY button (if it's not already active). Now, in any of your viewports, move the Select and Rotate cursor over the Torpedo object and rotate it drastically in the scene. As you do, you see the XYZ coordinates change. A suggested rotational setting is X -60, Y 50, and Z -180.

   (If you want, click on the other X, Y, and/or Z buttons to restrict rotation to that specific axis and, in any of your other viewports, rotate the torpedo object even more. Again, for the best effect, you'll want a multi-axis rotation on the torpedo object.)

3. When you've finished, activate the Camera01 viewport and click on the Animate button again to toggle animation mode off. Now, click again on the Play animation button.

You now see the Torpedo object start out on frame 0 in its original XYZ orientation, but then it rotates about its local axis during the course of the animation. Again, by rotating the 2D Quad Patches in relation to the camera, you can enhance the illusion that your Tachyon Torpedo effect is actually a 3D optical effect rather than a 2D texture applied to flat 2D shapes.

4. Click again on the Play Animation button to stop the animation; then, click on the Go to Start button to return to frame 0.

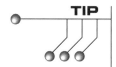

**TIP** If you want to impart a very frenetic, random rotation to the Torpedo object, select it and then go into Track View and assign a Noise controller to the Torpedo's Transform/Rotation track.

Now, if you want to render your own test animation of this sequence (and perhaps tweak the motion path), you can do so, but you'll need an appropriate starfield background that moves properly as the camera pans. (If you want to simply see a demonstration .AVI of this sequence, skip down to step #7.)

5. Return to the Material Editor and change the settings for your Environment Map in Slot #2. Under Coordinates, change the mapping from Screen back to Spherical Environment. Change the UV tiling from 1.0 to 4.0 on both U and V coordinates. Then, under Bitmap Parameters, double-click in the Bitmap Name Field to bring up the Select Bitmap Image File Browser.

6. From your *3D Studio MAX f/x CD-ROM*, go to the \MAPS\TGA directory and load the file STAR6402.TGA. This is a 640 x 320 pixel resolution image designed specifically to be used as a Spherical Environment starfield. After you load the file, close the Material Editor and render your sequence.

If you don't want to render your own version of this sequence, take a look at the following demonstration animation.

7. Select File/View File. From the \CHAP_12 directory, scroll down until you see the file TORPTEST.AVI, and click on it. When the Media Player appears, click on the Play button to play the 100-frame TORPTEST.AVI file.

See how the Torpedo object appears to be a 3D, solid, geometric optical effect rather than a "flat" 2D effect? By using 3D objects to represent optical effects in your space scenes, you can more easily control the placement and animation of the optical effects by simply animating them as 3D objects. In addition, by using this technique, you do not necessarily have to resort to Video Post processing using Glow or Blur filters.

Finally, note that if you want motion-blurred stars for this test sequence, you will either have to use a Starfield procedural filter loaded into Video Post or add Scene Motion Blur as a scene event in Video Post.

## Various Variations

What are some other ways in which you can vary this torpedo effect? Well, you can use different imagery for the Torpedo texture, of course. Another interesting effect you can try is to place an Omni light, with Ranges and Attenuation set, in the very center of your Torpedo object. By linking the attenuated Omni light to the Torpedo object, you can make your Torpedo object appear to actually illuminate scene elements as it flies by them—or violently impacts upon them! Adding interactive lighting in this way can greatly improve the verisimilitude of your 3D animations.

Another technique to try is to create a tachyon torpedo by using a volumetric Omni light with animated Noise (similar to what I discussed in Chapter 9, "Here Comes the Sun, Part I," when I showed you how to create volumetric sun effects). In this way, you can create the illusion of an intense ball of plasma energy fired from your spaceships' weapons ports.

Finally, you can even experiment with combining these two techniques. Try placing a volumetric Omni light in the center of your 3D tachyon torpedo object and then adjust the volume light parameters until you get the effect you want.

The animation file you've just created is saved in the \CHAP_12 directory of your *3D Studio MAX f/x CD-ROM* as TORPEDO3.MAX.

## Moving On

In the next three chapters, you'll take a look at how you can create laser beams in a variety of ways—from simple glowing cylinders to (yep, you guessed it) using Noise and bitmap textures. In addition, you'll see how you can use the techniques that I've just covered to create a sparkling highlight to represent the emanation point of a laser beam.

# 13

# Laser Beams 101

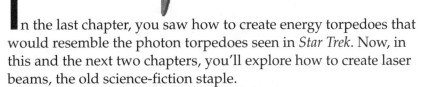

In the last chapter, you saw how to create energy torpedoes that would resemble the photon torpedoes seen in *Star Trek*. Now, in this and the next two chapters, you'll explore how to create laser beams, the old science-fiction staple.

As you saw when you previewed the space battle scenes, the battlecruiser fires off a volley of laser beams at the attacking fighters and succeeds in destroying one of the ships. I created the lasers in these scenes by using a variation of the tachyon torpedo effect that I discussed in the last chapter. By taking prerendered Autodesk Animator Pro flic files, converting them to .GIF image sequences, and then applying them to Quad Patches using Diffuse and Opacity mapping, I produced the illusion of crackling beams of energy.

In this chapter, you'll see how to duplicate this effect. You'll see how you can use a variation of the last chapter's tachyon torpedo effect to create a laser beam "muzzle flash." You'll also see how to enhance your laser beams by applying the Video Post Glow filter to add optical oomph to them.

Then, in the next two chapters, you'll see how you can take simple cylindrical meshes and turn them into nifty laser beams by applying layers of Noise materials.

## Creating Laser Beams With Geometry & Textures

Now you'll see how you can create a laser beam by applying Autodesk Animator Pro animations onto simple Quad Patch planar shapes.

1. In 3D Studio MAX, activate your Top viewport and press the W key on your keyboard to enlarge it to full screen. Press the S key on your keyboard to activate the 2D Snap Toggle. Then, from the Create Panel, select Create/Geometry, click on the Down arrow next to Standard Primitives, and pick Patch Grids. Under Object Type, pick Quad Patch.

2. In the Top viewport, move your cursor to approximate XYZ coordinates X -100, Y 10, and Z 0. Click and drag down diagonally to the right to approximately X 120, Y -10, and Z 0, until you have a Quad Patch object with a length of 20 and a width of 220. (This is for initial placement only, because you're going to change the proportions of this object drastically in the Parameters rollout.)

3. In the Parameters section of the Create Panel, change the Length from 20 to 5. Then, change Width from 220 to 500 and press Enter. In your viewports, you'll see the Quad Patch become a very long, thin object. Now, change its name from Quad Patch01 to Laser01.

4. In the Parameters rollout, click on the Generate Mapping Coordinates button.
   Although you want the Quad Patch's mapping coordinates active, you're not going to make use of them immediately— you'll see their effect later in this tutorial. Right now, you're going to apply a bitmap-fitted UVW map to the Quad Patch object, which will override the Quad Patch's current mapping. (After you apply your laser texture and render the first laser beam test image, you'll remove the UVW mapping, render another test image and compare the results.)

5. Click on the Modify tab to go to the Modify Panel, and from your Modifiers button set, pick UVW Map. (If it's not part of your default Modifiers set, click on the More button and then pick it from the Modifiers list.) The Mapping Parameters rollout appears and you see an orange UVW Mapping gizmo appear around the QuadPatch01 object.

**Note:** *The default UVW Planar Mapping gizmo is stretched to fit the parameters of your QuadPatch01 object. Consequently, the UVW Mapping will produce the same results as the original Generate Mapping Coordinates setting.*

## Fitting the Flic

Now you'll adjust the UVW Mapping gizmo so that it uses Bitmap Fitting. This will change its aspect ratio and make it less "stretched" along the Laser01 object.

1. In the Modifier Panel, go down to Alignment in the Parameters rollout and click on Bitmap Fit. The Select Image dialog box appears. From the \CHAP_13 directory of your *3D Studio MAX f/x CD-ROM*, find the file LASRMAX3.FLC and click once on it to highlight it. Then, click on the View button. The Media Player appears. Click on the Play button to play the LASRMAX3.FLC file.

   This flic was created in Autodesk Animator Pro. The flic has a resolution of 640 x 35 and is 60 frames long. As you preview this flic, notice that it consists of a rapidly flashing and vibrating inner core that flashes from white to yellow to orange; sparkling particles radiate from the central core.

   Although it's only an 8-bit (or 256-color) animation file, it's fine for your purposes because you need only a simple color gradient to provide the laser beam texture. The palette for this flic ranges from white to yellow, orange, red, and then to dark red, and finally black. At rendering time, the texture filtering in 3D Studio MAX converts 8-bit textures to 24-bit textures. This has the effect of smoothing out the textures and giving them richer color values.

The LASRMAX3.FLC file is also saved in the *3D Studio MAX f/x CD-ROM* \MAPS directory as individual .GIF files (LASR3000-LASR3059.GIF.)

**Note:** *If you use an animated texture such as a flic or an .AVI, 3D Studio MAX loads the entire animation into memory before it renders. Although the LASRMAX3.FLC that you're using is fairly small (approximately 650K), in general it's more memory efficient to load sequential images from an animated sequence to create your animated textures and/or backgrounds.*

*As you've seen earlier in the book, you can do this by saving your animation as individual images and then using 3D Studio MAX's .IFL creator in the Material Editor to create a list of image sequences. Remember, though, that 3D Studio MAX writes the .IFL file to the same directory in which it loads the images. If you are reading images from a CD-ROM or other read-only storage media, create an .IFL that contains the entire path name per bitmap, store the .IFL on your local hard drive, and load it from there.*

2. When you've finished previewing the LASRMAX3.FLC file, close the Media Player and load the file. When you return to your Top viewport, you should see that the UVW mapping icon has now shrunk in width to match the 640 x 35 pixel resolution size of the LASRMAX3.FLC.

Because I made the flic able to be tiled at each end, you can repeat it as many times as necessary down the length of your Laser01 object.

## Cloning Around

Now that you have applied the UVW mapping coordinates, you'll make one more change to the Laser01 object before you clone it.

1. Select Edit/Properties, turn off Cast Shadows and Receive Shadows for the Laser01 object, and click on OK. If you use a laser object like this in your own 3D scene, you don't want it casting or receiving shadows from any of the other objects in the scene. As an optical effect, this would look odd.

Now you'll clone your Laser01 object.

2. Click on the Min/Max Toggle button to return to your four viewports and then click on the Zoom Extents All button. Activate the Left viewport and press the W key to enlarge it to full screen. You want to Shift/rotate/clone the Laser01 object along its long (or Z) axis. To make this easier, click on the Angle Snap Toggle button. This will help you rotate the object in five-degree increments.

3. Click on the Restrict to Z axis button to restrict the rotation of the Laser01 object to the Z axis; then, click on the Select and Rotate button.

4. Now, holding down your Shift key, move your cursor over the Laser01 object until the Select and Rotate cursor appears; then, click and drag until you have rotated a clone of the Laser01 object. Rotate along the Z axis to -60 degrees and then release. As you do, the Clone Options dialog box appears. Click on Instance and then on OK to create the Laser02 object.

5. Hold down your Shift key again, move your Select and Rotate cursor back over the new Laser02 object, and rotate this again along the Z axis to -60. Release and create another Instance object, called Laser03, and then click on OK.

6. When you've finished, click on the Min/Max Toggle button to return to your four viewports. Activate your Perspective viewport and press the W key on your keyboard to enlarge it to full screen.

7. Now, using a combination of your Arc Rotate, Pan, and Zoom buttons, adjust your Perspective viewport until the three Quad Patch Laser objects are positioned as shown in Figure 13-1. The far end of the Laser objects should be in the upper-right corner of your screen, slanted diagonally down to the lower-left corner. You should be looking down on them at approximately a 45-degree angle.

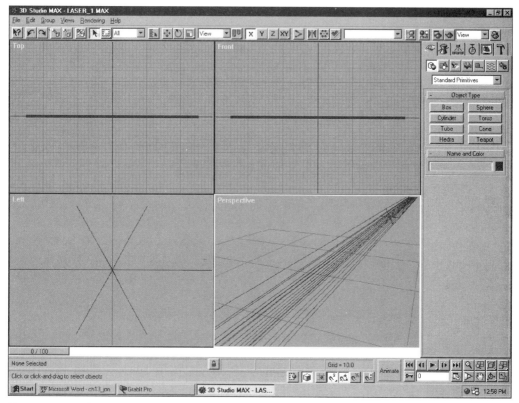

Figure 13-1: *The correct position for the test rendering of the Laser objects.*

8. Click on the Select by Name button; click on the All button under the list window to highlight all three Laser objects; then, click on Select.

You'll now apply your laser material to these selected three objects. So, it's time to build the material.

## Coherent Light

For your laser test renderings, you want to see your laser beams against a space backdrop, so you should load the standard STARS640.TGA bitmap as a Screen Environment background. You should already be familiar with how to do this from the previous tutorials. If not, go back to Chapter 9, "Here Comes the Sun, Part I," and follow the instructions on loading a bitmap Screen background for your scene. Place it in Slot #2 of the Material Editor.

**CD-ROM**

A copy of the STARS640.TGA image is included in the \MAPS directory of the *3D Studio MAX f/x CD-ROM*, as well as various chapter directories.

1. In the Material Editor, make Slot #1 active; you'll change its parameters to build your laser material. First, click in the check box next to 2-Sided (like the tachyon torpedo, you need to be able to see the texture on the 2D quad patches from any angle). Change Ambient and Diffuse colors to solid black, or RGB 0, 0, 0. Change Shininess and Shininess Strength to 0 and then change Self-illumination from 0 to 100.

2. Open the Extended Parameters rollout; under Opacity, change Falloff to Out and Opacity Type to Additive.

3. Now, open the Maps rollout. Click on the Diffuse Map button. When the Materials/Map browser appears, click on New under Browse From and then click on Bitmap in the list window. When the Bitmap rollout appears in the Material Editor, click on the Bitmap name button under Bitmap Parameters to bring up the Select Bitmap Image File dialog box.

**CD-ROM**

4. From the \CHAP_13 directory of your *3D Studio MAX f/x CD-ROM*, click on the file LASRMAX3.FLC. It should appear on the sample sphere in Material Slot #1. Click on the Go to Parent icon to return to the main Material #1 rollout; then, in the Maps rollout, click and drag the LASERMAX3.FLC Diffuse Map down to the Opacity Map slot. Check Instance in the Copy (Instance) Map dialog box and then click on OK. Now, change the name of this material to Laser 3 Flic.

5. When you've finished, click on the Assign Material to Selection button to assign this new Laser 3 Flic material to the selected Laser objects.

6. Activate your Perspective viewport and press Alt+R and Enter to render a single 640 x 480 test image. After a moment the image appears; it should look like Figure 13-2.

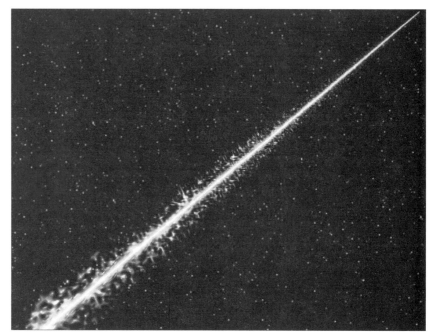

Figure 13-2: *The Laser Quad Patch objects with the LASRMAX3.FLC texture applied to them.*

If you look closely at your rendering, you'll see how 3D Studio MAX's texture filtering has softened and blurred the 8-bit texture that you've applied to these Quad Patch objects. In addition, you'll notice that by rotating and cloning the initial Quad Patch object twice along its Z axis, you've increased the intensity of the Animator Pro LASRMAX3 texture. The additive transparency of the texture creates a laser beam with an intense white core and with yellow, orange, and reddish-gold particles emanating from it.

As you see from this example, this is a modification of the technique discussed in the previous chapter to create tachyon torpedoes. By taking a flat bitmap texture, making it two-sided, and then applying it to 2D geometry, you've simulated a bright optical effect without post-processing. In addition, by duplicating the initial geometry along the Z-axis, you have created a laser effect that belies its original 2D nature. If you move the Laser object around your screen, or move the camera in relationship to it, the laser will not appear to be a "flat" effect at virtually any point of an animation. (The only exception to this is if you were to look dead-on down the length of the beam.) However, you can avoid this easily by judicious placement of your camera.

7. When you've finished examining this rendering, close your Perspective VFB window.

## Stretch to Fit

As I mentioned earlier, you can get different results for your laser beam renderings if you use the default UVW mapping coordinates applied to your Laser objects. By removing the bitmap-fitted UVW Mapping modifier from your Laser01 object, you get a stretched LASRMAX3.FLC texture for your laser beams. In most instances, stretching or smearing a bitmap texture on 3D geometry produces undesirable results, but for these optical effects, the results can be interesting.

Go ahead and take a look.

1. You want to preserve your current laser settings, so select Edit/Hold. You'll fetch your current settings after you do a test rendering.

2. Select the Laser01 object (either click on it or pick it from the Select by Name dialog box.) Because the other two laser objects are instances of Laser01, any changes that you make to it will be reflected on Laser02 and Laser03.

3. From the Modify Panel, go down to the Modifier Stack section of the rollout. You should see the UVW Mapping modifier at the top of the stack. Click on the Remove Modifier From the Stack button to remove the bitmap-fitted UVW Mapping gizmo.

4. Activate your Perspective viewport and render a test image. After a few moments, it appears and should look like Figure 13-3.

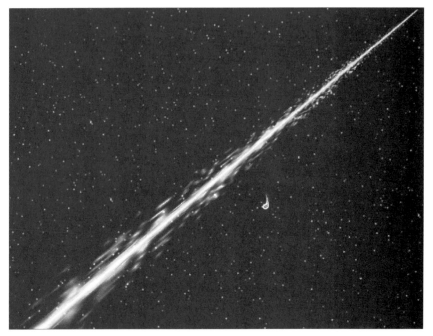

Figure 13-3: *The default mapping UVW coordinates of the Quad Patch laser objects creates a stretched bitmap texture.*

Notice how the stretched LASRMAX3.FLC bitmap makes the laser look more "fiery" instead of looking like a sparkling particle beam. Again, this is one instance in which altering a bitmap texture's coordinates drastically on a 3D mesh can produce a useful effect.

5. When you've finished viewing the rendering, close your Perspective VFB. Select Edit/Fetch and click on Yes to return to your original laser settings.

## Viewing the Laser Beam

Now take a look at a demonstration .AVI file to see your original laser beam effect.

1. Select File/View File, and from the \CHAP_13 directory of your *3D Studio MAX f/x CD-ROM*, double-click on the file

LASER_3.AVI. When the Media Player appears, click on the Play button to play the .AVI file.

This is a 320 x 240, 100-frame long .AVI file of your laser object. As you see, the LASRMAX3.FLC file, applied as an animated texture to the objects, creates the illusion of an intensely sparkling laser beam.

2. When you've finished viewing the LASER_3.AVI file, close the Media Player.

This Laser 3 Flic material is also in the 3DSMAXFX.MAT Material Library on your *3D Studio MAX f/x CD-ROM*.

 The scene file that you just created is included in the \CHAP_13 directory of your *3D Studio MAX f/x CD-ROM* as LASER_1.MAX.

## Adding a Starburst to the Laser Beam

In the last chapter, you saw how you can create tachyon torpedoes by using 2D geometry and sequential bitmap textures. In this chapter, you've created laser beams in the same way. Now you'll combine the two effects—tachyon torpedoes and laser beams—to create the effect of a "muzzle flash" appearing at the emanation point of the laser beam.

1. Click on the Min/Max Toggle button to return to your four viewports. You want to merge in the TORPEDO2.MAX demonstration file, so select File/Merge. When the Merge File  dialog box appears, go to the \CHAP_12 directory of your *3D Studio MAX f/x CD-ROM* and double-click on the file TORPEDO2.MAX.

2. When the Merge dialog box appears, click on All to select the Torpedo Group and the QuadPatch01, QuadPatch02, and QuadPatch03 objects comprising it; then, click on OK.

3. When the Torpedo group appears, click on the Min/Max Toggle button to return to your four viewports. You'll see the three Torpedo Quad Patch objects sitting in the middle of your viewports.

Now you'll move these selected objects to the end of the laser beam.

4. Activate the Top viewport and press the W key on your keyboard to enlarge the viewport to full screen. Click on the 2D Snap Toggle button; this will make it easier to align the Torpedo objects.

5. Click on the Select and Move button and then on the Restrict to X button. Now, drag the selected Torpedo group along the X axis to the right approximately 250 units, as indicated by the status bar at the bottom of the screen.

   Place the center of the selected Torpedo Quad Patches at the far right end of your three laser objects. Your screen should look something like Figure 13-4.

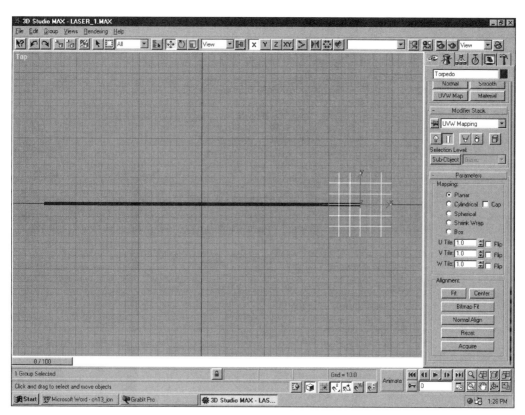

Figure 13-4: *The proper placement for the Torpedo group at the starting point of your laser beam.*

6. Click on the Min/Max Toggle button to return to your four viewports; then, activate your Perspective viewport. Press the W key on your keyboard to enlarge it to full screen.

7. Now, using your Arc Rotate, Pan, and Zoom functions, adjust your Perspective viewport until your screen looks something like Figure 13-5.

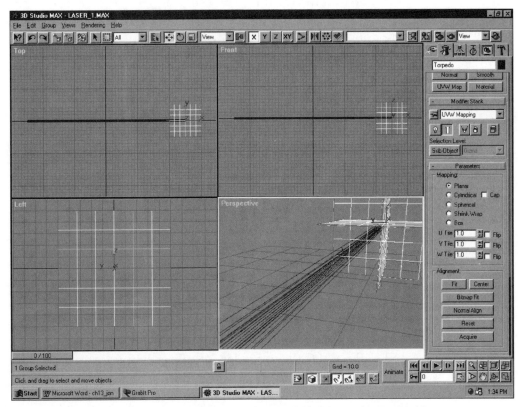

Figure 13-5: *The proper angle for the test rendering of the laser and torpedo objects.*

Don't worry about not being able to see the entire selected Torpedo group in your Perspective viewport. What's most important is that you see the center of the Torpedo objects; that is, the point at which they intersect the end of the laser objects.

8. Now, with the Torpedo group still selected, click on the Material Editor button to return to the Material Editor, and click in Slot #3 to make it active. Click on the Get Material icon to bring up the Material/Map Browser; under Browse From, click on Scene this time. You should see the STARS640.TGA image (used for the Screen Environment background) and the Laser 3 Flic and Torpedo Red materials. Double-click on Torpedo Red to load it into Slot #3.

   This is the tachyon torpedo texture that you created in the previous chapter; you'll modify this to create a starburst effect for the end of your laser.

9. In the Material Editor, go down to the Maps section of the rollout for the Torpedo Red material. Click on the Diffuse map name; you'll see the TORPR000.IFL loaded. This is the image file list for the 30 tachyon torpedo bitmaps.

10. Click on the Bitmap Name Field to bring up the Select Bitmap Image file browser. From the \CHAP_13 directory, highlight the file LSRBURST.FLC and click on View. When the Media Player appears, play the animation.

   The LSRBURST.FLC file is a 100 x 100 resolution flic that I created in Digimation's LenZFX plug-in for 3D Studio/DOS. It's very similar to the red tachyon torpedo images, but it's one-quarter the resolution. Its low resolution, however, actually makes it very suitable for creating a soft-focus muzzle flash effect for the emanation point of the laser beam.

11. Close the Media Player and double-click on the LSRBURST.FLC file to load it. You'll see it appear on the sample sphere of Slot #3. Click on the Go to Parent button to return to the main Material Editor rollout; you can see that the LSRBURST.FLC file is also loaded into the Opacity map slot. This is because the original TORPR000.IFL file was copied from the Diffuse to the Opacity map slot as an Instanced texture.

12. Activate your Perspective viewport again and then render another test image of the scene. After a moment, the image appears and should look like Figure 13-6.

Figure 13-6: *A laser beam with muzzle flash; the flash is produced by a varia-tion of the tachyon torpedo effect.*

Notice how 3D Studio MAX's texture filtering makes the low-resolution LSRBURST.FLC texture appear as a soft yet hot image.

13. When you've finished viewing the rendering, close your Perspective VFB window.

The muzzle flash material that you just created is in the 3DSMAXFX.MAT material library as Laser Burst; the scene file that you created is in the \CHAP_13 directory as LASER_2.MAX.

## Hot Flashes

Take a look at a demonstration .AVI of this laser beam with accompanying muzzle flash.

1. Select File/View File, and from the \CHAP_13 directory, load the file LASER_2.AVI. When the Media Player appears, click the Play button to play the laser animation.

   As you can see by looking at this .AVI file, the combination of 2D geometry with animated 8-bit laser and tachyon torpedo textures has produced a convincing illusion of an intense laser beam, with a bright muzzle flash from the emanation point.

   This variation of the torpedo effect can also show the point at which the laser beam impacts another surface, such as the skin of a spaceship, a spaceship's forcefield, or the body of an enemy robot.

2. When you've finished viewing the .AVI file, close the Media Player.

## Some Light Exercise

As I noted in Chapter 11, "Warp Speed!," for some optical effects, animation and timing are everything. To make your laser beam appear convincing, you would, of course, not confine yourself to these relatively short laser objects. Although they might be suitable for certain shots, for long shots you would probably want to drastically increase the length of the beam. Of course, in 3D Studio MAX, you can actually animate the beam's length during your animation.

One way to do this is to select the laser beam's end vertices, toggle on Animation Mode, and move the vertices to specific locations on specific frames. This enables you to animate the laser beam emerging from the barrel of a laser cannon and snapping outward suddenly to its target. (As you saw earlier, due to the nature of this effect, it doesn't hurt the laser beam imagery appreciably if the texture bitmap is stretched greatly down the length of the beam. It simply looks more fiery than particle-like.

Of course, seeing a beam of light actually traveling a short distance is scientifically nonsensical, but in many science fiction films, such effects are cheated for the sake of the viewer. Showing a beam of light actually "traveling" from the end of a laser weapon to its target helps provide extremely fast anticipation of the impending action (an impact) and reaction (an explosion, perhaps). Anticipation is one of the most common classical animation techniques, especially for the exaggerated movements of animated characters.

Another way to dress up this laser effect is to set Visibility keys in Track View to hide and unhide the laser objects in the scene. By setting groups of keys, you can create the effect of laser beams and muzzle flashes firing rapidly, like machine gun tracers. Of course, to control this effect better, you'll probably want to select all the laser objects in your scene (including the Torpedo muzzle flash group) and create a new group. This enables you to place and animate your Laser effect more easily in your scene.

## Adding Glow Effects in Video Post

Even though you can create convincing-looking optical effects by combining different textures with 3D geometry, you still might want to enhance your 3D Studio MAX optical effects by using the built-in Glow filter.

Glow is an image filter event in Video Post. You use it by assigning Glow to affect either an object in your scene or an object's Material Channel. By adjusting the color and size of the Glow filter parameters, you can add a little additional post-processing zest to your laser beams.

The following steps show how you do it.

1. Go to the Material Editor and make the Laser 3 Flic material in Slot #1 active.

2. Now, click and hold on the Material Effects Channel flyoff. As you do, you see a list of eight additional channels, numbered 1-8. Move your cursor down and select 1 to assign it to your Laser 3 Flic material. Now make your new Laser Burst material active (Slot #3) and assign Effects Channel 1 to it as well. When you've finished, close the Material Editor.

3. Select Rendering/Video Post; the Video Post menu appears. You'll want to set up a simple queue to demonstrate the Glow effect. Click on the Add Scene Event button; when the dialog box appears, click the Down arrow next to View: Front, select Perspective, and click on OK.

4. Click on the Add Image Filter Event button. Under Filter Plug-in, select Glow rather than Fade, and then click on Setup. Under Source, you'll see that the Material Effects Channel is set to 1 (the default). Leave the Material Color white, but change Size to 10. Click on OK twice to dismiss the dialog boxes.

5. Now, because you're just going to render a test image (and not save it to disk), click on the Execute Sequence button. Under Time Output, make sure that Single is selected, change Output Size to 640 x 480, and click on Render.

    Due to the processing involved in this rendering, the image may take a few minutes to appear on your screen. First, 3D Studio MAX renders the scene without Glow and then applies the Glow filter. When it does, it should look like Figure 13-7.

Figure 13-7: *Applying a Glow filter in Video Post creates a brighter, more intense laser beam and muzzle flash.*

Although it's processor-intensive, the Glow filter is very handy for enhancing your in-camera optical effects, especially self-illuminating textures.

6. When you've finished examining the rendering, close your Video Post Perspective VFB and return to your 3D Studio MAX desktop.

The scene file that you've just created and the Video Post .VPX file are in your \CHAP_13 directory as LASER_3.MAX and LASER_3.VPX.

## Moving On

In the next two chapters, you'll take a different approach to creating laser beam effects. You'll experiment with using simple 3D geometry—nested cylindrical shapes—and creating sparkling, animated effects with the Noise procedural texture.

# 14

# Advanced Lasers, Part I

In the last chapter, you saw how to create laser beams with "flat" elements—2D Quad Patch objects and Autodesk Animator Pro bitmaps.

In this chapter and the next, you'll explore how to create laser beams using combinations of solid geometry (cylinders) and the procedural Noise texture. You'll see how you can adjust the material parameters of the objects to simulate a gradient or glow (without using the Glow filter in Video Post). You'll also see how you can apply a Noise *controller* in Track View to animate the materials and produce sparkling effects.

First, you'll see how to create a very simple laser beam, and then you'll improve on it by adding more complex materials.

# Creating Laser Beams With Simple Geometry

Your first 3D laser beam is very simple—it's a series of nested cylinders that will represent the laser beam core and its surrounding glow. You'll map each of these cylinders with a basic, self-illuminated material that ranges from white to yellow and then, orange and red. You'll improve on this texture by adding a procedural Noise effect to the Diffuse, Self-illuminated, and Opacity map slots of the Material Editor.

It's time to get started.

1. In 3D Studio MAX, activate your Front viewport and press the W key on your keyboard to enlarge it to full screen. Select Cylinder on the Create panel.

2. Move your cursor to the center of the viewport and then click and drag to create a cylinder with an approximate Radius of 1 and a Height of about 50. Leave the Height Segments and Cap Segments both at 1. Click again to create the cylinder.

   Because these are just preliminary settings to aid in placing the cylinder, change the Cylinder01 Height from 50 to 2000 in the Create rollout. The cylinder changes to a long, thin tube. This stretched cylinder represents your initial laser beam core.

3. Change the Sides setting from 24 to 16; then, click in the Generate Mapping Coordinates check box to activate it. Finally, change the name of this object to LaserCyl01.

   Now that you've created an initial laser core object, you'll create the other five laser objects. To make creating the other lasers easier, you need to zoom in somewhat.

4. Click on the Zoom Extents All button. (If the LaserCyl01 object is not centered at the intersection of the grids, move it until its XYZ pivot axis is centered.)

5. Now, press the Shift+Z keys twice to zoom out from the LaserCyl01 object. You want to create another cylinder, so place your cursor in the center of the Front viewport, and click and drag outward until you've created another cylinder with

an approximate Radius of 3 and a Height of 2000. (Again, when you've finished, go to the Create panel and enter the exact values, if necessary.) Rename this object as LaserCyl02.

6. Click again in center of the Front viewport and create a third cylinder, with a Radius of 6 and a Height of 2000; name it LaserCyl03. At this point, you must zoom out from the three cylinders to leave room to create three more. Press Shift+Z again, and zoom out until LaserCyl03 is approximately one-third the height of your screen.

7. Create three more cylinders, each 2000 units in height and concentric about the first three. The fourth cylinder should have a radius of 9, the fifth a radius of 14, and the sixth a radius of 24. Name them LaserCyl04, LaserCyl05, and LaserCyl06, respectively.

8. When you've finished creating the six LaserCyl objects, click on the Min/Max Toggle button to return to four viewports and then click on the Zoom Extents All button so that the cylinders are visible in all viewports.

9. Now, you need to make sure that the lasers do not cast shadows on other objects. Select LaserCyl01 and then Edit/Properties; toggle off this object's Shadow Casting and Shadow Receiving attributes. Select each of the remaining LaserCyl objects in turn, and toggle off their Shadow attributes.

10. Activate the Perspective viewport and click on the Arc Rotate button. Move the Arc Rotate cursor inside the arcball, and click and drag until the six cylindrical objects are pointing diagonally down from the upper-right corner to the lower-left corner. (You should also adjust your Perspective viewport so that you're looking down on the LaserCyl objects at approximately a 45-degree angle.) Now, click on the Pan button and/or Zoom buttons, and adjust your Perspective viewport until it looks approximately like Figure 14-1.

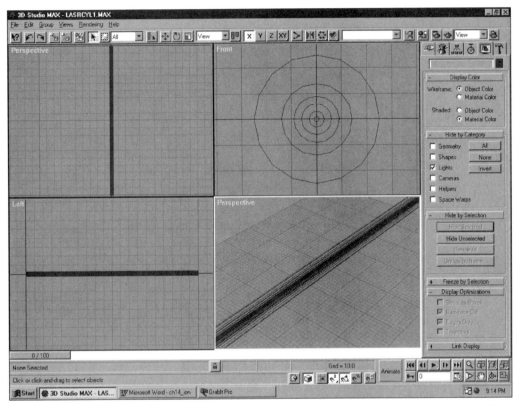

Figure 14-1: *The proper placement of the six LaserCyl objects for your laser beam test renderings.*

Now that you've gotten the LaserCyl objects placed correctly for your test renderings, it's time to set up their materials.

## I'd Like Half-a-Dozen Glowing Lasers, Please

At the moment, your six cylinders do not look very much like a laser beam. What you've done so far is create a laser beam "segment" so that you can see the effects of the various materials on these nested cylinder objects. As I mentioned in the last chapter, if you use physical laser beam objects in your 3D scene, you can adjust their length as necessary for any effects shot.

Now you'll create the materials that you're going to apply to these laser objects. But first, you'll set up your standard starfield background for your test renderings.

CD-ROM

1. Select Rendering/Environment, and from the \CHAP_14 directory, load the image STARS640.TGA and place it in Material Editor Slot #1. Then, go to the Material Editor, change it to a Screen background rather than Spherical Environment, and click on the Go to Parent button.

   Now you're going to create six simple materials to apply to each of your LaserCyl objects.

2. In the Material Editor, Slot #1 (your Starfield background) is active. You'll create a new material using this slot, which you'll place on the innermost LaserCyl object. (Remember that each slot is simply a place to display and manipulate materials; substituting a material for the starfield in Slot #1 does not delete it from the scene.) Click on the Get Material icon. Then, in the Material/Map browser, make sure that Browse From reads New, and double-click on Standard in the list window.

3. Increase Ambient and Diffuse to pure white or RGB values 255, 255, 255 and Self-illumination to 100. Reduce Shininess and Shininess Strength to 0. Leave Opacity at 100.

4. Open the Extended Parameters rollout; under Opacity Falloff, select Out, and change the Amount to 100. Under Opacity Type, click on Additive.

   As you do, the sample sphere in Slot #1 changes to a bright white globe with a darker halo around the edges. This will be the texture for LaserCyl01, which represents the white hot core of the laser. Change the material name to Laser 1.

   Now you'll want to create five other laser materials. To make keeping the same sets of parameters for these materials easier, you'll work from copies of Laser 1.

5. Click and drag the sample sphere in Slot #1 to copy the Laser 1 material to Slot #2. Then, click and drag to copy the same material to the remaining five material editor slots. When you have finished, all five slots should be filled with copies of Material #1. Change each material name to Laser 2, Laser 3, and so on, to Laser 6.

6. Now, click in Slot #2 to activate it. You'll want to change the Ambient and Diffuse parameters for Laser 2, so change both to RGB settings 255, 255, 0, or a bright yellow. Then, change Opacity from 100 to 75. You now have a bright but translucent glowing yellow.

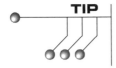

**TIP**

The quickest way to reduce a spinner value to zero (or its minimum value) is to position the cursor over the spinner and right-click.

7. Click on Slot #3 to activate it and change Laser 3's RGB settings to 255, 128, 0—a bright orange. Then, change Opacity to 65.

8. Activate Slot #4. Change Laser 4's Diffuse and Ambient colors to RGB 255, 0, 0, or pure red. Then, change Opacity to 50.

9. Activate Slot #5. Change Laser 5's Ambient and Diffuse colors to RGB settings 164, 0, 0, and change its Opacity to 25.

10. Finally, click on Slot #6. Change Laser 6's Ambient and Diffuse colors to RGB settings 128, 0, 0, and change its Opacity to 10.

You now have six materials ranging from a glowing white, to yellow, orange, red, a darker red, and then to an almost transparent, dark red. (These materials are in 3DSMAXFX.MAT on your *3D Studio MAX f/x CD-ROM*.)

## Faking Glows With Self-illuminated Materials

Now you'll apply these new materials to the six LaserCyl objects.

1. In your Front viewport, click on LaserCyl01 to select it; then, go to the Material Editor and make Slot#1 (Laser 1) active. Click on the Assign Material to Selection button to assign the white Laser 1 material to the innermost LaserCyl01 core object. In turn, click on each of the remaining LaserCyl objects, moving outward, and assign materials Laser 2 through 6 to each of them. When you have finished, all six material slots should have triangles in the window corners, indicating that they are "hot" materials.

2. Now it's time to do a test rendering. Activate your Perspective viewport and press Alt+R and Enter to render a single 640 x 480 still image. In a moment, the image appears, as shown in Figure 14-2.

Figure 14-2: *A laser beam object created with simple geometry and self-illuminated materials.*

Although the rendering on your screen isn't terribly exciting (at the moment), it does demonstrate how using self-illuminated materials mapped onto various layers of geometry can produce the suggestion of a glow effect. By building up layers of self-illuminated materials with Additive Transparency (and Falloff set to Out), you can create the illusion of an intense laser beam with a gradient glow radiating away from the core.

Of course, you could punch up your "faked" glow effect for these laser beam objects by assigning an Effects Channel to some or all of the materials and then applying several Glow filters in

Video Post. (This was demonstrated in the last chapter.) However, you created these laser objects to see how you can enhance simple geometry and material settings with more complex textures to create a scintillating energy beam.

The file you've just created is in the \CHAP_14 directory of your *3D Studio MAX f/x* CD-ROM as LASER_2N.MAX.

## Improving the Laser With Noise Textures

Now you're going to modify the simple Laser materials that you just created by using the Noise texture. With it, you can create the illusion of an intense beam of light, with sparkling fiery particles radiating away from the white-hot inner core.

1. Return to the Material Editor and make sure that the Laser 1 material is active. You're going to modify the settings of each Laser material and use each previous material to establish the basic parameters for the next. Many of the changes that you'll be making to each of the six materials are quite similar; however, they are also quite extensive, so follow along very carefully as you make the changes to Laser 1.

2. For the new Laser 1 Noise material, you want the inner core to be as bright as possible, so in the Basic Parameters rollout, click on 2-Sided. The sample sphere in Slot #1 brightens considerably. Leave the remaining Basic Parameter settings as they are and go down and open the Maps rollout.

3. In the Maps rollout, click on the Opacity name field to bring up the Material/Map browser. Under Browse From, select New and double-click on Noise in the list window. The Noise Procedural texture loads and the Noise rollout appears.

4. In the Noise Parameters rollout, change Noise Type from Regular to Fractal. Reduce Noise Size from 25 to 6. Leave the Noise Threshold, Levels, and Phase settings as they are.

5. Click on the Go to Parent icon to return to the top material level. You want to copy the Noise Opacity Map material to the Diffuse slot, so click and drag the Noise texture from the

A 3D flying saucer model in front of a digitized real-world image. A Quad Patch object with a Matte/Shadow material applied makes the saucer appear to cast a shadow on the "real" ground. (Chapter 2)

3D asteroid meshes, in front of 2D asteroid bitmaps applied to Quad Patch objects, create an asteroid field. (Chapter 3)

A warp drive "tunnel" effect created with a open-ended, 60-sided cone with a 3D Studio/DOS LenZFX bitmap sequence applied. (The LenZFX textures are included on the CD-ROM in the \CHAP_03 directory.)

A giant battlecruiser, protected by a forcefield, emerges from hyperspace. (The spaceship model and its texture maps are included on the \SCENES and \MAPS directories of the companion CD-ROM.)

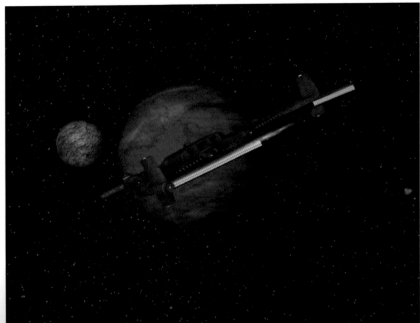

The battlecruiser heads off into deep space. Rocky bitmap textures, as well as digitized images of marbleized paper, provide the moon and planet textures.

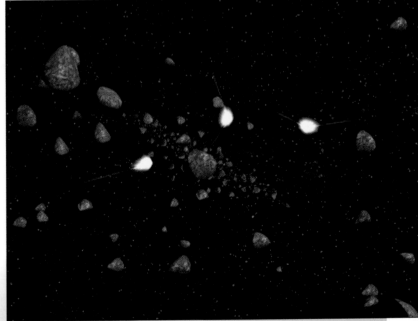

Three more warp bursts signify the appearance of three enemy fighter ships emerging from hyperspace. The nebula and starfield background image is mapped onto a sphere surrounding the other elements of this scene.

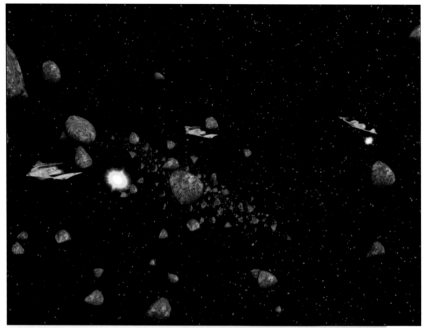

The fighters open fire on the battlecruiser with tachyon torpedoes. The torpedoes are a combination of 3D Studio/DOS LenZFX bitmap sequences and square Quad Patch objects.

The lead fighter heads towards the battlecruiser. This model, as well as multiple versions of its texture maps, is in the \SCENES and \MAPS directories of the companion CD-ROM.

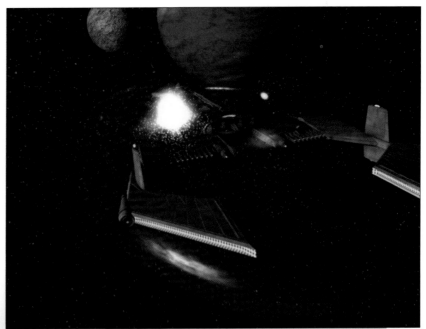

A torpedo impacts on the cruiser's forcefield. The explosion is a combination of an exploding sphere and the Video Post glow effect. (This effect is covered in Chapters 12 and 21.)

The fighter flies by on a strafing run. The fighters' and cruiser's glowing engines are created with the Video Post Glow filter.

The cruiser fires back with laser beams. (How to create laser beam effects is covered in Chapters 13, 14 and 15.) Various animated laser textures are also included in the \CHAP_13 and \MAPS directories of the companion CD-ROM.

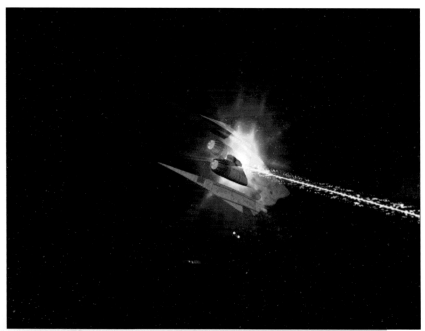

A fighter takes a direct hit from a laser beam. (This effect is covered in Chapters 13 and 21.)

The fighter explodes from the laser impact. The explosion is a combination of an exploding sphere with a self-illuminated material, Video Post Glow, and the 3D Studio MAX Combustion plug-in. (This plug-in is included on the companion CD-ROM.)

A 3D Studio MAX procedural Noise texture, used as an Environment map, provides both a starfield and nebula background. (See Chapter 6: "Nebulas Made Simple, Part I.")

A bitmap of a starfield and nebula background, loaded as a MAX Environment background, provides a deep-space vista. (Numerous starfield and nebula textures are included in the \MAPS directory of the *3D Studio MAX f/x CD-ROM*.)

A combination of shiny, transparent geometry, colorful Omni lights, and a starfield backdrop provide this nebula image. (From Chapters 6 and 7: "Nebulas Made Simple, Part I and Part II.")

**A** volumetric Omni light, with attenuation and Noise, provides a glowing sun effect. (See Chapters 9 and 10: "Here Comes the Sun, Part I and II.")

**A** combination of volumetric Omni light and a sphere with a self-illuminated Noise texture creates an animated physical sun object (with solar flares).

A modified 3D Studio/DOS LenZFX lens flare animation sequence provides a colorful warp drive effect.

A warp drive tunnel created with LenZFX bitmaps and 60-sided, open-ended cones. Two 30-frame LenZFX warp drive image sequences are included in the \MAPS directory of the companion CD-ROM.

Another modified LenZFX lens flare image sequence (also included on the companion CD-ROM); this one creates the illusion of a "tachyon torpedo.")

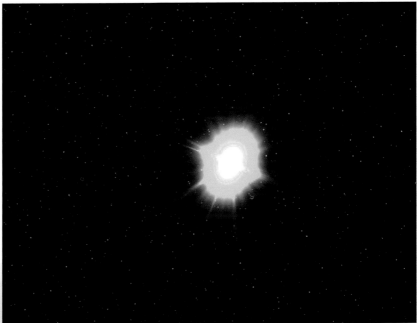

A "tachyon torpedo" effect created by applying 30-frame LenZFX bitmap image sequences onto three square Quad Patch objects. (See Chapter 12, "Tachyon Torpedoes Away!")

An Autodesk Animator Pro texture applied to rotated Quad Patches provides this laser beam effect (covered in Chapter 13, "Laser Beams 101"). Several laser textures are included on the companion CD-ROM.

Another laser beam; the sparkling "muzzle flash" is provided by a modified tachyon torpedo texture.

The laser beam/torpedo texture with a Video Post Glow filter applied.

A series of six concentric cylinders, each mapped with self-illuminated materials of varying transparency, creates the illusion of a glowing laser beam—without using the Video Post glow filter effects.

By using the Noise texture on six concentric cylinders, you can create a fiery, animated laser beam. (See Chapters 14 and 15, "Advanced Lasers, Part I and II.")

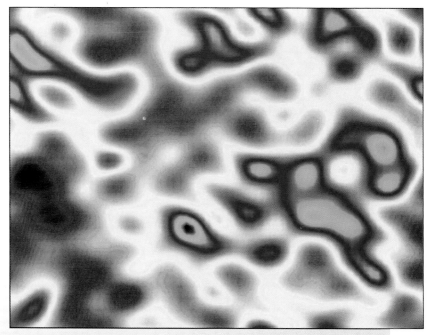

A psychedelic still image from an animated texture sequence. This image was created with James Gleick's CHAOS: The Software, from Autodesk. Although this software is now unavailable, several animation sequences from it are included in the \CHAP_ 16 and \MAPS directories.

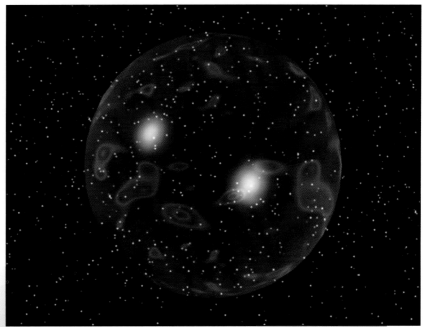

The CHAOS texture applied as a slight reflection map to a sphere. This "soap bubble effect" is covered in Chapter 16, "Shields Up, Captain."

By binding a Bomb Space Warp to a sphere, applying a self-illuminated material to the sphere, and then applying a Video Post Glow filter, you can create a white-hot explosion.

**A** marbleized texture pattern, combined with digitized cloud images, provides this Mars-like planet surface. (Variations of this texture are in the \MAPS directory of the companion CD-ROM.)

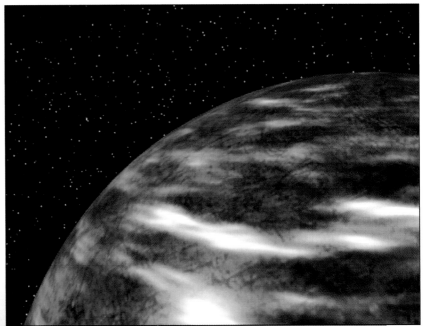

**B**y using 3D Studio MAX's Noise texture applied to a sphere surrounding a planet mesh, you can create animated cloud effects. (See Chapter 18, "Planets and Other Heavenly Bodies.")

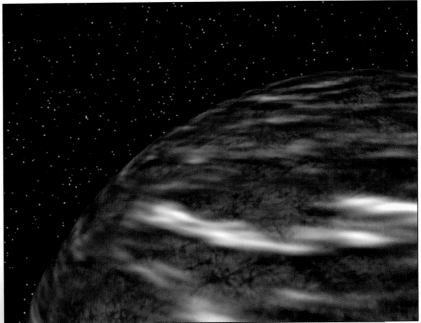

A ray-traced spotlight, shining on these Opacity-mapped Noise cloud textures, creates shadows on the planet surface.

A combination of a Noise Diffuse map and a Bump map creates this gas giant planet.

The *3D Studio MAX f/x CD-ROM* contains over 800 different textures, such as this image: ASTEROD1.TGA. (Note that the original image is 800 x 400 resolution, suitable for spherical mapping.)

The ASTEROD1.TGA texture applied to a complex 3D mesh. The mesh's craggy surface was created with a combination of Noise object modifiers and Edit Mesh: Face/Tessellate modifiers.

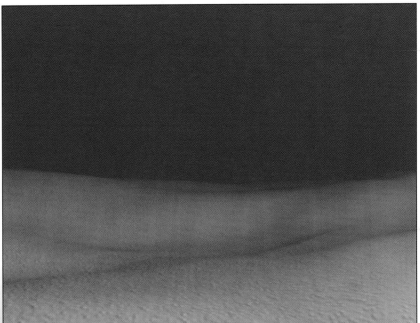

**F**rom Part IV, "Underwater Effects." 3D Studio MAX's Environmental Fog feature enables you to create the impression of underwater murkiness. A Quad Patch with a Noise object modifier provides the gently-rolling sandy ocean floor.

**A** Quad Patch mapped with a three-way Noise texture (Diffuse, Bump, and Reflection) creates this undersea effect. (See Chapter 23, "Under the Sea, White With Foam" for more on how to create this effect.)

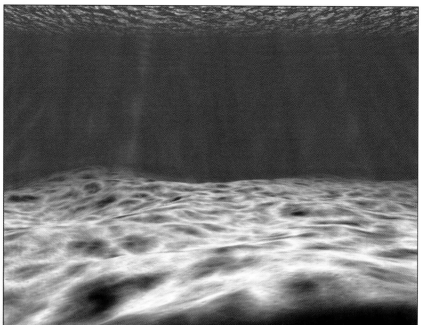

**B**y using projector spotlights, some with volumetric effects applied, you can create these distinctive water caustic patterns, as well as light rays. The dappled water caustics are provided by a Turbulence Noise texture loaded into a projector spotlight.

**3**D Studio MAX's particle effects enable you to fill your underwater scenes with particulate matter, such as plankton and bubbles.

A Wave Space Warp applied to a Viewpoint DataLabs hammerhead shark model makes the shark appear to swim through the scene. The shark model is included on the companion CD-ROM.

A replica of the Diving Bell from the 1960's Irwin Allen TV series "Voyage to the Bottom of the Sea" illustrates over half-a-dozen underwater effects covered in Part IV of this book. (Note that the Diving Bell model is included in the \DIVEBELL and \MESHES directory of the companion CD-ROM.)

The *3D Studio MAX f/x CD-ROM* contains some additional models not featured in the tutorials. One of them is this giant bug-shaped cruiser created by Michael Spaw, a noted 3D Studio MAX artist.

This model of a 688-I ("Los Angeles"-class) submarine is included in the \SCENES and \MESHES directory of the companion CD-ROM.

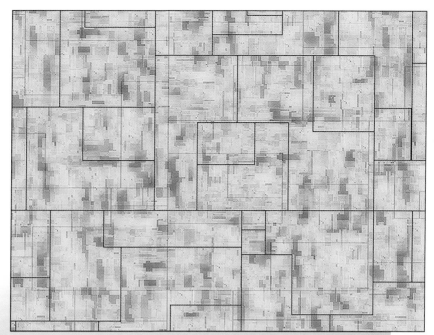

The \MAPS directory of the *3D Studio MAX f/x* CD-ROM contains a large number of texture maps. This 800 x 600 Targa bitmap is one of many "spaceship" textures found on the companion CD-ROM.

Many of the colorful texture maps on the *3D Studio MAX f/x CD-ROM* began as digitized images of real-world objects. Here, the heavily-retouched side of a dumpster provides another interesting "spaceship" texture.

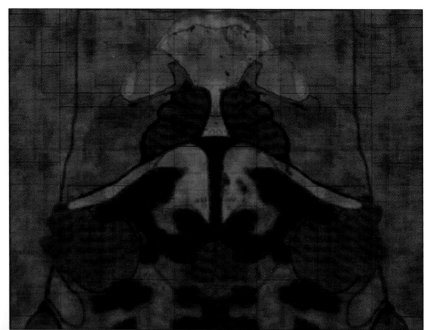

A close-up image of the top of Michael Spaw's hand-painted Bugship texture (included on the companion CD-ROM) combined with another industrial spaceship bitmap.

One of many "planet" textures included on the CD-ROM; the originals are at 800 x 400 resolution, perfect for spherical texture mapping.

Opacity map slot to Diffuse. In the Copy (Instance) Map dialog, click on OK for Copy and then click on the name button in the Diffuse name slot.

6. You'll want to change the settings of the Diffuse Noise material that you just copied. Click on the Black color swatch to the right of Color #1. You want to change this from black to bright yellow, so change the RGB settings to 255, 255, 0. Leave Color #2 (white) as it is; then, close the Color Selector. Click on the Go to Parent icon to return to the top material level. Now, rename this new material Laser 1 Noise.

## Modifying the Materials

If you take a look at the sample sphere in Material Slot #1, you'll see that the Laser 1 Noise material is a mottled yellow-white. The mottling comes from the Noise texture in the Diffuse and Opacity map slots. Although you set a bright yellow and white Noise texture for Diffuse, you left the Opacity map slot Noise color settings black and white for maximum masking. This provides a variance in the yellow and white values throughout the length of the LaserCyl01 object.

Now modify the settings of the next five laser materials.

### Laser 2 Noise

1. Drag the sample sphere in Laser 1 Noise to Slot #2 to copy the material and change the material name to Laser 2 Noise. Now, unlike the Laser 1 Noise core material, you'll want the remaining laser materials to be one-sided, so toggle off 2-Sided in the Basic Parameters section.

2. In the Basic Parameters rollout, change Ambient and Diffuse to RGB settings 255, 255, 0, or pure yellow.

3. Open the Extended Parameters rollout. Make sure that Falloff is set to Out, Opacity Type is set to Additive, and Opacity Falloff amount is set to 100.

4. In the Maps rollout, click on the Opacity name button to bring up the Noise material rollout. Under Noise Parameters, change Noise Type from Regular to Fractal. Change Size to 5. Under Noise Threshold, change the Low setting from 0.0 to 0.1.

5. Click on the Go to Parent icon to return to the top material level and copy the Noise Opacity map to Diffuse. Click on OK to make it a Copy rather than an Instance; then, click on the Diffuse name button. When the Noise rollout appears, click on the black Color #1 swatch and change the RGB values to 255, 0, 0, or pure red. Click on the Color #2 swatch and change it to RGB 255, 255, 0, or pure yellow.

6. When you've finished, click the Go to Parent icon to return to the main Material Editor rollout. Change the Diffuse percentage to 85.

## Laser 3 Noise

1. Drag the sample sphere in Laser 2 Noise to Slot #3 to copy the material, and change the new material name to Laser 3 Noise.

2. In the Basic Parameters rollout, change Ambient and Diffuse to RGB settings 255, 128, 0.

3. In the Maps rollout, click on the Opacity map name button. When the Noise rollout appears, change Noise Size to 4. Change Noise Threshold to 0.2.

4. Click on the Go to Parent icon and copy the Noise Opacity map material to the Diffuse map slot. Click on OK to make it a copy and then click on the Diffuse map name button.

5. Click on the Color #1 swatch and change its RGB settings to 255, 0, 0, or pure red. Click on the Color #2 swatch and change its RGB settings to 255, 255, 0, or pure yellow.

6. Click on the Go to Parent icon to return to the top material level and change the Diffuse percentage to 75.

## Laser 4 Noise

1. Drag the sample sphere in Laser 3 Noise to Slot #4 to copy the material, and change the new material name to Laser 4 Noise.

2. In the Basic Parameters rollout, change Ambient and Diffuse to RGB settings 255, 0, 0.

3. In the Maps rollout, click on the Opacity map name button. When the Noise Parameters rollout appears, change Noise Size to 3. Change Noise Threshold to 0.3.

4. Click on the Go to Parent icon and copy the Noise Opacity map material to the Diffuse map slot. Click on OK to make it a copy, and click on the Diffuse map name button.

5. Click on the Color #1 swatch and change its RGB settings to 255, 0, 0, or pure red. Click on the Color #2 swatch and change its RGB settings to 255, 255, 0, or pure yellow.

6. Click on the Go to Parent button to return to the top material level and change the Diffuse percentage to 50.

## Laser 5 Noise

1. Drag the sample sphere in Laser 4 Noise to Slot #5 to copy the material, and change the new material name to Laser 5 Noise.

2. In the Basic Parameters rollout, change Ambient and Diffuse to RGB settings 164, 0, 0.

3. In the Maps rollout, click on the Opacity map name button. When the Noise Parameters rollout appears, change Noise Size to 2. Change Noise Threshold to 0.4.

4. Click on the Go to Parent icon and copy the Noise Opacity map material to the Diffuse map slot. Click on OK to make it a copy, and click on the Diffuse map name button.

5. Click on the Color #1 swatch and change its RGB settings to 255, 0, 0, or pure red. Click on the Color #2 swatch and change its RGB settings to 255, 255, 0, or pure yellow.

6. Click on the Go to Parent button to return to the top material level and change the Diffuse percentage to 35.

## Laser 6 Noise

1. Drag the sample sphere in Laser 5 Noise to Slot #6 to copy the material, and change the new material name to Laser 6 Noise.

2. In the Basic Parameters rollout, change Ambient and Diffuse to RGB settings 128, 0, 0.

3. In the Maps rollout, click on the Opacity map name button. When the Noise Parameters rollout appears, change Noise Size to 1. Change Noise Threshold to 0.5.

4. Click on the Go to Parent icon and copy the Noise Opacity map material to the Diffuse map slot. Click on OK to make it a copy, and click on the Diffuse map name button.

5. Click on the Color #1 swatch and change its RGB settings to 255, 0, 0, or pure red. Click on the Color #2 swatch and change its RGB settings to 255, 255, 0, or pure yellow.

6. Click on the Go to Parent icon to return to the top material level, and change the Diffuse percentage to 25.

You have now created six Laser Noise textures. At this point, you may want to save each one of these textures to your 3DSMAX.MAT Material Library. Again, that the textures you've just created are on the 3DSMAXFX.MAT Material Library on your *3D Studio MAX f/x CD-ROM.*

# Adding It Up

Because you created new materials and changed their names from those assigned to the scene, you need to assign the six new materials to the six concentric cylinders.

1. Make Laser #1 Noise active in Slot #1 and select Laser Cyl #1 in the Top viewport. Click on the Assign Material to Selection icon to assign the material.

2. Repeat step #1 for each of the other five materials and the five concentric LaserCyl objects, matching the material number to the object number.

Now it's time to render a new test image.

Activate the Perspective viewport and then click on the Zoom button. You'll want to get a little closer to your six LaserCyl objects so that you can see the effects of the Noise textures better. Zoom in until your Perspective viewport looks like Figure 14-3.

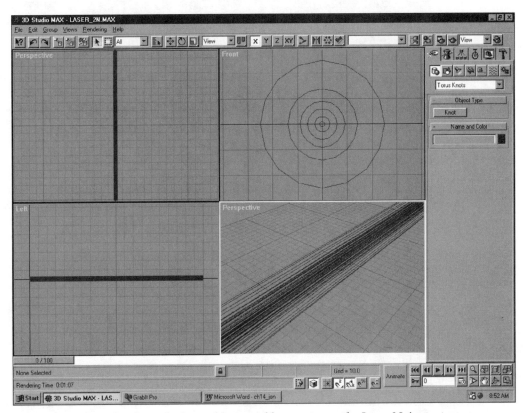

Figure 14-3: *Zooming in to the laser objects enables you to see the Laser Noise textures more clearly.*

Now without further ado it's time to render your laser objects and the new textures to see the effect.

3. Press Alt+R on your keyboard; then, press Enter to render a new 640 x 480 image of the Laser Noise effect. After a few moments, the image appears and should look something like Figure 14-4.

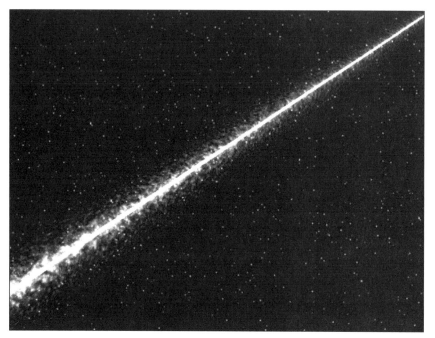

Figure 14-4: *The improved laser object using six layers of varying noise textures.*

Examine the image on your screen closely. As you can see, by using these layered Noise textures on the concentric cylindrical objects, you've created a fiery-looking laser effect. By using a combination of Noise textures with varying colors, you've created another 3D gradient that helps sell the idea of a powerful beam of energy.

In addition, by decreasing the size of each Noise texture on successive laser objects (working outward from the center), you create the effect that the energy beam is fragmenting into ever-smaller particles.

## Changing Your Core Values

Although this is a powerful and useful effect, you can punch it up even more by making the inner core much brighter.

1. Return to the Material Editor and click on Slot #1 (Laser 1 Noise). Then, in the Maps rollout, click in the Opacity map check box to turn it off. As you do so, the sample sphere becomes much brighter.

2. Activate your Perspective viewport again, and press Alt+R and Enter to render a new version of the laser effect. After a moment, it appears and should look like Figure 14-5.

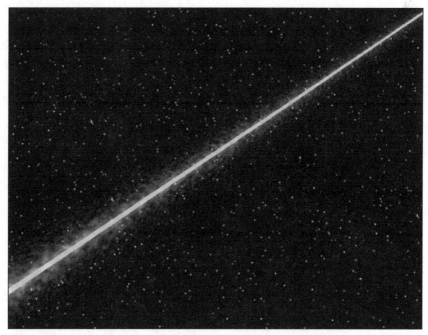

Figure 14-5: *The revised Noise laser effect with a brighter laser core object and material.*

As Figure 14-5 shows, by removing the Opacity map from the 2-sided Laser 1 Noise material, you've caused the LaserCyl01 inner core object to appear much brighter.

## Okay, So How Do I Use It?

Again, as I've discussed throughout this book, many ways exist to create the illusion of bright optical effects without necessarily having to create them entirely through post-processing. The examples that you've just covered demonstrate this. (However, there's no reason, of course, that you couldn't set Effects Channels for the new Laser materials and then apply a Glow filter to some or all of them.)

Now that you've created this laser Noise object, how can you use it in a scene? Well, you can select the six LaserCyl objects and Group them into a single object. Then, place one end of your new Laser Group inside the barrel of a laser cannon mesh and assign Visibility keys in Track View to make the laser beam flash quickly on and off.

In addition, if you assign a Look At Controller to the laser cannon barrel, you could make the laser beam point at and track an enemy spaceship mesh. Just have the Look At Controller looking at the spaceship itself, or even a Dummy target object that's parented to the spaceship and flying around it randomly. That way, you could have the laser appear to be missing, at first— until you had the Dummy swoop into the heart of the spaceship. (At that point, it would look as if the laser cannon operator suddenly got very lucky with his targeting.)

**Note:** *For more on Look At Controllers, see section 32-24, "Controlling Parameters: Look At Controllers," in the* 3D Studio MAX User's Guide, Volume 2.

Again, as I mentioned in the last chapter, you can also animate the length of the laser beam simply by scaling the individual laser objects and animating them. Or, you can select their end vertices and animate the vertices streaking outward from the barrel of the laser cannon. With these techniques, you can make the laser appear as short or as long as required for your particular scene.

## Animating the Textures (Without Animating the Textures)

Okay, so you can obviously move your laser objects around in space, but what about their textures? Shouldn't they appear to be moving as well?

Actually, you can make the Laser beam textures appear to be animated—but without even touching their material attributes. How do you do it?

The answer is simple—you use the "slot gag" technique that I covered in Chapter 11, "Warp Speed!" By animating the rotation of each LaserCyl object on its Z axis (making each object spin, preferably in varying directions, at various speeds), you can create a very convincing animated laser texture.

Take a look at a sample file that demonstrates this technique.

1. Save your current work as LASER_2N.MAX, and from the \CHAP_14 directory of your *3D Studio MAX f/x CD-ROM*, load the file LASER_3N.MAX. When the file appears, drag the Time Slider slowly from frame 0 to 100 and then back.

   In your viewports (most noticeably, the Perspective and Front views), you can see that each of the LaserCyl objects is rotating about its Z axis, at different speeds and in different directions from one another.

   Take a look at a demonstration .AVI of this animated effect.

2. Select File\View file, and from the \CHAP_14 directory, click on the file LASER_3N.AVI to load it. When the Media Player appears, click on the Play button.

   Notice how rotating the LaserCyl objects (but not animating their textures) creates the illusion of a fiery laser beam with a bright core.

3. When you've finished viewing the animation, close the Media Player.

## Moving On

Now, although you've just seen how you can animate the physical objects comprising the laser beam effect, there's no reason that you can't animate the actual Noise textures on the laser objects as well. By altering various parameters of each Noise texture, you can further enhance your laser beam imagery to create a sparkling beam of laser light.

You'll see how to do exactly that—by applying Noise controllers to Noise textures—in the next chapter.

# 15

# Advanced Lasers, Part II

In the last chapter, you saw how you could create striking laser effects by using simple geometry and nonanimated Noise textures. As you saw in the last part of that chapter, you can create the illusion of a swirling energy beam by simply animating the LaserCyl objects. As the example showed, by counter-rotating the LaserCyl objects on their Z (long) axis, the resultant "slot gag" effect suggests an actual animated texture.

However, there's no reason that you can't animate the LaserCyl Noise textures themselves. In this chapter, you'll see how you can animate just one Noise parameter to create the illusion of a sparkling beam of laser light.

## Checking Out the Laser Noise Parameters

First, load the laser file from the last chapter and then alter its material attributes.

1. From the \CHAP_15 directory of your *3D Studio MAX f/x CD-ROM*, load the file LASER_2N.MAX. (This file is identical to the LASER_2N.MAX file in the \CHAP_14 directory.) It

consists of the six LaserCyl objects, without Z axis animation. Each of these objects also has the Laser 1-6 Noise materials applied to it.

2. Animating the Noise parameters for all these materials is easy. Open the Material Editor and make sure that Slot #1 (Laser 1 Noise) is active. Go to the Maps rollout and click on the Diffuse name button to bring up the Diffuse Map Noise rollout.

Animating the Noise texture is as simple as pressing the Animate button, moving to any nonzero frame, and then adjusting your Noise settings as desired. (The one parameter that you can't animate is Noise Type; this remains fixed during the course of an animation.)

Take a look at all these settings. As you saw in the last chapter, by changing the Noise size, you can produce the illusion that your laser beam is fragmenting into smaller particles as they move away from the central core. By changing the Noise Threshold, you can "clamp" the range of gradation between the two Noise colors, making the Noise texture go from cloudy to wispy. (Of course, you can animate those colors, too, if you want.)

If you alter the Noise XYZ Offsets, you can move the texture relative to the object surface. Changing the Tiling will "stretch" it along the object's XYZ or UVW coordinates, and changing the Angle will—you guessed it—alter the angle at which the Noise pattern is applied to the surface of the object.

By modifying the Levels, you can increase or decrease the number of iterations for the Noise texture calculations. Finally, if you change the Noise Phase, it will shift the starting point of the sine wave that 3D Studio MAX uses to create the Noise function.

Although you can animate all of these aforementioned parameters, you need only to work with the last one—the Phase parameter.

## Automating the Process

Now, although changing a single parameter on each material is pretty easy, it's also tedious. For the best results, you'll want to enter different values for each Laser Noise material. (This is the old slot gag approach, so that the textures don't look as if they're moving in unison.) However, for best results, the values that you do enter for each material's Diffuse Noise texture need to be identical to that material's Opacity Noise texture. Otherwise, the Opacity "masking" will no longer fit the Diffuse Noise texture.

Again, although this isn't difficult to accomplish manually, it's laborious to open each material's Diffuse and Opacity maps, enter specific numeric values on specific frames, and keep track of each change without a scorecard. In addition, simply changing a Phase value from 0 to 10 during the course of an animation will produce a swirling movement—but what if you wanted frenzied particle action for your laser beam? You would then have to set multiple keyframes for each material, which vastly increases the number of variables that you have to monitor.

There's an interesting way to automate this process, though, and produce random, fast-moving laser particles. The key word in the preceding paragraph is "track"—you can animate each Laser Noise material's Noise parameters in 3D Studio MAX's Track View. In this case, you'll use a Noise Controller to modify the Noise materials.

## Phasing in the Lasers

For this example, you're going to open Track View and assign a Noise Controller to the Phase settings of each of the six materials' Diffuse and Opacity maps. Then, by simply changing the Noise Controller "seed" for each material (yet keeping the same seed for each material's Diffuse and Opacity textures), you can create a random laser particle effect.

Here's how to do it.

1. Click on the Track View button to bring up the Track View dialog box. Then, click on the Maximize button to enlarge Track View to full screen. This makes changing the material parameters easier.

2. Click on the Filters icon to open it. You want to adjust only the Materials/Maps and Material/Parameter settings, so in the Filters dialog box, click on None under Show and then click on

Materials/Maps and Material/Parameters to display just those parameters in the Track View. When you've finished, click on OK.

When you return to Track View, listed under World are the following parameters: Environment, Medit Materials, Scene Materials, and Objects.

3. Click on the + button to the left of Medit Materials. This opens the Laser 1 Noise (standard) through Laser 6 Noise (standard) materials. Click on the + button next to Laser 1 Noise. Another hierarchy tree opens up, listing Parameters and Maps. If the Parameters tree is open, click the - button to close it. You don't need to adjust any of the overall material parameters for Laser 1 Noise.

4. Click on the + button to the left of Maps to open this. You'll see Diffuse Amount and then Diffuse: Texture (Noise). Click on the + button to open the Diffuse: Texture (Noise) tree. When you do so, these tracks appear: Coordinates, Noise Size, Color 1, Color 2, Phase, Levels, Low Threshold, High Threshold, and Output. Now, open the Opacity: Texture (Noise) tree. The only parameter of these two maps that you'll adjust is Phase.

5. Go down to the Laser 2 Noise (Standard Material). Open the hierarchy tree and then the Maps tree. As you did with the Laser 1 Noise texture previously, click on the + button to open the Diffuse: Texture (Noise) and Opacity: Texture (Noise) trees only.

6. Now, working your way down the list, go to the remaining Laser 3-6 Noise materials. Open their Maps trees and then their Diffuse: Texture (Noise) and Opacity: Texture (Noise) trees only. You'll need to scroll down as you do this to keep the bottom tracks in view.

7. If you want, move your cursor to the bar dividing the hierarchy tree menu on the left from the Track View tracks on the right. As you move the cursor to the vertical dividing bar, you'll see the cursor change to a left and right arrow. Click and drag the vertical bar slightly to the right until you can see all of the listings present in each hierarchy tree, as shown in Figure 15-1.

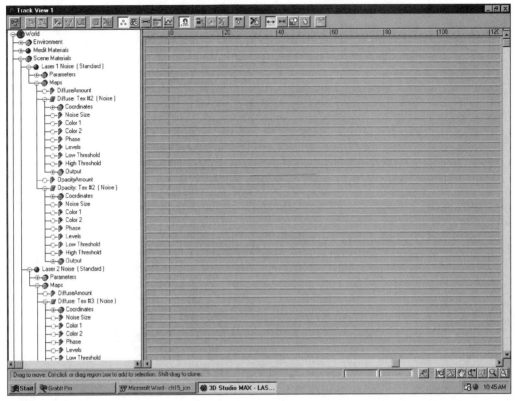

Figure 15-1: *The maximized Track View showing the materials and maps settings for the six LaserCyl objects.*

8. When you've finished, use the hand cursor to scroll the rollout down until you've returned to the Laser 1 Noise material.

## Pasting in the Controller

At this point, you'll want to paste a Noise controller to the Phase parameter of each materials' Diffuse and Opacity map settings. You'll then go in and vary the Noise controller seed settings for each of the materials.

1. Under Laser 1 Noise, go down to the Phase parameter of Diffuse. Click on it to highlight it.

2. Now, click on the Assign Controller button. The Replace Float Controller dialog box appears.

   If you haven't changed your 3D Studio MAX default controller settings, the default controller shown at the bottom of the dialog box reads Bezier Float. Replace this controller with the Noise Float controller.

3. From the Controller list, click on Noise Float and then on OK. As you do so, tracks appear for the Phase parameters of the Laser 1 Noise Diffuse texture and all tracks up the scene hierarchy from it. Now repeat this procedure for the Laser 1 Noise Opacity texture, as shown in Figure 15-2.

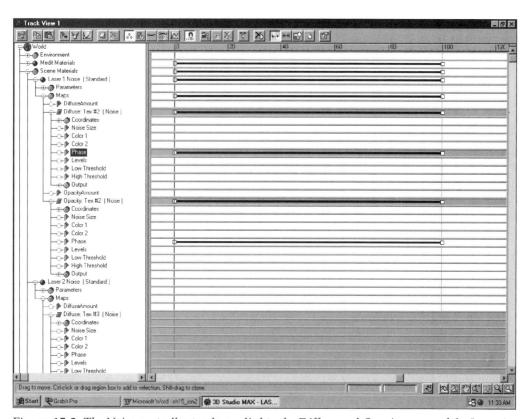

Figure 15-2: *The Noise controller tracks applied to the Diffuse and Opacity maps of the Laser 1 Noise material.*

4. Right-click on the Phase parameter of Diffuse: Texture (Noise) for the Laser 1 Noise material. As you do, a menu appears that includes Select All, Select Invert, Select None, and Properties. Select Properties and the Noise Controller dialog box appears, as shown in Figure 15-3.

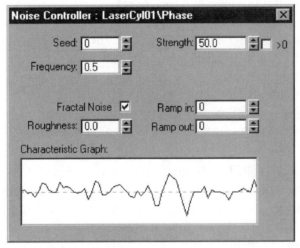

Figure 15-3: *The Noise Controller dialog box.*

Take a look at the Noise Controller parameters. The Noise Controller enables you to apply a random noise function, over time, to many different parameters in 3D Studio MAX—from materials to the translation, rotation, and scale of 3D objects themselves.

If you examine the default settings in the Noise Controller dialog box, you'll see that Seed is set to 0 and Frequency is set to 0.5. Fractal Noise is on and Roughness is set to 0.0. Strength is set to 50.

Now you'll alter the Noise Controller settings.

## Planting Seeds

You'll want to dampen down the roughness of the random Noise controller for each material. Then, you'll cut and paste the modified Noise Controllers to each material, and give each one a unique Noise Seed setting.

1. Because you're working with Laser 1 Noise, change the Seed from 0 to 1. This makes keeping track of the proper Seed number settings easier; you'll simply assign a Seed number that corresponds to the six Laser Noise materials. When you change the Seed setting, you'll see the graphical line representation of the Noise function change somewhat.

2. Click on the Fractal Noise check box to turn it off. This will smooth out the contours of the graph. Then, change the Frequency from 0.5 to 0.1. Press Enter or click in any other numeric fields to apply your change; the graph changes to a more gentle sine wave. Click on the Close button to dismiss the Noise Controller dialog box.

   Now you'll copy this Noise Controller from the Diffuse Texture Phase track of the Laser 1 Noise material to the other materials.

3. With the Diffuse Texture Phase parameter of Laser 1 Noise still selected, click on the Copy Controller button. This places a copy of the Noise Controller (and its revised settings) in the clipboard. To paste this Noise Controller to all other Phase parameters of the other materials, follow the next few instructions carefully.

4. Hold down the Ctrl key and click on the Opacity Phase parameter of Laser 1 Noise. Both the Diffuse and Opacity Phase parameters remain highlighted.

5. Holding the Ctrl key, move down the list of the remaining five Laser Noise materials and highlight the Phase parameter of each material's Diffuse and Opacity Noise texture.

6. When you've finished, release the Ctrl key but be careful not to click on any other parameter. This would deselect the selected Phase parameters and you would have to start over.

7. Click on the Paste Controller button; then, click on OK to paste a Copy—not an Instance—of the modified Noise controller to each of the Laser Noise materials. As you do, tracks appear for the remaining Phase parameters of each Laser material's Diffuse and Opacity maps, as shown in Figure 15-4.

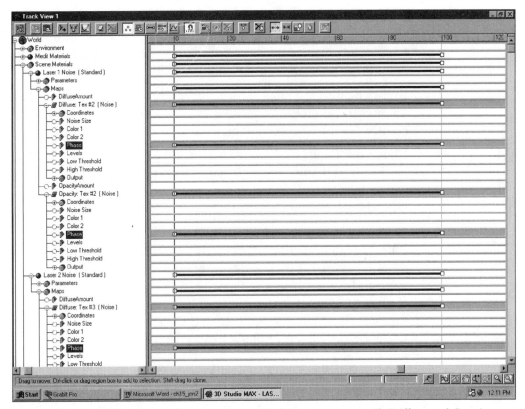

Figure 15-4: *The Noise Controller pasted to each of the Laser material's Diffuse and Opacity Phase parameters.*

## Plus Ça Change, Plus C'est la Même Chose

Whoever started that idea that the more things change, the more they remain the same could not have anticipated computer-generated special effects. It does hold true, however, for how you'll go about modifying the Noise Controller Seed settings for each material, as the following steps demonstrate.

1. Click on the Phase parameter of the Laser 2 Noise Diffuse: Texture track. (You don't need to change the Seed parameters of the Laser 1 Noise material, because you already set them at 1.)

When you click on this Phase parameter, the other Phase parameters become deselected. Because you've already copied Noise controllers to all these parameters, you don't need to keep all of them selected; you'll be adjusting them individually.

2. Right-click on the Phase parameter and select Properties from the menu. When the Noise Controller dialog box appears, change Seed to 2 and click on OK.

3. Click on the Laser 2 Noise Opacity: Texture Phase parameter to highlight it and then right-click and select Properties. When the Noise Controller dialog box appears, change Seed to 2 (as with the preceding Diffuse texture) and click on OK.

4. Now, working your way down the list, click on the individual Phase parameters of each of the remaining Laser 3-6 Noise textures; then, right-click and change the Noise Controller seed for both Diffuse and Opacity to the number that corresponds to the material number. (The Seed for the Phase parameter Laser 3 Noise: Diffuse and Opacity should be 3; for Laser 4 Noise, it should be 4, and so on.)

**Note:** *Make sure that the Noise Seed settings for Diffuse and Opacity are identical for each material. This ensures that the Noise Diffuse and Noise Opacity materials will change and evolve at the same rate. If not, the Diffuse and Opacity maps will get out of sync and possibly cause undesirable results. (On the other hand, you might want to play with this effect later. However, hold off for now—you've gotta get through the rest of this tutorial!)*

5. When you've finished, close the Track View.

## Previewing the Texture

Now you'll see how applying the Noise controller has affected your Laser materials.

1. Your Material Editor should still be up, so click on Slot #2 (the Laser 2 Noise material) to make it active. Because this is a more high-contrast material than Laser 1 Noise, seeing the results of the animated noise settings will be easier.

2. Under the Maps section of Laser 2 Noise, click on the Diffuse name field to bring up the Noise texture rollout. Under Noise Parameters, take a look at the settings for Phase. At the moment, they still say 0.0 because you're still at frame 0 of a (potential) 100-frame animation.

3. On your 3D Studio MAX desktop, click once on the Next Frame button to change from frame 0 to frame 1. As you do so, you'll see the settings change on the sample spheres of the six Laser Noise materials shown in the Material Editor. In addition, you'll see the Phase parameter of the Laser 2 Noise material change from 0.0 to 1.779. If you continue clicking through the subsequent frames of this 100-frame test animation, you'll see the Phase settings change for each of the materials. You can, however, use an easier way to get a preview of your animated material.

4. In the Material Editor, click on the Make Preview icon. The Create Material Preview dialog box appears. Under Preview Range, Active Time Segment should be selected. Under Image Size: Percent of Output, 100 percent should be active; the Resolution should be 99 x 98. Click on OK to create the preview.

   Over the next minute or so, 3D Studio MAX generates a small, 100-frame .AVI file showing the animated Laser 2 Noise materials on the sample sphere in Slot #2. Take a moment to relax from these tutorials and wait until the 100-frame animation is finished. You can see the progress of the preview generation at the bottom of your screen.

5. After a minute or so, when the preview finishes rendering, the Media Player appears along with a small preview window.

**Note:** *If you're running 3D Studio MAX under Windows 95 rather than Windows NT, the Media Player may not appear automatically after you render a material or scene preview.*

   Click on the Play button to play the Laser 2 Noise animated texture. As it plays, notice how the Noise Controller has randomized the Noise material that you applied to the Diffuse and Opacity map slots of Laser 2 Noise.

6. When you've finished viewing the Laser 2 Noise animated material preview, close the Media Player.

At this point, you may want to save both your 3D Studio MAX scene and the animated Laser Noise materials that you've just created to your local drive so that you can play with them later. However, the scene you've just created is in the \CHAP_15 directory of your *3D Studio MAX f/x CD-ROM* as LASER_NP.MAX (Laser Noise Phase). In addition, the six Laser Noise materials are in the 3DSMAXFX.MAT Material Library.

## If You Phase a Laser, Is It Then Called a...?

To get the full effect of this technique, render an .AVI animation test of the Laser Noise materials on the LaserCyl objects. However, at 320 x 240 resolution running on a Pentium 90, this animation would take approximately one hour to render.

No problem—I'll just save you the trouble of rendering this right now.

1. Select File/View File and, from the \CHAP_15 directory, pick the file LASER_NP.AVI. When the Media Player appears, click the Play button.

    Now you can see the effects of the animated Noise Phase settings. Notice how applying the random Noise Controller has resulted in a fiercely sparkling laser beam.

2. When you've finished viewing the file, close the Media Player.

## Varying the Effects

For your own laser beam effects, you may want to experiment with changing the Noise parameters. For example, you could apply different Noise controllers to the other Noise texture parameters, such as UVW Offset, Levels and so on. (For an odd multicolored rainbow effect, try putting a Noise controller on the Noise Color settings of the Diffuse map.)

Now, one thing that you may have noticed is that if you look closely at the end of each LaserCyl object, the Laser Noise textures wrap around on the endcaps of the objects. To some extent, this is a happy accident because, from certain angles, the effect is a bright sparkling emanation point of the laser where it's being fired from the barrel of a laser cannon. However, you might find this effect undesirable, depending upon the angle at which you will be viewing the laser objects.

To avoid this, you could simply move the endcaps into the barrel of whatever laser weapon mesh you have in your 3D scene so that you can't see them. Of course, you could also apply an Edit Mesh modifier to the objects, select the end faces of the cylinders, and then delete the offending faces.

Additionally, as I discussed at the end of Chapter 13, "Laser Beams 101," you could create a separate optical effect to produce a bright muzzle flash from the emanation point. This would also conceal the texture wrapping on these LaserCyl objects.

In Chapter 13, you saw how you could create a muzzle flash (or impact point) by using a variation of the tachyon torpedo effect. Other ways to accomplish this include placing a small volumetric Omni light at the barrel of the laser cannon. By using the same techniques discussed in Chapter 10, "Here Comes the Sun, Part II," you can make the laser beam appear to be emerging from a bright ball of light.

Finally, another technique with which to experiment is to create a series of six concentric nested spheres and place them at the very end of the six LaserCyl objects. By applying the animated Laser 1-6 Noise textures to each of the concentric spheres, you can create an animated Noise "fireball" at the end of your laser beam. As with the laser beams themselves, you'll want to select the spheres and then use Edit/Properties to turn off their Shadow Casting and Shadow Receiving Attributes.

## Moving On

As you've seen in this and in previous chapters, 3D Studio MAX's animated Noise texture is extremely versatile. With it, you can create evolving, organic textures; when Noise is combined with Self-illuminated materials and Diffuse and Opacity mapping, you can simulate glowing optical effects, such as the laser beam you've created here and in the last chapter.

Now that you've covered offensive weaponry in the last few chapters, you'll take a look at some defensive weaponry. In the next chapter, you'll see how you can create forcefields to protect your 3D elements from the effects of tachyon torpedoes and laser beams.

# 16

# Shields Up, Captain

**I**n the last four chapters, you saw the effects of offensive science-fiction weaponry, such as tachyon torpedoes and laser beams. Now it's time to turn your sights to defensive weaponry such as forcefields.

As you saw when you previewed the outer-space battle scenes, when the battlecruiser comes out of warp drive, it's protected by a science-fiction staple: a forcefield. Like the shield technology portrayed in the *Star Trek* universe, the forcefield that surrounds the battlecruiser is a protective bubble that protects it from asteroid impacts or from hostile alien spaceships. (That is, only up to a point, as the storyboards in Chapter 3, "Setting Up Your Scene," seem to indicate.)

You can create this effect quite easily in 3D Studio MAX. In this chapter, you'll see how you can use variations of the shiny Nebula materials that you created in Chapters 6 and 7 to create a glassy sphere. You'll also see how applying an animated reflection map enables you to create an interesting "soap bubble" effect.

# The Initiation of Forcefields

As you saw in the five space battle scenes, the forcefield surrounding the battlecruiser is a simple and subtle effect. The forcefield itself is a Sphere primitive (actually, an oblate spheroid), scaled nonuniformly on its Z axis to flatten it. After scaling the sphere, I linked it to the battlecruiser model.

I then used Edit/Properties to turn off Shadow Casting and Shadow Receiving for the sphere, and assigned it a material that was largely transparent. I set the transparency to Additive, set Shininess and Shininess Strength to high, and then loaded an animated bitmap sequence in the Reflection map slot. This creates the illusion of a "swimming" texture on the surface of the Forcefield object.

The reflection map consisted of a 320 x 200 flic file that I created in James Gleick's CHAOS: The Software program, from Autodesk. (Unfortunately, this program is no longer available.) This colorful and looping animated texture is reminiscent of the oily rainbow sheen that flows across the surface of a soap bubble. As it stands, it provides an interesting quality for your Forcefield effect.

Here's how you can simulate this effect in 3D Studio MAX. You want to create a very simple scene consisting of a sphere, an Omni light, and a camera. The sphere will act as your test forcefield, or shield object.

1. Activate 2D Snap and create a 100-unit radius sphere in the center of the Top viewport.

2. Change the sphere's default Segment setting from 16 to 36 and press Enter. Then, click on the Generate Mapping Coordinates check box to activate it. Finally, rename the sphere as Forcefield.

3. From the menu bar, select Edit/Properties, and toggle off Cast Shadows and Receive Shadows for the Forcefield object. (You don't want the Forcefield to cast or receive shadows, especially if it's surrounding another object, such as a spaceship.) Then, click on the Zoom Extents All button to center the Forcefield in your viewports.

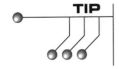

**TIP** You can reach the Properties dialog box more quickly by moving the cursor over the sphere and right-clicking to bring up the context menu. Then, select Properties from this menu.

4. On the Create Panel, click on the Lights icon and then on the Omni button. Change the V value from 180 to 255, or pure white. Because the Top viewport should still be active, press Shift+Z on your keyboard to zoom out from the Forcefield object. Then, move your cursor to approximate XYZ coordinates X -200, Y -200, and Z 0, and click to place the Omni light.

5. Click on the Zoom Extents All button to center scene in the viewports; then, click on the Select and Move button. Activate the Front viewport and move the Omni light up on the Y axis approximately 100 units.

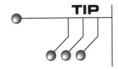

**TIP** The quickest way to select transform operations on an element in your scene is to move the cursor over the selected objects and right-click. The context menu that appears not only lets you reach the Properties dialog box but also select transform operations without moving up to the toolbar.

6. On the Create Panel, select Create/Camera and click on the Target button. Activate the Top viewport again and then press Shift+Z to zoom out further in the viewport.

7. Place your cursor below the Forcefield sphere in the Top viewport at approximate XYZ coordinates X 0, Y -400, and Z 0. Then, to place Camera01, click and drag vertically upwards along the Y axis to place the Camera01 target in the center of the Forcefield sphere.

8. Activate the Perspective viewport and change it to Camera01. At this point, your viewports should resemble Figure 16-1.

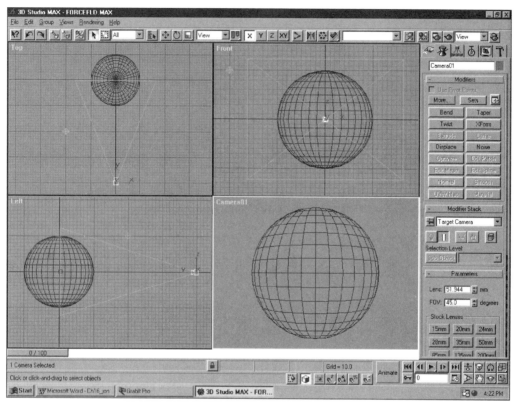

Figure 16-1: *The basic setup for the Forcefield test renderings.*

9. To make it easier to see the effects of the Forcefield material, load the standard STARS640.TGA bitmap into your scene as a Screen background. (By this point, you can probably do this in your sleep.) Place it in Material Editor Slot #2.

## An Agent of Chaos

Now you'll create the actual Forcefield texture.

1. Select the Forcefield object, return to the Material Editor, and activate Slot #1. You want to alter Material #1's attributes to create your Forcefield texture. This will look something like a soap bubble, with multicolored swirls of energy crawling over the Forcefield surface.

2. Click on the Assign Material to Selection button to assign Material #1 to the selected Forcefield object.

3. Under Basic Parameters, click on 2-Sided and change the Ambient color to solid black, or RGB values 0, 0, 0. Now, change Diffuse and Specular to pure white, or RGB 255, 255, 255.

4. Change Shininess to 50, Shininess Strength to 75, and Opacity from 100 to 7. This will create a nearly transparent object, looking almost like a piece of tinted glass.

5. Open the Extended Parameters rollout. Under Opacity, leave Falloff set to In but change the Amount from 0 to 100. Change Opacity Type to Additive to give the illusion of a halo around the edges of the Forcefield. When you've finished, close the Extended Parameters rollout and open the Maps rollout.

6. Under Maps, click on Reflection to activate it, and change the amount from 100 to 20. Click on the Maps name field next to Reflection. When the Material/Map Browser appears, make sure that New is selected and then click on Bitmap. When the Reflection rollout appears, change the coordinates from Environmental Mapping: Spherical Environment to Texture.

7. Click in the Bitmap name field to bring up the Select Bitmap Image File browser. From the \CHAP_16 directory of your *3D Studio MAX f/x CD-ROM*, click once on the file FORCEFLD.FLC file to highlight it, and click on View. When the Media Player appears, click on the Play button.

This is a 320 x 200, 8-bit flic that I created in James Gleick's CHAOS: The Software, originally from Autodesk. Developed by chaos theory specialist James Gleick, this MS-DOS-based program let you create fractal landscapes as 3D .DXF files, plus low-resolution animations of various fractal phenomena, such as landscapes, clouds, and 256-color contour patterns. Frame 30 from the animation is shown in Figure 16-2.

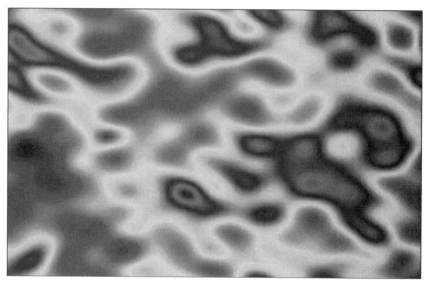

Figure 16-2: *A still image (frame 30) from the FORCEFLD.FLC animation.*

I created the FORCEFLD.FLC file that you're viewing by animating various parameters of the Chaos Contour function across 120 frames. I then loaded this flic into Autodesk Animator Pro and cross-faded the first 30 frames of the animation into the last 30 frames, resulting in an endlessly looping, 90-frame animation.

I converted this animation to a 256-level grayscale palette and then mapped a custom palette to it, without color fitting. The custom palette consisted of wildly ramped colors—from black to red, yellow, green, orange, blue, and then black again. Thus, the final result is this somewhat psychedelic or solarized-looking animated texture. For your purposes, it's perfect to convey the illusion of a "soap bubble" forcefield effect.

8. Click the Close button to dismiss the Media Player.

## Flic Files versus .IFLs

Although you could load the FORCEFLD.FLC file as a reflection map, instead you're going to load up a series of .GIF images created from this flic. This will speed up overall rendering time because 3D Studio MAX does not have to load the entire FORCEFLD.FLC into memory and has more memory available for rendering.

1. From the \CHAP_16 directory, load the file FORCE000.IFL. This will load the 90 sequential .GIF frames of the FORCEFLD.FLC animation frame by frame as they are needed during rendering; the first bitmap appears on the sample sphere of Material Editor Slot #1.

2. In the Coordinates section of the Reflection rollout, change UV Tiling from 1.0 to 2.0 for both U and V. This quadruples the number of reflection image maps being applied across the surface of your Forcefield object.

3. When you've finished, click on the Go to Parent button to return to the top material level. Change the name of Material #1 to Forcefield 1.

    This material is included in the 3DSMAXFX.MAT Material Library on your *3D Studio MAX f/x* CD-ROM.

4. Activate the Camera01 viewport; then, press Alt+R and Enter to render a single frame of this object. After a moment, the image appears and should look something like Figure 16-3.

Figure 16-3: *A test rendering of the Forcefield object.*

If you take a look at Figure 16-3, you can see how using an almost completely transparent material with a slight reflection map has resulted in a glassy object that looks like a soap bubble.

5. When you're finished with the rendering, close the Camera01 VFB window.

## The Animated Forcefield Effect

If you want, you can now render a low-resolution .AVI file to see the effect of the texture moving across the surface of the Forcefield. However, I've already rendered a test animation of this sequence, so you can take a look at that.

1. Select File/View and, from the \CHAP_16 directory, click on the file FORCEFLD.AVI. When the Media Player appears, click on the Play button to play through this demonstration .AVI file.
    As you can see, the animated Chaos texture produces an ever-changing, solarized effect.

2. Click on the Close button to dismiss the Media Player.

Of course, you can vary this effect in many ways. You can change the tiling of the Reflection map or the Reflection map percentage. Or you can use a completely different texture for the Reflection.

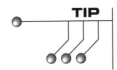

**TIP**

One interesting thing to try is Add a Noise texture into the Reflection map slot. Play around with the various Noise parameters, including Color #1 and Color #2, and the Threshold settings. Then, as you explored in the last chapter, go into Track View and apply a Noise controller to both Noise Phase and the Noise colors. With a little experimentation, you can create your own psychedelic texture effects without prerendered bitmaps.

## Altering the Forcefield With Noise Shininess Maps

Now you'll alter this Forcefield effect further. You'll load a Noise texture as a Shininess map to add another level of energy to the Forcefield.

1. Return to the Material Editor and go down to the Basic Parameters section of Forcefield 1. Change Shininess from 50 to 35. Next to Highlight, click on the Soften check box. This will further soften the specular highlight of the Forcefield object.

2. Go to the Maps section and click on the Shininess Maps name button. When the Material/Map browser appears, click on Noise.

By loading the Noise texture as a Shininess map and then animating the settings, you can create another level of energetic movement on the surface of your Forcefield. As the Noise texture evolves during the course of an animation, you'll see the various patterns appear in the Specular highlight, producing an interesting effect similar to the Nebula effects that you covered in Chapter 6, "Nebulas Made Simple, Part I" and Chapter 7, "Nebulas Made Simple, Part II."

Now you'll adjust the Noise parameters of your Shininess map to produce an interesting specular effect.

3. In the Noise rollout, go to Noise Parameters and change Noise Type from Regular to Turbulence. Change Size from 25 to 10.

4. When you've finished, activate the Camera01 viewport and press Alt+R and Enter to render another test image, as shown Figure 16-4.

Figure 16-4: *The Forcefield object with a Turbulence Noise texture loaded as a Shininess map.*

**Note:** *The Noise Shininess map has broken the Specular highlight on the Forcefield up into a complex pattern resembling a spider web. Of course, you can animate this Specular highlight simply by turning on the Animate button and adjusting the parameters of the Noise texture at a nonzero frame. By changing the XYZ Offset, Tiling, Angle, Levels, and/or Phase, either singly or in combination, you can produce quite striking results.*

Take a look at a demonstration of this effect.

5. Select File/View File and, from the \CHAP_16 directory of the *3D Studio MAX f/x* CD-ROM, pick the file FORCEFL2.AVI and click on it. When the Media Player appears, click on the Play button to play this 320 x 240 .AVI file.

   I created the animated Specular highlight shown in this .AVI file by simply animating the Phase attribute of the Noise Shininess map. On frame 0 of this 100-frame animation, Phase is at 0. I then turned on the Animate button, went to frame 100, and changed Phase to 10.0. This animated Phase parameter produces the "crawling" Specular highlight effect.

   The material you just created is in the 3DSMAXFX.MAT Material Library as Forcefield 2. In addition, the scene file used to create this animation is in the \CHAP_16 directory as FORCEFL2.MAX.

6. When you've finished viewing the animation, click the Close button to dismiss the Media Player.

## Using Animated Bump Maps

Now you'll alter the material on your Forcefield object one more time.

1. Return to the Material Editor. If you're still in the Noise Parameters rollout of the Forcefield 1 material, click on the Go to Parent button to return to the top material level.

2. In the Maps section, click and drag the Noise texture map from the Shininess slot down to Bump. Click on Copy and then OK. This will copy the Noise material parameters from

Shininess to Bump. Now, click again in the check box next to Shininess to turn off the Shininess map.

3. Activate the Camera01 viewport again; then, press Alt+R and Enter to render another test image of the Forcefield effect. After a few minutes, the image appears; it should resemble Figure 16-5.

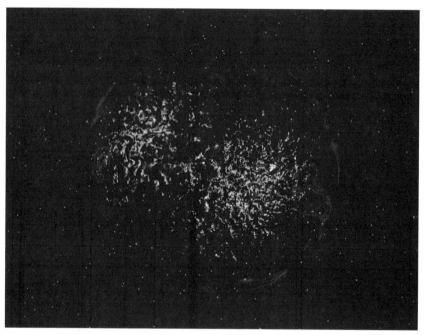

Figure 16-5: *By using a Noise texture as a bump map, you can subtly distort the surface of your Forcefield object and pick up unusual Specular highlights.*

Notice that by copying the Noise texture from Shininess to the Bump map slot, you've changed the appearance of the Forcefield surface again. The procedural Noise texture produces a look similar to that of old-fashioned, leaded glass. The Noise Bump map creates the illusion of ridges and valleys with Specular highlights produced by the Omni light running over their surfaces.

Of course, if you were to animate these Noise Bump map parameters, you would see the Specular highlights appear to crawl across the surface of the Forcefield. This might suggest an interesting electrical effect, or how the Forcefield is reacting to impacts from tachyon torpedoes or asteroids.

Take a look at one final .AVI demonstration of this effect.

4. Select File/View File and, from the \CHAP_16 directory, pick the file FORCEFL3.AVI. When the Media Player appears, click on the Play button.

In this animation, notice how the animated Bump map produces the illusion that the leaded-glass texture is actually crawling across the surface of the object. (As with the previous Noise Shininess map example, the only Noise parameter that has been changed is Phase, going from 0.0 to 10.0 from frames 0 to 100.) An interesting side effect, of course, is that the animated bump map also distorts the ebb and flow of the Reflection map on the surface of the Forcefield object.

5. When you've finished viewing this file, close the Media Player.

The file you've just created has been included in the \CHAP_16 directory as FORCEFL3.MAX. In addition, this last texture is in the 3DSMAXFX.MAT Material Library as Forcefield 3.

## Moving On

Okay, now what happens when you cross offensive science-fiction weapons such as lasers and tachyon torpedoes with defensive weaponry such as forcefields? In the case of the space battle scenes you saw earlier, the effect could be summarized succinctly as "BOOM!"

In the next chapter, you'll see how you can create dazzling explosion effects, using 3D Studio MAX's Bomb Space Warps, some simple geometry, and the Glow filter in Video Post.

# 17

# Things That Go Boom in the Night

In this chapter, the last in the Part II tutorials, you'll examine how to use the 3D Studio MAX built-in Bomb Space Warps and Video Post Glow filter to create impressive explosion effects.

In one of the space battle shots, you saw the enemy fighters' tachyon torpedoes hit the battlecruiser's shields and trigger explosions on impact. As the torpedoes hit, bright flashes of light and glowing particles blasted outward. You also previewed the shot where the battlecruiser's lasers hit one of the fighters, causing it to disintegrate in a fireball and a burst of glittering sparks.

By using the 3D Studio MAX's Bomb Space Warp linked to simple geometry (in this case, high-resolution sphere primitives) you can create dynamic particle effects. Then, by applying animated, self-illuminated materials and the Video Post Glow filter to these spheres, you can create the illusion of a bright flash of light, which then dissipates from white to yellow, orange, red, and then to black.

You'll see how to create this effect in the following sections.

## Ties That Bind

Now you'll experiment with 3D Studio MAX's Bomb Space Warps and Video Post Glow Filter to see how to create a simple yet striking explosion effect.

First, you need to create a simple sphere object to blow up with a Bomb Space Warp.

1. In 3D Studio MAX, press the S key on your keyboard to activate 2D Snap Toggle; then, create a Sphere in the center of the Top viewport with a Radius of 30 units. Don't change the Segments value.

2. Although you won't be texture-mapping this object until later, click on the Generate Mapping Coordinates check box so that you don't have to worry about this later.

   Now you'll create and place the actual Bomb Space Warp.

3. Press the W key to enlarge the Top viewport to full screen. From the Create Panel, select Space Warps, and click on Bomb. Move the cursor to the very center of the Sphere01 object and single-click. A white triangular pyramid appears, which represents the Bomb.

   Now you'll bind the Bomb Space Warp to the Sphere01 object.

4. Click on the Space Warp to deselect it and select the Sphere01 object. Click on the Bind to Space Warp button in the toolbar and then press the H key on your keyboard to bring up the Select by Name dialog box.

   Although you could move the cursor over the Bomb Space Warp and the Sphere01 object and link them manually, it's sometimes easier to simply select an object and then pick the correct Space Warp modifier from a name list (especially if your scene contains extremely complex or closely spaced geometry.)

5. From the Select Space Warp list, click on Bomb01 and then click on the Bind button in the Select by Name dialog box. Both objects flash white briefly, indicating that they are now bound together.

6. Press the W key again, or click the Min/Max toggle button to return to your four viewports. Then, click on the Zoom Extents All button to center the Sphere01 and Bomb Space Warp objects in each viewport.

## We're Having a Blast

Now you'll zoom away from these objects in the Perspective viewport so that you can see the overall effect of the Bomb blast.

1. Click on the Zoom All button; then, click and drag until you've reduced the Sphere01 object to approximately one-sixth the height of the screen in each of your four viewports.

2. Click on the Degradation Override button (if it's not already active). You want to see the effects of the Bomb Space Warp, so drag the Time Slider bar to the right slowly until you see the Sphere01 object explode. Now, drag the Time Slider bar back and forth (scratching through the animation) to see the entire explosion effect.

3. Move to frame 5. Notice that the Sphere01 object faces shatter into their component triangles beginning on this frame. Then, as you progress through the next couple of frames, you see how the triangles begin to blast apart from the center of the Bomb Space Warp.

4. At this point, make sure that the Perspective viewport is active and then click on the Play button and play through the entire 100-frame animated sequence on your 3D Studio MAX desktop.

    As you can see, on frame 5 the Sphere01 object explodes. The pieces blast outward quite regularly and then arc downward. This is because Gravity in the Space Warp binding is set at its default value of 1.0. Although this is interesting, you want to create a space effect—where there is no Earth-like gravity. So, in a completely omnipotent fashion, you'll turn Gravity off.

5. Click on the Select button to deselect Bind to Space Warp mode. Now, in any of your viewports, click on the Bomb Space Warp to select it.

6. Click on the Modify tab to bring up the Modify Panel for the Bomb Space Warp (or press Ctrl+2). Reduce Gravity to 0.0 (right-click on the spinner) and then click on the Play Animation button again. As you do, you see the Sphere01 particles fly straight outward from the center, and not arc "down" the Z axis toward the construction grid. They simply fly outward into space.

At the moment, you're still a little way from creating an acceptable explosion. Right now, the particles don't tumble as they should. The explosion looks simply like a rapid "expansion" of the faces flying from the centerpoint of the Sphere01 object, as shown in Figure 17-1.

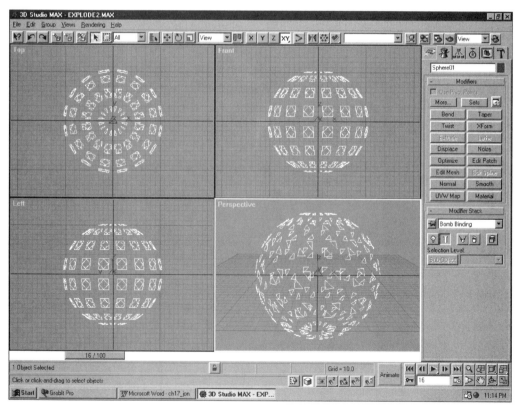

Figure 17-1: *Frame 16 of the initial bomb explosion effect. The current Bomb settings result in a uniform expansion of the faces.*

7. Click on the Play button again to stop the playback, and return to frame 0.

## Now Cause Total Chaos

Now you'll modify your Bomb settings to produce an honest-to-gosh explosion.

1. Take a look at the Bomb Parameters under the Modify Panel. Strength is at 1.0. This determines the initial speed of the blast. Gravity is now at 0.0, so there is no longer a downward force working on the Z axis of the faces of Sphere01 as they blow outward from the initial bomb blast. Because Chaos is at 0.0, the flying triangular faces do not spin and tumble during the course of their flight. This is why the Sphere01 object looks as if it's simply expanding at the seams instead of actually blowing apart violently.

   Now you'll change some of these parameters and see the effects.

2. Change Chaos from 0.0 to 5.0; then, click on the Play animation button again.

   Notice how chaotic movement in both translation and rotation is present on the triangular faces as they blow apart from the Bomb Space Warp. This is a much more realistic explosion effect.

3. Stop the animation and return to frame 0. Change Chaos from 5.0 to 10 (its maximum setting) and click the Play animation button again. See how the particles tumble and vary in their positions even more greatly? Now you have the beginnings of an interesting explosion effect, as shown in Figure 17-2.

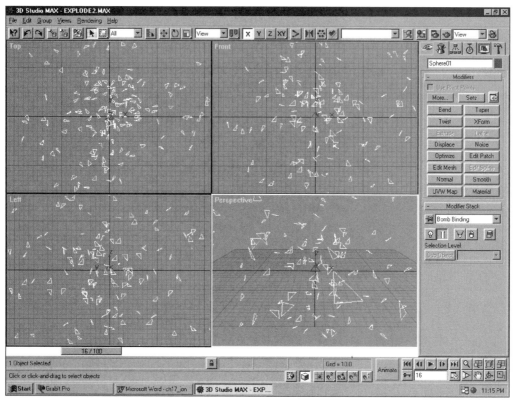

Figure 17-2: *Frame 16 of the bomb animation with Chaos set to its full range of 10.0. Note how the increased Chaos setting has resulted in the triangular faces being blow completely across the screen in random patterns.*

4. Click on the Go to Start button to return again to frame 0.

## Increasing Complexity

Of course, if you want to make a more realistic explosion effect, in terms of pure geometry, you need more particles. Although you could apply an Edit Mesh modifier to the Sphere01 object and then tessellate it to produce more faces, there's an easier way. You simply increase the number of segments of the original Sphere01-object.

1. Click on the Sphere01 object to select it. From the Modify Panel, go to the Modifier Stack and click on the Down arrow to open the Modifier stack. Move down the stack to Sphere and, in the Parameters rollout, increase Segments from 16 to 36. As you do, the number of faces on the sphere increases (of course).

2. Now, click on the Play animation button to take a look at the effect. Note the increased number of particles blasting outward during the course of the animation. It is now a much more complex explosion, as shown in Figure 17-3.

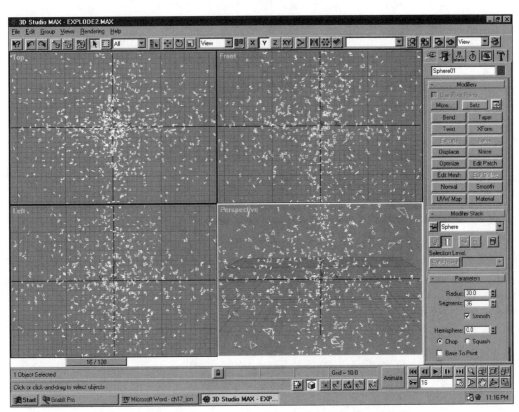

Figure 17-3: *Frame 16 of the explosion test with a 36-segment sphere.*

3. When you've finished viewing the animation, return to frame 0.

## Setting Up Your Own Explosion

Now that you have the basic elements for creating an explosion, you'll actually set up a 60-frame animated sequence.

1. Right-click on the Play animation button to bring up the Time Configuration menu. Under Animation, click on the Rescale Time button. You'll see that the current time is set to the 3D Studio MAX defaults as Start Time 0, End Time 100, and Overall Length 100. You're going to scale your animation sequence from 100 frames down to 60.

2. Under New, change Length from 100 to 60. As you do, you see the End Time also change to 60. Close the Time Configuration window. Now you have a 60-frame sequence.

3. Click on the Play button again. The Sphere01 object now explodes across 60 frames. Notice also that because you scaled the overall sequence down from 100 frames to 60, the explosion effect starts on frame 3 instead of frame 5. Now, return to frame 0.

## An Animated Bomb Texture

In this section, you'll create an animated texture that will correspond to this 60-frame explosion animation.

1. Make sure that the Sphere01 object is selected; then, click on the Animate button. It will turn red, indicating that you are now in animation mode.

2. Click on the Material Editor button to bring up the Material Editor. Notice that the active sample has a red outline around it, indicating that you are in Animate mode. Click on the Assign Material to Selection button to assign Material #1 to Sphere01. It's now a "hot" material in the scene. (You're going to be changing its parameters in a moment.) Then, change its name to Explode 1.

3. Change the following parameters: On the Basic Parameters rollout, click on 2-Sided. Change both the Ambient and Diffuse colors to RGB 255, 255, 255, or pure white. Reduce Shininess

and Shininess Strength both to 0. Then, change Self-illumination to 100. You now have a pure white, self-illuminated, 2-sided material.

4. Drag the Time Slider from frame 0 to frame 3. As you do, you'll see the Sphere01 object begin its explosion.

   Now you'll set another material key. You'll want to keep the material that you applied to the Sphere01 object as (mostly) white for frames 0 to frame 3. From frame 3 to frame 10 and subsequent frames, however, you're changing the color substantially.

   One way that you can "hold" this color from frame 3 to frame 5 is to simply go into Track View, select the keys for Ambient and Diffuse, and copy them from frame 3 to frame 5. However, for your purposes, you can do something a little easier.

5. With Animate mode still active, return to the Material Editor and change the RGB settings for either Ambient or Diffuse (whichever is active), to RGB 255, 255, 254. This will change the overall material color a negligible amount; yet, because you've made a slight change in the material, it will set a new key on frame 3.

6. Click on the Next Frame button to go to frame 4. The pieces of the Sphere01 object begin their rapid expansion as the object explodes. Return to the Material Editor and change the RGB settings of either the Ambient of Diffuse colors (whichever is last active) to 255, 255, 255. This will set "bracketed" keys of a nearly pure-white material for frames 0 to 3 and 4.

7. Drag the Time Slider from frame 4 to frame 10. The pieces of Sphere01 blast further outward. In the Material Editor, change both the Ambient and Diffuse colors to RGB 255, 255, 128. You now have a bright, washed-out yellow.

8. Drag the Time Slider from frame 10 to frame 20 and then change the Explode 1 Ambient and Diffuse colors to RGB 255, 255, 0, or a pure lemon-yellow.

9. Go to frame 30, and change the Explode 1 RGB settings for Ambient and Diffuse to 255, 128, 0, or a bright orange.

10. Now, go to frame 40 and change the RGB settings for Ambient and Diffuse to 255, 0, 0, or a pure red.

11. Finally, drag the Time Slider all the way to frame 60 and change the RGB values of the materials to 0, 0, 0, or pure black. This will fade out all the particles by frame 60.

12. When you've finished, click on the Animate button again to toggle Animation mode off; then, drag the Time Slider back to 0. In the Material Editor, you see the color changes that you set cycling back from black, through red, to orange, yellow, bright yellow, to white.

This scene is saved to the \CHAP_17 directory of your *3D Studio MAX f/x CD-ROM* as EXPLODE1.MAX.

## That Blowed Up Real Good

It's time to do a test rendering of one of the frames.

1. First, you're going to place this explosion against a suitable starfield backdrop, so select Rendering/Environment, and from the \CHAP_17 directory, load the image STARS640.TGA and place it in Material Editor Slot #2. In the Material Editor, change it to a Screen background rather than Spherical Environment.

2. Now, drag the Time Slider from frame 0 to frame 8. Then, make sure that your Perspective viewport is activated, and press Alt+R and Enter to render a single 640 x 480 image of your Perspective window. After a moment, the image appears and should look like Figure 17-4.

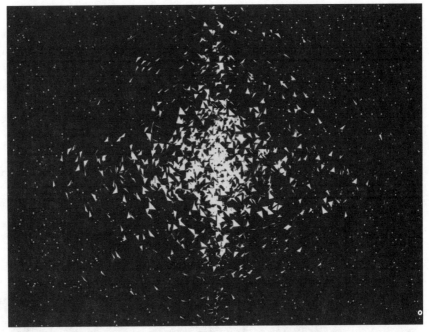

Figure 17-4: *Frame 8 of the EXPLODE1.MAX explosion test rendering.*

As your rendering shows, although the motion dynamics of your explosion are impressive, the appearance of the yellowish, blown-apart triangles of the Sphere01 object is less than impressive. You need to camouflage the fact that the particles of this explosion effect are actually two-dimensional triangular faces.

You can do this by using an Opacity map to change the appearance of the triangular faces. Here's how to do it.

3. Return to the Material Editor. On the Basic Parameters rollout for the Explode 1 material, click on Face Map. Then, open the Maps rollout. You're going to load an Opacity map to create a face-mapped material. Click on the Opacity map button, and when the Material/Maps Browser appears, make sure that New is selected and click on Bitmap.

CD-ROM

4. Under Bitmap Parameters, double-click in the Bitmap name field. From the \CHAP_17 directory, select the file PARTICLE.GIF and then click on View. PARTICLE.GIF is a 65 x 65 grayscale image of a soft white sphere; it provides a fine Opacity Face Map to camouflage the triangular faces appearing in your explosion.

5. Close the PARTICLE.GIF image window and then click on OK to load the image and return to the Material Editor. The PARTICLE.GIF image is now loaded as an Opacity map for the Explode 1 material.

6. Activate the Perspective viewport again and render another test image of frame 8. After a moment, the image appears and should look like Figure 17-5.

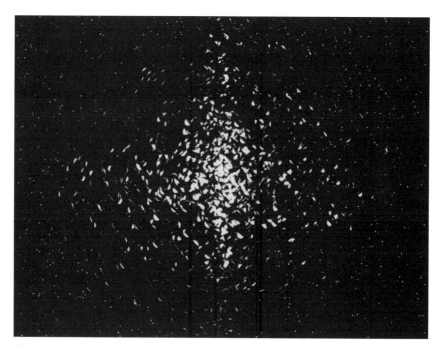

Figure 17-5: *By using a face-mapped opacity map, the triangular faces look more like rounded particles.*

As you can see, by using the PARTICLE.GIF image as an Opacity map, you have camouflaged the fact that the particles present in your explosion are actually just 2D triangular faces.

**Note:** *An interesting experiment for you to try to improve your explosion effects is to use a face-mapped Noise texture as an Opacity map. By adjusting the Noise Size, Type, and Threshold settings and by animating parameters such as UVW Offset or Phase, you can further "rough up" the edges of the triangular face particles appearing in your explosions. In addition, an animated Noise opacity map can create the illusion that each individual particle is sparkling as it flies outward from the center of the explosion.*

Now, if you wanted to render a test .AVI file of this animation sequence, seeing more of the particles as they blast out from the center would be nice.

7. Drag the Time Slider from frame 6 to frame 10; the particles blow outward a little further. With your Perspective viewport active, click on the Zoom Extents button to reduce the size of the exploded imagery on frame 10 so that you can see all of the particles present on that frame.

8. If you click on the Play animation button or simply go to the last frame (frame 60), you see more of the overall particles and their dispersal pattern during the course of the animation.

The file you have just created is in the \CHAP_17 directory as EXPLODE2.MAX.

## The Explosion Rendering

At this point, you may want to do your own test rendering. However, the *3D Studio MAX f/x CD-ROM* already contains a 320 x 240 .AVI demonstration file of this explosion effect.
To take a look at it, use the following steps.

1. Select File/View File and, from the \CHAP_17 directory, click on the file EXPLODE2.AVI to load it. When the Media Player appears, note that the first frame of the EXPLODE2.AVI file

shows how the face-mapped material, using the PARTICLE.GIF Opacity map, has given your sphere sort of a honeycomb appearance. (You'll fix that in a moment.) Now, click on the Play button.

As you can see, the particles blast outward from the center of the sphere where the Bomb Space Warp was attached; in addition, the particles change color and finally fade to black.

2. When you've finished previewing the animation, close the Media Player.

## Creating a Big Bang in Video Post

Although this is now a more interesting effect because of the motion dynamics, something is still missing. You need not only to obscure the face-mapped "honeycomb" pattern of the initial Sphere01 object on the first few frames but also to impart a feeling of energy to the individual particles.

You can do this by applying a Glow filter in Video Post. By applying a large Glow effect to the particles, you can create the effect of a fiery explosion.

1. Return to the Material Editor. Assign an Effects Channel to your revised Explode 1 material (called Explode 2 in the 3DSMAXFX.MAT Material Library.) At the moment, the current Effects Channel is set to 0, so you're going to "change the channel."

2. Click and hold on the Effects Channel button until the rollout appears. Select Channel 1 rather than 0 and release the mouse button. This assigns the Explode 1 material to Channel 1 (or vice-versa).

Now you'll go to Video Post to assign the Glow Filter.

3. Select Rendering/Video Post. You'll want to set up a simple Video Post queue to provide a glow effect for these particles. In the Video Post menu, click on the Add Scene Event button. Under View, change the viewport to Perspective. Under Video Post parameters, make sure that the VP End Time is set to 60

and that Video Post parameters are enabled. Then, click on OK. The Perspective viewport is now added to the Video Post queue.

4. Click on the Add Image Filter event button. Under Filter Plug-in, click on the Down arrow and change from Fade to the Glow plug-in. Click on Setup. For Source, make sure that the Material Effects channel is set to 1. Then, change Size from 20 to 15 and click on OK. Make sure that the VP End Time is set to 60 and then click on OK again.

5. Now, you need to add an Image Output Event, so click on the Add Image Output Event button. Under Image File, click on Files. At this point, you would probably want to render an .AVI file to your 3DSMAX/IMAGES directory. So, under filename, highlight it, type **EXPLODE2,** and click on OK. For your purposes, the default Radius Cinepak video compression is sufficient, so you don't need to change your setup for the .AVI file. Click on OK. Again, under Video Post parameters, make sure that the VP end time is to 60; then, click on OK to return to the Video Post dialog box. It should look like Figure 17-6.

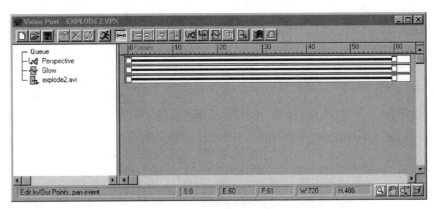

Figure 17-6: *The Video Post settings for the Explode2 animation.*

6. Now, if you want, you can save your Video Post settings; to do this, click on the Save Sequence button and save these Video Post settings to your \VPOST directory as EXPLODE2.VPX.

## A Brief Digression

At this point, you may ask why you went through this entire exercise if I'm providing all the elements on the CD-ROM that are necessary to create these effects. There are a couple of reasons.

First, knowing the exact procedures required to create an elaborate effect is important. Second, you should set up these effects yourself so that, in the process, you can see points at which you might diverge from the tutorials (not right now, though) in your own work, and customize the effects for your own needs.

One of the primary purposes of this book is not just to lead you by the hand and show you one or two specific ways of creating an effect, but to give you ideas on how you can modify these techniques to create even more elaborate effects.

## Back On Track

Okay, now you can get back to seeing something blow up.

1. Click on the Execute Sequence button to bring up the Execute Video Post menu. Under Range, the range of the sequence should be 0 to 60. If you want to render this sequence relatively quickly (at least, on a Pentium 90 MHz PC), set the output to 320 x 240.

   Before you do that, however, you'll create a final 640 x 480 still image rendering with the Video Post Glow filter.

2. Under Time output, click on Single rather than Range. Then, enter 8 for the frame number. Under Output Size, make sure that 640 x 480 has been selected and then click on Render.

**Note:** *It may take a couple of minutes for your final image to appear. Although the initial Perspective viewport rendering of frame 8 will appear fairly quickly, even at 640 x 480 resolution, the Glow Filter may take an additional minute or so to finish processing the image. However, after a few minutes, the still image rendering will appear in the Video Post queue Virtual Frame Buffer window, and it should look like Figure 17-7.*

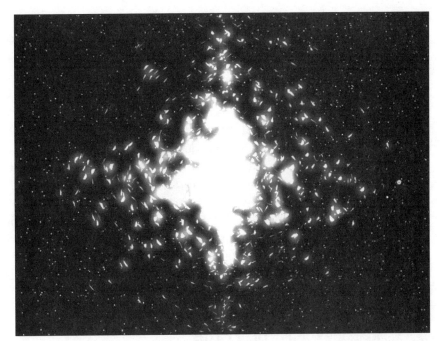

Figure 17-7: *Frame 8 of the test explosion routine, with a Video Post Glow filter applied to the particles.*

Now you have something that looks a little more like a fiery explosion. Notice how, in the center of the image, the glow effect produced by the Video Post filter creates an irregular hot-white fireball where the clusters of particles are spaced closely together. Subsequent clusters of particles radiating out from the center of the blast also have an intense glow effect around them.

## Blow Something Up, Already!

Okay, now (finally) you'll take a look at a demonstration .AVI file of this sequence with the final Glow effect added.

1. Minimize both the Video Post queue Virtual Frame Buffer window and the Video Post dialog box.

2. Select File/View File. From the \CHAP_17 directory, load and play the file EXPLODE3.AVI.

Boom! Note how the Glow filter applied to the white Sphere01 object has resulted in a bright glowing sphere on the first few frames. In addition, notice how the Glow effect creates an irregularly shaped fireball, which very quickly dissipates as the particles blow outward from the center. You now have a cool explosion effect, perfectly suited for outer space pyrotechnics.

Again, you can vary this effect in many ways. You could, for example, create several nested spheres, each with different materials animating at different rates and also each with different detonation times, bomb speeds, and other parameters to create a multiple explosion effect. You could also alter the Glow filter settings in Video Post and assign different material channels to each of the materials applied to the objects to create additive glow effects and additive color for the nested objects.

The file you've just created is saved in the \CHAP_17 directory of your *3D Studio MAX f/x CD-ROM* as EXPLODE3.MAX.

## Tweaking the Particle Paths

As you play through the animation, you will notice that, even though you set the Chaos factor to 10.0, the particles still tend to blow outward from the centerpoint of the Bomb Gizmo, mostly in a straight line. You can distort the particle paths as the faces fly outward in other ways, however.

One thing to try is to apply a Noise Object Modifier to the actual Sphere01 object. By animating the Noise settings and/or rotating or translating the Noise Gizmo, you can apply an additional level of chaotic motion to your particles. You can also apply a Displace modifier and load an irregular, high-contrast bitmap to use as a displacement map. (You'll be experimenting with the Displace modifier in Chapter 19, "Space Rubble: Creating Asteroids.")

In addition, you can try animating the position of the Bomb Space Warp itself during the course of the animation.

## Even More Ways to Blow Up Stuff

As with almost all the techniques covered in this book, you can vary the effects parameters in many ways to get the look that you want. What are some other ways that you can incorporate explosions into your scenes?

Well, using the techniques you've just covered, you can render a sequence of custom explosion images and then map those prerendered sequences onto 2D Quad Patch objects (as you did to create the tachyon torpedo imagery for Chapter 13, "Laser Beams 101"). By placing these planar shapes into your 3D Studio MAX scene and adjusting them so that they always face the camera (perhaps using a Look At controller), you could choreograph an extremely complex series of explosions without having to manually set up all the different explosion parameters as physical 3D objects within your space scene.

Of course, if you do this, you'll need to make careful use of .IFL (Image File Lists) to have the explosion imagery appear on the 2D shapes at the specific points in the animation in which you need the effect. (Check 3D Studio MAX's Help file for more information on using .IFLs.)

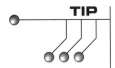

**TIP**

An excellent resource for explosion imagery is VCE's Pyromania and Pyromania 2 CD-ROMs. The Pyromania CDs contain high-quality, 24-bit digitized images of cinematic-style explosions. The images, taken from 35mm movie film, let you put *Star Wars*-quality explosions in your 3D scenes. For more information, see Appendix C, "3D Studio MAX Resources."

Although you can use the 3D Studio MAX Bomb Space Warps to disintegrate your actual spaceship models, the Bomb Space Warp blows objects apart into their component faces. Although this may be an acceptable effect for certain scenes, you may want to produce something a little more believable.

When you blow a 3D mesh apart into its triangular faces, you notice immediately that the mesh isn't "solid." Although it may be a representation of a spacecraft (presumably filled with bulkheads, circuitry, and piping), in actuality it's a 3D model composed of 2D faces. And, if you simply blow it apart into faces, it may look no more substantial than a hollow eggshell with a firecracker inside.

A way around this is to place combinations of Bomb Space Warps and Sphere geometry (with the appropriate materials) inside your spaceship or other models. At the point at which the ship explodes and the Video Post Glow filter overwhelms the effect, you could "hide" your original spaceship model, using the Visibility keys in Track View. Then, you could "unhide" either a predamaged version of your ship (with custom texture maps and mangled geometry) or even unhide rough pieces of debris. By animating these pieces tumbling out of the explosion, you could produce a spectacular pyrotechnic effect.

Finally, another way of creating an explosion effect (or augmenting an existing one) is simply to animate a volumetric Omni light. As you saw in Chapter 9, "Here Comes the Sun, Part I," you could animate the Ranges, Attenuation, Density, and Noise factors of a volumetric Omni light to produce the illusion of a brilliant fireball. For some scenes, simply creating a bright flash that engulfs an object, and then having debris tumbling out of the dissipating fireball may be sufficient to convey the feeling of an extremely powerful explosion.

## The Combustion Plug-in (Free Inside!)

Finally, there's another excellent way to produce explosion effects in 3D Studio MAX—use Rolf Berteig's freeware Combustion plug-in. Combustion is a volumetric plug-in that produces layered fog, smoke, flame, and explosion effects. This plug-in is included on the *3D Studio MAX f/x CD-ROM* in the \COMBUSTN directory.

For more information on how to use Combustion in your 3D Studio MAX scenes, see Appendix B, "Combustion: A Free Plug-in For 3D Studio MAX."

## Moving On

You've just come to the end of the space optical effects. In the next three chapters of "Part III: Modeling Effects," you'll see how to create nifty-looking planets and asteroids. By using bitmap textures and the Noise texture to create gaseous effects and cloud patterns, you can create worlds that your starships will be proud to orbit.

In the two chapters after that, you'll see how to create not just rocky-looking asteroids, but entire asteroid fields—and without using enormous numbers of 3D objects.

Shields up!

# Part III

# Modeling
# Effects

# 18

# Planets & Other Heavenly Bodies

**O**kay, enough pyrotechnic stuff. It's time to work on some effects that are a little more placid in nature.

When you viewed the space battle shots, you probably noticed a bright-orange, Mars-like planet in the background of a couple of shots. Like the physical sun object that you created in Chapter 10, "Here Comes the Sun, Part II," creating planets in 3D Studio MAX is very easy.

## Okay, But Where's the Turtle It Sits On?

In most earthly religions and mythologies, creating planets is a relatively large task for the deities involved. For you, however, it's simply a few mouse clicks away.

In the beginning of this book, you created the heavens. Now you'll create, if not the earth, then another planet suitable for some form of life. Ideally, this won't take you six days to do (but then again, you're not putting an entire menagerie on it, either).

1. In 3D Studio MAX, activate 2D Snap and create a Sphere with a radius of approximately 200 units in the center of the Top viewport. (You may want to enter the exact value in the Radius section of the Parameters rollout.) Change the Segments value from 16 to 60, and click in the Generate Mapping Coordinates check box to activate it. Finally, rename this object Planet.

2. Click on the Zoom Extents All button so that you can see the entire Planet object in all the viewports.

3. To make your Planet test renderings more realistic, load your standard starfield backdrop. Select Rendering\Environment, and from the \CHAP_18 directory, load the image STARS640.TGA and place it in Material Editor Slot #2. Go to the Material Editor and change it to a Screen Background rather than a Spherical Environment.

4. Now, click on Slot #1 to activate Material #1. You need to change these material settings to create your first planet material. Change the Ambient and Diffuse colors to pure black, or RGB settings 0, 0, 0. Change Shininess and Shininess Strength to 0.

    You'll want to give the planet a matte surface to keep it from looking like a plastic globe. When I was in high school in the mid '70s, I shot some planet special effects on Super-8 film for "Buck Cosmo, Space Ranger," the sci-fi "epic" mentioned in this book's introduction. The planets were rubber bounce balls spray-painted flat white, with 35mm slides of painted artwork projected on them. Even with flat paint, eliminating a specular hotspot on the "planets" was still difficult, although the effect was surprisingly convincing.

    (Don't laugh; in *2001: A Space Odyssey*, some of Jupiter's moons during the latter half of the film were created by projecting artwork onto matte white spheres. On the other hand, they probably weren't rubber bounce balls bought at K-Mart for $1.69.)

    With CGI, of course, you don't have this problem; you can just turn off the shininess component of a material.

5. Open the Maps rollout and click on the Diffuse Map name button. When the Material/Map browser appears, under Browse From, make sure that New is selected, and click on Bitmap. Under Bitmap parameters, click on the Bitmap name field. From the \CHAP_18 directory or the *3D Studio MAX f/x CD-ROM*, click once on the file ORN_MIST.TGA to highlight it, and click on View.

   **CD-ROM**

   I created this texture, a 1024 x 512 pixel .TGA image, by scanning a piece of orange marbleized paper. I then brought this 24-bit image into Adobe Photoshop, where I retouched it and combined it with a heavily retouched image of clouds at sunset. Finally, I used Photoshop's Offset filter (with Edge Wrapping activated) to modify the edges of the texture so that it would be tileable with no visible seams.

6. Close the View Image window and double-click on the ORN_MIST.TGA image to load it. When the image loads, click on the Go to Parent button to return to the top level of the Material Editor.

7. With the Planet object still selected, click on the Assign Material Selection button to assign the new planet material to the object. Change the name of this material to Planet 1. Minimize the Material Editor (but don't dismiss it).

## Let There Be Light (& a Targeted Camera)

Now you'll place a camera and a directional light in the scene.

1. Activate the Top viewport; then, press Shift+Z twice to zoom away from the Planet. Press the W key to enlarge the Top viewport to full screen. Now, create a targeted camera at approximate XYZ coordinates X 0, Y -800, Z 0 with the target at the center of the planet of the Planet.

2. Return to the Create Panel, click on Lights, and select Directional. Change the RGB settings to 255, 255, 255, or pure white. Change the Hotspot to 250, and click in the Show Cone checkbox to activate it. Scroll the Directional light rollout up and click on Cast Shadows to activate it.

3. Move the cursor to approximate XYZ coordinates X –600, Y –600, Z 0, and click to place the Directional light.

4. Press the W key again to return to four viewports and click on the Zoom Extents All button. Right-click in the Left viewport to activate it and then right-click on the selected Directional light. Make sure that Move is selected and then drag the light upward on the Y axis to Y 600.

5. Click on the Zoom Extents All button again; then, activate the Front viewport, right-click on the Directional light, and select Rotate. Rotate the light on its Z axis approximately 50 degrees, activate the Top viewport, and rotate the light again, on the Z axis approximately 45 degrees. Click on the Zoom Extents All button again. The screen should look like Figure 18-1.

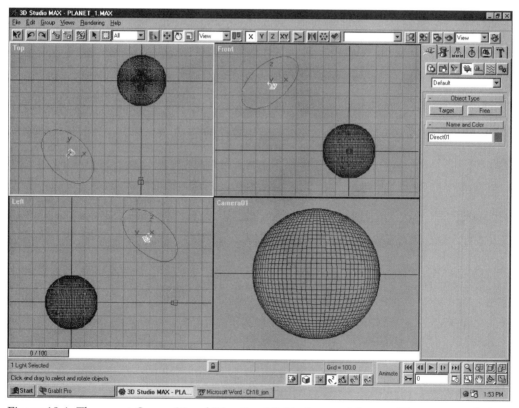

Figure 18-1: *The correct Camera01 and Directional light placement for your Planet test rendering.*

6. Now you'll render a test image. Activate the Camera01 viewport; then, press Alt+R and Enter to render a 640 x 480 still, as shown in Figure 18-2.

Figure 18-2: *A test rendering of a basic planet texture.*

Figure 18-2 represents a Mars-type planet covered in wispy clouds. For long to medium shots, this texture is sufficient to convey the image of a realistic planetary surface.

7. When you've finished viewing the image, close the VFB.

The scene that you have just created is in the \CHAP_18 directory as PLANET_1.MAX.

**Note:** *The \MAPS directory of the* 3D Studio MAX f/x CD-ROM *has several variations of this texture, including some additional planet textures with clouds that you may want to use in your own space scenes. You'll play with variations of this original orange planet texture in a moment.*

## Getting Closer

Now you can see what this planet looks like close up.

1. Activate the Top viewport, turn off 2D Snap, select the Camera01 body, and drag it to approximate XYZ coordinates X –150, Y 550, and Z 0.

2. Activate the Left viewport and drag Camera01 to approximate XYZ coordinates X 0, Y 175, and Z 0. Now, click on the Camera01 Target (you can either use the Select by Name menu or click several times on the Target to let 3D Studio MAX cycle through the objects located there). Drag the Camera01 Target upward on the Y axis to approximately Y 150. Activate the Top viewport and drag the Target to the left along the X axis to approximately X -150. When you've finished, the screen should look something like Figure 18-3.

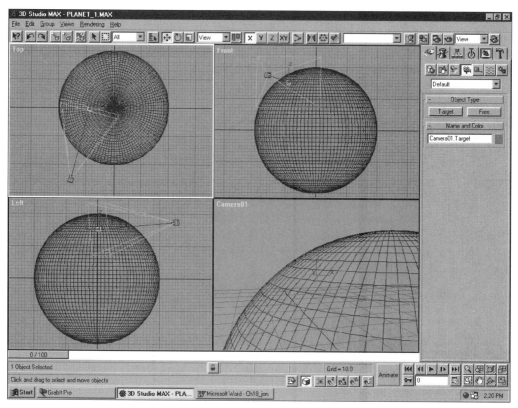

Figure 18-3: *The proper placement for the close-up Planet rendering.*

For best results, you'll need to increase the segment count on your Planet object.

3. Click on the Planet to select it; then, in the Modify Panel, increase the Segments value from 60 to 100. This increased complexity will ensure a smooth silhouette at this close camera range.

4. Activate the Camera01 viewport again, and press Alt+R and Enter to render a close-up image. After a few moments, the new rendering appears, as shown in Figure 18-4.

Figure 18-4: *A close-up rendering of the Planet using the ORN_MIST.TGA texture.*

## Toiling on Tiling

Although this texture may be suitable for long shots and medium shots, for close-ups it seems a little fuzzy. This is caused both by the 3D Studio MAX renderer's texture filtering and the inherent quality of the original texture map used on this object. You can do a couple of things to correct this.

One, obviously, is to increase the resolution of the original texture map applied to the planet object. The other thing, however, is to simply increase the tiling of the texture on the object. If you are merely going to be rendering a close-up of a planet surface, you can probably get away with tiling the texture, especially if the texture has no visible seams like your ORN_MIST.TGA texture here.

Return to the Material Editor and change the tiling of this Planet texture.

1. Close the Camera01 VFB and return to the Material Editor. Go down to the Map slot of the Planet 1 texture and click on the Diffuse map name button to go to this level of the material. On the Coordinates rollout, change both U and V Tiling from 1.0 to 2.0. The ORN_MIST.TGA texture changes visibly on the sample sphere in Slot #1. Click on the Go to Parent button to return to the top material level.

   Again, because this material is "hot" in the scene on the Sphere01 Planet object, you don't need to click on the Assign Material Selection button again. The changes you've made to the texture map tiling have already been updated on the Planet object.

2. Activate the Camera01 viewport again and render another view of this close-up planet image. After a moment, the image will appear as shown in Figure 18-5.

Figure 18-5: *The Planet object with the ORN_MIST.TGA texture tiled twice across the U and V mapping coordinates.*

Now you can see how increasing the texture tiling on the Planet has shrunk the size of the detail (and increased the apparent level of detail) on the Planet's surface. You can now see, more distinctly, the dark, canal-like detail that gives this planet its Mars-like quality.

## Bumping Up the Detail

Now, you may still want to increase the apparent level of detail on your Planet object. Obviously, you can simply return to the Material Editor and increase your texture tiling even further.

However, another way to increase the apparent level of detail on this Planet is to use a Bump map. In the following steps, you're going to load a bitmap into the Bump map slot to increase the apparent amount of surface relief visible on the planet surface.

1. Close the Camera01 VFB window and return to the Material Editor. On the Maps rollout, click on the Bump map name button to bring up the Material/Map browser. Make sure that New is selected from the Browse From section and then double-click on Bitmap in the list window. When the Bitmap rollout appears, click on the Bitmap name button to bring up the Select Texture Image File browser.

2. From the \CHAP_18 directory, click on the file ORNPLNTS.TGA to highlight it and then click on the View button. When the image appears, you'll see that it's a variation of your original orange planet texture.

   This started out as a scan of the marbleized paper used for the ORN_MIST.TGA texture; however, I altered it further in Photoshop to add greater detail; for this example, you don't need to tile it. In addition, I have omitted the cloud patterns on this image. This bitmap, like ORN_MIST.TGA, is a 1024 x 512 resolution, seamless texture map designed for spherical mapping.

3. Close the View Image window and click on the ORNPLNTS.TGA texture to load it into the Material Editor. When you do, notice that the material sphere in Slot #1 has changed to show a slight amount of surface relief provided by this new Bump map. At this scale, it's not yet too noticeable.

4. Click on the Go to Parent button to return to the main Material Editor rollout. Activate the Camera01 viewport and render a new version of the close-up Planet image.

   Notice how, on the screen, the ORNPLNTS.TGA Bump map creates slight surface relief on the Planet object.

5. When you've finished viewing the image, close the Camera01 VFB window.

   The scene you've just created is in the \CHAP_18 directory as PLANET_2.MAX.

## Rising Above It All

The level of detail shown in this latest Planet rendering may be sufficient for animation or animated video sequences. However, for high-resolution still images, you may want to increase the detail further.

To do this, you can reduce the Bump map setting so that the surface relief is not quite so pronounced and then increase the UV Tiling to provide finer detail. Of course, you can experiment with other Bump map images or change the Bump map Output settings to soften the effect.

One drawback of placing a Bump map on this Planet surface is that the ORN_MIST.TGA cloud patterns now seem to be part of the actual Planet landscape instead of looking like faint wispy clouds above the surface. However, you don't need to sacrifice surface relief for the sake of creating realistic clouds on your Planet surfaces. In fact, you don't necessarily have to have the clouds painted on your original planet texture maps at all.

You can create a Planet surface using texture maps, and then build the clouds as a separate layer using 3D Studio MAX's Noise effects in the Material Editor. In addition, you can make the clouds appear to move across the surface of the planet, and even cast shadows on its surface.

The next section shows you how you do it.

## Creating Cloud Effects With Noise

Before you create the Noise cloud effect, you'll need to change the texture on your existing Planet object so that you can more easily see the clouds.

1. Return to the Material Editor and go to the Maps section. The file ORNPLNTS.TGA is now loaded in the Bump map slot. Drag it up to the Diffuse map slot to replace the ORN_MIST.TGA bitmap. Click on Copy and then OK to copy the file. This will be your new Planet surface texture.

In a moment, you'll create a new texture for the clouds, but first you need to build another sphere object on which you'll map the cloud material. You'll do that by Shift-cloning the current Planet.

2. Activate the Front viewport and then enlarge the Front viewport to full screen. (The next few steps will be easier if you minimize the Material Editor first.)

3. Click on the Select and Uniform Scale button; then, in the Front viewport, click on the Planet object to select it. Now, holding down the Shift key, click and drag on the Planet object to scale it outwards to XYZ percentages X 101, Y 101, and Z 101. When you release the mouse button, change the name of the object to Atmosphere and then click on OK. It should be a copy of the Planet, of course, rather than an instance or reference.

   You now have two concentric spheres, and you may be thinking that, because the outer Atmosphere object is surrounding the Planet, you should turn off its Shadow Casting and Shadow Receiving properties. Ordinarily, you would. However, in a few moments, you're going to change your Directional light from using Shadow Maps to using Ray-Tracing. This allows the Opacity maps that you'll be using for the cloud texture to actually cast shadows on the Planet surface.

4. Return to the four viewports and activate the Camera01 viewport again. Now, restore the Material Editor. Because you created a copy of your original Planet object, the Atmosphere object also has a copy of the Planet 1 texture on it. You're going to build a new material to create the cloud effect.

5. Click in Slot #3 to make it active. Change both Ambient and Diffuse to pure black, or RGB 0, 0, 0. Change Shininess and Shininess Strength to 0. This creates a matte black object. Now, open the Extended Parameters section. Change Falloff to Out, change Amount to 100, and Under Opacity Type, click on Additive.

6. Open the Maps rollout and click on the Diffuse map name button to bring up the Material/Map browser. Under Browse From, make sure that New is still selected, and click on Noise. In the Noise material level, go to the Coordinates rollout.

Change Coordinates from XYZ to UVW. Under Tiling, change U to 2.0, change V to 6.0, and W to 0.0. Under Noise Parameters, change Noise Type to Fractal, and change Size from 25.0 to 0.1. Under Noise Threshold, leave High at 1.0, but change Low from 0.0 to 0.35.

7. Finally, open the Output rollout and change Output Amount from 1.0 to 2.0. This will make the clouds brighter in the scene.

8. Click on the Go to Parent button to return to the top material level, and drag the Noise texture from the Diffuse map slot down to the Opacity map slot. Under Copy Method, click on Instance; then, click on OK to accept these changes. In Slot #3, you should see that the sample sphere now has what looks like a cloud pattern. In addition, by copying the Noise texture down to the Opacity map slot, you have created a transparent sphere that is revealed only by the cloud patterns placed upon it.

9. Change the name of this material to Clouds Noise, and click on the Assign Material to Selection button in the Material Editor to assign this new material to Atmosphere.

 This material is included in the 3DMAXFX.MAT Material Library.

10. When you've finished, close the Material Editor.
Now you'll move the Directional light to a better position.

11. Click on the Zoom Extents All button; then, in the Top viewport, move the Directional light upward on the Y axis to approximate XYZ coordinates X 0, Y 600, Z 0. Right-click on it again and select Rotate. Rotate it on its Z axis –45 degrees.

12. Activate the Camera01 viewport and render another test image of the Planet with the new Clouds Noise material. After a few minutes, the rendering appears; when it does, it should resemble Figure 18-6.

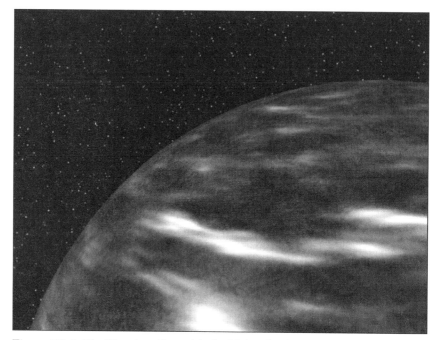

Figure 18-6: *The Planet surface with the Noise cloud material applied to the Atmosphere object.*

13. When you've finished viewing the image, close the Camera01 VFB.

This scene is included in the \CHAP_18 directory as PLANET_3.MAX.

## Partly Cloudy, Slight Chance of Meteor Showers

As you examine the rendering on the screen, notice how the Noise material on the Atmosphere object provides soft, wispy clouds, apparently over the surface of the planet.

If you want to change the density of the clouds, there are several things you can do. One is to return to the Material Editor and increase the Noise Threshold of the clouds (try changing it from 0.35 to 0.5). However, this also decreases the apparent size of the clouds, so you may want to increase the Tiling of the Clouds Noise texture also.

Now you'll see what you can do to make the clouds "pop out" more from the Planet surface. If you change your Directional light shadow parameters from using Shadow Maps to using Ray-Traced Shadows, you can make the opaque parts of Opacity maps cast shadows on other objects.

1. Select Light01; then, in the Modify Panel, go down to the Shadow Parameters rollout. Make sure that Cast Shadows is on, and click on Cast Ray-Traced Shadows to activate it.

2. Activate the Camera01 viewport and render another test image of the Planet with the new Clouds Noise material. (Using Ray-Traced lights and Opacity maps in the scene increases the rendering time noticeably. At 640 x 480 resolution, this image may take a few minutes to render on a Pentium 90.)

   When the image appears, it should resemble Figure 18-7.

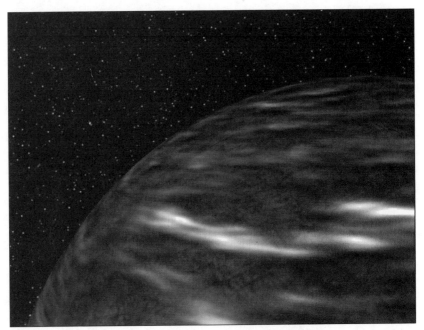

Figure 18-7: *Using Ray-Traced shadows enables the Opacity-mapped clouds to cast shadows on the Planet object.*

3. When you've finished viewing the image, close the Camera01 VFB.

## Blowin' in the Wind

Although it may increase the rendering time, using 3D Studio MAX's Noise to create Opacity-mapped clouds can produce striking effects. By animating the Tiling and/or Phase values of the Noise texture, you can make the clouds appear to crawl across the Planet surface. This can provide greater realism for your space animation sequences.

Here's a quick way to set up the cloud animation. All you have to do is change the UVW offset of the Clouds Noise texture.

1. Click on the Animate button to toggle animation mode on; and then move to frame 100.

2. Open the Material Editor and click on the Diffuse map name button to go to the Noise rollout. Under UVW Offset, change U from 0.0 to -0.1, change Phase from 0.0 to 1.0, and press Enter to accept these changes.

3. Click on the Animate button again to toggle Animate mode off; then, drag the Time Slider back to frame 0. As you do, you should see the Clouds Noise texture on the sample sphere change.

   Now you'll take a look at a demonstration .AVI of this animated Noise parameter.

4. Select File/View File, and from the \CHAP_18 directory, click on the file PLANET_4.AVI. When the Media Player appears, click on the Play button.

   As the .AVI file shows, increasing the V Offset just a slight amount during a 100-frame animation creates the illusion of rolling clouds over a rotating planet surface.

5. When you've finished viewing the animation, close the Media Player.

This file, with the animated cloud parameters, is saved in the \CHAP_18 directory as PLANET_4.MAX.

## Creating Planet Textures With Noise

Now that you've seen how to create moving clouds over your planet using the Noise texture, you'll see how you can use the Noise texture to create a planet surface as well.

To better see the effects of the Noise texture on your Planet surface, you're going to hide the Atmosphere object.

1. Click on the Select by Name button, then pick Atmosphere from the list and click on Select. Click on the Display tab of the Command Panel and click on Hide Selected to hide the cloud object.

2. Now, to speed up your rendering, you'll change your Directional light back to using shadow maps rather than Ray-Traced shadows. Click on the Directional light in any of the viewports to highlight it, and click on the Modify tab of the Command Panel. Under Shadow Parameters, click on Use Shadow Maps.

3. Now, return to the Material Editor. You'll want to change the texture on your Planet object, so click on Slot #1 to make it active. Go to the Maps section and click on the Diffuse map name button to go to the Bitmap Parameters rollout. You need to change the Diffuse map type from Bitmap to Noise. Next to Type, click on the word Bitmap to bring up the Material/Map browser. Under Browse From, click on New and then Noise. When the Replace Map dialog box appears, click on OK to discard the old texture map.

   Now you need to change the Noise settings.

4. Under Coordinates, change from XYZ to UVW Coordinate mapping. Under UVW tiling, change the U tiling to 2.0, change the V tiling to 8.0, and keep the W tiling at 1.0. Under Noise Parameters, change Noise Type to Fractal rather than Regular. Leave the Noise Threshold as it is but change Size to 0.1. Press Enter to accept these changes.

5. Go to the Color #1 and Color #2 color swatches. Click on Color #1 to bring up the Color Selector. You want to change this from black to a reddish brown, so change the RGB settings to 216, 58, 27. Click on the Color #2 slot and change the white color

setting to RGB settings 234, 196, 34. When you're finished, close the Color Selector and click on the Go to Parent button in the Material Editor to return to the top material level.

6. Go to the Maps section and click on the Bump map name button. When the Bump map rollout appears, change UV Tiling for both U and V from 1.0 to 2.0, and press Enter. This will increase the Bump map detail created by the ORNPLNTS.TGA bitmap. Click on the Go to Parent button to return to the main Material Editor screen.

7. Now you'll preview this new texture. Activate the Camera01 viewport and render another test image. After a few moments, the image appears; it should look like Figure 18-8.

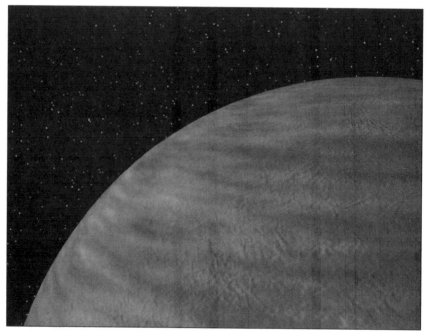

Figure 18-8: *The procedural Noise texture used as the primary Planet texture.*

Take a look at this rendering. By changing the UV Tiling so that the V value is four times that of U, you've smeared the texture around the Planet's equator. This makes it look something like Jupiter with bands of colorful gas wrapping around its circumference. In addition, by doubling the tiling of the Bump map, you produce subtle relief features that resemble canyon ridges and valleys on the Planet surface.

Again, as you've seen in the previous chapters, you could modify this effect in many ways. You could create a series of nested concentric spheres, each with a different Noise texture applied, at varying levels of opacity. Opacity on the innermost sphere would be set at 100 percent; as you worked your way out, the opacity level on each sphere would diminish. This would create planet textures of extreme depth. By applying different Noise textures onto these spheres, with varying colors, you could create very elaborate worlds resembling the gas giants Jupiter or Saturn.

In addition, by varying the Noise settings on each one of the spheres (as you saw in the moving cloud animation), you could even create the illusion of a fast-moving, turbulent atmosphere.

The texture you've just created is in the 3DSMAXFX.MAT Material Library as Planet Noise. In addition, this scene file is in the \CHAP_18 directory as PLANET_5.MAX.

8. When you've finished viewing the image, close the Camera01 VFB.

## Moving On

For your own planet textures, you should experiment with a variety of different materials and bitmaps. For instance, scanned photographs of stone formations, such as sandstone and granite, or other natural phenomena such as cracked earth, mud, or marble patterns, can produce interesting-looking planet textures. You can also take digitized photographs of the Earth and manipulate them in Photoshop. If you cut and paste various elements, such as continents or cloud patterns, you can create entirely new earth-like worlds ("Class-M planets," in "Star Trek" parlance).

Now, speaking of rocky textures, you're going to be experimenting with quite a few of them in your next two chapters. Coming up: how you can create not just a single asteroid, but an entire asteroid field, at costs far less than what your parents paid 20 years ago.

# 19

# Space Rubble: Creating Asteroids

In the opening shot of the five space battle scenes, the camera is on the periphery of an asteroid field. As it pans and tilts across the spacescape, numerous asteroids tumble slowly in their long, lonely orbits. Behind these, clusters of other asteroids recede in the distance. A few seconds later, the battlecruiser emerges from warp drive.

Although hundreds of asteroids may seem to be in this scene, only about 70 actual asteroid objects are really there. To produce the impression of thousands of asteroids, I created "real" 3D mesh asteroids for the foreground, and applied rendered asteroid images to distant Quad Patches, using Diffuse and Opacity maps. In addition, after I created and texture mapped the initial asteroid meshes, I duplicated many of them as Instance objects. This helps keep the overall face count down, thus speeding up the rendering.

Creating the appearance of hundreds or even thousands of asteroids—or an entire asteroid belt—in your space scenes is easier than you may think, if you use these techniques.

Now you'll see how you can create these effects. You'll start off with one asteroid and then see how to propagate it into a dense field worthy of *The Empire Strikes Back*.

## Stacking on the Modifiers

In Chapters 6, "Nebulas Made Simple, Part I," and Chapter 7, "Nebulas Made Simple, Part II," you saw how you could use 3D Studio MAX's object modifiers to distort the surface of a sphere to create a nebula object. After you had subtly distorted the sphere, you applied a glassy material and placed Omni lights inside; the Specular Highlights on the distorted surfaces of the sphere created the illusion of nebulous gas clouds.

For this tutorial, you're going to build an asteroid by applying a number of the Edit Mesh modifiers to a simple sphere. By stacking these modifiers one on top of the other and examining the cumulative results, you can see how to take very simple geometry and turn it into a complex organic shape, such as a rocky asteroid surface.

Here's how to do it.

1. In the Top viewport, create a sphere in the center with a radius of approximately 100 units. Decrease the number of Segments from 16 to 8; then, click on the Generate Mapping Coordinates field to activate that field. Finally, change the object name from Sphere01 to Asteroid.

   Now, you'll want to distort the surface of this basic asteroid object. If you want, you can create an irregularly shaped asteroid by applying an Edit Mesh modifier, selecting individual vertices, and pulling them into different positions manually. You can rough out your asteroid shape that way, and then tessellate the surface to smooth it out.

   Although the general idea is fine, you don't need to go to all this trouble. You can distort the Asteroid's vertex positions very quickly by using an Edit Mesh modifier on the vertices but then using a Noise modifier to distort their positions. You'll then apply additional modifiers to produce the detail you need.

   First, you'll select all the vertices.

2. Add an Edit Mesh modifier to the Asteroid. In the Selection Level section of the Edit Mesh rollout, the default is Sub-Object: Vertex.

3. Click on the Zoom Extents All button to center the Asteroid object in all of the viewports. In any viewport, drag a Select

bounding box around the entire Asteroid object. Its vertices turn red, indicating that they're selected.

Now it's time to add the next item to the stack.

4. From the Modifiers Panel, click on Noise. When you do, the Noise rollout appears, and an orange bounding box representing the Noise Gizmo appears around the Asteroid object. Under Noise Parameters, leave Seed and Scale at their default settings of 0 and 100, respectively. Click on the Fractal button to activate it. Under Strength, change X to 35, Y to 50, and Z to 75. Press Enter to accept these settings.

As you can see, the Noise Gizmo distorts the selected vertices of the Asteroid object, using these XYZ coordinate distortion settings; the screen should look something like 19-1.

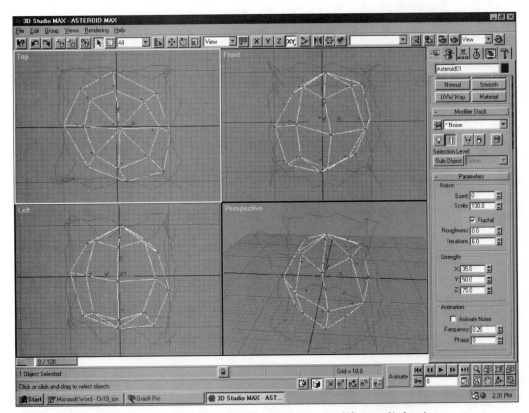

Figure 19-1: *The basic Asteroid object with the first Noise modifier applied to it.*

## A Flagrant Distortion of Reality

At this point, you've distorted your basic sphere Asteroid object, but it doesn't look much like an asteroid. Instead, it looks like an irregularly shaped piece of crystal. So, you need to keep going and apply some more distortion to its surface.

1. Return to the Modifier Panel and click again on Edit Mesh. Once again, the Edit Mesh rollout appears. Under Selection Level, change the Sub-Object from Vertex to Face. In the Top viewport, drag a bounding box around the entire Asteroid object to select all the faces. As you do so, the entire Asteroid object turns red.

**Note:** *Every time you change the Sub-Object selection—even in the same Edit Mesh Modifier—you must choose a selection set of Sub-Objects to which to apply the modifier.*

2. Scroll the Edit Mesh rollout up until you see the Tessellation section. By applying a Tessellation modifier to the Asteroid, you can smooth out its blocky contours by creating more faces. You can then further distort them. Leave the Tessellation settings at their defaults and click on the Tessellate button once. As you do, the rough contours of the Asteroid smooth out; the object also becomes more complex, as shown in Figure 19-2.

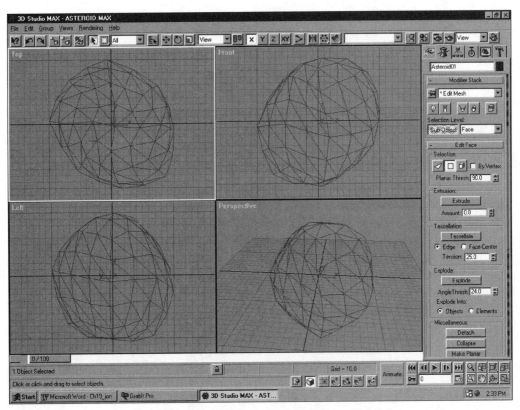

Figure 19-2: *The Asteroid object with one level of tessellation applied to it.*

You now have a simple, roughly spherical asteroid that might be suitable for long shots. However, because of the relatively low number of faces on the Asteroid, you need to increase its complexity further, particularly if it's going to be in a close-up.

At this point, you have several different options. You can apply additional levels of Tessellation to further smooth the surface of the object, you can apply another level of Noise, or you can do a combination of the two.

That sounds best, so you'll do both.

3. Return to the Modifiers Panel and click on Noise again. This applies another Noise modifier to the Asteroid object, and you can see that Noise has been added to the top of the modifier stack. Now, under Noise Parameters, click on Fractal to activate it. Change Roughness to 0.25 and press Enter to accept these changes. This applies another layer of surface distortion to the Asteroid object. Under Strength, change X to 25, Y to 35, and Z to 50. When you do so, the Asteroid surface is distorted even further, and it should appear something like Figure 19-3.

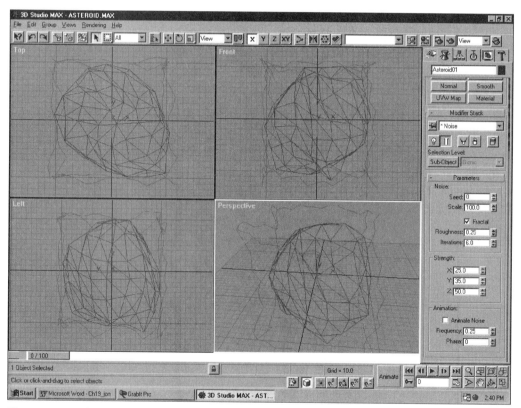

Figure 19-3: *The Asteroid object with another level of Noise applied to its faces.*

Now you've made your Asteroid look less like a cobblestone and a little more like a jagged hunk of rock. However, you should still increase the overall face count to make the object more suitable for close-up rendering.

4. Add a third Edit Mesh modifier to the Asteroid. Change the Sub-Object selection to Face and tessellate the Asteroid again. This again smoothes the contours of the Asteroid and adds face complexity to it, as shown in Figure 19-4.

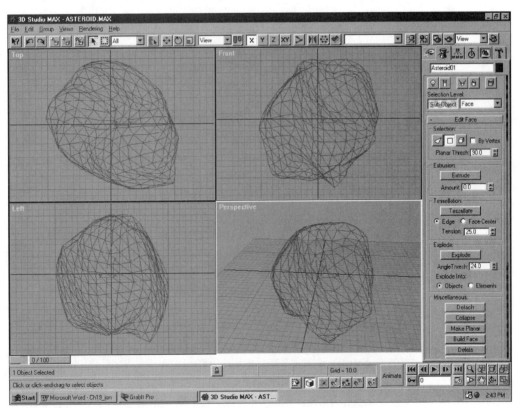

Figure 19-4: *A second level of tessellation applied to the Asteroid object.*

## Bumps & Hollows

At this point you have a fairly decent-looking asteroid, at least for medium shots. However, for close-ups you may still want to increase the complexity of its surface. So, you'll continue adding modifiers to this object and see how it changes the topology of the Asteroid.

1. In the Edit Mesh Panel, click again on the Tessellate button. This further smoothes the Asteroid surface and subdivides its faces. Scroll back up to the Modifiers Panel and click on Displace. (Again, if Displace is not part of the default modifier settings, click the More button and pick Displace from the Modifiers list.) When you do so, the Displace rollout appears and an orange UVW Mapping Gizmo, representing a planar map, appears in the viewports.

   The Displace object modifier enables you to distort the topology of a 3D Studio MAX object by using the luminance values of a bitmap; it applies the distortion to the object using the standard UVW mapping coordinate types.

2. Under the Parameters section of the Display rollout, click on the Name button under Image to bring up the Select Displacement Image browser. From the \CHAP_19 directory of the *3D Studio MAX f/x CD-ROM*, click on the file DISPLACE.GIF to highlight it; then, click on View.

   The DISPLACE.GIF image is a 320 x 160 resolution, grayscale bitmap. I created this simple texture in Autodesk Animator Pro to be used specifically as a Spherical displacement map. Its high contrast enables you to create the illusion of pockmarks, hills, and valleys on your asteroid surface.

3. Click on OK to load the DISPLACE.GIF image into the Displacement rollout. Under Map, click on Spherical. Go back up to the Displacement: Strength section under Parameters, change from 0.0 to 25, and press Enter. Now you will see the tessellated Asteroid surface take on a much more craggy and rocky appearance, as shown in Figure 19-5.

CD-ROM

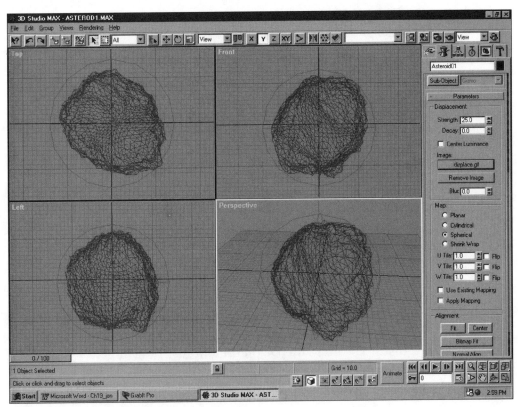

Figure 19-5: *The asteroid object with a Displacement map applied to it.*

As you can see in Figure 19-5, the high-contrast displacement map that you applied to the Asteroid results in a craggy, rocky object. The higher luminance values of the bitmap produce bumps and hills on the rocky surface, whereas the darker areas of the bitmap push down the surface to create pockmarks and valleys.

**Note:** *Displacement mapping is a versatile modeling tool. For example, you can create the illusion of extruded text in a high-resolution Quad Patch. Simply apply a Displace modifier (loaded with a text bitmap) to the object and then set Strength to the appropriate level. If the bitmap consists of a black background with the word "MAX" printed on it in white, you can create the effect of "MAX" extruding from the surface of the object. If you enter a negative Strength value, you make it appear as if "MAX" is carved into the Quad Patch object.*

## Rolling With the Changes

Now, if you want to modify the effect that this Displacement map has on the Asteroid, you don't have to use a different texture. By changing the relationship of the Displacement Mapping Gizmo applied to the 3D object, you change how the Displacement affects the object's surface.

You're going to check out this effect, but first you need to hold your current settings.

1. Select Edit and then click on Hold. This holds the current 3D Studio MAX settings in the Hold buffer. Now, from the Displace rollout of the Modify Panel, under Selection Level: Sub-Object, click on Sub-Object to activate the Displacement Mapping Gizmo. The Gizmo changes from orange to yellow.

   In the Left viewport, you can see that one side of the Gizmo—the left side—is still orange. This represents the back of the spherical mapping coordinates. However, because the DISPLACE.GIF image is a seamless texture, you won't see a distinct seam in the Displacement mapping effect as you alter its position relative to your object.

2. Click on the Select and Rotate button; then, in any of the viewports, move the cursor over the Displacement Mapping Gizmo, and click and drag to rotate the Gizmo. As you do, the surface of the Asteroid object distorts. Click in any other viewport and continue rotating the Gizmo to examine the effect.

   You can alter the Distortion effect drastically on the Asteroid simply by rotating the Displacement Mapping Gizmo. You can also animate the translation, rotation, and scale of the Gizmo, creating very unusual effects, but it wouldn't look much like a dead hunk of rock, of course. By animating the Gizmo relative to the 3D object upon which it's applied, you can create the illusion of an undulating object surface. You can also create a specific distortion effect appearing across the surface of the object, and then disappearing, as you move the Gizmo around on the surface of the object, or literally off the object altogether.

Of course, you could also apply a series of bitmaps or an animation file as a Displacement map to an object. If you had an animation, for instance, of a white line tracing itself across a dark background, and applied that to a complex Quad Patch as a Displacement map, you could create the effect of a snake crawling beneath a carpet. (Why you would necessarily *want* to animate something this, um, Freudian, is a question that you'll have to ask yourself.)

Nevertheless, Displacement mapping is a powerful modeling tool. If you liked the specific asteroid object that you created by rotating the Gizmo, then you might want to save it to your own 3DSMAX\SCENES directory.

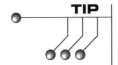

**TIP** Any time that you want to save an object or group of objects separately from the scene they're in, simply select them and use Save/Selected.

3. When you've finished playing with the Modifier, select Edit/Fetch from the menu bar and click on Yes to restore the Asteroid object to its earlier form.

4. Now, click again on the Asteroid object to select it and then return to the Modifiers Panel and click on the various mapping types, such as Planar, Cylindrical, and Shrinkwrap, to examine how the application of these different mapping types changes the surface of the Asteroid object. When you've finished, click again on Spherical to restore the asteroid to its previous settings.

## Step by Step, Inch by Inch...

Although it seems as if you've taken a great number of steps to get to this point of creating an asteroid, there is a reason that you've done all this work. By employing all these steps, you've explored a number of 3D Studio MAX's Object modifiers and their cumulative effects. You can apply as many of these modifiers as necessary (and as your PC resources can handle) to create the effect you want. Just keep adding or popping them off the stack as necessary.

Now you'll see how this effect works.

1. Go back to the Modifier rollout. Displace is at the top of the Modifier stack. Click the Down arrow to the right of Displace; the entire Modifier Stack appears. You now see the history of all the changes you're applied to the Asteroid object, and the order in which they occurred.

   Remember, however, that you haven't permanently distorted the Asteroid object itself. You haven't modified the object; you've applied modifiers *to* it. You can also just as easily (actually, more easily) remove those modifiers.

2. Click again on the Down arrow to close the Modifier stack, and click on the Remove Modifier from Stack button. The Displacement Mapping button and the Displacement map itself are removed from the Asteroid, and it returns to an earlier, smoother configuration.

   If you go through the Modify Stack and delete all the modifiers, eventually you return to the original 100-unit Radius, 8-segment sphere that you created at the beginning of this tutorial. Don't worry about losing the changes, though; although you can't undo these specific actions, you can do a Fetch to return to your distorted Asteroid object.

3. Select Edit/Fetch and then click on Yes to bring back the Asteroid.

## Render That Rock!

Now it's time to set up your asteroid scene for rendering.

1. Activate the Top viewport and press Shift+Z twice to zoom away from the Asteroid object. Now, create a Target Camera at approximate XYZ coordinates X 0, Y 550, and Z 0. Place the target in the center of the Asteroid.

2. Place a Target Spot in the Top viewport at approximate XYZ coordinates X -500, Y -500, and Z 0; place the target in the center of the Asteroid. Change the value from 180 to 255 to make a pure white spotlight; activate Cast Shadows.

3. Now you'll change the spotlight parameters to narrow the cone of light from it. In the Spotlight rollout, change Falloff to approximately 25. Click on the Zoom Extents All button, activate the Left viewport, and move the spotlight up its Y axis to approximately Y 500.

4. Activate the Perspective viewport and assign the Camera01 view to it. The spotlight shines down on the Asteroid at a 45-degree angle from the upper-left side of the screen down to the lower right.

5. Select the Asteroid object so that you can create and assign an Asteroid texture to it in preparation for a test rendering.

6. First, you'll load the standard starfield background and place it in Material Editor Slot #2. (Review Chapter 4, "Starlight, Star-bright, Part I," and Chapter 9, "Here Comes the Sun, Part I," for instructions on how to do this.) You'll modify Material #1 to create your Asteroid texture.

7. In the Material Editor, click on the sample sphere in Slot #1 to activate it. Change the Ambient and Diffuse color settings to pure black, or 0, 0, 0, and reduce Shininess and Shininess Strength to 0. As with the Planet in the last chapter, you want the Asteroid to be a totally matte object.

8. Go down to the Maps rollout and open it; then, click on the Diffuse map name button. When the Material/Map browser appears, make sure that New is selected under Browse From and then click on Bitmap. When the Bitmap rollout appears, click on Bitmap name button. From the \CHAP_19 directory, click on the file ASTEROD1.TGA to highlight it and then click on View.

**CD-ROM**

The ASTEROD1.TGA texture is an 800 x 400 resolution image that I created by combining several scanned photographs. One photograph depicted the side of a cliff showing a complex rocky texture; the other photos showed cracked mud and a rocky, pebbly surface. I brought these textures into Adobe Photoshop, layered them together, and made them seamlessly tileable using the Offset filter.

9. If you would like to see some alternative rocky texture maps, view the remaining ASTEROD textures.

   ❋ ASTEROD2.TGA is the original rock surface used in the previous texture, but without the cracked mud texture added to it.

   ❋ ASTEROD3.TGA is a variation of the ASTEROD2.TGA texture, but with higher contrast and a slightly darker palette.

   ❋ ASTEROD4.TGA texture is a variation of the first asteroid texture. Again, the palette on this one has been changed and composited with several other rocky images to present a more granular appearance.

   ❋ ASTEROD5.TGA is a variation of the previous ASTEROD4.TGA texture, but with a slightly different palette.

   ❋ ASTEROD6.TGA returns to a striated rocky face and is darker in texture than the previous asteroid images.

   ❋ ASTEROD7.TGA is an even more complex variant of the ASTEROD6.TGA image.

   ❋ ASTEROD8.TGA is a largely blue/gray rocky surface with very few earth tones.

   ❋ ASTEROD9.TGA is a lighter version of ASTEROD2.TGA; this texture is used on the asteroids in the space battle scenes.

   All these texture are 800 x 400 resolution, designed for Spherical texture mapping, and all are seamlessly tileable.

10. When you've finished viewing these textures, close the View Image window and load the original ASTEROD1.TGA bitmap.

11. In the Material Editor, click on the Go to Parent button; then, in the Maps section, drag the ASTEROD1.TGA texture from the Diffuse Bitmap slot down to the Bump map slot. Click on Instance rather than Copy; then, click on OK. Increase the

Bump map amount from 30 to 50. With the Asteroid object still selected, click on the Assign Material to Selection button to assign your new asteroid material to the Asteroid object.

12. Now, finally, it's time to do a test rendering of the Asteroid. Activate the Camera01 viewport; press Alt+R and Enter to render a 640 x 480 resolution image. After a few moments, the image appears and should look something like Figure 19-6.

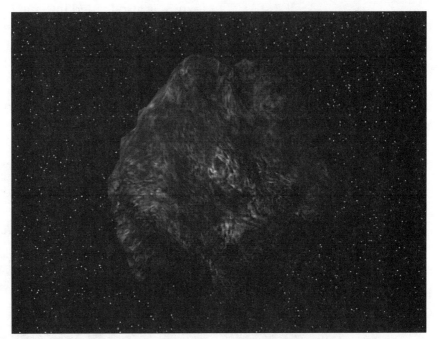

Figure 19-6: *The Asteroid object with a rocky asteroid texture applied to it.*

After considerable work applying Object Modifiers such as Edit Mesh, Noise, and Displace, and applying a "crunchy" bitmap, you've created a pretty believable asteroid—at least, one that has not gone through the "heat-treating" of an Earth reentry. First, applying multiple layers of Object Modifiers such as Noise, Tessellation, and Displacement mapping distorted your original low-res sphere; then, by using a Bump map, you created even greater detail on the Asteroid surface.

Now you'll change your asteroid material once again and re-render the Camera viewport.

13. Return to the Material Editor; then, under the Maps section, click on the Diffuse map name button to bring up the Bitmap Parameters rollout. Click on the ASTEROD1.TGA name, and from the \CHAP_19 directory, load the file ASTEROD2.TGA. You see the sample sphere in Slot #1 change from brown tones to a blue/gray texture. Click on the Go to Parent button to return to the top material level.

    If you look under the Maps section, you'll see that the ASTEROD2.TGA texture is also loaded into the Bump map slot. When you first copied the Diffuse map to the Bump map slot, you made it an Instance rather than a copy. Therefore, any change that you make in the Diffuse map slot will also update the Bump map slot.

14. Activate the Camera01 viewport again and render another test image; it should look something like Figure 19-7.

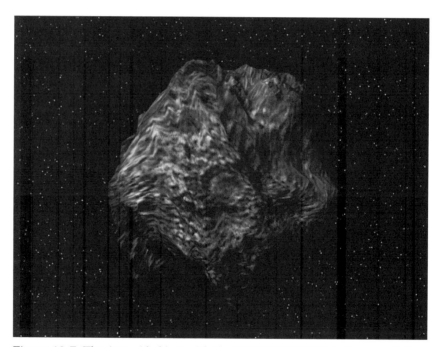

Figure 19-7: *The Asteroid object with the ASTEROD2.TGA texture applied to it. The lighter tones of the texture make the asteroid look more like a chunk of lunar rock.*

15. When you've finished viewing the image, close the Camera01
    VFB window.

The asteroid textures you've just created are in the
3DSMAXFX.MAT Material Library as Asteroid 1 and Asteroid 2.
In addition, the scene that you've just created is in the \CHAP_19
directory as ASTEROD1.MAX.

## Collapsing the Asteroid Modifier Stack

By now, you should be very familiar with 3D Studio MAX's Object
Modifiers such as Edit Mesh, Noise, and Displace. (And if you
aren't, then you didn't read my admonishment at the beginning of
this book about going through all the 3D Studio MAX tutorials
first, or else you're skipping around in these tutorials. If you're the
kind of person who skips to the end of a book to see whodunnit,
then let me tell you: Rosebud was his *sled*, Darth Vader is *Luke's
father*, and in *The Crying Game*, she's a *he*.)

Joking aside, although 3D Studio MAX's modifiers are powerful
modeling tools, they do add some memory overhead to each 3D
Studio MAX scene. (3D Studio MAX has to keep track of each
object's modifier history, which is contained within the object file
itself.) When you render an animation, 3D Studio MAX has to
calculate all the modifiers present on each object, for each frame of
the animation.

Consequently, if you're rendering and/or modifying a large
number of objects with modifiers applied to them, or if the objects
themselves are extremely complex and have modifiers applied,
then not only rendering but also manipulating the objects may
pose a computational problem.

One solution to this is to create the complex object that you
want, using the object modifiers, and then save a copy of it to disk.
Then, if you're satisfied with the final results of your modified
object, you can collapse the stack. When you do so, the history of
each modifier applied to the object is removed and the object is
frozen in its final state. You cannot then go back and transform the

object back to its original state, but you can work forward; you can apply new object modifiers to this editable mesh object and further refine its surface.

Unless you have a specific need to animate the object modifiers applied to your mesh objects, you can speed up both object manipulation and rendering time by collapsing the stack. For objects such as your Asteroid, you may want to get the shape as complex as you deem necessary for the scene, and then collapse it into an editable mesh object.

Here's how to do it.

1. Select Edit/Hold; this will store your current 3D Studio MAX Asteroid settings. Make sure that the Asteroid object is selected and then click on the Modify tab of the Command Panel.

2. Click on the Edit Stack button and the Edit Modifier stack dialog box appears. You should see the stack history as Displace, Edit Mesh, Noise, Edit Mesh, Noise, Edit Mesh, and then, at the bottom, the original Sphere object.

   If you click on the Collapse All button, the cumulative result of the object modifiers applied to the original sphere collapses into an editable mesh Asteroid object.

3. Click on the Collapse All button. When the warning dialog box appears, click on Yes. The Modifier stack disappears and you are left with a simple mesh object. Click on OK to dismiss the Editor Modifier stack dialog box.

Now, don't fetch the Asteroid geometry just yet. You want to keep it for your next rendering test.

## "Lay in the Coordinates, and Engage."

At this point, you could begin applying new modifiers again, if you wanted. However, the only new modifier that you'll apply in the final part of this tutorial is a UVW map.

When you created your original sphere, you activated the Generate Mapping Coordinates option. This option enables the original sphere's UVW texture coordinates to be retained, even after applying all the modifiers and collapsing the modifier stack.

However, after all these vertex and face transforms, you may want to apply new mapping coordinates so that the textures conform better to the Asteroid's surface. (If you were to render the current Asteroid mesh, it would be indistinguishable from the original Asteroid with all the modifier history retained.)

1. From the Modifier Panel, click on UVW Map. Under Mapping parameters, click on Spherical. The Spherical UVW mapping Gizmo appears around the Asteroid, and you see UVW Mapping added to the Modifier Stack above Mesh.

2. Activate the Camera01 viewport again and render a new test image, as shown in Figure 19-8.

Figure 19-8: *Applying a UVW map to the collapsed mesh Asteroid changes the appearance of the Asteroid's original texture.*

Notice how the appearance of the Asteroid 2 texture varies from the previous rendering, where the original UVW mapping coordinates were altered by the additional modifiers.

3. When you've finished viewing the image, close the Camera01 VFB window and select Edit/Fetch to return to the original Asteroid object.

The editable mesh object you created is saved in the \CHAP_19 directory as ASTEROD2.MAX.

## Moving On

Now you've seen how to create a single complex asteroid. In the next chapter, you'll see how you can propagate it into the illusion of hundreds or even thousands of new asteroids. By using a combination of rendered images (of 3D effects) and 2D Quad Patch objects, you can simulate an asteroid field so dense and impenetrable, it would make your starship insurance rates become…well, astronomical.

# Asteroid Fields

**I**n the last chapter, you explored various methods by which you can use 3D Studio MAX's object modifiers to turn a simple sphere into a rocky asteroid. In this chapter, you conclude your tutorials on individual space effects by looking at how to simulate a dense asteroid field without using a huge number of 3D mesh objects.

In the opening shot of your sample space battle scenes, the battlecruiser comes roaring out of warp drive at the outskirts of an asteroid field. In the foreground are 3D asteroid meshes, rotating and moving slowly through the scene. As the camera tilts down, the asteroids continue in the background until they form a dense oval patch, sprinkled like dust across the cosmos.

Although the foreground asteroids are obviously 3D objects, the asteroid field in the distance is a modification of a cyclorama object, as described in Chapter 5, "Star Light, Star Bright, Part II." Again, a cyclorama, in theater, TV, or film parlance, is usually a painted or photographic backdrop that simulates a distant background; it's often placed behind the "windows" of a theater stage or movie set.

In the case of the distant asteroid field, I first rendered a series of generic 3D asteroid bitmaps in 3D Studio MAX. I then took these bitmaps, loaded them into Adobe Photoshop, and did a considerable amount of cutting, pasting, duplicating, and scaling until I'd created five different asteroid images. Each image depicted numerous asteroids arranged in a rough oval configuration. On each successive image, the asteroids both increased in number and diminished in size until the final asteroids in the fifth image were simply scatterings of tinted single pixels. I then created Opacity maps (or holdout mattes) from each of the five asteroid images.

When I had finished with these images, I loaded them into 3D Studio MAX and mapped them onto five curved Quad Patch objects—a multiplanar 2D asteroid backdrop. By placing 3D asteroid meshes of diminishing size directly in front of the asteroid backdrop, I created the effect of far more 3D asteroids being in the scene than were actually there.

Now you'll examine how this effect works.

## Flying Around in His Astral Plane

As with the warp drive effect described in Chapter 11,"Warp Speed!," in this chapter you're going to load an existing 3D Studio MAX scene and then deconstruct it rather than build everything from scratch. Later, you'll take a quick look at how you can use an "asteroid kit" to create the 3D asteroid bitmaps that you might need for your own asteroid fields. By rendering a series of asteroid images and then loading them into a paint program, you can cut and paste individual asteroids as needed to create the effect you want.

1. In 3D Studio MAX, select File/Open or press Ctrl+O. Then, from the \CHAP_20 directory of your *3D Studio MAX f/x* CD-ROM, load the file ASTPLANE.MAX. When the file loads, the screen should look like Figure 20-1.

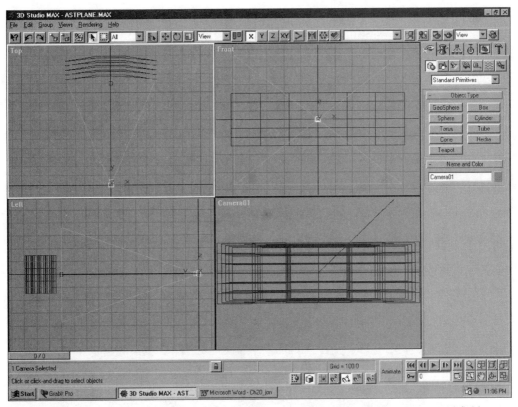

Figure 20-1: *The five curved Quad Patch objects used to create a multiplanar asteroid field background.*

As you should see on your screen, there are five levels, or layers, of 2D Quad Patch objects.

2. In your Top viewport, click on the first Asteroid Plane object (the one closest to the camera) to select it. Click on the Modify Panel and take a look at the Modify Stack. The top item listed is a Bend modifier; if you look down through the stack, you'll also see a UVW Mapping modifier and, at the bottom, the original Quad Patch object. Close the Modifier Stack listing.

As you'll see in a moment, the proportions of each object correspond to their respective asteroid bitmap textures. (The maps are quite wide, at 1024 x 300 resolution.)

It's time to do a test rendering of the scene to see the effect.

3. Activate your Camera01 viewport; then, press Alt+R and Enter to render a test image. When the image appears, it should look like Figure 20-2.

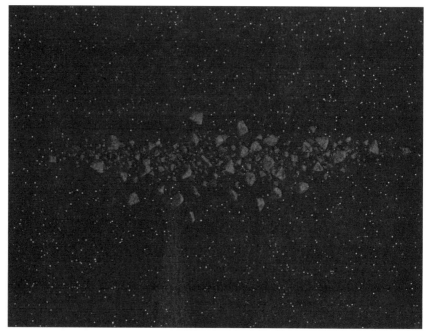

Figure 20-2: *A distant asteroid belt created with 2D imagery on multiplanar 2D geometry.*

Notice the illusion of the many levels of asteroids. The Quad Patch closest to the camera is mapped with an image of the largest asteroids. As you work your way back, the successive patch objects feature images of asteroids that increase in number but decrease in size, giving the illusion that they are receding a great distance. Asteroid Plane 05 (the one furthest from the camera) is mapped with an image that consists simply of airbrushed single pixels created in Autodesk Animator Pro. For consistency, these pixels use the same color palette as the foreground asteroid images.

By layering bitmaps depicting various sizes of asteroids onto multiple 2D Quad Patches such as these, I've produced an impression of considerable depth. The asteroid images mapped onto the Quad Patches consist of a separate Diffuse and Opacity map for each texture. The Opacity map for each image consists simply of a solid white holdout matte, or silhouette, of each asteroid in its matching Diffuse map. This uses the alpha channel to prevent the starfield background from bleeding through the shadowed areas of the asteroids.

You can create your own alpha masks for your asteroid images by rendering them as Targa-format images and using the 3D Studio MAX Alpha Split option. However, if you load the original rendered bitmap into a capable paint program such as Adobe Photoshop, and then cut and paste asteroid elements, you must use Photoshop's layering features to extract a new opacity mask for your final asteroid texture.

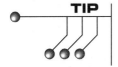

**TIP** | If you want to render Targa files from 3D Studio MAX with the Alpha Split option, select Rendering/Render and press Enter. When the Render Scene dialog box appears, click on Files; under List Files of Type, select Targa Image File. In the Render Output dialog box, click on Setup. The Targa Image Control dialog box appears. Click on Alpha Split and then on OK. When you then render your image, a separate alpha channel image is saved as a Targa (.TGA) file. This .TGA file has the prefix A_ followed by the rest of the original image file name. You can use this alpha channel image in the Opacity Map slot of the Material Editor for its related texture map.

## The Asteroid Bitmaps

Take a look at the individual images making up each layer of the asteroid 2D Quad Patch objects.

1. Select File/View File, and from the \CHAP_20 directory, click on the file AST_BK1.TGA to view it.

   This image consists of just over three dozen asteroids. The asteroids themselves are simple mesh objects mapped with a basic asteroid texture, such as the one you used in the previous tutorial. In the original 3D scene used to render these aster-oids, I placed a non–ray-traced spotlight at a 45-degree angle off to the left and above the camera viewpoint. (The asteroid meshes retained their Shadow Casting and Shadow Receiving attributes.) I then rendered the image with some of the aster-oid objects cloned as Instance objects, which helped speed up rendering time. The final bitmap, like all the other asteroid bitmaps, is 1024 x 300 resolution.

Now you'll take a look at the Opacity map, or mask, for the first Asteroid Quad Patch object.

2. Select File/View File and, from the \CHAP_20 directory, click on the file AST_AM1.TGA to view it.

As you can see, this consists simply of solid white silhou-ettes of the asteroids present in the AST_BK1.TGA image. When it's used as an Opacity map, everything that is white is opaque; everything black is transparent.

3. Select File/View File and, from the \CHAP_20 directory, click on the file AST_BK2.TGA.

This image is used on the second 2D Quad Patch object (working backward from the camera view). As you can see, there are a greater number of asteroids in the image; they're also smaller, to create the illusion that they're receding in the distance.

4. Select File/View File, and from the \CHAP_20 directory, click on and view, in turn, the files AST_BK3.TGA, AST_BK4.TGA, and AST_BK5.TGA. In each image, the asteroids increase in number while decreasing in size, until the final image shows nothing but a faint dusting of pixels.

5. If the screen is getting cluttered with View windows, close them all and click on File/View File to view the files AST_AM2.TGA, AST_AM3.TGA, AST_AM4.TGA, and AST_AM5.TGA. Again, these are the Opacity maps for each of the asteroid Diffuse maps. The final image, AST_AM5.TGA, shows clearly the single pixels used to create the most distant asteroids.

6. When you've finished viewing the images, close all your View windows.

## Building a Better Asteroid

Now that you've seen the images comprising the five asteroid textures, take a look at the asteroid material settings themselves.

1. Click on the Material Editor button to bring up the Material Editor. When the Material Editor appears, you see that Slot #1—the Asteroid Plane 1 material—is active.

    Now you'll examine the settings for this material. Ambient and Diffuse are both solid black. Shininess and Shininess Strength are set to 0. For the purposes of this tutorial, I've set Self-illumination to 100 to make the asteroid images render more brightly.

2. Open the Extended Parameter rollout. Under Opacity Type, notice that Subtractive rather than Filter or Additive is set. This ensures that the asteroids are completely opaque and do not appear translucent if viewed against a lighter-colored background such as a nebula. (If you set the Opacity Type to Additive and render a test image of the asteroids, you would see the stars shining through the shadowed areas of the asteroids.)

3. Now, finally, open the Maps rollout; notice that the Asteroid images you previewed earlier are loaded into their respective Diffuse and Opacity map slots.

4. If you examine each of the remaining materials, you'll notice that their parameters are identical with the first Asteroid Plane 1 material; only the maps differ.

All these textures are saved in the 3DSMAXFX.MAT material library on your *3D Studio MAX f/x CD-ROM*.

## Building Your Own Asteroid Kit

Probably the best way to create your own multiplanar asteroid images is by building an "asteroid kit." This is simply a small collection of asteroid 3D mesh objects that you can render and use to create the illusion of many more asteroids. Now you'll load a simple demonstration file to see how this is done.

1. Select File/Open or press Ctrl+O on your keyboard, and from the \CHAP_20 directory, load the file ASTRDKIT.MAX. When the scene file appears, your screen should look something like Figure 20-3.

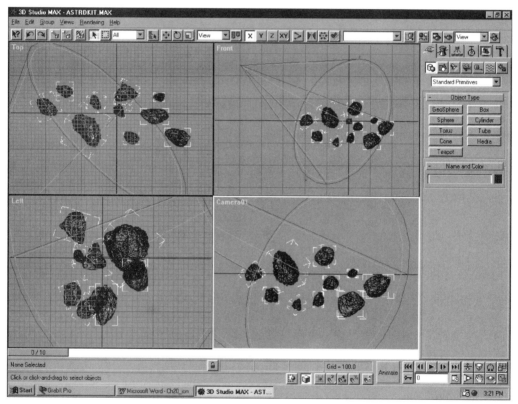

Figure 20-3: *A basic asteroid kit for creating multiplanar asteroid images.*

This asteroid kit consists of ten different asteroid meshes of various sizes. One spotlight is placed approximately 45 degrees to the left of the asteroids and above them. A camera with a standard 50mm lens looks directly at the front of them. It's time to do a test rendering of this first frame.

2. Select Alt+R and Enter to render a single image of the Camera01 viewport; it should look like Figure 20-4.

Figure 20-4: *The asteroid kit with the Asteroid 1 texture applied to the mesh objects.*

3. When you've finished viewing the image, close the Camera01 VFB window.

    Now you'll take a look at a quick way to create varying asteroid maps for your rendered asteroid images. Notice that in all viewports, the asteroid objects all have Key Brackets surrounding them. This indicates that the asteroids all have animation keys set for them.

4. If your Camera01 viewport is still active, click on the Next Frame button to go from frame 0 to frame 1. Continue moving from frame 1 all the way to frame 10. As you do, the asteroids rotate on their XYZ axes.

Very simply, you have a group of ten asteroids, each spinning on multiple axes across ten frames of animation. Although this is not particularly useful as an animation by itself, it is very useful for creating a series of ten Targa files of different asteroid images.

As the asteroids rotate across the ten frames of animation, their contours change drastically from one frame to the next. Consequently, during the range of ten rendered frames, the ten or so asteroids revolve (and evolve) into a hundred different-looking asteroids of various sizes and shapes.

If you want, you can render and save each of these ten frames as separate .TGA files (with Alpha Split active). These ten frames then become the basis for your own multiplanar asteroid artwork. By loading these images into a 24-bit paint or image editing program such as Adobe Photoshop, you can cut, paste, and resize the asteroids and their alpha channel masks to produce the illusion of hundreds—even thousands—of new "space rocks." The settings shown in this 3D Studio MAX file are suggested for the asteroid plane closest to your camera.

If you want to render additional asteroids (for Quad Patches receding from the camera), you can simply move the camera further away from the asteroids; or, just change the Camera01 lens setting from 50mm to something more wide-angle such as a 35mm, and then a 28mm, a 22mm, and so on. This shrinks the asteroids further in the frame. Finally, if necessary, you can render the images all at one size and then use your image editing program to shrink and composite the final images. This may give you greater flexibility and be faster than creating and rendering all your asteroid images in 3D Studio MAX as 3D mesh geometry.

When the images are to your liking, map them onto 2D Quad Patches. The overall configuration of the 2D Quad Patches is up to you; however, it's best if the 2D shapes have aspect ratio as your final asteroid bitmaps. After you've created the Quad Patches, you can activate their Generate Mapping Coordinates option or apply a UVW mapping Gizmo and set it for Planar mapping.

One thing to remember: When you create your own Quad Patch asteroid field object(s), you will probably want to turn off the objects' Shadow Casting and Shadow Receiving attributes so that a spotlight in your scene won't cast a rectangular shadow from the Quad Patches on any other objects.

However, if you are using ray-traced spotlights in your space scene, you may actually want to leave the Shadow Casting and Shadow Receiving on for the Quad Patch asteroid field objects. As you saw in Chapter 18, "Planets & Other Heavenly Bodies," using ray-traced lights let Opacity-mapped "2D" asteroids cast shadows onto other objects.

You should bear a few other things in mind when using this technique. If you're placing 3D asteroid meshes in front of the 2D Quad Patch asteroid field images, ensure that the lighting in your foreground 3D scene matches that of the prerendered asteroid field images on the Quad Patches. For best results, you should probably set up the 3D scene in which you're going to be using your 2D asteroids first, determine the exact lighting angles, and then determine where the asteroid field is going to be located. After you do that, you can load up your asteroid kit, adjust your materials as necessary, change the lighting to the correct angle, and then render your asteroid kit frames to match your final 3D scene.

## Moving On

That's it! You've now covered twenty different chapters describing, detailing, and deconstructing different types of outer space special effects. In the next chapter, you'll wrap up your examination of space effects by revisiting the five demonstration space battle scenes. You'll load each scene and then take a quick look at how all the techniques covered so far come together to create the final effects shots.

# 21

# The Space Battle: Dissecting the Effects

**W**ay back in Chapter 3, "Setting Up Your Scene," you took a look at five shots that represented scenes depicted in the space battle storyboards. These five shots, comprising almost 1,000 frames, helped to illustrate the effects that have been covered in the last 17 chapters.

In this chapter, you'll load each of the 3D Studio MAX files used to create these shots and examine how the elements covered in the previous 17 chapters combine to create these outer space pyrotechnics. By this point, you should be familiar enough with the effects to need just a brief overview of "what's happening where" in these sequences. That's what I'll present now. I'll touch on all the elements in the first shot and then run through the remaining shots quickly, dissecting their effects.

## The Space Battle: Shot #1

Not surprisingly, the best place to start is with the first space battle shot. So…

1. From the \CHAP_21 directory of the *3D Studio MAX f/x CD-ROM*, load the file SPACEBT1.MAX. Figure 21-1 shows the Camera01 viewport during frame 257 of the sequence. (In this figure and in most of the other screen captures, I've hidden the Grid, Axis Tripod, and Lights for clarity; in addition, I've changed the Nebula sphere display to Box mode so that you can see the foreground elements more easily.) A full rendered version of frame 267, showing a closer view of the battlecruiser, is shown in Figure 21-2.

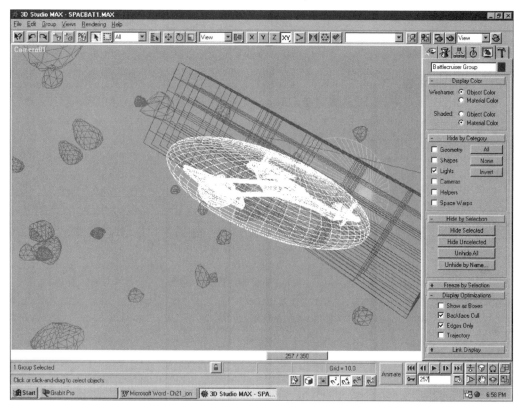

Figure 21-1: *Frame 257 of the SPACEBT1.MAX scene. The battlecruiser emerges from the warp drive tunnel; the asteroid field Quad Patches are directly behind it.*

Figure 21-2: *The rendered version of frame 267 of the SPACEBAT1.MAX scene.*

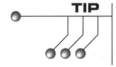

**TIP**    The texture maps for the five .MAX scene files discussed in this chapter are *not* included in the \CHAP_21 directory, but are instead in the \MAPS directory. If you have any difficulty rendering test images of these scenes, make sure that you have added the *3D Studio MAX f/x CD-ROM* \MAPS directory in your bitmap paths. Use the File/Configure Paths option in 3D Studio MAX to add the \MAPS directory to your bitmap paths.

Before you read the discussion of the various effects elements used in this scene, you should review the first space battle shot again. Then, you can take a look at a wireframe preview of the same shot.

2. Select File/View File, and from the \CHAP_21 directory, click on the file SPACEBT1.AVI to load it. When the Media Player appears, play the animation.

Again, as I mentioned previously and in Chapter 3, "Setting Up Your Scene," this 350-frame opening shot sets up the space environment for the numerous modeling, optical, and post-processing effects discussed in Chapters 3 through 20.

3. When you've finished watching the scene, stop the animation; then, in the Media Player, select File/Open. From the \CHAP_21 directory, click on the file PREVIEW1.AVI to load it. When it loads into the Media Player, play the animation.

This is a wireframe preview of the first space scene. It's useful to see how these wireframe mesh objects reveal their true selves in the SPACBTL1.AVI demonstration rendering that you've just previewed.

Approximately 70 asteroid meshes move slowly in front of the five asteroid field Quad Patch objects. Again, these Quad Patches create the impression that the asteroid field stretches back much further in the scene and you are merely on the periphery of it.

*Note: For the purposes of this book's tutorials, I've scaled down the asteroid field effect to keep it from becoming unwieldy for your examination and further experimentation. Of course, for your own asteroid field effects, you may want to expand on the number of asteroids depicted on both the background Quad Patch cyclorama objects and on the foreground asteroid meshes.*

In the background, you should see the large sphere comprising the Nebula and starfield effect surrounding the various elements in the scene—from the entire asteroid field, warp drive tunnel, and emerging battlecruiser to the planet and moon that the cruiser is approaching.

4. When you've finished viewing the animation, close the Media Player.

Now you'll examine briefly the elements making up this scene.

## The Starfield & Nebula Background

For this and the other four space shots, I combined the starfield and nebula image elements into a single large bitmap, which I then applied to the Nebula Sphere object.

If necessary, you can apply a nebula bitmap only to the Nebula Sphere (as a Diffuse and Opacity map) and then either load a starfield background into 3D Studio MAX's Environment Background, or (if available) load a procedural starfield filter into the appropriate queue of Video Post.

1. Press the H key to open the Select by Name dialog box. Holding down the Ctrl key, go down the list and deselect Camera01, the Camera01.Target, Nebula Sphere, and Nebula Path. Click on Select.

2. Go to the Display panel and click on Hide Unselected to hide the remaining elements in the scene. Now you're looking at just the Camera and the Nebula object, with its assigned path.

3. Enlarge the Top viewport to full screen and then click on the Zoom Extents icon to center the elements in this viewport. Click on the Z key five times to zoom close into the center of the Nebula Sphere and Camera01. You should be able to see the paths for both the Camera01 body and its target.

4. Click on the Camera01 path or else press the H key. Select the Nebula Path.

   This is the spline path derived from the Camera01 path. As you saw in Chapter 8, "Nebulas on the Move," by converting (that is, extracting) the camera path to a spline object, you can have the Nebula object and its textures follow along precisely with the camera movement. This lets you lock the nebula imagery to the camera movement and not have it slide relative to the Environment starfield background, a procedural Video Post starfield, or foreground elements. Again, however, you can roll the camera or set up outrageous camera moves—and the nebula sphere will stay in perfect registration.

5. Return to four viewports and unhide the remaining elements in the scene.

## The Asteroids & Asteroid Fields

The asteroid effects are fairly obvious. The bracketed boxes surrounding the asteroid meshes indicate that translation and rotation keys have been set on the asteroids.

Drag the Time Slider to the middle of the scene (approximately frame 175). You can see the asteroids moving and rotating slowly through the scene. Notice that the Asteroid Field Quad Patch objects do *not* move at all during the scene; this would spoil the illusion of a distant, large field of asteroids.

## The Space Warp

On frame 175, notice the large Warp Drive cones dominating the Camera01 viewport; the cruiser is just beginning to emerge from the center. The Warp Drive effect, as you explored in Chapter 11, "Warp Speed!," consists of animated bitmaps applied to morphing cones. The morphing effect creates the illusion that the warp drive tunnel appears out of nowhere, holds for a moment, and snaps back.

1. Select the objects Warp_1 Large, Warp_1 Small, Warp_2 Large, and Warp_2 Small.

2. Click on the Track View icon. When the Track View window appears, click on the Filters icon. Under Show Only, click on Selected Objects, and click on OK. Open the Objects track and then the Warp_1 and Warp_2 object tracks (including Morph), but don't open the Warp 1 or Warp 2 material tracks. You may want to Maximize the Track View window and then click on the Zoom Horizontal Events icon to see the tracks for the objects, as shown in Figure 21-3.

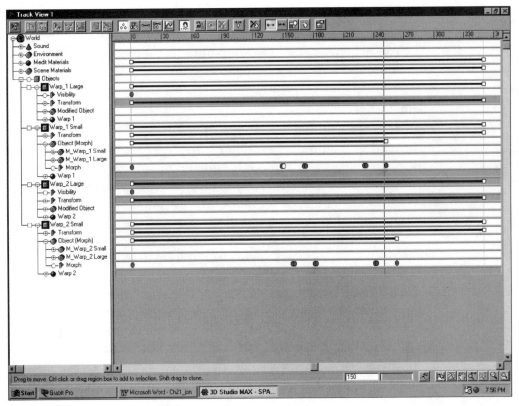

Figure 21-3: *The Morph Tracks for the Warp Drive objects.*

3. Click on the first Morph key for Warp_1 Morph; then, right-click on the key to bring up the Key Info dialog box. Click on the Right arrow to cycle through the keys; you can see that the Warp_1 Morph effect is dormant from frames 0 to 149, begins on 150, and opens completely by frame 170. It holds from frame 171 to frame 231 and then recedes on frame 251.

4. Click on the Warp_2 Morph keys and repeat the preceding procedure. You can see how the Warp_2 Morph effect is offset from the first Warp effect by 10 frames (frames 0 to 159, 160 to 180, 181 to 240, and 241 to 261).

5. When you've finished, close the Key Info dialog box, and Minimize—but don't dismiss!—your Track View window. You're going to use it throughout this chapter for all five space battle shots.

## The Battlecruiser

The battlecruiser model used in the five space battle scenes has an interesting history. Although I built and textured this model (primarily in 3D Studio/DOS), unlike the fighter ships, I didn't design it. The battlecruiser model was inspired by a original design created by my friend Bill George.

Bill, an Academy Award winner (for the models in *Innerspace*, 1987), is a special-effects supervisor at Industrial Light and Magic (ILM) in San Rafael, California. ILM, of course, is the special-effects company founded by George Lucas to create the effects for the original *Star Wars*. (This model, as well as other vehicles included on the book's CD-ROM, is shown in several figures in the Color Gallery section in the middle of this book.)

1. In any viewport, click on the battlecruiser model to select it (or use the Select by Name dialog box to pick the Battlecruiser Group).

2. Maximize Track View and open the Battlecruiser Group; then, open the Transform tracks. If you look at the Visibility, Position, and Scale Tracks, you'll see that keys are set on frames 0, 159, 160, and 350 (Position and Scale only). Click on the first Scale key and then right-click to bring up the Key Info dialog box. Click on the Right arrow to cycle through the keys and examine their values. On frames 0, 159, and 160, the XYZ Scale values are held at 5.394; however, when you get to frame 350, the values jump to 107.875.

    What's happening is a bit of 3D cinematic sleight-of-hand. To make the cruiser appear to be emerging from the warp drive tunnel, I scaled down the ship, placed it behind the warp drive cones, and added Visibility and Scale keys to it, unhiding the ship starting on frame 160. As the cruiser begins to move forward on frame 160 (and emerge from the warp drive optical effect), it grows—it scales outward as it flies by the camera. This gives the impression that the ship is coming from a much greater distance than it really is.

By using the Scale keys in this manner, you can suggest a forced perspective effect, suggesting that objects are much bigger or much smaller (relative to the camera) than their actual scene dimensions indicate.

3. Minimize Track View and return to four viewports.

4. If you open the Battlecruiser group, you'll see that it's composed of a separate Forcefield object and another ship group; if you open the latter group, you'll see all the components making up the vessel.

*Note: If you want to change the battlecruiser's appearance, a huge variety of "spaceship-style" textures is on the CD-ROM. Just pick and choose the ones you want to create your own warship.*

## The Planets & Moon

As you saw above, by using forced perspective, you can "cheat" certain effects. When you see the planet and the moon in any non-camera viewport, they are obviously both (relatively) tiny and close together. (At that size and distance, compared to the cruiser, if the planet had any inhabitants, they wouldn't even need a space program to land on their moon—just a grappling hook and some rope.)

However, during the course of any of the five effects shots, the action never takes you close to either world—so their small scale is fine for these shots.

## The Lighting: Where's the Sun?

In this book, I've spent a great deal of time discussing how to create a certain effect—but it's not even shown in any of the five shots. There's no point in asking "what is it?," even rhetorically, since the subhead gives it away. (I'll have to talk to myself about that.) The answer to this nonexistent question is—the sun.

I didn't show a volumetric sun in any of the animations for a couple of reasons—one practical, the other cinematic.

First, when I set up these shots, I decided to front-light most of the elements to make them easily visible for the test animations. Although this method is not nearly as stylish as backlighting or rim lighting, you the reader had to be able to see all the elements in the demo animations, so I made the lighting deliberately bright and the lights' placement conservative. (I'll hold off on discussing moody, film-noir lighting for 3D until a later book.)

*Note: For higher-resolution renderings (such as video), you can be much more dramatic with your lighting. In fact, in conventional special-effects photography, miniatures are often backlit to provide a greater sense of mass and to camouflage their reduced scale. You should experiment with this to enhance the appearance of your CGI miniatures, too.*

Second, when I choreographed the animation, I determined that most of the action would take place with the camera to the left of the primary elements in each shot (as seen from above). This enables the shots, when run in sequence, to cut together properly—and it obeys the #1 rule of camera direction: *don't cross the line.* (This is also called the "180-degree rule.")

When you're directing and composing a shot, you should always draw an imaginary line between your subject and another point of interest, or the direction in which the subject is moving. If you're going to have the subject move past the camera in one shot, and you cut to a reverse angle, you should stay on the same side of the subject as in the previous shot, as shown in Figure 21-4.

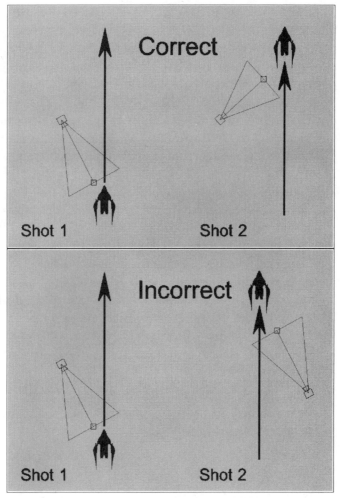

Figure 21-4: *The correct and incorrect way's to place a camera for a standard 2-shot cut.*

Take, for example, SPACEBT2.AVI, when the cruiser passes by the camera and the fighters appear. If I had placed the camera on the right side of the ship, pointing up so that I could see a cool sun effect, I would have had to pan further back to see the emerging fighters—a somewhat awkward maneuver. In addition, since the cruiser is passing from right to left in shot #1, changing the camera position to the other side of the cruiser would have made the vessel appear to have suddenly switched direction. (This effect would be especially jarring if you were to cut to a reverse angle of the ship, from behind, with the camera placed on the right.)

This is the most basic rule of direction, one that's evolved in the course of 100 years of cinematic language. Unfortunately, it's also violated regularly by fledgling 3D artists enamored of their ability to make movies on their desktops. There are other ways to move your camera, of course (including continuous floating shots around your subject—also overused in the 3D realm), but knowing a bit about real film direction when creating your own "desktop movies" is always helpful. (For more information, see Appendix D, "Special Effects & Filmmaking Resources.")

Now, notice that several spotlights and a couple of Omni lights are used in this scene.

1. Press the H key to bring up the Select by Name dialog box; then, Under List Display, click on None and then Lights. The following lights are shown:

   ※ Omni Asteroid Plane: This illuminates just the Quad Patch asteroid objects.

   ※ Omni Nebula: This illuminates just the Nebula object; even though this is a Self-illuminated material (go to the Material Editor and examine it), this light makes the material even brighter in the scene.

❧ Omni Sun: This is the unseen volumetric sun. If you were to choreograph and render the entire 13-shot space battle, you might see this sun during some of the shots. (Check out the Environment dialog box to see the volume light settings, although, again, this effect doesn't appear in the current camera angles.)

❧ Spotlight Asteroids: This is a spotlight that illuminates just the 3D mesh asteroids.

❧ Spotlight Battlecruiser: This is a spotlight that illuminates just the battlecruiser group. (Notice how its target pans with the battlecruiser as it flies by. The spotlight target is keyframed manually, not linked to the cruiser.)

❧ Spotlight Planet/Moon: This light is for the Planet and Moon objects only.

*Note: All of these lights have Exclusion sets turned on for various objects so that they don't provide unwanted illumination.*

2. As an exercise, select each light in turn; then, click on the Modify Panel and click on the Exclude button. You can then check each light's Exclude/Include object sets.

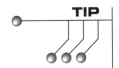

**TIP**

Another way to use volumetric Omni lights is to place them on the ends of your spacecraft engines and link them to the spacecraft model itself. This way, you can create a visible glow emanating from the engines, even when you don't directly see the engine exhausts themselves. This technique may be a little more versatile than using the Glow filter in Video Post on the engine exhaust material.

# The Space Battle: Shot #2

Now that you've examined the various parameters in the first space battle shot, you can run through the remaining shots quickly and see how the various effects elements that you've learned are incorporated.

**CD-ROM**

1. From the \CHAP_21 directory, load the file SPACEBT2.MAX. When the file loads, select File/View File, and from the same directory, click on the file SPACEBT2.AVI to load it. When the Media Player appears, play the animation.

   This 208-frame animation depicts the battlecruiser, now out of warp drive and safely out of the asteroid field, heading beneath you, as shown in Figures 21-5 and 21-6.

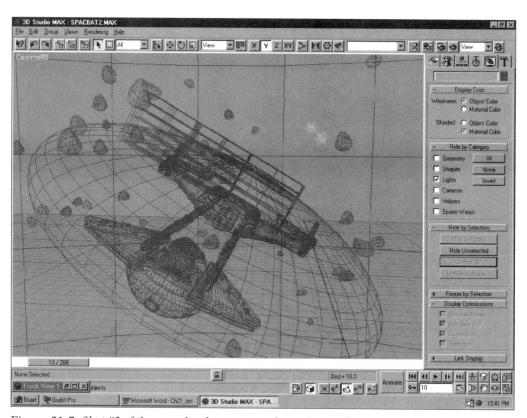

Figure 21-5: *Shot #2 of the space battle sequence, shown in wireframe mode.*

Figure 21-6: *The full rendered version of shot #2 (frame 0).*

However, no sooner does the cruiser arrive in "normal" space than it has unexpected company—three small fighter ships warp into the scene and the lead ship immediately launches an attack. As the ship gets into range, it fires off two tachyon torpedoes, which zip by the camera as the three fighters fly to attack.

2. Stop the SPACEBT2.AVI playback; then, in the Media Player, click on Open/File. From the \CHAP_21 directory, click on the PREVIEW2.AVI file to load it; then, play the animation. This is a wireframe preview of the sequence.

In this scene, note how the torpedoes unleashed by the lead fighter are actually in the scene all the time. What's more, they seem to be rotating wildly.

3. Close the Media Player and press the H key. When the Select by Name dialog box appears, select the Torp1 and Torp2 grouped objects and then maximize the Track View dialog box. In Track View, open the tracks for the Torp1 and Torp2 objects, including their Visibility and Transform tracks.

4. Take a close look at these keys. (If you want, click on their keys singly and then right-click to examine the key values, including the Transform function curves.) Torp1 is invisible until frame 173; on frame 174, when the first fighter ship is in the right position, the torpedo "unhides" and also moves quickly through the scene, from frames 174 to 188. Torp2 unhides on frame 184 and then fires off as well on frames 184 to 194.

   The torpedo objects simply hang around in the scene until they're needed because of the Visibility keys. In setting up this shot, I simply determined at what frames I wanted the torpedoes to fire; then, at the right frame, I moved the torpedoes into the correct positions. (In this case, that was directly in front of the fighters' wing cannons.) Then, by copying the Transform keys for those frames to frame 0, flattening their function curves, and setting Visibility keys for the appropriate frames, I made the torpedoes appear to fire from the cannons.

5. Click on the Rotation track of either Torp object and then click on the Assign Controller icon. As you can see, I've assigned a Noise Rotation controller to these objects' Rotation tracks. This imparts a frenetic, back-and-forth rotational movement that makes the sparkling torpedo effect more pronounced, particularly on higher-resolution renderings. Without the rendered imagery, however, they look a bit odd.

Other items that you might want to examine in this scene are the fighter's Scale keys. Like the cruiser in shot #1, the fighter ships are scaled down and placed behind the morphing warp drive cones. Then, they appear and "grow" quickly as they emerge from warp drive. In addition, you may notice that, to simplify and speed up the warp drive effect, I used only one morphing warp cone per ship.

6. When you've finished looking at these items, minimize the Track View window.

## The Space Battle: Shot #3

Now you'll run quickly through shot #3.

1. From the \CHAP_21 directory, load the SPACEBT3.MAX file. When the file loads, select File/View File and then the SPACEBT3.AVI file. When the Media Player appears, click on Play to view the animation.

   In the previous shot, you saw how the lead fighter opened fire with torpedoes. In this shot, the torpedoes enter the frame and impact on the cruiser's forcefield with a bright flash of light. The fighters zoom by, preparing (presumably) for another strafing run.

2. When you've finished viewing this animation, select File/Open in the Media Player, and from the \CHAP_21 directory, load and play the PREVIEW3.AVI file.

   Now that you've seen the final animation, you might find comparing it with the wireframe preview (the first frame of this sequence is shown in Figure 21-7) to be interesting.

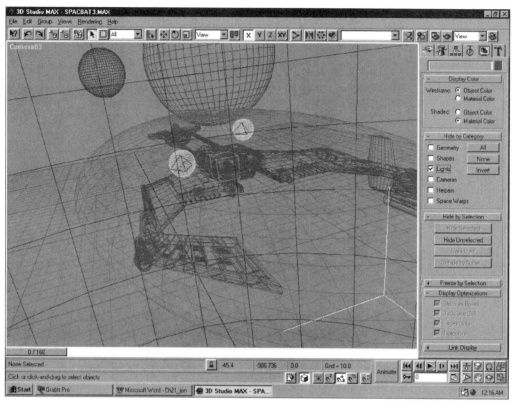

Figure 21-7: *The opening shot of the SPACEBT3.MAX scene. Note the two explosion spheres and Bomb Space Warps attached to the top of the cruiser forcefield.*

Notice how the Quad Patch torpedoes enter the frame and impact directly on two Spheres, linked to the top of the forcefield. You can also see two pyramidal Bomb Space Warps linked to the forcefield. As the torps hit, the spheres detonate, blasting pieces through the scene, as shown in the test rendering in Figure 21-8.

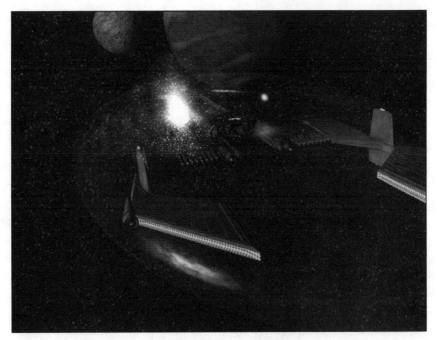

Figure 21-8: *Frame 33 of the SPACEBT3.MAX scene.*

3. Close the Media Player.

By applying a Glow filter (set to 20 pixels) in Video Post, and applying an animated, self-illuminated material to the two spheres, I created a bright flash with glowing particles blasting away from the forcefield. As the camera tracks forward with the slowly moving cruiser, the camera flies through the fading, glowing particles—a nice effect. (Note that you can make the explosion more or less "chunky" by selecting the Explosion Spheres, going to the Modify Panel, and changing the spheres' segment counts.)

Also notable in this and the other space battle shots: Any scene elements not visible during the course of a given shot aren't just hidden, they're deleted. Because the five shots contain all the elements necessary to create the entire 13-shot storyboarded sequence described in Chapter 3, "Setting Up Your Scene," you can simply merge in elements that you need from any given shot if you want to choreograph the remaining space battle scenes.

4. Select the various pyrotechnic elements, such as the tachyon torpedoes, the Bomb Space Warps, and/or the Explosion Spheres, and examine their keys in the Track View window. In a reversal of shot #2, the torpedoes enter the frame and then, as they impact on the Explosion spheres, they disappear using Visibility keys. Simultaneously, the Spheres "unhide" and detonate.

5. Open the Material Editor and examine the Explosion materials applied to the spheres. (You can use the Get Material/Scene option to load the materials, if they're not visible in the current Material Editor. You can also examine these materials' settings in Track View.) Observe how the materials are animated to correspond with the point of detonation. In addition, I set Effects Channels for these materials, as well as the cruiser's window material, and the Red Glowing Grid material making up the cruiser's and the fighter's engines.

6. Select Rendering/Video Post and examine the Glow Filter queue settings.

7. When you've finished examining this scene, close Video Post and/or the Material Editor and minimize Track View.

## The Space Battle: Shot #4

1. From the \CHAP_21 directory, load the SPACEBT4.MAX file. Select File/View File, and from the same directory, load and play both the SPACEBT4.AVI and the wireframe PREVIEW4.AVI files.

    This 90-frame shot—in which the cruiser retaliates against the strafing fighters—demonstrates an application of the LASER_3.MAX effect discussed in the latter part of Chapter 13, "Laser Beams 101." In this shot, you see both laser beams and their associated muzzle flashes erupting from the top of the cruiser's weapons towers. (Two versions of this effect are shown in Figures 21-9 and 21-10.)

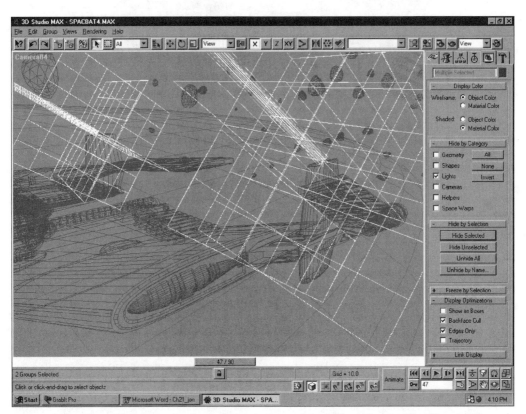

Figure 21-9: *The MAX setup for the battlecruiser Quad Patch laser beam effect (frame 47).*

Figure 21-10: *The final rendered image of shot #4 (frame 47).*

I produced both of these optical effects by mapping a rendered laser beam flic texture (and the modified tachyon torpedo flic texture) onto Quad Patch objects. Notice how the torpedo effect on the square Quad Patches simulates a bright lens flare-type muzzle flash.

By grouping the laser and torpedo objects, using the Hierarchy/Adjust Pivot Point option to center the pivot in the torpedo Quad Patch, and then linking these objects to the cruiser towers, I created lasers that could rotate and fire from the tops of the towers.

2. Select the Laser1 and Laser2 groups and maximize the Track View. Open the Laser1 and Laser2 groups and examine their settings. As with the tachyon torpedoes in the previous two examples, you can see Visibility keys set for the lasers. Click on the Visibility keys and then right-click on a selected key

and examine its values. By setting multiple Visibility keys, I made the lasers flash on and off rapidly, creating a staccato machine-gun effect.

For this scene, however, I did not apply a Glow filter to the lasers. Because the laser Quad Patch objects run through the forcefield bubble, and 3D Studio MAX's Video Post Glow filter works on the Z axis of the camera, the laser glow effect would be obscured by the bubble.

*Note: If you wanted to create a glow for the entire laser beam in this scene, you could render multiple passes and composite them in Video Post. You would first render the existing scene with no Glow filter. Load that rendering into the background of this scene, hide all objects except for the cruiser, and open the Battlecruiser group. At that point, you would either hide or delete the forcefield mesh and then apply a matte material to the entire cruiser model [except for the lasers]. The matte material would enable the previous rendering to "show through" the cruiser model. Then, by applying the Glow filter to the lasers and re-rendering the scene, you could impart a glow effect to those parts of the lasers within the forcefield.*

3. Minimize the Track View when you've finished examining the scene.

## The Space Battle: Shot #5

Now it's time to examine the last test shot in the space battle scenes.

1. From the \CHAP_21 directory, load the SPACEBT5.MAX file. (If you get a warning saying that you are missing the Combustion plug-in .DLM or .DLL files, you should ignore it for the moment. You can install the Combustion plug-in, included on the *3D Studio MAX f/x CD-ROM*, after you've finished this tutorial; placing it in your 3DSMAX\PLUGINS directory will let you reproduce the explosion effect shown in the upcoming SPACEBT5.AVI file. (For more information, see Appendix B, "Combustion: A Free Plug-in for 3D Studio MAX.")

2. Select File/View File, and from the \CHAP_21 directory, load and play the SPACEBT5.AVI and PREVIEW5.AVI files.

As these animations indicate, the three fighters are swooping through space in front of the (apparently distant) planet and moon, preparatory to another strafing run on the cruiser. However, as the previous shot indicated, the cruiser has begun to return fire. Laser beams flash through the scene, with the two most distant fighters avoiding the blasts. But after a moment, the closest fighter to you runs out of luck; one of the cruiser's lasers lances the fighter amidships and then blasts it into atoms (or at least into very thin triangular polygons).

Two examples of this shot, both wireframe and final rendered version, are shown in Figures 21-11 and 21-12.

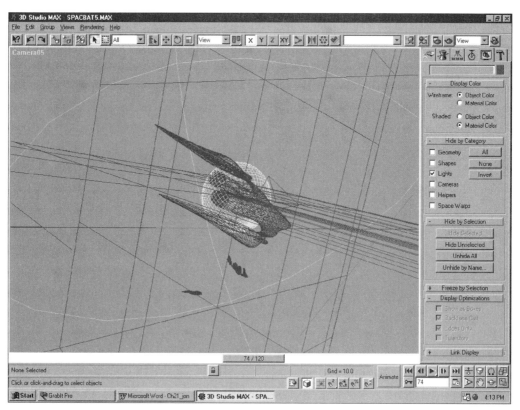

Figure 21-11: *Frame 74 of the SPACEBT5.MAX sequence, shown in wireframe.*

Figure 21-12: *The final rendered version of frame 74.*

Notice in this shot how the 3D elements have been pared down to just what's necessary for the sequence. Off-camera is the Laser and Torpedo Quad Patch object. In front of the camera are the Nebula sphere, the planet and moon meshes, and the three fighters.

3. Close the Media Player and select the Laser beam object. Drag the Time Slider to frame 69 and observe the Laser's position. At this point, it's still attempting to lock on to the fighter.

4. Now, click the Next Frame button to advance to frame 70. You'll now see how the Laser object has flipped completely around and how the Quad Patch on its end is sitting in the middle of the fighter.

As you saw in the SPACEBT5.AVI rendering, when the laser beam actually connects with the ship, there's a brief moment (five frames, to be exact) when you see a sparkling highlight engulfing the fighter. As I mentioned in Chapter 13, "Laser

Beams 101," the same Tachyon Torpedo modification used to create the laser beam muzzle flash at its emanation point can also be used to create an impact point of the laser.

5. Click on the Next Frame button to advance from frame 70 to 75 and then 76 and 77.

As the viewports indicate, the laser beam with its impact point effect remains on the fighter until frame 75, when it is yanked off-camera on frame 76, where it remains. (You'll find out why in a moment.) On frame 76, the actual explosion effect begins.

I created the fighter's explosion much the same way as the tachyon torpedo hits on the cruiser forcefield in shot #3. By parenting a sphere (with a self-illuminated, animated material applied) and a Bomb space warp to the fighter, I created a particle explosion that destroys the hapless ship. (In addition, the Glow filter in Video Post turns the sphere into a white-hot fireball that engulfs the vessel.)

However, I've also augmented this explosion effect with Rolf Berteig's Combustion plug-in for 3D Studio MAX. As mentioned earlier, Combustion is a volumetric effect loaded into the Environment editor that lets you create smoke, fog, fire, and explosions such as the one seen here. (Again, for more information on how to use the Combustion plug-in, see Appendix B, "Combustion: A Free Plug-in for 3D Studio MAX.")

The reason that I yanked the Laser object off-camera, instead of simply hiding it, is that the volumetric Combustion effect would show the outlines of the Laser and Tachyon Torpedo Quad Patch objects, even if they were hidden (using Visibility keys) or otherwise made invisible by altering their material attributes. Because the Combustion gaseous explosion effect overwhelms the ship, removing the Laser object from the scene entirely prevents undesirable effects.

6. Finally, another Bomb Space Warp parented to the fighter ship itself finishes the job; if you click to frame 80 and beyond, you'll see how the fighter itself blows into fragments.

7. As an exercise, select the various laser beam and/or explosion elements, Maximize the Track View window, and examine the key settings and frame timings for these objects.

## Moving On

If you've completed all these tutorials in order, by now you should have a thorough grounding in how to create a variety of science fiction-style visual effects in 3D Studio MAX. However, you don't have to limit yourself to these types of effects. Many of the techniques you've seen—from optical effects to modeling— can be expanded and modified to create unusual terrestrial effects as well.

Coming up in Section IV, "Underwater Effects,"—you'll journey from the realm of outer space to inner space.

# Part IV

# Underwater Effects

# 22

# Seawater?
# See—Water!

**N**ow that you've spent a few hundred pages in outer space, it's time to bring your effects down to a more terrestrial realm: that of inner space.

In this and the next five chapters, you'll see how to build an entire underwater environment, piece by piece. You'll start off using Environmental Fog to create underwater haze, and then create the illusion of the ocean surface, water caustic patterns, volumetric light rays, plankton, and bubbles. In Chapter 26, "Swimming With the Fishes," you'll see how to place a shark in your scene and make it swim. Finally, in Chapter 27, "The Diving Bell & Wrapping It Up," you'll see how placing a human-made object in your underwater scene enables you to use the aforementioned effects in different ways.

## Making Murk

If you've seen various nature documentaries de[...]
sea life or have experience with snorkeling or scub[...]
you've seen the effects of a large body of water on lig[...]
absorbs light much more rapidly than does air (not sur[...]
and it also absorbs specific colors, or light wavelengths, m[...]
rapidly than others. If you're scuba diving within 30 feet of t[...]
surface in clear Caribbean water on a sunny day, you may not
notice the effect; the bright tropical fish and coral surrounding you
still retain their vibrant colors.

But the deeper you go, or the more the surface light dims, the
more you'll notice the colors diminishing. Reds tend to disappear
first, followed by yellows and then greens. The last color in the
spectrum to go is blue, which is why in underwater photography,
the colors tend to range from bright blue-green in shallow water
to darker blues, cobalts, and finally black as you hit the abyssal
depths. (The chemical composition of the water also tends to affect
its color absorption; lake water or cold ocean water tends to be
much more greenish and murky, due to the presence of algae, soil
runoff, or plankton.)

To duplicate the murkiness inherent in underwater photography, you need to set up atmospheric conditions in your 3D scene
that mimic the light absorption and visibility attenuation present
in underwater environments. You can do this in 3D Studio MAX
by using the Fog feature of the Environment Editor. In addition,
you can create the illusion of depth drop-off by applying a gradient to the Environmental Fog shader, and vary the effect by adding Noise to the Fog.

## Underwater Fog?

Here's how you can create the illusion of hydronamic haze (murky water) in 3D Studio MAX. You want to create a simple underwater scene to illustrate the effects of the environmental fog attributes in 3D Studio MAX.

*Note: For best results, you should do the tutorials in this chapter and in Chapter 23, "Under the Sea, White With Foam," in one session.*

1. Reset 3D Studio MAX and activate the 2D Snap toggle.

2. In the Top viewport, create a Quad Patch grid with its upper-left corner at approximate XYZ coordinates X -100, Y 100, and Z 0; and its lower-right at approximate XYZ coordinates X 100, Y -100, and Z 0. Note that this Quad Patch object should have a length and width of 200 units.

3. Change the name of this object from QuadPatch01 to Ocean Floor. Under Parameters, click on Generate Mapping Coordinates. You're going to apply a sandy ocean floor texture to this Quad Patch object in a moment.

4. In your Top viewport, create a Target Camera with the camera body at approximate XYZ coordinates X 0, Y -40, and Z 0. Click and drag vertically upward until the Camera01 target is touching the far end of the top of the Ocean Floor Quad Patch object. You should move it on vertically on the Y axis approximately 102 units.

   In the Left viewport, move the Camera01 body on the Y axis upward 10 units.

5. In the Modify Panel, scroll up to the Environment Ranges section of the Parameters rollout. You'll want to set the Camera01 ranges for the fog effect, so click on Show and change the Far Range from 1000 to 125. The Camera01 Ranges sphere appears, showing the Far Range sphere encompassing most of the Ocean Floor Quad Patch object. Now, change the Perspective viewport to the Camera01 view.

## Deep Light

Now it's time to create an Omni light to illuminate your Ocean Floor object.

1. From the Create Panel, select Create/Lights and click on Omni. Change the colors to pure white, or RGB values 255, 255, 255. In the Top viewport, click to place an Omni light at approximate XYZ coordinates X 50, Y -50, and Z 0.

2. In the Left viewport, move the Omni light up on the Y axis approximately 50 units.

   You're going to change your Ocean Floor Quad Patch object from a flat shape to something a little more topographically interesting. First, you'll have to make it a bit more complex, however, using several levels of tessellation.

3. Click on the Ocean Floor object to select it. Add an Edit Mesh modifier and change the Sub-Object Selection Level to Face.

4. Because you changed the Sub-Object selection, you must select the faces that you want to edit. In any viewport, select the entire Ocean Floor Quad Patch object. From the Modify Panel, scroll the Edit Face rollout until you see the Tessellation section. Leave the settings as they are and click on the Tessellate button; the number of faces increase on the Ocean Floor object.

5. Click on the Tessellate button twice more. The Ocean Floor object has now become much more complex in terms of its overall face count. Scroll the rollout up to the Modifiers rollout. You'll want to apply a Noise modifier to sculpt the flat Ocean Floor into a sandy bottom.

6. Click on Noise. When the Noise parameters rollout appears, click on Fractal to activate it and then, under Strength, change X to 10, Y to 10, and Z to 15. The Ocean Floor Quad Patch object is now distorted into a gently rolling surface, as shown in Figure 22-1.

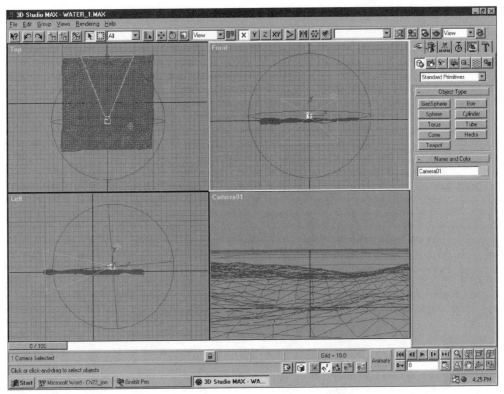

Figure 22-1: *Your Ocean Floor Quad Patch object with three levels of tessellation applied and a Noise object modifier distorting its surface.*

## Still Water, White Sand

Now you'll load the material that you're going to use for the Ocean Floor object.

1. In the Material Editor, click on the Get Material icon. Under Browse From, select Material Library, select Open, and from the \MATLIBS directory of your *3D Studio MAX f/x CD-ROM*, load the 3DSMAXFX.MAT Material Library. When the Material Library loads, scroll down to the material White Sand and double-click on it to load it into Material Editor Slot #1.

    Take a look at the parameters for this material— it's fairly simple.

2. In the Maps rollout; notice that the WHTESAND.TGA file is loaded as a Diffuse, Shininess, and Bump map. Use File/View File to examine this bitmap file; it's in the \MAPS directory of your *3D Studio MAX f/x CD-ROM*. This is a 640 x 480, 24-bit Targa image that I created in Adobe Photoshop. I produced the texture very simply by creating a solid white field and applying Photoshop's Noise filter to it. This resulted in a noisy pattern of multicolored pixels across the white field. I then adjusted the color to eliminate most of the yellow tones from the image.

3. When you've finished viewing this bitmap, close the View File window and return to the Material Editor.

   Notice that the White Sand material has a fairly high Shininess and Shininess Strength value. Notice also that the WHTESAND.TGA bitmap is loaded into the Shininess mapping slot.

4. Open the Shininess bitmap rollout and then the Output rollout. The WHTESAND.TGA output is inverted, creating a black field with light speckles. This produces the illusion of tiny sparkling grains of sand on the surface. After you've examined these sections, click on the Go to Parent icon to return to the top material level. Click on the Assign Material to Selection icon to assign the White Sand material to the selected Ocean Floor object. Finally, close the Material Editor.

   It's time to set your environment fog parameters to create the illusion of a murky underwater scene.

5. Select Rendering/Environment. When the Environment Map appears, under Atmosphere: Effects, click on Add and then Fog. On the Fog Parameters rollout, click on the Color Swatch to bring up the Color Selector. You'll want to change the fog color from pure white to a dark blue-green to imitate the color of underwater, so set the RGB values to 0, 96, 128. This gives you a moderately dark blue-green shade. Close the Color Selector.

6. For now, you can leave the remaining Fog parameters at the default settings. Because you are not using transparent objects in the scene, you don't need to change the Exponential switch. (You'll explore this setting and the effect of transparent objects in Fog in Chapter 25, "Plankton & Bubbles.") In addition,

because you have no other foreground objects in the scene, you can leave the Near Percentage at 0; the Far Percentage remains at 100. Close the Environment dialog box.

7. It's time to do a test rendering, so activate the Camera01 viewport and then render a single 640 x 480 image. After a few moments, the image appears as shown in Figure 22-2.

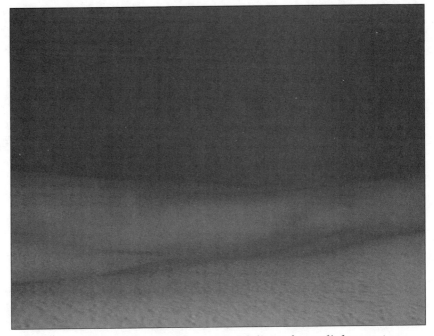

Figure 22-2: *The basic underwater scene with linear fog applied to create an underwater effect.*

In Figure 22-2, the basic Fog settings create the impression of an underwater scene. The Noise modifier applied to the Ocean Floor Quad Patch object creates the feeling of a gently rolling, sandy bottom; the White Sand texture completes the illusion. The scene looks something like the ocean floor near the Caribbean or Hawaii.

8. When you've finished viewing the rendering, close the Camera01 VFB window.

## Gradients & Color Banding

You can modify this underwater scene in several ways to make it more interesting. To start, you can add a gradient effect to the Fog so that the underwater murk appears to become darker the deeper you go.

1. In the Fog Parameters rollout of the Environment Editor, click on Use Map under Environment Color Map. Then (again under Environment Color Map), click on Assign. When the Material/Map Browser appears, click on New under Browse From and then double-click on Gradient. When you return to the Fog Parameters rollout, click on Map #1 (Gradient); under Put to Material Editor, click on Slot #2 and then on OK.

2. Because you'll be using specific color gradient to color the Fog in the Material Editor, you don't have to tint the fog here to its present blue-green color. Click on the Fog color swatch and change the fog back to pure white, or RGB values 255, 255, 255. Close the Environment Dialog box.

3. Click on the Material Editor icon to bring up the Material Editor and then activate Slot #2. Because you selected a gradient, Slot #2 already contains a grayscale gradient set up as a Spherical Environment map. You need to change the colors on this to something more suitable for an underwater environment, so change the RGB values for Color #1 to 0, 96, 128; for Color #2 to 0, 64, 96; and for Color #3 to 0, 48, 64. Now, change the Color 2 position from 0.5 to 0.65 to move up the midpoint of the gradient effect.

4. Re-render a test image of the Camera01 viewport. After a few moments, the image appears as shown in Figure 22-3.

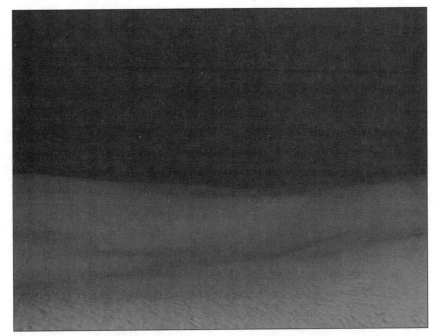

Figure 22-3: *By using a gradient Environmental map, you can create a gradient fog effect in your underwater scene.*

Notice that using a Spherical Environmental map with a Gradient tints the fog color in the background of your underwater scene. The very slight gradient in the color fog enhances the impression of water depth in the background. The middle part of your screen is darker than the upper part, near the water surface. This makes the sandy bottom seem to be both disappearing in the distance and slanting on an incline to a drop-off with deeper water beyond it.

Study this rendering carefully. A slight amount of banding is present in the color gradient of the background. You can mitigate this banding and produce a more unusual underwater effect by adding Noise to the Fog color gradient.

5. Close the Camera01 VFB window and return to Slot #2 in the Material Editor. Open the Noise rollout and change both Noise Size and Amount to 0.1. In the Coordinates rollout, change the U tiling from Tile to Mirror. This ensures that the Environmental Noise effect does not produce a vertical seam in your rendering.

6. Activate the Camera01 viewport again and do another rendering to test this effect.

After a few moments, a new version of your familiar scene appears on your screen. (Due to the subtlety of this effect, I haven't reproduced it in this book.) Notice how adding a slight bit of Noise to your Environment gradient has "fuzzed up" the fog. This slight noise effect has also eliminated color banding in the gradient background.

7. Close the Camera01 VFB.

## "Pushing the Film"

This technique of modifying Fog with Noise in a gradient Environmental map can be very useful. By breaking up the linear gradient effect of the fog in your underwater scene, you can make the scene seem less artificial.

In addition, by adjusting the Noise Amount and Noise Size, you can create an interesting filmic effect that you may have seen during the course of some underwater documentaries. For many underwater shots captured on motion picture film, because of the low light levels underwater, the documentary makers often must "push the film." To push a piece of film means to increase the exposure of the film during the developing process. This tends to increase the film grain. If you're rendering one of your 3D Studio MAX underwater scenes to video, it might actually help the verisimilitude of your shot to add artificial film grain. Experiment by adding a very small amount of Noise in the Environmental Gradient used as your background. Set the Noise Size very low to simulate film grain. In addition, by animating the Noise parameters, you can even simulate the "swimming" effect of grainy film—no pun intended.

Feel free to play with the various parameters of this simple underwater scene. You may want to adjust the fog colors, the Gradient, and the amount of Noise used in the scene to see their effects. However, before you do so, save your scene to your 3DSMAX\SCENES directory as WATER_1.MAX. In the next chapter, you're going to load the WATER_1.MAX file as the established environment for the ocean surface effects.

The file you've just created is also in the \CHAP_22 and \CHAP_23 directories of your *3D Studio MAX f/x CD-ROM* as WATER_1.MAX. If you want, you can simply load and use either of these files for the next tutorial.

## Moving On

In this tutorial, you've seen the effect of underwater "fog" used to simulate murkiness. In the next chapter, you'll add to this underwater environment by creating the underside of the ocean surface. By using a variation of your Ocean Floor Quad Patch object, and applying liberal amounts of Noise bump, reflection and shininess maps, you can create anything from a placid pond to a stormy sea surface.

# 23

# Under the Sea, White With Foam

**N**ow that you've seen how to create the illusion of underwater murkiness in Chapter 22, "Seawater? See—Water!," you'll examine how to create the effect of the underside of the ocean surface. If you've seen any nature documentaries dealing with undersea life, or if you have personal experience with snorkeling or scuba diving, you've probably noticed the effect of the underside of the ocean surface.

Just as the top of a body of water acts something like a mirror reflecting its surroundings, the underside of a body of water also reflects its surroundings, and also refracts light rays passing through it. It's like a moving mirrored surface that provides ever-changing shiny reflective patterns, depending upon the wind on the surface and the currents beneath the waves.

You can duplicate this effect in 3D Studio MAX by using a combination of animated bump, shininess, and reflection mapping on a relatively simple Quad Patch object, similar to the one you used for your Ocean Floor. In addition, you'll see how you can create a more complex ocean surface effect by increasing the face count of the Quad Patch object and animating its face parameters.

## Mirror, Mirror

Now you'll explore the simplest technique to create an undulating, undersea effect—simple geometry with complex textures.

1. If you're still in 3D Studio MAX with the WATER_1.MAX file loaded, you can proceed from there. If you don't have this file loaded, then load it either from the 3DSMAX\SCENES directory or from the \CHAP_22 or \CHAP_23 directory of the *3D Studio MAX f/x CD-ROM*.

2. Activate the left viewport and select the Ocean Floor object.

3. Click on the Mirror Selected Objects icon at the top of the screen. When the Mirror: Screen Coordinates dialog box appears, for Mirror Axis, check Y and set Offset to 50. Under Clone selection, select Copy and then click on OK. This creates a mirrored duplicate of the Ocean Floor object, labeled Ocean Floor01, 50 units above the ocean floor. Change its name from Ocean Floor01 to Ocean Surface. (You may also want to change its object color to make distinguishing it from the Ocean Floor object easier.)

4. In the Left viewport, move the Camera01 body to the right to XYZ coordinates X 60, Y 0, and Z 0. Click on the Camera01 Target to select it (or press the H key to bring up the Select By Name dialog box, and select the Camera01 Target). In the Left viewport, drag the Camera01 target up on the Y axis to XYZ coordinates X 0, Y 30, and Z 0. The screen should now look like Figure 23-1.

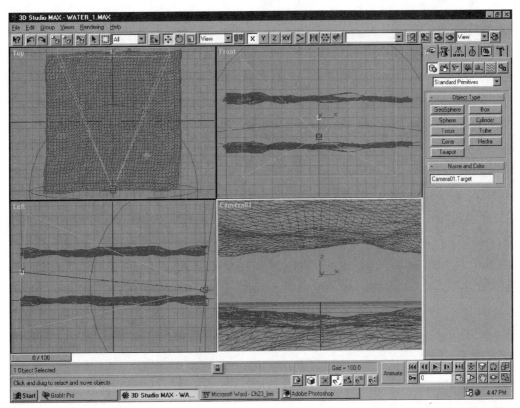

Figure 23-1: *The mirrored copy of the Ocean Floor object provides the basis for the Ocean Surface effect.*

5. Move the Omni light down to XYZ coordinates X -50, Y -40, and Z 0. In the Front viewport, drag it to the left along the X axis to X -50. This centers the Omni light in the scene.

## Popping the Stack

Now you'll remove the object modifiers from your Ocean Surface object to return it to a flat Quad Patch object.

1. Select the Ocean Surface object and click on the Modify tab of the Command Panel. As you do, you see Ocean Surface object turn bright red, indicating that it has an Edit Mesh modifier applied to it and that its faces are ready for modification. Under the Modifier Stack, you see that Noise is the last Object Modifier applied to the object.

2. Click on the Remove Modifier from the Stack icon. As you do, the Ocean Surface Quad Patch object flattens out and the Edit Mesh modifier appears in the Modifier Stack. This is the modifier that you applied earlier to the original Ocean Floor object to tessellate the surface.

3. Click again on the Remove Modifier from the Stack button. The Ocean Surface object has been reduced to the original simple Quad Patch with which you started. Under Parameters, make sure that Generate Mapping Coordinates is checked.

## Imperfect Reflections

Now it's time to apply a texture that will be appropriate for your undersea surface effect.

1. Click on the Material Editor icon to bring up the Material Editor. If you're working with your original WATER_1.MAX file, material Slot #1 should have the White Sand texture and Slot #2 should have the Spherical Environment gradient map used for tinting the fog background.

2. Click on Slot #3 to activate it. You're going to build a new material to represent the underside of the Ocean Surface object. First, you'll change the Ambient and Diffuse colors. Activate Ambient and change its RGB values to 0, 8, 16, or a

very dark blue-green. Change Diffuse to RGB values 64, 160, 196, or a medium blue-green. Change Specular to pure white, or RGB values 255, 255, 255. Change Shininess to 50 and Shininess Strength to 100. Next to Highlight, click on Soften. This will blur the specular highlight slightly on the undersea Ocean Surface object.

3. Open the Maps rollout and click on the Shininess Map name button. When Material/Map browser appears, click on New. Then, click on Noise to load it. Under Noise Parameters, change Noise Type from Regular to Fractal. Under Size, change this from 25 to 4. Click on the Color #1 color swatch. When the Color Selector appears, change Color #1 to RGB values 0, 16, 32. Keep Color #2 as pure white, or RGB 255, 255, 255, and close the Color Selector.

4. Click on the Go to Parent icon to return to the top material level; then, drag the Noise texture from the Shininess Map slot down to Bump Map. When the Copy Method dialog box appears, click on Instance rather than Copy and then click on OK. Next, increase the Bump Map setting to maximum, or 999. Now, drag the Noise Texture from the Shininess Map slot down to Reflection, but instead of placing an Instance, click on OK to place a Copy of this texture (you're going to modify its settings slightly). As you can see, the material on the sample sphere in Slot #3 becomes much brighter.

5. Now you'll make a final change to this material. Click on the Reflection map button, change the Noise Type from Fractal to Turbulence, and change the Noise Size from 4.0 to 1. Click on the Go to Parent icon to return to the top material level, and click on the Assign Material to Selection icon to assign this material to the Ocean Surface object.

    It's time to do a test rendering of this scene.

6. Make sure that the Camera01 viewport is active; then, press Alt+R and Enter to render a 640 x 480 test image of this scene. After a few moments, the image appears and should look like Figure 23-2.

Figure 23-2: *The illusion of an undersea surface created with shininess, bump, and reflection mapping.*

As shown in Figure 23-2, dusk appears to be falling "topside" in your underwater scene. The Noise gradient in the Environmental Map produces a varied pattern in the blue-green murky water, and the Omni light in the center of scene provides a soft glow on the sandy ocean floor; it also picks up the Noise bump map on the flat Ocean Surface object.

7. Close the Camera01 VFB window of the Camera01 rendering.

## Light 'em Up

You can change the look of this undersea effect easily by simply increasing the light level in the scene.

1. Click on the Omni01 light to activate it. From the Modify section of the Command Panel, go to the Omni01 light's general parameters and change the multiplier from 1.0 to 2.0.

2. Activate the Camera01 viewport again and render another test image, as shown in Figure 23-3.

Figure 23-3: *By increasing the multiplier on the Omni light used in the scene, you've created the illusion of brighter highlights reflecting off of the underside of the Ocean Surface object.*

3. Close the Camera01 VFB window.

At this point, you may want to return to the Material Editor and save the material that you just created in your own 3DSMAX.MAT Material Library as WATER 2. This material is also included in the *3D Studio MAX f/x CD-ROM* Material Library.

## Animating the Water Noise Texture

In Chapter 15, "Advanced Lasers, Part II," you saw how you can create an interesting laser beam effect by applying a Noise material and then animating its parameters. If you animate the Noise material parameters applied to the underwater Ocean Surface, you can create the illusion of a very realistic, undulating, rippling water surface.

Here's how to do it.

1. Because you're going to be concentrating on the Ocean Surface, you don't need to show the Ocean Floor object. Click on the Ocean Floor object to select it, and use Hide by Selection on the Display panel to hide the Ocean Floor object.

    Now you'll tilt the camera target up slightly so that you can see a little more of the Ocean Surface.

2. Make sure that 2D Snap is still active; then, move the Camera01 target in the Left viewport up on the Y axis 20 units. Reactivate the Camera01 viewport.

3. To set up animated parameters, click on the Animate button and move to frame 100. In the Material Editor; Slot #3 should still be active, showing the WATER_2 texture for the Ocean Surface. Go to the Maps rollout and click on the Shininess Noise Map button. In the Coordinates rollout, change the Z Offset from 0.0 to 10. Click on the Go to Parent icon to return to the top material level.

    Because you placed an Instance of the Shininess Noise Map in the Bump Map slot, the Bump Map follows the changes made in the Shininess Noise Map. However, you do still need to animate the Reflection Map.

4. Click on the Reflection Noise Map button and change the Noise Coordinates Z Offset to 10 as well. Click on the Go to Parent icon. The texture on the sample sphere in Slot #3 changes to reflect the animated Z coordinate settings. Turn off the Animation mode.

By animating the Z coordinates of all three Noise texture maps applied to your Ocean Surface object, you create the illusion of water movement across the 100 frames of animation set up in the 3D Studio MAX scene.

The scene you've just created is saved in the \CHAP_23 directory as WATER_2.MAX. If you want, you can also save it under the same file name to your 3DSMAX\SCENES directory; you'll be using this scene file for the tutorials in the next chapter.

## Render, Man

Now you can render your own 320 x 240 test .AVI of this animation, but if you'd rather, you can look at the rendering that I already did with these scene parameters.

1. Select File/View File, and from the \CHAP_23 directory of the *3D Studio MAX f/x* CD-ROM, click on the file WATER_2.AVI. When the Media Player appears, click on the Play button to play the animation.

   Notice how animating the Z Offset coordinate of the noise textures results in the textures appearing to move through the Ocean Surface Quad Patch object. If you were to animate the X and Z or the Y and Z Offsets of the three Noise textures applied to Ocean Surface object, you would not only get the illusion of ripples constantly undulating across the surface, but also the impression of a specific current or wind direction, moving on either the X or the Y axis. (You can also reverse the direction of the current, or wind effect, by typing in negative Offset values.)

   Of course, by simply rotating the Ocean Surface Quad Patch object to any orientation, you can "point" the water ripples in any direction you want. In addition, by increasing or decreasing either the number of frames or the Offset value, you can speed up or slow down the apparent ripple effect. For your purposes, using an Offset value of 10 on the Z axis, for a 100-frame sequence playing at 30 frames per second, creates a gently rippling ocean surface.

2. When you've finished viewing the sequence, close the Media Player.

## Enhancing the Ocean Surface Effect

Now you'll beef up the movement on your Ocean Surface object. As you've seen in the previous example, you can create a realistic undersea surface by using a flat Quad Patch object with an animated Noise bump map applied to it. However, you may sometimes want to create an even more dynamic ocean surface effect (for instance, a storm occurring on the surface).

For this effect, you'll animate the faces and vertices of the actual Ocean Surface Quad Patch object itself. To do that and make it look realistic, you need to greatly increase this object's complexity.

1. Close the Material Editor, if it's still open, and select the Ocean Surface object. Just as you did in Chapter 22, "Seawater? See—Water!," you need to add an Edit Mesh modifier to the Ocean Floor object to tessellate the Ocean Surface object. Follow the procedure outlined in that chapter and tessellate the Ocean Surface four times using the default settings.

*Note: Depending upon the speed of your computer, the Object Modifier may take a few moments to finish tessellating the entire Ocean Surface. When it's finished, you should see an extremely complex Quad Patch.*

2. From the Modifiers rollout, click on Noise to apply a Noise Object Modifier to the Ocean Surface object. In the Parameters section, change Noise Scale from 100 to 25. Click on Fractal to activate it; then, under Strength, change the Z value from 0.0 to 10. Finally, under Animation, click on Animate Noise.

The combination of Edit Mesh Tessellation modifiers and the Noise modifier distort the surface of the original simple Quad Patch, as shown in Figure 23-4.

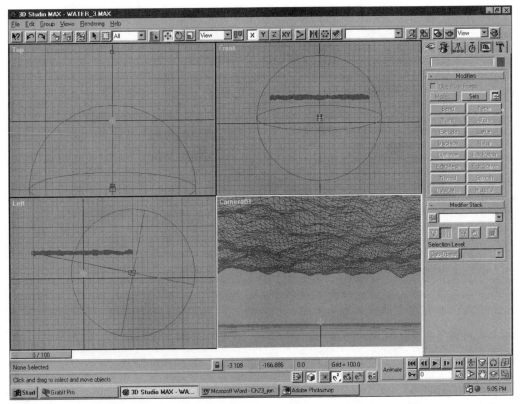

Figure 23-4: *A combination of Edit Mesh and Noise Object modifiers has produced an undulating Ocean Surface.*

3. Drag the Time Slider from frame 100 all the way back to frame 0 and observe the Camera01 viewport. The topology of the Ocean Surface object changes because you activated the Animate Noise function.

    Now you'll look at a test rendering of this effect.

4. Select File/View File, and from the \CHAP_23 directory, select the file WATER_3.AVI. When the Media Player appears, click on the Play button to play the animation.

    You can now see that the combination of the original WATER_2 texture applied to the animated Ocean Surface object has resulted in a dynamic water surface.

5. When you have finished previewing the file, close the Media Player.

At this point, you may want to play around with other material and geometry settings to create your own water effects. For instance, you could change the WATER_2 Bump, Shininess, and Reflection maps; in addition, rather than use Noise textures, you could use bitmap textures. Again, the key to interesting effects is to experiment.

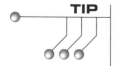

**TIP** If you want this new Ocean Surface object to revert back to its original simple geometry, just return to the Modifiers Panel and click on the Remove Modifier from the Stack button as many times as needed. This will delete the Modifier Stack history of the various modifiers that you've applied to your Ocean Surface object.

The scene you've just created (with the enhanced Ocean Surface topography) is in the \CHAP_23 directory as WATER_3.MAX.

## Moving On

Now that you've seen how to create the illusion of both a sandy ocean floor and the underside of the ocean surface above it, how can you tie these two elements together? In the next chapter, you'll see how, as you use 3D Studio MAX's projector spotlights and the Environmental Volumetric light functions, to create the effects of water caustic patterns and light rays coming from the ocean surface.

# 24

# Light Rays, Not Stingrays

**N**ow that you've created the effects of underwater murkiness, the ocean floor, and the underside of the ocean surface, you need a way to tie these elements together. One way to do this is to create interactive lighting effects, creating the illusion that light from the animated ocean surface is actually casting patterns on the ocean floor.

In this chapter, you'll create the effect known as *water caustics*. In 3D graphics terminology, a water caustic is the pattern that light produces when it passes through a body of water onto an underwater surface. You may have noticed this effect any time that you've walked around a swimming pool on a bright sunny day. On the bottom of the pool, undulating patterns of light wax and wane, causing flickering in constant motion.

You can mimic the effect of water caustics in 3D Studio MAX by using projector spotlights with different textures loaded in them. These textures will attenuate some of the overall light and create patterns on the Ocean Floor object. In addition, you can create animated water caustics easily. You can either use the slot gag technique (counter-rotating two or more projector spotlights with bitmaps) or you can load animated textures—either bitmap sequences or procedural textures—into the projector lights.

*Note: For true realism, water caustic patterns tend to disappear relatively close to the surface. For example, if you're scuba diving in clear water, as in the Caribbean or Hawaii, and are down only 30 feet or so, you won't see the distinctive water caustic patterns that you see sharply defined on the bottom of a swimming pool. (The slight murkiness of ocean water as opposed to filtered pool water is a factor in this, of course.) The patterns still move but they tend to be very soft and amorphous. However, there may be times when you want to cheat realism by forcing a particular effect. Therefore, placing strongly delineated caustics on, say, a submarine or a swimming shark—as long as neither is in the abyssal depths—may help sell the overall underwater scene. (In Chapter 26, "Swimming With the Fishes," you'll explore how to create the aforementioned swimming shark.)*

## Caustic Humor

Creating water caustics in 3D Studio MAX is very simple.

1. First, load the WATER_2.MAX file that you created for the previous chapter. If you didn't save a finished version, load it from the \CHAP_24 directory of the *3D Studio MAX f/x* CD-ROM. (Be sure to unhide the Ocean Floor object if it's still hidden.)

2. Camera01 should still be pointed toward the Ocean Surface as you left it. In this chapter, you're looking at both the Ocean Surface and the Ocean Floor, so you need to move the Camera01 target back down. In the Front or Left viewport, move it down along the Y axis -50 units.

3. Select Camera01, and in the Modify Panel, change the camera lens to a 35mm lens, a semi-wide angle lens. It lets you see more of both the Ocean Surface and Ocean Floor objects.

   You'll be using a projector spotlight to illuminate the Ocean Floor in this scene, so you need to set the Omni01 light in the scene to exclude the Ocean Floor object.

4. Select the Omni01 light, and in the Modify Panel, make sure that the Omni light multiplier is set at 2.0. On the General Parameters rollout, click on the Exclude button. When the Exclude/Include dialog box appears, click on Ocean Floor and then on the Right arrow to place the Ocean Floor object in the list of Excluded objects. Click on OK.

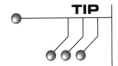

**TIP** Use Exclude to help keep control of special lighting effects. It's especially useful in complex scenes in which you need a number of lights for different purposes. For example, if you want a light simulating a rocket engine exhaust to light the surrounding geometry but not the nearby (and supposedly distant) planet, simply exclude the planet from the exhaust light. Excluding unnecessary objects from light effects also speeds up rendering calculations.

Now you'll create the projector spotlight used for your water caustic pattern.

5. Create a Target Spot in the Left viewport at approximate XYZ coordinates X 0, Y 0, and Z 49. (You may need to make the viewport full screen to do this accurately.) Place the target approximately in the middle of the ocean floor.

Now you'll modify the Spot01 settings.

6. In the Modify Panel, change the spotlight color to pure white, or RGB 255, 255, 255. Make sure that the Multiplier is set at 2.0; under Attenuation, click on Use and Show, and then change the Start Attenuation Range to 95 and the End Attenuation to 100. Under Spotlight Parameters, change the Hot Spot to 120 and the Falloff to 125; click on Show Cone to activate it, and change the Spotlight Aspect from a Circle to a Rectangle. Finally, go down to Shadow Parameters section and click on Cast Shadows.

7. Click in the Projector check box to turn Spotlight01 into a projector light; then, click on Assign. When the Material/Map Browser appears, make sure that New is selected under Browse From; then, click on Bitmap. In the Command Panel,

on the Spotlight Parameters rollout, click on the Bitmap name button, put the Bitmap to Material Editor slot #4, and click on OK in the Put to Material Editor dialog box.

8. In the Material Editor, activate Slot #4. You need to load a water caustic bitmap, so click on the Bitmap name button. From the \CHAP_24 directory of the *3D Studio MAX f/x CD-ROM*, click once on the CAUSTIC.GIF image to highlight it; then, click on View.

   CAUSTIC.GIF is a grayscale bitmap of a medium-gray field with antialiased, white, wavy lines traversing it vertically and horizontally. I painted this artwork originally in Autodesk Animator Pro, brought it into Adobe Photoshop, and applied heavy blur to the image. Then I made it seamlessly tileable along all four sides. When it's loaded into a projector spotlight, this image creates a reasonable facsimile of a stationary water caustic pattern.

9. Close the CAUSTIC.GIF image and click on OK to load it into the Material Editor.

10. Now you'll render a test image, so activate the Camera01 viewport and then press Alt+R and Enter. (If you've previously rendered your own WATER_2.AVI or WATER_3.AVI file, you must change back to Single Frame with an Output Size of 640 x 480. Last, make sure that Save File isn't checked under Render Output.) Click on Render. After a few moments, the image appears; it should look like Figure 24-1.

Figure 24-1: *The CAUSTIC.GIF image, loaded into a projector spotlight, creates stationary water caustic patterns on the ocean floor.*

In Figure 24-1, notice how using the CAUSTIC.GIF image in the projector spotlight creates water caustic patterns on the sandy Ocean Floor object.

## Increasing the Depth

Although this is an interesting effect, you could make it a little more realistic for your underwater scene by changing the size of the pattern. You may want to suggest that the ocean depth in your scene is perhaps 20 to 30 feet. However, due to the large size of the caustic pattern on the Ocean Floor, the floor seems to be only a mere five feet or so below the surface. So, you need to change this.

1. Close the Camera01 VFB window and return to the Material Editor. Because the CAUSTIC.GIF image is seamlessly tileable, you can use the UV Tiling options to decrease the size of the water caustic patterns simply by quadrupling the texture across the projector spotlight. On the Coordinates rollout, change UV Tiling from 1.0 to 2.0, for both U and V.

2. Activate the Camera01 viewport again, and press Alt+R and Enter to render another test image. After a few minutes, the image appears as shown in Figure 24-2.

Figure 24-2: *Increasing the tiling of the CAUSTIC.GIF image makes the ocean floor appear to be at a greater depth from the ocean surface.*

3. When you've finished viewing the image, close the Camera01 viewport.

## Making It Move

Although this projected bitmap technique may be useful for quick-and-dirty still imagery, the chief characteristic of water caustic patterns is that they move. So, you must make your water caustic pattern move, too.

You can do this in several ways. The easiest way, using a still bitmap, is to create two projector spotlights, each with the same (or similar) water caustic bitmap, and then counter-rotate the lights. This creates a slot gag—a moving moiré or interference pattern, as explained in Chapter 11, "Warp Drive!" In addition, you can both rotate the individual projector spotlights and animate the UV Offset of the caustic bitmap patterns in each spotlight. By turning on the Animate button and then changing the UV Offset in the Material Editor on a non-zero frame, you can make the bitmaps "slide" across the projector spotlight target.

(One thing to remember if you use this technique: you must make sure that your water caustic bitmaps are seamlessly tileable. Otherwise, as you either Tile them in the Material Editor or scroll them using animated UV Offsets, you will see an obvious seam at their edges.)

Of course, one of the easiest ways to create animated water caustic patterns in a projector spotlight is to use an animated bitmap sequence. By loading an animated sequence of water caustic bitmaps (or a .FLC or .AVI file) into a projector spotlight, you can create the appropriate caustic effect without moving the spotlights. Again, make sure that the animated map loops seamlessly to avoid jumps in your placid water patterns.

## Using Noise to Create Water Caustic Patterns

Another way to create animated water caustic patterns in projector lights is to not use bitmaps, but to use your old Material Editor favorite instead—the procedural Noise texture. The following steps show you how to do this.

1. Return to the Material Editor. Make sure that Slot #4 is active; then, click on the Bitmap name button next to Type. When the Material/Map Browser appears, make sure that Browse From is selected, click on New, and click on Noise. When the Replace Map dialog box appears, click on OK to discard the old CAUSTIC.GIF texture map. The Noise texture appears on the sample sphere in Slot #4.

   You're going to change some of these Noise parameters on the Noise Parameters rollout.

2. Under Noise Type, change from Regular to Turbulence. Change the Size from 25 to 5. Finally, go down to the Noise Parameters rollout and click on swap next to Color 1 and Color 2. This reverses the order of colors in the Turbulence Noise function.

3. Activate the Camera01 viewport, and press Alt+R and Enter again to render a test image with the new Noise texture. After a few moments, the image appears as shown in Figure 24-3.

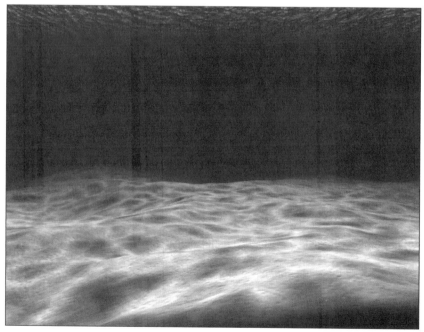

Figure 24-3: *The Turbulence Noise function loaded into the projector spotlight.*

Notice how the Noise texture produces a much more irregular, organic-looking pattern on the Ocean Floor object. Because this is a procedural texture loaded into the projector spotlight, it actually occupies less RAM than a large bitmap and may therefore render faster.

4. When you've finished viewing the image, close the Camera01 VFB window.

## Looking Sharp Underwater

Now, how about enhancing this effect? You're going to sharpen the Noise texture and see what happens.

1. Return to the Material Editor, and in the Noise Parameters rollout, change the Noise Threshold High value from 1.0 to 0.75.

2. Activate the Camera01 viewport again and do another test rendering. If you compare this image to that in Figure 24-3, you'll see that altering the High Threshold value results in a higher-contrast Turbulent Noise caustic effect.

3. Close the Camera01 VFB window.

## Animating the Noise Texture

Now you'll see how you can animate this projected Noise caustic texture. You can produce a striking effect by changing the Z Offset values of the Noise texture, much as you did to create the animated texture for the Ocean Surface object.

1. Click on the Toggle Animation Mode button to turn Animation Mode on, and move to frame 100.

2. Return to the Material Editor and change the Noise Z Offset from 0.0 to 10. Click on the Toggle Animation Mode button again to turn Animation Mode off.

At this point, you could render your own 320 x 240 .AVI file of this animated water caustic pattern. However, again, I've already rendered a test animation of this effect to save you some time and to keep from wearing out all those monitor electrons.

3. Select File/View File, and from the \CHAP_24 directory, click on the file WATER_4.AVI to load it. When the Media Player appears, click on the Play button to play the animation.

Pretty cool effect, huh? As you can see, by animating the Z offset for the Noise Turbulence texture in the projector spotlight, you've created very realistic-appearing water caustic patterns on the Ocean Floor. In addition, by combining this with the animated Noise texture for the Ocean Surface object, the light coming from the Ocean Surface seems to be producing these varied light patterns.

4. When you've finished previewing this file, close the Media Player and save this file to the Scenes Directory as WATER_4.MAX. This file is also saved in the \CHAP_24 and \CHAP_25 directories.

## Creating Volumetric Light Rays

Now that you've seen the effect of a projector spotlight on the Ocean Floor, you'll see what happens when you turn a projector spotlight into a volumetric spotlight. This will produce the illusion of beams of lights flashing from the Ocean Surface down onto the Ocean Floor, and will look much like the actual source of the caustic patterns you've already seen.

To create the illusion of shafts of light coming from the ocean surface, you'll need a second spotlight.

1. Enlarge the Left viewport to full screen. You'll want to duplicate your Spot01 spotlight, so click on the Select and Move icon (if it's not already selected) and then click on the Restrict to Y button to restrict the movement to the Y axis. Holding

down the Shift key, click and drag the Spot01 spotlight vertically upward on the Y axis 100 units. When you release the Shift key, click on OK to create a copy of original Spot01 light, now called Spot02.

2. In the Modify Panel for Spot02, make the following changes. Under Attenuation, set the Start Range to 190 and the End Range to 200. On the Spotlight Parameters rollout, change the Falloff to 75. (The Hot Spot should automatically go to 73.) Change the Multiplier from 2.0 to 5.0—you want the light rays to be quite noticeable.

3. On the General Parameters rollout, click on the Exclude button. You'll want to exclude the new Spot02 light from affecting the Ocean Surface (and, surprisingly enough, the Ocean Floor as well. You want to make the light rays simply appear in the open water of the scene.) When the Exclude/Include dialog box appears, click on Ocean Floor and Ocean Surface and then click on the Right arrow to Exclude them from both Illumination and Shadow Casting of the Spot02 light. Click on OK to dismiss the dialog box.

4. Projector should still be active, so click on the Assign button and, when the Material/Map Browser appears, click on Bitmap. Under Map, click on the Name button, put the new map to Material Editor Slot #5, and click on OK.

    It's time to return to the Material Editor and load the bitmap that you'll use to produce the light rays.

5. Click on the Material Editor icon to bring up the Material Editor and then click on Slot #5 to make it active. Click on the Bitmap name button under Bitmap Parameters, and from the \CHAP_24 directory, click on the file WATERVL1.GIF to highlight it; then, click on View.

    WATERVL1.GIF is essentially a variation of one of the starfield bitmaps. I created this image in Adobe Photoshop by taking the original STARS640.GIF image, cropping it to 320 x 240, and layering it. Click the Close button to dismiss this image, and click on OK to load this bitmap in Material Editor Slot #5.

    Now you'll make Spot02 a volume light.

6. Select Rendering/Environment; under Atmosphere Effects, click on Add. Click on Volume Light and click on OK. On the Volume Light Parameters rollout, click on the Pick Light button. Click on Spot02. You've now assigned the default Volume Light parameters to the Spot02 light.

7. Now, click on the Min/Max Toggle icon to return to the four viewports. Activate the Camera01 viewport and render another test image. (Because you're rendering a volume light effect, which is processor-intensive, the image may take a few minutes to appear.) When it appears, it should look like Figure 24-4.

Figure 24-4: *A volumetric spotlight produces the illusion of shafts of light coming from the ocean surface down to the ocean floor.*

By using the WATERVL1.GIF texture in a volumetric projector spotlight, you create shafts of light emanating from the ocean surface. (The slight "banding" in the shafts of light is caused by having the Environment Volume Light Filter

Shadows parameter set to Low. For best results, you should set the parameters to High; however, this increases the rendering time substantially. For the purposes of this tutorial, you'll leave Filter Shadows at the default setting.)

8. Close the Camera01 VFB window.

## Moving the Light Rays

Now, if you want to make the light rays move in the scene, how do you do it? Well, you can simply rotate the Spot02 light, making the shafts of light rotate in relationship to one another. Or you can simply animate the angle of the projected WATERVL1.GIF bitmap from within the Material Editor. You'll try the latter now.

1. Click the Animate button to toggle Animation mode on and move to frame 100.

2. Return to the Material Editor and go to the Coordinates rollout for Slot #5. Change the Angle from 0.0 to 90. As you do so, the .GIF texture on the sample sphere rotates.

**CD-ROM**

3. Click again on the Animation button to turn off animation mode; if you want, save this file to the 3DSMAX\SCENES directory as WATER_5. (This file is also saved in the \CHAP_24 and \CHAP_25 directories of the *3D Studio MAX f/x* CD-ROM.)

    At this point, you could render your own 320 x 240 test .AVI file of this animation, but once again, I've already provided a demonstration of this animation on the *3D Studio MAX f/x* CD-ROM.

4. Select File/View File, and from the \CHAP_24 directory, click to load the file WATER_5.AVI. When the Media Player appears, click on the Play button to play the animation.

    As you can see, by changing the angle of the WATERVL1.GIF bitmap, you can create a simple effect of the shafts of light rotating and sparkling in the scene.

5. When you've finished viewing the file, close the Media Player. You should experiment with different ways of varying this effect. To improve it, you could Shift-clone this spotlight and then counter-rotate the two textures to create a light ray slot gag effect. You could also vary the fog density, the light attenuation, and of course, the type of texture that you use to create the shafts of light. (The \MAPS directory of the *3D Studio MAX f/x CD-ROM* has additional WATERVL.GIF images to try.)

## Moving On

Now that you've seen how to create animated lighting effects, you'll continue building up your underwater scene. So far, you've created a beautiful ocean environment with rippling blue-green water, a sandy ocean floor, and sparkling water highlights. Now, you'll add some more dynamics to this scene. In the next chapter, you'll see how to use 3D Studio MAX's particle systems to create both plankton and bubbles.

# 25

# Plankton & Bubbles

**O**kay, in the space of a few short chapters, you've created underwater murkiness, a realistic ocean surface, and water caustic patterns. Now you'll add a few more elements to your underwater scene. Again, if you've seen some underwater nature documentaries or have experience with snorkeling or scuba diving, you have probably noticed just how much debris there is underwater, particularly in the ocean.

If you've dived in either a warm-water environment such as Hawaii or the Caribbean, or a cold-water environment such as the waters off Monterey, California, you've probably seen how the water is filled with tiny bits of material. This material ranges from fragments of seaweed to microscopic plankton, brine shrimp, and suspended particles of silt. Therefore, to create more realistic underwater scenes, having the suggestion of tiny bits of material drifting through the water helps.

## A Belief in Suspension

You can help "suspend disbelief "and create the suggestion of tiny debris drifting through your underwater scene by using 3D Studio MAX's Particle systems.

Here's how to do it.

1. If you still have your WATER_5.MAX file loaded from the previous chapter, you can proceed from this file. If you took a break and don't have this scene in 3D Studio MAX, you can load it from the \CHAP_25 directory of the *3D Studio MAX CD-ROM*.

   You have to make a couple of changes to this file. First, to speed up your test renderings, you'll turn off the volumetric light effects that you applied to the Spot02 spotlight.

2. In the Atmosphere section of the Environment dialog box, click on Volume Light to highlight it. Click on Active to toggle the Active Volume Light effect off. When you're finished, close the Environment dialog box.

   Now it's time to place the particle system that you'll use to create your plankton effect. After that, you'll modify its parameters.

3. Enlarge the Left viewport and make sure that 2D Snap is active. In the Create Panel, select Create/Geometry. Click on the Down arrow and select Particle Systems. On the Object Type rollout, click on Spray.

4. Place the cursor at approximate XYZ coordinates X 0, Y 40, and Z 50. Click and drag diagonally downward to the right to approximate XYZ coordinates X 0, Y -50, and Z 0, and release the mouse button to set the Spray emitter. Change its name to Plankton and return to four viewports.

   Now you'll change the angle on the emitter.

5. Activate the Top viewport and press the W key to enlarge to full screen. Click on the Select and Rotate icon and click on the Restrict to Z button to restrict rotation to the Z axis. Move the Select and Rotate cursor over the Plankton emitter and rotate it on the Z axis to approximately Z -45. Return to your four viewports.

The Plankton particle emitter is in the middle of the viewports; in the Camera01 viewport, you'll see it pointing diagonally off to your right.

6. Select Edit/Properties, toggle off the Plankton emitter's Shadow Casting and Shadow Receiving attributes and click on OK. You don't want the final rendered particles to cast disproportionately large shadows on your Ocean Floor mesh.

## Perusing the Plankton Particle Parameters

Now that you've created the Plankton Spray emitter, you need to go back and examine some of its settings.

1. In the Modify Panel, go to the Parameters rollout. In the Particles section, change Viewport Count to 1000. Change Render count to 5000. Change Drop Size to 10.0. Make sure that Speed is set to 0.1 and Variation to 0.5. For the display in your four viewports, make sure that Dots is selected. Under Render, the default should be Tetrahedron.

Now you'll adjust the Spray particle Timing.

2. In the Modify Panel, set Start to -300. Set Life to 300 and click on the Constant check box to make sure that a constant number of particles—in this case, 5000 particles—will appear in your renderings. Finally, under Emitter, the Width should be 200 units and the Length should be 50. Your screen should look like Figure 25-1.

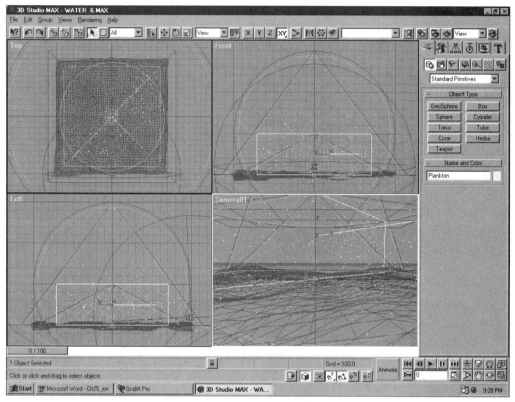

Figure 25-1: *The Spray emitter set up to create the plankton effect.*

It's time to return to the Modify Panel and examine what each of the Spray parameters means in the context of this scene.

## Particle Count & Render Count

Under Particles, the Viewport Count simply specifies how many particles are actually displayed in your viewports. Note that 3D Studio MAX offers this to speed up the screen refresh rate; it also helps speed up preview renderings and manipulation of 3D elements. (If you designated the same number of particles in the viewports as for final rendering, you may find that working in the MAX environment becomes very slow, especially with a slower computer.) Render Count designates the number of particles that are actually rendered.

## Size & Speed

Drop Size indicates the unit size of the actual particles; Speed indicates the rate at which particles erupt from the emitter. In the case of the Plankton, you've set the speed to 0.1 so that the particles drift slowly through the screen. Variation, which you've set at 0.5, determines the initial rate of the particles in both speed and direction.

## Particle Display

The Drops, Dots, or Ticks check boxes indicate how 3D Studio MAX displays the particles in the viewports. Drops are actual 3D objects in your scene and are affected by the Size parameter. Ticks and Dots are 2D representations of the final 3D particle effect; they render faster and display faster in 3D Studio MAX viewports.

## Render (Particle Types)

Under Render, Tetrahedron is set rather than Facing particles. Tetrahedron is the default setting for the Spray emitter; these particles are long, thin polygons.

The default mapping coordinates set for each Tetrahedron particle are cylindrical, which lets you use animated texture maps to determine the opacity and color of each drop. This can be very useful in depicting raindrops, for example. (For the Plankton effect, you'll apply a face-mapped material to change the tetrahedron particles' appearance slightly.)

## Timing

Under Timing, you've set the Start Timing of the particles as -300 frames and their life as 300 frames, with a constant Birth Rate. The reason that you're setting the Start Timing to a negative value is that the initial particle speed is so low. You want the particles to drift slowly through the scene and be present in the first frame. Their drift has some speed variation, however.

If you had set the Start Time for the particles at frame 0, the particles wouldn't begin to appear until later in the animation, when you would see them emerging from the murk. By setting the Start Time to a negative frame value and setting the Birth Rate to Constant, the particles appear on frame 0 already drifting through the scene. By setting the life of the particles to 300, you create the impression that the particles are drifting for a long time through the underwater scene before they disappear and are replenished.

# Previewing the Plankton Particles? Precisely!

Now that you've examined the particle parameters, you'll take a look at a preview of these particle settings. Although you could render your own preview to check out the effect, again, I've saved you the trouble.

1. Select File/View File, and from the \CHAP_25 directory, click on the file PREVIEW1.AVI. When the Media Player appears, click on the Play button to play the animation.

    This is a 100-frame, 320 x 240 wireframe .AVI file depicting the parameters that you just established for the Plankton emitter. Notice how the plankton particles drift through the scene; in addition, the Variation setting makes some of the particles drift in chaotic paths.

2. When you've finished viewing the animation, close the Media Player.

    Now you'll create a simple texture map for these plankton particles.

3. Click on the Material Editor icon to bring up the Material Editor. The White Sand texture is loaded in Slot #1, the Noise Gradient for the ocean background in Slot #2, the Water Texture Noise material in Slot #3, the Water Caustic Noise texture for the projector Spotlight (Spot01) in Slot #4, and the WATERVL1.GIF file for the volumetric light ray spotlight (Spot02) in Slot #5. So, click on Slot #6 to activate it. You're going to alter its settings to create a new Plankton material.

4. Under Basic Parameters, click on 2-Sided and Face Map. Change both Ambient and Diffuse colors to pure white, or RGB settings 255, 255, 255. Change Shininess and Shininess Strength both to 0. Change Self-illumination to 100 percent. Open the Extended Parameters rollout to make sure that Falloff is set to Out, and change Opacity Type to Additive.

5. Open the Maps rollout and click on the Diffuse Map name button to bring up the Material/Map Browser. Under Browse From, make sure that New is selected; then, click on Bitmap. When the Bitmap parameters rollout appears, click on the Bitmap name button. From the \CHAP_25 directory of the *3D Studio MAX f/x CD-ROM*, click once on the PLANKTON.GIF image to highlight it, and then click on View. This is a 65 x 65 resolution, soft white dot that I created in Adobe Photoshop. This will form the basis for your face-mapped plankton texture. When you've finished viewing the image, close the View window. Click on OK to accept the map and return to the Material Editor.

6. Click on the Go to Parent to return to the top material level; then, drag the PLANKTON.GIF Diffuse map down to Opacity. Under Copy Map, click on OK to put a Copy rather than an Instance in the Opacity Map slot. Make sure that the Plankton emitter is still selected; then, click on the Assign Material to Selection icon to assign this material to the plankton emitter. Finally, change the name of the material to Plankton. When you've finished, close the Material Editor.

Now it's time to do a test rendering of your plankton effect, but to speed things up, you'll turn off the volumetric light rays.

7. Press the H key on your keyboard to open the Select by Name dialog box. Pick Spot02 and click on Select. Go back to the Modify Panel and, on the General Parameters rollout, click in the On check box to turn the Spot02 light off.

8. Activate the Camera01 viewport and render another test image. After a few moments, the image appears and should look like Figure 25-2.

Figure 25-2: *The Plankton effect using the Spray particle emitter.*

In this rendering, notice how using the PLANKTON.GIF as a Face Map on the small Tetrahedron particles has produced the illusion of tiny bits of debris drifting through your underwater scene.

9. When you've finished viewing the image, close your Camera01 VFB window.

## Varying the Particle Effect

You can vary this effect in your scene in several ways. You can change the size and position of the emitter, and the size, speed, and number of rendered particles in your scene. In addition, you might experiment with different textures, including the use of nonface-mapped textures and nonopacity-mapped textures for the Plankton effect.

Other things to try include adding various Space Warps to your scene to alter the particle paths. By using Space Warps such as Wind, Deflector, or Gravity, you could create the suggestion of tiny currents and eddies swirling different clumps of particles throughout the underwater landscape.

Now you'll take a look at a demonstration .AVI file of the plankton effect.

1. Select File/View File, and from the \CHAP_25 directory of the *3D Studio MAX f/x CD-ROM*, select the file WATER_6.AVI. When the Media Player appears, click on the Play button to play the animation.

    Now you can see the effect of the Spray Plankton particles drifting through the scene. The face-mapped PLANKTON.GIF image helps break up the long, thin particles into softer, more rounded particles.

2. When you've finished viewing the animation, close the Media Player.

The scene you've just created is included in the \CHAP_25 directory as WATER_6.MAX.

## Swimming in Champagne: Creating Bubbles

In the eastern Caribbean, there is an island called Dominica. Dominica is a study in contrasts; it's an island of lush green vegetation growing from rich black volcanic soil. The island boasts 365 rivers and the world's second-largest boiling lake (it boils because of volcanic activity; the largest boiling lake is in

New Zealand.) Dominica is also renowned for its excellent scuba diving. Surrounding the island's black rock beaches are several world-famous scuba sites.

One of the most unusual of Dominica's dive sites is called Champagne. This site is noteworthy for the mild geothermal activity that takes place beneath the ocean floor. When you dive at Champagne, you see, approximately 30 to 35 feet down, streams of tiny bubbles pouring out of the ocean floor from small vents. The effect occurs over an area of about 100 square feet. Scuba diving through this area is quite amazing. It's like being inside a giant aquarium, especially when you are surrounded by the colorful tropical fish.

Although you don't ordinarily see air bubbles simply erupting from the ocean floor, I'm going to use the example of the Champagne dive site off the coast of Dominica to illustrate the next underwater effect. You're going to create another Spray emitter in 3D Studio MAX, but instead of creating Plankton, you'll use it to create bubbles! By applying an Opacity-mapped bubble texture to face-mapped particles, you can create the illusion of bubbles coming from your sandy ocean floor.

The following steps show you how to create this effect.

1. You should still have your current 3D Studio MAX scene loaded; if not, then from the \CHAP_25 directory, load the file WATER_6.MAX. You'll create the Bubble emitter in this scene.

2. Enlarge the Top viewport to full screen and make sure that 2D Snap is active.

3. Create a Spray particle system beginning at approximate XYZ coordinates X -40, Y -20, and Z 0. Drag the cursor diagonally downward to the right to XYZ coordinates X 40, Y -90, and Z 0, and release.

4. In the Create Panel, make the following changes. Change the Spray01 particle emitter name to Bubbles. Under Parameters, set both Viewport Count and Render Count to 1000. Change Drop Size to 0.2 and change Speed to 0.5. Change Variation to 0.25; for the Viewport Display, click on Dots. Under Render,

click on Facing rather than Tetrahedron. You'll want to change the bubbles to the two-triangle-square Facing particles. (These tiny quad shapes will always be perpendicular to the camera viewpoint.) Under Timing, change Start to -100, change Life to 300, and make sure that Constant is checked.

5. Return to four viewports and activate the Left viewport. Rotate the Bubbles emitter 180 degrees so that the bubbles rise properly in the scene. The emitter should be pointing up, of course, on the Y axis. Now the bubbles will appear to rise from the sandy Ocean Floor object directly in front of the camera.

   So that you can see the effect of the new Bubble particles more easily, hide the Plankton emitter.

6. In any viewport, select the Plankton emitter and then use Hide Selected.

7. Select the Bubbles emitter again and click on the Modify tab of the Command Panel. You'll want to examine the Bubbles parameters, as you did with the Plankton emitter earlier.

Both the Bubbles Viewport and Render Count are 1000. You'll want fewer bubble particles in the final rendered scene. Even though the dive site off Dominica is called Champagne, you don't want to present the impression that you're scuba diving through carbonated water.

Under Render, you've changed from the default of Tetrahedron (3D) particles to Facing (or 2D) particles. Facing particles consist simply of square 2D quad shapes made up of two triangles. By applying a Diffuse and Opacity map to Facing particles, you can have the texture always present itself perpendicular to the camera view. This obviates the need for two-sided materials, naturally. (However, in a moment you'll see that you must keep in mind some special considerations when you're using transparent objects like these with linear fog.)

Again, under Timing, you see that the Start Time is set to -100; the bubbles are already present in the scene in frame 0 of the sequence. By setting the Life to 300 and the Birth Rate to Constant, you can create the impression of long-lived bubbles in the scene.

## Bubble, Bubble...

Now you'll go to the Material Editor and create a bubble material for these new particles.

1. In the Material Editor, click in Slot #6 to activate it. It should now have the Plankton texture present, so drag it to Slot #5 to make a copy of this texture. In Slot #5, highlight the name Plankton and type **Bubble 3** to change its name.

   Now you'll make the following changes to this material.

2. Because you're using Facing particles, you don't need 2-Sided or Face Map active, so click in both of their check boxes to turn off these options. Change Ambient and Diffuse to solid black, or RGB settings 0, 0, 0. Go down to Filter and change this to RGB settings 255, 255, 255, or pure white. (You'll notice that Filter is not highlighted. This is because the Opacity map that you were using for the original Plankton texture used Additive transparency rather than Subtractive or Filter.) Open the Extended Parameters rollout and change Falloff from Out to In; under Opacity Type, change this to Filter.

3. Go down to the Maps rollout and click on the Diffuse map button to go to the Bitmap Parameters Rollout. Click on the Bitmap Name button, and from the \CHAP_25 directory, click once on the BUBBLE3.TGA file to highlight it. Click on View.

   When the image appears, notice that it's a clear white bubble with sharp specular highlights. It looks something like a soap bubble, although it doesn't have the swirling colors that you saw on the forcefield in Chapter 16, "Shields Up, Captain." I rendered this image in 3D Studio MAX. First, I created a sphere, assigned a Glass texture to it, and made it Additively transparent with Opacity Falloff set to In rather than Out. At that point, I aimed a bright spotlight at the sphere and rendered it. I then loaded this image into Adobe Photoshop and cropped it to make it square. It now suffices as your Bubble Diffuse and Opacity map.

4. Close the BUBBLE3.TGA View window and then click on OK to load the BUBBLE3.TGA image as the Diffuse Map. When you return to the Bitmap Parameters rollout, open the Output

rollout and change the Output Amount from 1.0 to 2.0. This will brighten the RGB output of the BUBBLE3.TGA Diffuse map. Click on the Go to Parent icon to return to the main Material Editor rollout, and drag the BUBBLE3.TGA Diffuse map down to the Opacity map slot to copy it. When the Copy Method dialog box appears, click on Instance and then on OK.

5.  With the Bubbles particle emitter selected, click on the Assign Material to Selection icon. This assigns the new Bubble 3 material to the Particle System Bubbles.

6.  It's time to render a test image of the Camera01 viewport. After a few moments, the image appears; it should resemble Figure 25-3.

Figure 25-3: *The bubble texture applied to the particle bubbles in your 3D Studio Max underwater scene.*

## ...Toil and Trouble

Although the image shown in Figure 25-3 is striking (and the bubbles in the middle of the open water look fine), this scene has a problem. If you look closely at the rendering, you'll notice that the bubbles in the center, over the bright part of the sandy ocean floor, are dark rather than bright. You can actually see faint, dark corners of the square-facing particles from the Bubbles spray emitter. This is a rendering attribute of 3D Studio MAX's Linear Fog setting that you need to correct.

The issue lies with 3D Studio MAX's new Linear Fog algorithms, which differ from those of 3D Studio/DOS. In 3D Studio MAX, if you place Opacity-mapped or other transparent objects in Linear Fog, you may notice parts of the object that are still visible even if the opacity map applied should make them transparent.

To see this effect more clearly, you'll increase the particle size and do another test rendering.

1. Close your Camera01 VFB, if you want, and then go to the Modify Panel and change the Bubble Drop Size from 0.2 to 1.0.

2. Activate the Camera01 viewport and render another test image.
   When the image appears on your screen, the Linear Fog/transparent object problem is quite obvious. You can see the corners of the face-mapped Bubble particles quite easily over the light-colored Ocean Floor surface. (Note that changing the particle Opacity Type will not fix this rendering problem.)

3. Close the Camera01 VFB window.
   You can fix the problem by changing the Fog parameters from Linear to Exponential. This is a new Fog setting in 3D Studio MAX that enables you to render transparent objects properly in your foggy scenes. When you check Exponential, the density of the fog also increases exponentially with distance—that is, with the ranges you've set for your camera. However, because it increases the density of the fog from that of the Linear settings, you have to make corresponding changes to the camera ranges and lights in your scene to match the look of your original Linear Fog settings. (You'll do all this in a moment.)

4. To see the new Exponential Fog effect more easily, leave the current Bubble size at 1.0. (When the shot is "fixed," you can then reduce the Bubbles' size back to their original setting.) Click on Rendering/Environment to bring up the Environment dialog box. Under Atmosphere: Effects, you see Fog and Volume Light. Volume Light is not active because you turned off the volumetric light rays for your Spot02 light to speed up your rendering, so ignore this setting. Click on Fog to open up the Fog Parameters Map. Under Standard, click on the Exponential check box, and close the Environment dialog box.

5. Activate the Camera01 viewport again and render another test image. (Again, let this image render completely before you go on.)When the image appears, take a close look at the rendering.

## Making Your Bubbles Pop (Out)

Now it's time, once again, for a good news/bad news evaluation of this effect. The good news is that, by checking the Exponential Fog parameter, you've eliminated the face-mapped particle corners; the bubbles are now completely transparent.

The bad news is that, unless you change the camera ranges and lighting settings substantially, your underwater scene will remain much darker than the earlier renderings using Linear Fog. To fix this, you must adjust the camera and lighting parameters to make the scene resemble that shown in Figure 25-1. Here's how to do so.

1. Close the Camera01 Virtual Frame Buffer window and the Material Editor. You're going to change the Camera01 ranges. Activate the Left viewport and select Camera01. In the Modify Panel, note that Environment Ranges are set with the Near range at 0 and the Far range at 125. Change the latter parameter to 250.

   The Far Camera01 range now exceeds the size of the Ocean Surface Quad Patch object. Consequently, you must increase the size of this object so that its edges don't appear in the rendering.

2. Click on the Ocean Surface object; then, in the Modify Panel, go to the Parameters rollout and change Length and Width from 200 to 400. Press Enter to accept these changes. The Ocean Surface object has doubled in size.

*Note: Because you're using a procedural Noise texture on this object, increasing the size of the object does not affect the size of the Noise texture mapped to it. To change the Noise scale, you would have to alter this parameter in the Material Editor.*

Now you'll change the Omni light that is lighting the ocean surface.

3. In the Left viewport, select the Omni01 light. In the Modify Panel, change the Omni light's Multiplier to 4.0. Under Attenuation, click on Use and Show. Keep the Attenuation default settings as 80 and 320, respectively.

4. Click on the Spot01 spotlight; this is projecting the Noise water caustic pattern on the Ocean Floor. Change the Multiplier to 3.0. Under Attenuation, change the Start range from 95.0 to 110 and change the End range to 120. The Start and End range spheres expand to encompass more of the Ocean Floor object. Under Spotlight Parameters, change Hot Spot from 120 to 150. This opens the light up even further; it now overshoots the entire Ocean Floor object.

5. Because you're going to do another test rendering, keep the Bubble size at 1.0 and activate the Camera01 viewport again to render another test image. After a few moments, it appears as shown in Figure 25-4.

Figure 25-4: *The Exponential Fog settings with the revised camera ranges and light attenuation ranges has produced the proper bubble effect.*

You've now returned largely to the luminance values that you had when you used the original Linear Fog settings, and the bubbles are appearing properly over the bright Ocean Floor.

6. When you've finished viewing this rendering, close the Camera01 VFB window.

7. In any of the viewports, click on the Bubbles emitter, and in the Modify Panel, change Drop Size from 1.0 back to 0.2. This changes the bubbles back to a more appropriate size for this underwater scene. If you want, render another image of the resized exponential bubbles; it should look like Figure 25-5.

Figure 25-5: *The re-scaled Bubbles with the proper Exponential Fog settings.*

## Animated Bubbles

Earlier in this chapter, you viewed a wireframe .AVI preview to gauge the bubble movement. Now you can take a look at a full-rendered preview.

1. Select File/View File and, from the \CHAP_25 directory, select the file WATER_7E.AVI. (The E represents Exponential Fog.) Click on it to load it. When the Media Player appears, click on the Play button to play the animation.

    A realistic animated sequence of bubbles now drifts upwards in this underwater scene.

2. When you've finished viewing the rendering, take your computer out for dancing and drinks—it's earned it. (No, actually, just close the Media Player and continue; you still have one more underwater tutorial to do.)

The Plankton file you created earlier in the chapter is saved in the \CHAP_25 directory as WATER_6.MAX. The first version of the bubbles file with Linear Fog is saved as WATER_7.MAX; the revised, "fixed" version, with Exponential Fog, is saved in the \CHAP_25 directory as WATER_7E.MAX.

## Moving On

Okay, now you've created an appealing underwater environment, rife with bubbles and plankton, but there's no larger sea life in the area. Or is there? In the next chapter, you'll see how to load a hammerhead shark, and then breathe life into its gills and make it move with a Wave Space Warp. With just a few mouse clicks, you can create a fearsome pelagic predator guaranteed to chase hapless swimmers from the scene.

# 26

# Swimming With the Fishes

**Y**ou've now come to the last major tutorial chapter of this book. In this chapter, you'll build on the techniques that have been covered in the last five chapters about creating underwater scenes.

Here, you're going to load a shark model and merge the WATER_7E.MAX scene from the previous chapter to make the shark appear to swim through the scene. By applying a 3D Studio MAX Wave Space Warp to the shark, you can impart a realistic swimming motion to it. The shark model that you'll use is provided through the courtesy of Viewpoint Datalabs International of Orem, Utah. Viewpoint Datalabs is the largest distributor of datasets for 3D programs in the country. The company provides 3D models for everything from military and industrial uses to film and TV effects.

It's time to get started.

## Fishy Business

Again, you're going to load the shark first and then merge the WATER_7E.MAX file into the shark scene. This will make seeing the shark's position in relation to its surroundings easier. (I've already scaled the shark model and placed it properly in the 3D scene to make this tutorial a little easier.)

1. From the \CHAP_26 directory of your *3D Studio MAX f/x CD-ROM*, load the file SHARK_FX.MAX. The screen should look like Figure 26-1.

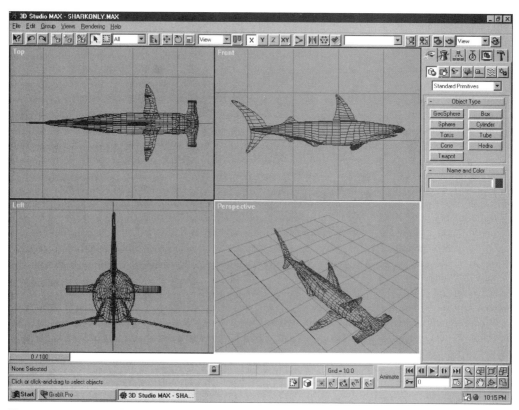

Figure 26-1: *A modified version of the Viewpoint Datalabs hammerhead shark model.*

The shark model you're looking at is a little different from Viewpoint's standard hammerhead shark model. I modified it slightly to enhance its appearance. First, I made the original's tall, thin dorsal fin shorter and more hooked; conversely, I changed the pectoral fins to make them longer and thinner. (The original, unmodified Viewpoint shark model is included in the \MESHES directory of your *3D Studio MAX f/x CD-ROM*. In addition, it's available on the World Creating Toolkit CD-ROM accompanying 3D Studio/DOS.)

Now that you've loaded the shark model, you'll merge the WATER_7E.MAX file to check the shark's placement in the underwater scene.

2. Select File/Merge, and from the \CHAP_26 directory, click on the file WATER_7E.MAX. When the Merge dialog box appears, click on All, and then OK. When you do so, the Ocean Floor, the Ocean Surface, and the particle Bubbles appear in your viewports.

3. Activate the Perspective viewport and press the C key on the keyboard to change it to the Camera01 view. As the screen indicates, the shark is positioned midway through the underwater scene and off to the left, heading from left to right.

   Because you already have the shark placed properly in the scene, hide the surrounding 3D meshes to make manipulating the actual shark model easier.

4. Using Hide by Selection, hide all the selected WATER_7E.MAX elements that you merged into the existing shark scene. (Because they are selected when merged, this is easy.)

## Er, Warp Swim & Engage!

Now you'll apply a Wave Space Warp to the shark model. This will add a basic swimming movement to the shark. After doing so, you'll adjust the shark's orientation in the scene and then animate it. When you've finished, the shark will look as if it's cruising low over the sandy ocean bottom.

1. Enlarge the Front viewport to full screen. Click on the Create Panel and select Space Warps. Under Object Type, click on Wave. The Wave rollout appears.

2. Place the cursor at approximate XYZ coordinates X -31, Y 0, and Z 13. Click and drag outward to create the initial Wave Space Warp. Watch Wave length, and drag it approximately 8.5; then, release the mouse button. Move the mouse again to set the Amplitude to approximately 1.5, and click again. This sets the initial Wave Space Warp settings.

   These are just temporary settings; you're going to alter the position of the Wave Space Warp and then change its parameters further to create the proper swimming effect that you need for the shark.

3. Under Display, leave Size at 4 but change Segments from 20 to 12. The Wave Space Warp shrinks along its Y axis. Leave Divisions set at 10.

4. Turn on Angle Snap. Rotate the Wave Space Warp on its Z axis to Z -90 degrees.

5. Move the Wave Space Warp up on the Y axis to approximately 1.65 to ensure that the Space Warp completely encompasses the Y axis of the shark from the viewport axis perspective. Return to the four viewports.

## Scale the Warp, Not the Fish

As you can see, you need to scale the Wave Space Warp along its X axis to provide the proper swimming movement for the shark. So, you'll do a Non-uniform Scale on the Wave Space Warp.

1. Select Non-uniform Scale from the Scale flyoff. (If you're unsure about the exact icon, consult the 3D Studio MAX manuals.) In the Front viewport, move the cursor over the selected Space Warp and scale the Wave Space Warp along its X axis to approximately 375 percent.

2. Move the Wave Space Warp to the left along the X axis to approximately X -2.05. When you've finished, the screen should look something like Figure 26-2.

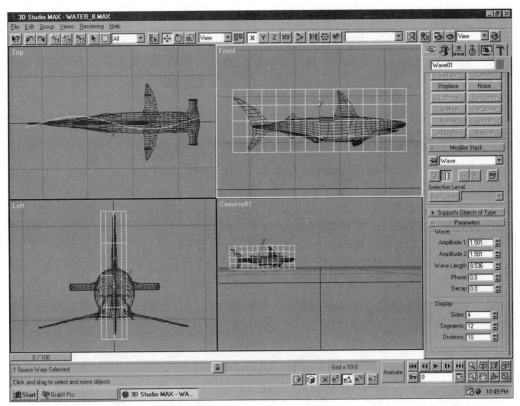

Figure 26-2: *The proper placement for the Wave Space Warp to produce the swimming movement for the hammerhead shark.*

**Note:** *Doing a Non-uniform Scale on the X axis of the Wave Space Warp smoothes out the sine wave that will create the shark swimming motion. This means that the shark will not shimmy like a small snake or a worm, but instead will be imparted with a graceful, flowing swimming motion.*

Now you'll bind the Wave Space Warp to the shark.

3. Click on the Bind to Space Warp icon. In any viewport, move the cursor down over the selected Wave Space Warp until the Bind to Space Warp cursor appears. Click and drag the cursor down over the body of the shark until you see the small Bind to

Space Warp cursor box change from blue to yellow. When it does, release the mouse button. The shark turns white briefly, the Wave Space Warp Gizmo turns yellow, and the "sine wave" effect is applied to the shark geometry, as shown in Figure 26-3.

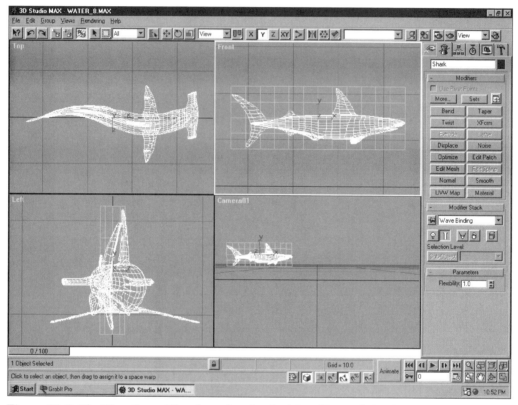

Figure 26-3: *The Wave Space Warp bound to the shark has distorted the shark's geometry to produce a sine wave swimming movement.*

4. When you've finished, click on the Select Object icon to deselect the Bind to Space Warp tool.

Now, take a closer look at the effect that the Wave Space Warp has on the shark. As you can see, the effect is not quite perfect. For instance, notice that, in the Top viewport the Wave Space Warp has distorted the ends of the hammerhead's distinctive eye stalks. This is unnatural, of course: the eye stalks of real hammerheads are relatively rigid, and the swimming movement that the Wave Space Warp provides to the shark shouldn't be carried forward to the entire shark head. For the purposes of this tutorial, however, this is adequate. (The swimming movement is subtle enough that you probably wouldn't notice aberrant movement on the shark's head unless you rendered it in a tight close-up.)

In the future, however, if you want to fine-tune this effect, you can select the shark and then apply an Edit Mesh Modifier to it. You can then select Sub-object: Vertex (or Face) and select almost all of the vertices of the shark model—with the exception of the tips of the eye stalks. Then, when you bind a Wave Space Warp to the selected vertices of the shark, you won't affect the ends of the eye stalks. You should experiment with this after you finish this tutorial; to get the proper effect, you may have to adjust the sub-object selection set several times. Again, for your purposes, this slightly unnatural effect won't show up in your final rendering.

## Positioning the Shark

Now that you've applied the Wave Space Warp to the shark, it's time to test the effect and see how the Wave Space Warp actually changes the shark's geometry as you move the shark through the scene.

1. Activate the Top viewport and press the W key to enlarge it to full screen. You want to zoom away somewhat from the shark, so press Shift +Z twice to reduce the size of the shark and Wave Space Warp in the scene. Click on the Pan button and drag the Top viewport to the left until the hammerhead shark is on the far left of the screen. Right-click to get out of Pan mode; then, click on the shark to select it.

2. Make sure that the Restrict to X button is active so that you'll be moving the shark only along its X axis. Before you move the shark, click on Edit/Hold to freeze the current configuration. Move the Select and Move cursor back down to the shark and drag it to the right side of the screen slowly. As you do so, you'll see that the Wave Space Warp imparts a sinuous swimming movement to the shark.

3. After you play with this effect, either click on the Undo button to return the shark to the original position or Fetch the previous configuration. Either returns the shark to its original position.

Now, before you place the shark in position for the final test rendering, take a look at the shark's material.

4. Bring up the Material Editor. Slot #1 should be active, so click on the Get Material button, and when the Material/Map Browser appears, click on Scene. At the top of the list of materials, you should see a Multi/Sub-Object with Shark Noise underneath. Double-click on Shark Noise to load it into Slot #1. Shark Noise is simply a mottled gray, Noise-generated material.

5. Open the Maps rollout and click on the Diffuse map button. The Noise rollout contains a Fractal Noise texture, Size 25, of slate gray and lighter gray. This is the basic shark material. The only other material on the shark is a Black Plastic material, used for the shark's eyes. When you've finished looking at this material, close the Material Editor.

Now you need to adjust the shark's position in the underwater scene and then animate it to produce the final effect of a shark swimming over the ocean floor.

6. Drag a bounding box around the entire hammerhead shark and Wave Space Warp to select both objects. Unhide all of the WATER_7E.MAX scene elements. To make things easier to see, press the Shift+Z key to zoom out in the Top viewport. You can now see the shark in the top view just to the left of center of the Ocean Floor object.

To test the swimming effect, you want to make the shark swim from left to right, diagonally toward the camera.

7. Press the spacebar to lock the selection to the shark and Space Warp, and rotate both of them on the Z axis to -45 degrees.

## Making It Swim

Now it's time to set up the actual shark swimming animation.

1. Press the H key on the keyboard or click on the Select by Name icon. When the Select Object dialog box appears, notice that both the shark model and the Wave01 Space Warp are selected. Deselect the Wave01 Space Warp and click on Select.

2. Click on the Animate button at the bottom of the screen and move to frame 100.

   To make moving the shark forward (albeit diagonally) easier, you must change the XYZ axis orientation.

3. Click on the Down arrow in the Transformation Coordinate System pop-up. View (the default) should be active; select Local instead. As you do, you see the XYZ axis tripod orientation on the shark change to its own coordinate system so that the shark's nose points along the Y vector. Click on Restrict to Y; then, move the cursor over the shark and click and drag the shark along its Y axis diagonally downward to approximate XYZ coordinates Z 0, Y 105, and Z 0. Release the mouse button.

4. When you've moved the shark into proper position, click on the Animate button again to toggle animation mode off. Drag the Time Slider slowly back from frame 100 to frame 0. As you do so, you'll see the shark moving backwards (of course); however, the swimming motion on it is apparent in this Top view. (Because you are dealing with so many elements in the scene, the movement may be somewhat slow, depending on the video card and the CPU speed of your PC.)

5. Press the W key on the keyboard to return to four viewports and activate the Camera01 viewport.

   To see this effect of the swimming shark, you can render a 320 x 240 preview. However, I've already rendered a wireframe version of this scene so that you can take a look at it now.

6. Select File/View File, and from the \CHAP_26 directory, select the file PREVIEW1.AVI. When the Media Player appears, click on the Play button.

A wireframe animation of the hammerhead shark swimming through the scene plays. (It looks somewhat busy because you have both the plankton and bubble particles drifting through the scene.)

## Making It Swim More Slowly

Notice in the preview that the shark seems to be swimming rather quickly. This is because you set up only a 100-frame animation sequence and you're playing this sequence back at 30 frames per second. If you want to retain the parameters that you've established, you can simply scale the overall time. This will slow down the movement of all the elements in the scene, including the shark. You'll do this in a minute.

1. First, close the Media Player; then, click on the Time Configuration icon (under the Go To End icon) at the bottom of the screen. In the Time Configuration menu, under Animation, click on Rescale Time. In the Rescale Time dialog box, change the length from 100 to 200, and click on OK. This doubles the number of frames in the sequence.

   In addition, the new frame 100 now marks the halfway point of the sequence (of course).

   Before doing a test rendering, you need to change some of the lighting parameters so that the shark isn't improperly lit.

2. Click on the Select by Name icon or press the H key on the keyboard. When the Select Object's dialog box appears, click on the Omni01 light and then on Select. Click on the Modify tab of the Command panel. Because you set this light originally to affect just the Ocean Surface object, and that was before you added the shark to the scene, you now need to exclude the shark from the light's effects as well. Otherwise, it will create undesirable illumination on the hammerhead.

3. Under General Parameters, click on the Exclude button. When the Exclude/Include dialog box appears, click on Shark and then on the Right arrow to add the shark model to the list of Excluded objects. Click on OK.

4. Activate the Camera01 viewport. But before you render a test image, you'll set a couple of additional parameters. When you merged the WATER_7E.MAX file, the Fog parameter wasn't merged, so you'll need to reset fog for this scene.

5. Select Rendering/Environment. When the Environment Dialog box appears, under Atmosphere/Effects click on Add; then, under Add Atmospheric effect, click on Fog. When Fog appears, make sure that it's highlighted and then go down to the Fog parameters section. Under Environment Color map, click on Assign. When the Material/Map Browser appears, click on New and then on Gradient. Under Environment Color Map, you'll see that Map #1 should be Gradient. Click on this name button, and when the Put to Material Editor dialog box appears, click on OK to place this material in Slot #1. Under Standard Parameters, click on Exponential. (Remember the bubble effect in the last chapter.)

6. For an added bonus, go back up to the Atmosphere section and, under Effects, click on Add again. Under Add Atmospheric Effect, click on Volume Light and click on OK. You want to recreate the Volumetric light effects from Chapter 24, "Light Rays, Not Stingrays," so under Volume Light Parameters: Light, click on Pick Light. Click on the Select by Name icon and, under Pick Object, click on Spot02 and click on Pick or press Enter. This will assign the Volume Light effect to the Spot02 light.

7. Under Fog Color, click on the Color swatch and make sure that this is set to pure white, or RGB settings 255, 255, 255. Close the Color Selector. When you've finished, close the Environment dialog box.

8. Bring up the Select Objects dialog box and select Spot02. In the Modifier panel, on the General Parameters rollout, turn this light back on. The Multiplier should be set to 5.0; if you scroll the rollout up, note that this is still a projector spotlight, with the WATERVL.GIF image loaded.

9. Activate the Camera01 viewport. Make sure that the time slider is at frame 100; then, press Alt+R and Enter to render a test image. After a few minutes, the image appears and should look like Figure 26-4.

Figure 26-4: *The underwater scene with the hammerhead shark, volumetric lighting, and particle systems.*

In this scene, particle systems create plankton and bubbles, a projector spotlight creates the effect of water caustic patterns, and a projector volumetric spotlight creates the effect of light rays coming from the ocean surface.

10. When you've finished looking at the rendering, close the Camera01 VFB window.

## Making it Swim—in Color!

Now you'll take a look at a 320 x 240 .AVI file of this animation. This represents the culmination of all the techniques that you have covered in five chapters of Section IV, "Underwater Effects."

1. Select File/View File, and from the \CHAP_26 directory, click on the file WATER_8.AVI. When the Media Player appears, click on Play.

   The shark now swims more slowly through the scene, and you see the various parameters such as the animated volumetric light rays, the animated Noise texture for the water surface, particle systems bubbles and plankton, and the water caustics on the ocean floor. In addition, notice how the Wave Space Warp creates a realistic swimming movement for the hammerhead shark.

2. When you've finished viewing the animation, close the Media Player.

The file you've just created, with all the proper parameters, is saved in the \CHAP_26 directory of the *3D Studio MAX f/x CD-ROM* as WATER_8.MAX.

## Moving On

Now you've finished the individual effects tutorials for this book. In the next chapter, you'll take a look at a nifty bathysphere model that serves as the centerpiece of the underwater effects you've just covered. (The model is the Diving Bell from the old 1960s TV series, "Voyage to the Bottom of the Sea.") You'll take a brief look at the various effects techniques present in the scene. When you've finished with that chapter, you should be able to create your own underwater scenes and populate them with all manner of spirits from the vasty deep.

# 27

# The Diving Bell & Wrapping It Up

**A**s I mentioned in the introduction to this book, when I was a kid, I enjoyed watching science fiction TV shows in the mid-1960s such as the original "Star Trek." However, my favorite show at that time was Irwin Allen's "Voyage to the Bottom of the Sea." I was thrilled by the design of the sleek, glass-nosed Seaview and the other vehicles presented on the show, such as the Flying Sub, the Minisub, and the Diving Bell.

To this day I'm a fan of the series (at least for the nostalgic memories it invokes), and I still enjoy watching occasional episodes. (About every five years or so, I buy a box of Cap'n Crunch cereal, pour a bowl, and watch a bunch of the first season black-and-white "Voyage" episodes, just to time-travel back 30 years to my childhood. My wife has learned to put up with it.) Regardless of the show's hokey episodes and rubber-suited monsters, "Voyage" and the other sci-fi and fantasy shows of the 1960s sparked my interest in other realities—both underwater and in distant space. That interest continues today, and indeed is one of the motivating factors behind my writing a book on space and underwater special effects.

At any rate, I'm still enamored enough of the vehicle designs from "Voyage" that I'm using one—the Seaview's Diving Bell—to cap off the underwater effects that have been covered in the last five chapters. During the four-year run of "Voyage" (1964-1968), the crew of the Seaview would sometimes deploy a diving bell—a small bathysphere about eight feet in diameter—from the aft belly of the Seaview. The Diving Bell (also known as Apple 1 in some episodes) enabled its crew to explore deep ocean crevasses. It also allowed the crew to arouse the ire of giant monsters, including a huge sperm whale that swallowed the Diving Bell whole in the show's memorable second-season premiere, "Jonah and the Whale."

Today, the Diving Bell exists mainly in "Voyage" reruns on cable TV's Sci-Fi Channel. 20th Century Fox Studios auctioned off the full-size fiberglass Diving Bell prop in 1974, and its design is in the public domain. Since then, the Diving Bell has gone through several private collections and has now surfaced (pardon the pun) on the roof of the Aquatech Scuba Diving shop in San Diego, California. (No joke; you can drive right by on Interstate 5 and see it sitting there.)

However, the Diving Bell has been given another lease on life as a 3D Studio MAX model. To serve as a focal point for the underwater effects you've just created, I've constructed a duplicate of "Apple 1" from reproductions of the original 20th Century Fox blueprints, and I have included the Diving Bell on the *3D Studio MAX f/x CD-ROM*. You'll find it in the \DIVEBELL and \MESHES directories as DIVEBELL.MAX and DIVEBELL.3DS, respectively. In the scene, the Diving Bell sits on a sandy ocean floor in shallow ocean water (the Caribbean, possibly) and is witness to the lone Viewpoint hammerhead shark, cruising in search of a meal.

So, take a look at the last underwater demonstration scene and the revival of "Apple 1." It just goes to show that you can't keep a good Diving Bell down (or should that be up?).

## Previewing the Diving Bell Scene

Now you'll take a look at the Diving Bell scene, and then some demonstration .AVI files.

1. From the \CHAP_27 directory of your *3D Studio MAX f/x CD-ROM*, load the file WATER_DB.MAX. The file loads and you see a rather complex 3D Studio MAX scene. The Diving Bell model sits on a heavily tessellated (and then optimized) Ocean Floor Quad Patch surface, as shown in Figures 27-1 and 27-2.

Figure 27-1: *Frame 265 of the WATER_DB.MAX scene. (Note that the Grid and Lights are hidden in this figure.)*

Figure 27-2: *The rendered version of frame 265. Note the volumetric light beams coming from the Diving Bell's floodlights.*

Now, take a look at a wireframe preview and then a full rendered version of this sequence.

2. Select File/View File, and from the \CHAP_27 directory of the *3D Studio MAX f/x CD-ROM*, select and play the file PREVIEW1.AVI.

3. When you finish viewing the preview, load and play the WATER_DB.AVI scene. Both animations are 300 frames long.

In WATER_DB.AVI, you're in blue-green water, looking up at the underside of the ocean surface. A steel cable stretches to the surface, with faint bubbles rising alongside it. (Because the Seaview isn't visible in this scene, you assume that the Diving Bell has been lowered from the crane of a surface vessel off-camera.)

As the camera tilts down to the ocean floor, you see the source of the bubbles: the carbon dioxide vent of the "Apple 1" Diving Bell sitting on the sandy bottom. Its floodlights are active, revealing tiny bits of plankton drifting by on the current. And, as you tilt down, you see the Viewpoint hammerhead shark swim by the Bell, whose crew members are safe inside its thick steel walls. (Trivia note: The "NIMR" on the side of the Bell stands for Nelson Institute of Marine Research, named for Admiral Harriman Nelson—Richard Basehart's character in "Voyage.")

## The Penultimate Subhead

This Diving Bell shot illustrates the half-dozen 3D Studio MAX underwater effects that you've just covered in the last five chapters. Environmental Fog creates underwater haze and murk. Shininess, Reflection, and Bump mapping create the ocean surface. 3D Studio MAX's Spray particle systems produce the plankton and bubbles; volumetric and projector lights produce the Diving Bell's spotlight beams and water caustic patterns. Finally, as you saw in the last chapter, a Wave Space Warp produces the swimming shark movement.

You may notice a few more things about this scene. First, unlike the last few underwater examples, I've replaced the projector spotlight that creates the water caustics on the ocean floor and the Diving Bell with a Directional light. If you're lighting large scenes (whether under water or above it) and you want to simulate parallel light, then a Directional light is more realistic than a spot. You could get away with it in the previous chapters because of the limited range of the camera, and because the camera didn't move in the scene.

One thing you may also have noticed in the full rendered .AVI file: In lieu of the volumetric light rays coming from the ocean surface, I've placed volumetric spotlights inside the floodlights on the sides of the Diving Bell. (The circular 2D faces making up the self-illuminated floodlights have had their Shadow Casting and Shadow Receiving Properties toggled off.)

In addition, although the Diving Bell is designed for crushing depths, it appears to be joyriding here; it's sitting in a mere 25-30 feet of water. (Perhaps the Nelson Institute now makes more money taking tourists down to sightsee in the Caribbean, instead of descending into the Marianas Trench to photograph seven-gilled sharks.)

Finally, note that this complex Diving Bell model is Grouped; if you Open or Explode the Group, you'll see virtually all of the model's components as separate pieces, which you can modify or remap as you wish. Separate versions of this model (without the underwater surroundings) are included on your *3D Studio MAX f/x* CD-ROM in the \DIVEBELL and \MESHES directories.

When you've finished viewing the animation, close the Media Player and then go on to create your own original effects in 3D Studio MAX.

## Moving On . . . for the Last Time

As I mentioned in the introduction, when I sat down at my computer to begin work on the various effects for this book, my wife Joan commented on how much I enjoy what *isn't* rather than what *is*. (That comment was more apt in light of the fact that I wrote most of this book while beta-testing 3D Studio MAX, with no final documentation until several months later. It's also funny because Joan is an author in her own right, and creates inspirational products born from her considerable talent and imagination.)

Some people might interpret her comments to mean that many artists seem to enjoy the world of the imagination more than the so-called "real" world. However, I think that most creative people—and perhaps computer graphics artists in particular—don't really make a major distinction between these two "worlds." Your imagination—the worlds it creates, the visions it makes into reality—is as tangible and as much a "real" part of you as the color of your eyes and the sound of your voice. The landscape of your imagination is a part of your "real" world, too.

In that sense, computer graphics artists have it perhaps more easy than other artists. Painters can capture real-world or imaginary scenes on canvas, and photographers and filmmakers can capture moving simulations of reality, but with a computer and the right software, you can have the best of both worlds. You can capture the stylized reality of painting with the kinetic movement of filmmaking—and you can do it on your own. You don't need teams of programmers, art critics, or a committee of bean counters to help you envision, create, and visit computer-generated realities. Ultimately, I hope that this book and the examples contained here have stimulated your creativity, and that you'll go off to not just duplicate the effects contained here, but to improve on them.

Now, I have one final story.

Although I worked on this book for more than six months, in one sense I've been working on it for about 30 years. When I was a kid in first grade (1966-1967), I used to flip over my classroom assignment paper and, using Crayolas, draw cartoon spaceships exploding and the Seaview firing torpedoes at giant monsters.

It amuses my wife to no end that, 30 years later, I'm still doing that—and what's most hilarious is that I get paid for it, as well.

The only difference is that now, rather than crayons, I use a computer.

# Part V

# Appendices

# About the Companion CD-ROM

The CD-ROM included with your copy of *3D Studio MAX f/x* contains valuable software programs and example files from the appropriate chapters.

## To view the CD-ROM

Windows NT: Double-click on the LAUNCHME.EXE file from your Windows Explorer or File Manager. You'll see a menu screen offering several choices. See "Navigating the CD-ROM" below for your option choices.

## Navigating the CD-ROM

Your choices for navigating the CD-ROM appear on the opening screen. You can quit the CD, browse the Hot Picks, or learn more about Ventana.

## Using the Programs on the CD-ROM

You can access the material on the CD-ROM directly through Windows Explorer (Windows NT).

## Technical Support

Technical support is available for installation-related problems only. The technical support office is open from 8:00 A.M. to 6:00 P.M. Monday through Friday and can be reached via the following methods:

Phone: (919) 544-9404 extension 81

Faxback Answer System: (919) 544-9404 extension 85

E-mail: help@vmedia.com

FAX: (919) 544-9472

World Wide Web: http://www.vmedia.com/support

America Online: keyword Ventana

## Limits of Liability & Disclaimer of Warranty

The author and publisher of this book have used their best efforts in preparing the CD-ROM and the programs contained in it. These efforts include the development, research, and testing of the theories and programs to determine their effectiveness. The author and publisher make no warranty of any kind expressed or implied, with regard to these programs or the documentation contained in this book. The author and publisher shall not be liable in the event of incidental or consequential damages in connection with, or arising out of, the furnishing, performance, or use of the programs, associated instructions, and/or claims of productivity gains. Some of the software on this CD-ROM is shareware; there may be additional charges (owed to the software authors/makers) incurred for their registration and continued use. See individual program's README or VREADME.TXT files for more information.

# Combustion: A Free Plug-in for 3D Studio MAX

*Copyright © 1996 Rolf Berteig*

*(Author's note: Rolf Berteig is one of the developers of 3D Studio MAX and has graciously offered permission to include this plug-in on the 3D Studio MAX f/x CD-ROM. This plug-in, as well as other freeware 3D Studio MAX plug-ins, is available on the Kinetix WWW site and on the Kinetix Forum on CompuServe. Note that the source code for Combustion is included in the \COMBUSTN directory of this book's CD-ROM.)*

*Combustion is an atmospheric plug-in for 3D Studio MAX that produces animated fire, smoke, and explosion effects using the Environment/Atmosphere plug-in interface. Ergo, no geometry is required to produce these effects (making them virtually RAM-free) and they render much more quickly than a particle system effect would.*

## Installing Combustion

Use the following steps to install Combustion for use with 3D Studio MAX:

1. Go to the \COMBUSTN directory of your *3D Studio MAX f/x CD-ROM* and copy the COMBUST.ZIP file into your 3DSMAX\STDPLUGS subdirectory (or any other plug-in subdirectory in which 3D Studio MAX is looking for plug-ins at load-in time). Using PKWare's PKUNZIP program, unzip the COMBUST.ZIP file in your \STDPLUGS subdirectory.

2. Copy the .AVI files 4EXPLODE.AVI, CAMPFIRE.AVI, FOGYLAKE.AVI, and MAXBURN.AVI to your 3DSMAX\IMAGES subdirectory.

3. Copy the files 4EXPLODE.MAX, FOGYLAKE.MAX, MAXBURN.MAX, and CAMPFIRE.MAX to your 3DSMAX\SCENES subdirectory.

(Note that Combustion's original name was Inferno, but I changed it to eliminate confusion with Digimation's LenZFX Inferno plug-in. So, you may see some occasional references to Inferno in this context, but it's really referencing Combustion.)

## The Demonstration Files

Here's a description of the .AVI files created from the .MAX files of the same names.

※ CAMPFIRE.AVI (from CAMPFIRE.MAX) shows a campfire in the desert at night.

※ EXPLODE.AVI (from EXPLODE.MAX) shows a simple explosion using a few instances of the Combustion flame effect.

※ FOGYLAKE.AVI (from FOGYLAKE.MAX) shows how you can make very cool, localized 3D fog. You can use this routine in place of 3D Studio MAX's Environmental Layered Fog option, since Combustion is a full 3D localized effect.

※ MAXBURN.AVI (from MAXBURN.MAX) shows more flames burning under the word "MAX."

## The Combustion Effect

A Combustion effect consists of two parts in a 3D Studio MAX scene:

1. A Combustion apparatus lets you position and size the effect in the scene relative to other objects.
2. An atmospheric effect added in the Rendering\Environment dialog controls most of the effect's parameters.

To create a fire or explosion effect, you must first create a Combustion Apparatus in the scene. The Combustion Apparatus object is found in the Helpers section under Atmospheric Apparatus. The size and position of the apparatus lets you place the location of the effect in the scene.

Next, you must add a Combustion atmospheric effect to the list of effects in the Environment dialog. Finally, use the Pick Object button to bind the Combustion effect to the apparatus.

## Combustion Apparatus Object Parameters

Below are the parameters for the Combustion Apparatus; you can adjust these as necessary for your scene.

### Radius

This parameter specifies the radius of the apparatus. This defines the extent of the fire effect.

### Hemisphere

When this parameter is turned on, the apparatus becomes a hemisphere rather than a sphere. This is useful when you're trying to simulate a flame (or other directed) effect.

### Seed

This parameter is a seed to the random number generator. When multiple apparatuses are present in the scene, each one should be given a different seed value so that the effects will be different for each apparatus even if they have the same parameter values.

### New Seed

Selecting this button will randomly generate a new seed value.

## Combustion Atmospheric Effect Parameters

Again, here are the Atmospheric Effect parameters; adjust these as necessary to create the effect you need.

### Pick Object

Selecting this button places 3D Studio MAX in a pick mode. You may then select a Combustion Apparatus object in the scene with the mouse, or use the H key to bring up the Hit/Select by Name dialog. After an apparatus is picked, it will be added to the drop-down list of Combustion Apparatuses that are currently bound to the Combustion atmospheric effect.

A Combustion Apparatus does not produce any effect until it is bound to one or more Combustion atmospheric effects. A single Combustion atmospheric effect can be applied to more than one Combustion Apparatus, and multiple Combustion effects can be added to the environment.

### Remove Object

This command removes the Combustion Apparatus that is currently selected in the drop-down list from the list.

### Colors

Two colors define the color of the fire effect and an optional third color defines the color of the smoke that follows the fire in an explosion.

- *Inner Color:* The color of the fire at its densest part. This could be considered the hottest part of the fire.

- *Outer Color:* The color of the fire at its sparsest part. This would be the cooler part of the fire. The fire is then shaded using a gradient made from the inner and outer colors. Denser parts of the flame use a color closer to the inner color and the outer edges of the flame use a color closer to the outer color.

* *Smoke Color:* If the explosion and smoke options are turned *on*, then the inner and outer colors will animate to the smoke color during the final phase of the explosion. If explosion is off, this has no effect.

## Flame Type

There are two types of flames from which to choose:

* *Tendril:* This is more of a traditional campfire flame look. The flames are pointed at the ends and have veins along their centers.

* *Fire Ball:* Flames are more puffy and round, as if they were balls of fire. This works well for explosions.

## Stretch

This parameter scales the flame effect along the Z axis of the Combustion Apparatus. Stretch values that are greater than 1 make the flame longer and skinnier pointing in the direction of the Z axis. Values that are less than 1 compress the flames along the Z axis. A stretch value of 1 has no effect. Stretch can be very helpful when you're trying to simulate fire effects. You can achieve good results by setting the Flame Type to Tendril and setting Stretch to around 2-3. You can also produce a similar effect by nonuniform scaling the Combustion Apparatus.

Unlike using the Stretch parameter, scaling the Apparatus will also scale the boundaries of the effect. The Stretch parameter does not make the size of the effect larger, but instead scales the flames within the volume. If you scale the apparatus into an egg shape, you can use the stretch parameter (with a value less than 1) to counter scale the flames. This way, the flames will have the same overall appearance, but the volume that is filled with the effect will be an egg shape rather than a sphere.

## Regularity

The regularity parameter affects the overall shape of the fire. When Regularity is set to 1, the overall shape of the fire will resemble the shape of the Combustion Apparatus. Therefore, it will be a perfect sphere or hemisphere, depending on the Combustion Apparatus settings. The fire effect will still taper off toward the edges of the sphere but it will be easy to identify the spherical shape. When regularity is 0, the overall shape will not be spherical but instead very irregular. The actual shape will depend on other settings such as Flame Type and Flame Size. The irregular shape is constructed by trimming out chunks from the original regular shape; therefore, the actual effect may appear smaller than the apparatus appears in the viewports.

## Flame Size

This parameter specifies the size of the individual flames or tendrils. This will not affect the overall size of the effect but instead affect the characteristic appearance of the fire. A value of 35 seems to work well for explosion effects. When attempting to simulate fire, smaller values such as 18-20 seem to be better.

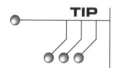

**TIP** *The size depends on the scale of the scene.* If you are working on a larger scale, then you will need to use larger flame sizes. Also, if the flame size is considerably small, you may need to increase the number of Samples to capture the detail; otherwise, you may get aliasing artifacts.

## Flame Detail

This parameter specifies the amount of detail within the individual flames. If this parameter is low, then the flames will be smooth with little detail. Larger values will provide more detail, and, of course, slower rendering times. A value of 3 (the default) is pretty good most of the time. If you are using a larger value for the Flame Size and the flames appear too smooth, increasing flame detail may help. If you use values larger than around 3 or 4 for Flame Detail, you may need to increase the number of Samples in order to capture the extra detail.

## Density

This parameter specifies the density or overall strength of the effect. Smaller values for density will make the fire effect more transparent and less noticeable. Larger values make the fire brighter and more opaque. This parameter depends on the overall scale of the scene. If you are working on a larger scale, and therefore the Combustion Apparatus is larger, then the effect will appear brighter and more opaque unless you lower the density.

If the Explosion parameter is turned on, then the actual density used for the effect is automatically animated. The actual density used will be 0 before and after the explosion and will vary during the explosion. When Phase is 100, the density used will peak reaching the density specified by this parameter.

## Samples

This parameter specifies the rate at which the volume is sampled. Higher values give more precision and generally produce better results, but at the expense of slower rendering times. The default value of 15 works pretty well most of the time. The following are some cases when you may want to increase the number of samples:

1. If the Flame Size parameter is relatively small.

2. If the Flame Detail parameter is greater than 3 or 4.

3. If a flat surface of an object is inside the effect's volume (to avoid banding).

4. Any time that you see a banding effect, increasing the number of samples will probably help.

## Phase

The fire effect is animated by animating the Phase parameter. As the Phase value changes, the fire changes in appearance. The faster the Phase value changes, the faster the animation of the fire. In effect, the Phase parameter acts as an ease curve for the fire effect.

When Explosion is turned on, the Phase parameter also controls the timing of the explosion. An explosion has three phases through which it goes:

| Phase Value | Description |
|---|---|
| 0-100 | The explosion starts at 0 and peaks in intensity at 100. |
| 100-200 | The explosion burns off and the fire turns into smoke. |
| 200-300 | The smoke dissipates. The explosion is completed at 300. |

So, to animate an explosion, the Phase value should be set to 0 when the explosion is supposed to start, and 300 when it is supposed to end. The shape of the curve in between controls the timing of the explosion. Typically, the curve should be steep at first and then round off so that it is nearly flat as the value approaches 300. The following is an example of a typical explosion Phase curve:

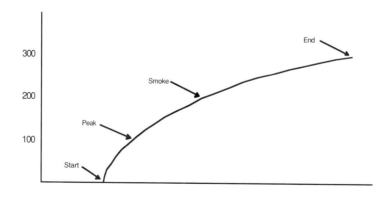

This shape of curve causes the explosion to peak quickly and then slow down as it turns to smoke and dissipates. The Setup Explosion button will bring up a dialog that will automate setting up a Phase curve with these characteristics so that you don't have to go into the Track View and set it up by hand.

When Explosion is not turned on (the default), the Phase parameter will just control the rate at which the fire effect "churns." The numbers that you would use would typically be about the same, although you would probably want to use a straight line rather than a curve. Animating Phase to go from 0 to 300 over a 100-frame animation seems to be about right for a typical fire effect.

## Drift

This parameter causes the flames to move in the direction of the apparatus's local Z axis. Essentially, this parameter represents an offset along the Z axis. So, if you animate it to go from 0 to 100, then the fire effect will appear to drift 100 units over the animation. Note that the bounds of the effect will not move; instead, the flames will drift inside the effect. When you're trying to simulate fire, animating this parameter is essential to make the flames appear to rise.

## Explosion

When this parameter is turned on, several parameters are automatically animated based on Phase to simulate an explosion effect. The size, density, and colors are animated as the Phase parameter changes from 0 to 300. When this parameter is turned off, the Phase parameter just animates the amount that the flames churn over time.

## Smoke

When this parameter is turned on, the flame colors will turn to the smoke color as the Phase parameter goes from 100 to 200. If this parameter is not turned on, then the flame colors will remain the same over the duration of the explosion.

## Setup Explosion

This button brings up a dialog that will automate the task of setting up a typical explosion curve. There are two spinner controls in the dialog that allow you to specify a start and end time for the explosion. After you OK this dialog, the existing Phase curve will be discarded and a new phase curve will be created that represents an explosion over the specified interval.

## Fury

When Explosion is turned on, the Phase parameter controls the timing of the entire explosion in addition to the churning effect of the flame. This parameter allows you to control the rate at which the flames churn independent of the explosion itself. So, if you want the fire to burn more furiously, set this parameter to something greater than 1 (perhaps 2 or 3); if you want it to churn slower, set it to something less than 1.

## A Note About Transparent Objects Inside the Effect

When 100 percent transparent objects go into the Combustion effect, they will still appear slightly opaque. This is because the integration function required to do an exponential falloff curve would require huge sample rates (which would slow the effect way down) and that's not in the scope of this version of this plug-in at this time. If you use particle system effects to augment these volume effects, use 3D particles rather than 2D opacity-mapped particles.

# 3D Studio MAX Resources

**T**he following 3D Studio MAX Resources information was provided courtesy of the Kinetix World Wide Web site (http://www.ktx.com) and the 3D Artist MAX WWW site (http://www.3dartist.com).

Kinetix is the new multimedia division of Autodesk, Inc. and is responsible for marketing 3D Studio MAX, the 3D Studio MAX VRML Plug-in, and several other multimedia packages.

*3D Artist* magazine, published in Santa Fe, New Mexico, is an excellent resource for the latest tips and tricks on a variety of 3D programs, including 3D Studio/DOS and 3D Studio MAX. In addition, *3D Artist* presents a weekly online "newsletter" called The Tessellation Times (http://tgax.com/tess/) which is offered to *3D Artist* subscribers. The Tessellation Times offers late-breaking news and commentary on the state of the 3D graphics industry. (For more information, see the *3D Artist* listing under "Magazines" later in this appendix.)

In addition, *3D Artist* magazine offers The MAX Page, a WWW site devoted to MAX resources news (http://www.3dartist.com/3dah/max/themaxpg.htm).

Every effort has been made to ensure that the information is accurate; however, at press time, final product prices and even final product names may have been undecided. For the most up-to-date information, please contact the respective companies directly. Neither the author nor Ventana can be responsible for errors in the content.

For more information on 3D Studio MAX resources, check out the Ventana Online Updates for *3D Studio MAX f/x* at http://www.vmedia.com/updates.html.

*Key:* Vx *stands for voice;* Fx *stands for fax;* E *stands for email;* B *stands for bulletin board system.*

## 3D Datasets

### Acuris
931 Hamilton Ave.
Menlo Park, CA 94025
Gen: Vx 415/833-4990
http://www.acuris.com

### Syndesis Corp.
235 S. Main St.
Jefferson, WI 53549
http://www.webmaster.com/syndesis/
Gen: Vx 414/674-5200 Fx 414/674-6363 E: syndesis@inc.net

### Viewpoint DataLabs International
625 S. State St.
Orem, UT 84058
Gen: Vx 801/229-3000 Fx 801/229-3300
Inq: Vx 800/328-2738
1-800-DATASET
http://www.viewpoint.com

## 3D Studio MAX Plug-ins & Other Software

### 4DPAINT

4DPAINT brings high-end 3D paint *functionality* to the PC in a fully interactive 3D environment. 4DPAINT invites you into a virtual paint world with natural media painting tools. 4DPAINT is a real-time modular brush and paint system with unlimited, uniquely individual painting effects.

*Available May 1996 from 4DVISION LLC at $1,495 U.S. list.*

### Sculptor NT

Sculptor NT brings full trimmable 3D NURBS modeling to 3D Studio MAX. Open and closed smoothed surfaces may be instantly created and deformed intuitively and interactively. Sculptor creates objects that can be modified by moving control points to achieve shape changes on coarse or fine detail levels. Multiple Sculptor objects may be joined to form composite objects, and objects can be deformed or stretched and retain their smooth, flexible joints.

*Available August 1996 from 4DVISION LLC at $495 U.S. list.*

### MetaREYES Metaballs NT

MetaREYES creates complex surfaces using a technique called Metaballs. Metaballs creates objects with an organic look. Animating Metaballs allows users to quickly create lifelike characters, animals, or liquids.

*Available August 1996 from 4DVISION LLC at $595 U.S. list.*

### Puppeteer NT

Puppeteer NT combines smooth skin deformation, real-time motion capture, constraints-based motion editing, and the ability to load predefined motion files. The face tracking and skeletal skin modules allow for vertex level mesh animation based upon captured motion data or the movement of underlying skeletal mesh objects. The system's real-time motion capture capability provides a direct interface with Flock of Birds motion-capture hardware from Ascension Technology Corp. Motion data files for most motion-capture systems are supported directly, including Ascension, Motion Analysis, Adaptive Optics, Viewpoint, SuperFluo, Polhemus, Biovision, and other popular formats.

*Available September 1996 from 4DVISION LLC at $795.00 U.S. list.*
4DVISION LLC
formerly Schreiber Multimedia, Inc. & Schreiber Instruments, Inc.
4800 Happy Canyon Rd. #250
Denver, CO 80237
ftp.4dvision.com - http://www.4dvision.com/
Gen: Vx 303/759-1024 Fx 303/759-0928 B: 303/759-3598
E: corp@4dvision.com
Inq: Vx 800/252-1024

### RayMax

The first raytracer for 3D Studio MAX! The Plug-in is fully integrated into 3D Studio MAX, does selective raytracing (objects for raytracing are selectable), and has a programmable shader (Material, Texture, Shadow, Volume, Light, Lens, Output). In addition, it supports multi-threading and distributed network rendering. Planned for the future: hardware-supported raytracing from ART.

*Available August 1996.*
ABSOLUTE Software GmbH
Dammtorstr. 34 B, 20354
Hamburg, Germany.
Contact: Ruediger Hoefert, 100136,1105@compuserve.com

### GAMUT-SGm

For Sega Saturn developers, this professional file conversion and preview application simplifies Saturn game development using 3D Studio MAX. GAMUT-SGm converts geometry, materials, textures, and bitmaps to standard file formats, with automatic quad generation. An interactive preview function displays converted objects on the Saturn.

*Available July 1996 from Animetix Technologies, Inc. at $995 U.S. list.*

### GAMUT-PSm

For Sony PlayStation developers, this professional file-conversion application simplifies PlayStation development using 3D Studio MAX. GAMUT-PSm converts geometry, materials, textures, and bitmaps to standard file formats, with optional quad generation. GAMUT-PSm also exports and imports standard PlayStation file formats.

*Available July 1996 from Animetix Technologies, Inc. at $995 U.S. list.*

### GAMUT-DXm

For Windows 95 game developers, this professional file-conversion and preview application simplifies game development for Windows 95 titles. GAMUT-DXm converts geometry, materials, textures, bitmaps, and animation to Microsoft's Direct3D format. An interactive preview mode shows converted objects with animation.

*Available August 1996 from Animetix Technologies, Inc. at a price to be announced.*

Animetix Technologies, Inc.
1745 W. 12th Ave., Vancouver, BC V6J 2E5
http://www.animetix.com/

### BauMAX

BauMAX is an interactive prototyping tool for Architecture. In the old days, users doing architectural renderings would create 95 percent of their construction in AutoCAD and AutoCAD applications and then export these drawings to 3D Studio MAX via .DXF or .3DS. This resulted in a bunch of problems that took a long time to correct (such as flipping normals manually). BauMAX changes your way of working. The user models complex architectural models inside 3D Studio MAX and visualizes these extremely fast! BauMAX provides architecture specific commands and tool sets. The user builds models including all parameters such as Textures and material. Walls, windows, and doors are inserted based on a parametric database.

*Available July 1996.*

Contact: Cebas Computer, Edwin Braun, +49-6221-760038, http://www.cebas.com

### 3D/AV Digital Production Suite

3D/AV synchronizes 3D graphics with full-motion video and audio to provide nonlinear movie play, animation recording, digital compositing, and real-time AV capture and record within

3D Studio MAX. Running on Truevision's Targa 1000/2000 cards, 3D/AV integrates render previews, video texture maps, motion tests, and true video display in NTSC and PAL.

*Available May 1 from Diaquest at $795 U.S. list.*

### 3D/Digital Disk

3D/Digital Disk provides direct access via Ethernet or SCSI connection to Accom, Abekas, and Sierra Design Labs recorders. DDR functions are remotely controlled from 3D studio MAX and image sequences are automatically color converted and transferred for video capture and recording. The VTR Auto-Edit option provides editing between the DDR and RS-422 VTRs.

*Available May 1996 from Diaquest at $795 U.S. list.*

DiaQuest
1440 San Pablo Ave.
Berkeley, CA 94702
http://www.diaquest.com/
Gen: Vx 510/526-7167 Fx 510/526-7073
Sales: sales@diaquest.com

### Sand Blaster

Sand Blaster, a next-generation particle system, allows 3D Studio MAX artists to use any object as a particle. Animators can explode an object into particles and reassemble the particles into another object. Sand Blaster features vortex, swarm, and collision detection space warps for intelligent particle motion.

*Available July 15, 1996 from Digimation; $495.*

### Fractal Flow

Fractal Flow is an image-processing plug-in application that uses fractal technology to distort images or specific parts of an image. 3D Studio MAX users can simulate cloaking space ships, rain drops, fire, water, smoke, and more. Each effect can be animated over time using the Track Editor.

*Available July 15, 1996 from Digimation; $395.*

### Image Master

This essential utility for 3D Studio MAX allows artists to instantly view thumbnail pictures of images created or used inside the application. Features include the ability to easily view, move, delete, and resize groups of images at once. Users can also convert between any 3D Studio MAX file format.

*Available July 15, 1996, from Digimation; $95.*

### Bones Pro MAX

Based on the award-winning product for 3D Studio, Bones Pro provides skeletal deformation with an easy and straightforward approach. This plug-in allows artists to animate any mesh object with 3D MAX Studio bones, and comes with a Blend plug-in to smooth joints between connected objects.

*Available July 15, 1996 from Digimation; $495.*

### LenZFX MAX

This award-winning special-effects software includes Glow, Hilight, Depth of Field Blur, and Lens Flare. Each module features total user control and animatable options. Lens Flare features a unique and powerful lens flare construction kit.

*Available July 15, 1996 from Digimation; $495.*

Digimation
1000-L Riverbend Blvd.
St. Rose, LA 70087
800/854-4496
Quarterly Catalog
Contact: David Avgikos, 504/468-7898; davida@digimation.com;
http://www.digimation.com

### SPRN.DLL

SPRN.DLL is a system printer driver for 3D Studio MAX. It allows you to render directly to a Windows configured printer driver. It's possible to determine resolution of the output and runs integrated as a 3D Studio MAX Plug-in. Price is $49.

Contact: netnice GbR, Horst Brueckner, +49-9195-946612, CIS 100015.1534@compuserve.com

### CyberMesh: The Mesh Modeling Tool for Photoshop

CyberMesh is a plug-in module for Adobe Photoshop that allows you to save grayscale images as 3D models in .DXF or ElectricImage FACT formats. Cybermesh lets you use the full

arsenal of Photoshop's painting and image processing tools to generate and modify 3D models.
Knoll Software
P.O. Box 6887
San Rafael, CA 94903
Gen: Vx 415/453-2471; fx 415/499-9322

### PRIMATTE S-100 for 3D Studio MAX

This high-quality chromakey and image composting package offers blue (or any color) screen removal to any size image supported by 3D Studio MAX.

*Available May 15, 1996 from P.E. Photron at $400 U.S. list.*
Photron, Ltd. - P.E. Photron (U.S. office)
4030 Moorpark Ave. #108
San Jose, CA 95117
http://www.photron.com/
Gen: Vx 408/261-3613 Fx 408/261-3628 E: tak@photron.com
Tech: E: sgross@photron.com

### Moritz

Moritz is a toolbox for technical visualisation, steel construction, and piping. With only a few keystrokes, you build up a tube construction with bends, flanges, and fittings, or simply choose a steel beam from a Database, determine the length parameter, and put it into 3D Studio MAX. You can generate steel profiles such as T-beams or U-beams either by choosing them from a standards library or determining the parameters in the menu. Building up a tube construction is done by creating only the central axis; Moritz generates pipe bends and pipe skin. Generate flanges or reductions either by choosing them from a library or determining the parameters in the menu. Price: $250 + shipping costs.

*Available September 1996.*
Contact: Schneider & Partner, Rolf Peter Gansel, +49-203-26155, CIS 100121.3336@compuserve.com

### MaxParticles II/All-Purpose-Emitter

These particle systems provide trails, shaped bursts, fountains, explosions, streams, bubbles, sparks, and fireworks. The application supports multiple particle types, multiple mapping options, secondary motion inheritence configuration, burst shaping, and emission bias control. It also provides simple vapor and smoke plumes.

*Available April 1996 from Sisyphus Software and from Independent Kinetix and Graphics Software Dealers at a recommended price of $70.*

### MaxTrax

MaxTrax provides procedural and permanent object trails. Useful for skid marks, jet trails, boat wakes, footprints, painting, hand-writing, animated map development, banners, and tire tracks, the software supports multiple mapping options, trail fade, and scale inheritance. It provides for the ability to switch between procedural trails and permanent trails for completely unique effects.

*Available May 1996 from Sisyphus Software and from Independent Kinetix and Graphics Software Dealers at a recommended price of $70.*

### Max'Plode (MaxParticles III)

This plug-in generates explode geometry and shape-filling, all-purpose-emitter routines. Max'Plode provides an intelligent fragmentation engine with the configurable vector controls of Sisyphus All-Purpose-Emitter to fragment geometry by faces, clumps, and smoothing. Provides arbitrary particle distribution and stable particle replacement systems. Provides 'blowaway,' explode, and disintegrate effects. Blast centers are configurable, and it provides volume-filling bubbles.

*Available June-July 1996 from Sisyphus Software and from Independent Kinetix and Graphics Software Dealers at a recommended price of $75.*

### MaxParticles I

This software provides specialized particle effects: fast bursts, halos, and planar fields. It approximates running water, rapids, planar force fields, cylindrical fields, jumpgates, black holes, and whirlpools.

*Available July-August 1996 from Sisyphus Software and from Independent Kinetix and Graphics Software Dealers at a recommended price of $70.*

### MaxSolids

MaxSolids provides extended primitives for use in the 3D Studio MAX create/geometry mode, including parameterized filleted cubes, prisms, spindles, tanks, filleted n-gonal extrusions, channels, and standard extrusions.

*Available August-September 1996 from Sisyphus Software and from Independent Kinetix and Graphics Software Dealers at a recommended price of $50.*
Sisyphus Software
6402 Stable Dr., Leon Valley, TX 78240
http://www.sisyphus.com/
Gen: Vx 210/543-0665 E: CIS 74461,157

## Character Studio

Two 3D Studio MAX plug-in components (Biped and Physique) provide revolutionary character animation abilities. Biped realistically animates any two-legged creature using a unique footstep-driven and physically based approach. Physique gives precise muscle bulging control over continuously surfaced models.

*Available from Kinetix. (Development by Unreal Pictures.)*
Kinetix (formerly Autodesk Multimedia)
111 McInnis Pkwy.
San Rafael, CA 94903
http://www.ktx.com/
Gen: Vx 415/507-5000 Fx 415/491-8311
Inq: Vx 800/879-4233
Educ: Vx 415/507-6415

## Interchange for Windows v 3.5—with 3D Studio MAX plug-in

File conversion for more than 40 formats including support for LightWave LWO and LWS, Alias polysets, BRender, RenderMorphics, and Wavefront, as well as DEM and STL. Also exports RenderWare, RIB, and POV-Ray 2 files. The new 3D Studio MAX plug-in allows importing and exporting from within 3D Studio MAX .
U.S. list price $495, inquire for upgrade pricing.
Syndesis Corp.
235 S. Main St.
Jefferson, WI 53549
http://www.webmaster.com/syndesis/
Gen: Vx 414/674-5200 Fx 414/674-6363 E: syndesis@inc.net

## Books

### 3D Studio MAX Design Guide
The Coriolis Group, 1996
Anthonly Potts, David H. Friedel, Jr., Anthony Stock
ISBN 1-883577-83-7
$39.99 (includes CD-ROM, 16 color pages)
The Coriolis Group
http://www.coriolis.com
7339 E. Acoma Drive, Suite 7
Scottsdale, AZ 85260
602/483-0193

### 3D Studio Hollywood & Gaming Effects
New Riders Publishing, 1996
To order from publisher: 800/428-5331
$50.00 (for 3D Studio/DOS; includes CD-ROM)
ISBN 1-56205-430-9

### 3D Studio IPAS Plug-In
Tim Forcade
New Riders Publishing, 1995
$55.00 (for 3D Studio/DOS; includes CD-ROM)
ISBN 1-56205-431-7

### 3D Studio Special Effects
New Riders Publishing, 1994
$50.00 (for 3D Studio/DOS; includes CD-ROM)
ISBN 1-56205-303-5

### Inside 3D Studio Max
New Riders Publishing, 1996
Steven Elliott & Phillip Miller
ISBN 1-56205-427-9
$60 (includes CD-ROM)
New Riders Publishing
http://www.mcp.com/newriders
Macmillan
201 W. 103rd St.
Indianapolis, IN 46291
Sales: Vx 800/428-5331, 317/581-3500 Fx 317/581-3535

## CD-ROMS & Textures

### Pyromania and Pyromania II
This collection of pyrotechnic effects is invaluable for 3D artists who want to simulate science-fiction-style effects. The effects, digitized from 35mm motion picture film, range from zero-gravity explosions to smoke and flame.
VCE Inc.
13300 Ralston Ave
Sylmar, CA 91342-7608
800/242-9627

### Xeno-1
A collection of unusual "alien" textures perfectly suited for games and multimedia development.
Positron Publishing
1915 N. 121st St. #D
Omaha, NE 68154
Gen: Vx 402/493-6280 Fx 402/493-6254 E: positron@radiks.net CIS 73131,2027
Sales: Vx 800/365-1002

## Heidi™ Graphics Hardware Accelerators

### 3Dfx Interactive, Inc.
For availability and pricing, contact 3Dfx Interactive, Inc.
Contact: Alma Ribbs, 415/919-2405; almar@3dfx.com;
http://www.3dfx.com

### 3Dlabs
For availability and pricing, contact 3Dlabs, Inc.
3Dlabs
2010 N. 1st St. #403, San Jose, CA 95131
Gen: Vx 408/436-3455
Contact: Neil Trevett, 408/436-3456; neil.trevett@3dlabs.com;
http://www.3dlabs.com

### AccelGraphics

AccelR8 and AccelPRO family available now. For further information and pricing, contact AccelGraphics.
AccelGraphics
1942 Zanker Rd.
San Jose, CA 95112
General: Vx 408/441-1556 Fx 408/441-1599
Contact: Greg Milliken, 408/467-5021; greg_milliken@ag3d.com

### Diamond Multimedia

FireGL available now. For further information and pricing, contact Diamond Multimedia.
Diamond Multimedia Systems, Inc.
2880 Junction Ave.
San Jose, CA 95134
http://www.diamondmm.com/
Gen: Vx 408/325-7000 Fx 408/325-7070
Inq: Vx 800/468-5846 E: info@diamondmm.com
Contact: Ed Huang, 408/325-7930; edh@diamondmm.com

### Dynamic Pictures, Inc.

For availability and pricing, contact Dynamic Pictures, Inc.
Contact: Dinesh Sharma, 408/327-9004; sharma@dypic.com

### ELSA

Gloria Series available now. For further information and pricing, contact ELSA.
ELSA, Inc.
2150 Trade Zone Blvd. #101, San Jose, CA 95131
http://www.elsa.com/
Gen: Vx 408/935-0350 Fx 408/935-0370 B: 408/935-0380
Inq: Vx 800/272-3572
Contact: Joy Li, 408/935-0350; sales@elsa.com;
http://www.elsa.com

### Fujitsu Microelectronics, Inc.

Sapphire Designer available now. For further information and pricing, contact Fujitsu Microelectronics, Inc.
Fujitsu Microelectronics, Inc.

San Jose, CA
800/558-2494; 408/922-9149
Contact: Hiten Patel, 408/922-9770; hpatel@fmi.fujitsu.com;
http://www.fmi.fujitsu.com

### Intergraph Computer Systems Division

TDZ workstations available now. Call 800/763-0242 for Intergraph
authorized resellers.
Intergraph Corp.
Huntsville, AL 35894
http://www.intergraph.com/ics
Gen: Vx 205/730-5441
Inq: Vx 800/763-0242
Contact: Aggie Frizzell, 205/730-6139; alfrizze@ingr.com;
http://www.intergraph.com/ics

### Matrox Graphics Inc.

MGA Millennium available now. Heidi drivers for 3D Studio
MAX will be available in the third quarter 1996. For further infor-
mation and pricing, contact Matrox Graphics Inc.
Matrox Graphics Inc.
1055 Saint-Regis
Dorval, Canada, PQ H9P 2T4
Gen: Vx 514/685-2630
Contact: Caroline Debie, 514/969-6300 x2606;
Caroline.Debie@matrox.com; http://www.matrox.com/mga

### Omnicomp

3Demon Series available now. For further information and pricing,
contact Omnicomp.
Omnicomp, Inc.
Houston, TX
800/995-6664; 713/464-2990
Contact: Kelly D. Stuart, 713/464-2990;
omnicmp@phoenix.phoenix.net;
http://www.phoenix.net/~omnicmp

### Rendition Inc.

For availability and pricing, contact Rendition, Inc.
Contact: Tami Bhaumik, 415/335-5900 x177; tami@rendition.com;
http://www.rendition.com

### Symmetric

GLyder available now. For further information and pricing, contact Symmetric.
Symmetric Simulation Systems, Inc.
http://www.symmetric.com/
Gen: Vx 214/931-5999 Fx 214/931-7028
Contact: Perry Copus, 214/931-5999; pcopus@symmetric.com;
http://www.symmetric.com

# Hardware

### SpaceArm 3D Digitizer SpaceSculpt Interface

Designed for 3D Studio MAX, this driver allows the modeler to create true 3D datasets from a sculpted model in record time. Artists can digitize points or splines and create simple or complex models in a matter of minutes. By enabling the automatic surface generator, models come to life.
*Available May 1996 from FARO Technologies, Inc. Call for pricing.*
FARO Technologies, Inc.
125 Technology Park, Lake Mary, FL 32746
Gen: Vx 407/333-9911 Fx 407/333-4181
Inq: Vx 800/736-0234
Contact: Jon Houston, 800/736-0234; houstonj@faro.com

### SpaceWare AniMotion

SpaceWare AniMotion is a plug-in and SpaceController (3D control device) bundle that gives animators real-time, 3D motion control of objects, cameras, and light sources. Automatic animation recording captures the motion as it happens and the dynamic camera gives animators simultaneous, hand-held control of subject, path, and field of view for impressive 3D animation.
*Available June 24 from Spacetec IMC at $495 U.S. list.*
Contact: Stas Mylek, 508/970-0330 ext. 123; stas@spacetec.com;
http://www.spacetec.com

### TARGA 1000 Pro & 3D/AV Digital Production Suite

This is a digital video suite within 3D Studio MAX. Features include synchronization of 3D graphics and animation with AV movies, real-time compositing and effects using the TARGA 1000, design and preview of fast-rendered 3D graphics, and audio/video capture and record with remote control of VTR inside 3D Studio MAX.

*Available April 29, 1996 from Truevision and Diaquest at $3,495 through Dec. 3, 1996.*
Truevison
2500 Walsh Ave., Santa Clara, CA 95051
Gen: Vx 408/562-4200 Fx 408/562-4065
Tech: E: support@truevision.com
Contact: Truevision, 408/562-4200 or 800/522-TRUE; info@truevision.com; http://www.truevision.com

## Magazines

### 3D Artist
Columbine, Inc.
P.O. Box 4787, Santa Fe, New Mexico 87502
505/982-3532
$5.00
Bi-monthly

### 3D Design
Miller Freeman Inc.
600 Harrison St., San Francisco, CA 94107
415/905-2200
$3.95, subscriptions: $29.95/year
Monthly

### Advanced Imaging
PTN Publishing Co.
445 Broad Hollow Road,
Melville, NY 11747-4722
516/845-2700
No charge to qualified professionals
All others, $60/year
Monthly

### Digital Imaging
Micro Publishing Press, Inc.
2340 Plaza del Amo, Suite 100
Torrance, CA 90501
310/212-5802
Free to qualified professionals
All others $24.95/year
Bi-monthly

### Digital Video Magazine
IDG Company
600 Townsend St., Suite 170 East,
San Francisco, CA 94103
800/998-0806
$4.95 subscription: $29.97/year
Monthly

### New Media
Hyper Media Communications
901 Mariner's Island Blvd., Suite 365
San Mateo, CA 94404
415/573-5170
Free to new media pro's, $4.95 for others,
and subscription $52/year
Monthly

### Wired Magazine
Wired Ventures Ltd
PO Box 191826, San Francisco, CA 94119-9866
415/222-6200
$4.95, $39.95 subscription for 12 issues
Monthly

## Miscellaneous

### Astronomical Slides and Photos
The Finley Holiday Film Corporation markets astronomical slides
from NASA. Contact the company for permission to use their
NASA material in your own 3D renderings.

Space & Science Products
12607 E. Philadelphia St., P.O. Box 619
Whittier, CA 90601
800/345-6707

## Online Sites (World Wide Web)

| | |
|---|---|
| http://www.coherentlight.com | Coherent Light |
| http://www.gsfc.nasa.gov/NASA_homepage.html | NASA Information Services |
| http://www.ktx.com | Kinetix |
| http://www.rhythm.com | Rhythm & Hues Studios |
| http://www.adobe.com | Adobe Systems Inc. Home Page |
| http://www.disney.com | Walt Disney Pictures |
| http://www.rhythm.com/~goodman | John Goodman site (Rhythm & Hues) |
| http://www.viewpoint.com | Viewpoint DataLabs |
| http://www.viewpoint.com/avalon/ | Viewpoint Datalabs: Avalon PD 3D site |
| http://www.bio-vision.com | BioVision (motion capture data) |
| http://www.digitaldirectory.com/animation.html | The Digital Directory |
| http://www.rga.com | R/GA Digital Studios |
| http://www.cgw.com | Computer Graphics World |
| http://www.baraboo.com/3dcafe/ | 3D CAFE (3D Mesh Model Geometry and Graphical Imaging) |
| http://www.3dscanners.com | 3D Scanners |
| http://cedar.cic.net/~rtilmann/mm/ | Mesh Mart Home page |

| | |
|---|---|
| http://arachnid.cs.cf.ac.uk/ Ray.Tracing | The Ray Tracing Home Page |
| http://www.dataspace.com/ WWW/vlib/comp-graphics.html | The World-Wide Web Virtual Library: Computer Graphics and Visualization |
| http://siggraph.org/ | ACM SIGGRAPH Online! |
| http://www.cs.unc.edu/graphics/ | Graphics groups, The University of North Carolina-Chapel Hill Computer Science Department |
| http://www.bergen.gov/AAST/ ComputerAnimation/ CompAn_TopPage.html | Computer Graphics and Animation Home Page |
| http://cruciform.cid.com/ ~werdna/sttng | Star Trek: The Next Generation |
| http://www.ugcs.caltech.edu/ st-tng/ | Star Trek: The Next Generation |
| http://www.linder.com/ newmedia.html | Pacific Interactive Media presents New Media Pioneers [Muybridge] |
| http://www.amazon.com | Amazon.com Books! Earth's Biggest Bookstore |
| http://www.nsf.gov/ | National Science Foundation World Wide Web Server |
| http://www.3dsite.com | 3DSite |
| http://www.cinesite.com | CineWebSite:Animation |
| http://www.cartoon-factory.com/ wb_bc.html | Animation Art by Bob Clampett |

## Online Sites (Newsgroups)

**The Kinetix Forum** on the CompuServe Information Service (type GO KINETIX at any CompuServe prompt) comp.graphics.packages.3dstudio.

# Special Effects, Animation & Film-making Resources

**T**he following books, magazines, and World Wide Web sites may be useful to 3D graphics artists, animators, and filmmakers.

## Books

Arijon, Daniel, ***The Grammar of the Film Language***
Reprint Edition
Paperback
$24.95
Samuel French Trade, 1991
ISBN: 187950507X

Culhane, Shamus, ***Animation: From Script to Screen***
Reprint Edition
Paperback
$14.95
St. Martin's Press, 1990
ISBN: 0312050526
*An Ex-Disney animator describes the animation process.*

Halas, John, **Contemporary Animator**
Hardcover
$54.95
Focal Press, 1991
ISBN: 0240512804

Hoffer, Thomas W., **Animation, a Reference Guide**
Hardcover
$59.95
Greenwood Publications Group, 1982
ISBN: 0313210950

Muybridge, Eadweard, **The Human Figure in Motion**
Hardcover
$24.95
Dover Publications, 1989
ISBN: 0486202046

Muybridge, Eadweard, **Animals in Motion**
Hardcover
$29.95
Dover Publications, 1957
ISBN: 0486202038
*The Muybridge books have long been considered indispensable reference works for artists and animators studying motion. Muybridge's photographic motion studies, done in the late 1880's, are still invaluable today.*

Russet, Robert and Starr, Cecile, **Experimental Animation: Origins of a New Art**
Reprint Edition
Hardcover
$14.95
Da Capo Press, 1988
ISBN: 0306803143

Straczynski, J. Michael, **The Complete Book of Scriptwriting**
Revised
Hardcover
$19.99
Writer's Digest Books, 1996
ISBN: 0898795125
*J. Michael Stracynski is also the Executive Producer of the syndicated science fiction series, "Babylon 5," which relies almost exclusively on computer-generated imagery for its special effects.*

Thomas, Frank and Johnston, Ollie, **The Illusion of Life : Disney Animation**
Revised
Hardcover
$60.00
Hyperion, 1995
ISBN: 0786860707
*Many people regard this as the definitive work on classical animation; computer animators should also study it.*

## Magazines

### American Cinematographer
ASC Holding Corporation
1782 N. Orange Dr., Hollywood, CA 90028
800-448-0145
$5.00 Subscription: $35/year, Monthly
American Cinematographer *often has articles on special visual effects for both film and TV.*

### Animation
30101 Agoura Court, Suite 110
Agoura Hills, CA 91301
818-991-2884
$4.95, subscribe: $45/year, Monthly

### Animerica
Viz Communications, Inc.
PO Box 77010, San Francisco, CA 94107
415-546-7073
$4.95, subscription: $58/year, Monthly

### Cinefantastique
7240 W. Roosevelt Rd., Forest Park, IL 60130
708-366-5566
$5.95, subscription: $48/year, Monthly
*This science-fiction magazine occasionally features in-depth coverage of special visual effects.*

### Cinefex
Box 20027, Riverside, CA 92516
$8.50, subscription: $26.00 four issues, Quarterly

*The definitive resource for the special visual effects aficionado. Should be required reading for anyone interested in the visual effects field; includes numerous articles on computer graphics.*

### Cinescape
Cinescape Group, Inc.
1920 Highland Ave, Suite 222
Lombard, IL 60148
708-268-2498
$4.99, $29.95/year, Monthly

### Sci-Fi Universe
L.F.P. Inc
8484 Wilshire Blvd., Suite 900
Beverly Hills, CA 90211
800-217-9306
Cover price $4.99, $29.95 for year, 9 times a year

### Starlog
Starlog Group
475 Park Avenue South
New York, NY 10016
800-877-5549
$4.99
Subscription Rate: $39.97 for 1 year, Monthly
Starlog *magazine runs periodic articles on special visual effects in science fiction and fantasy TV shows and films.*

## Online Sites (World Wide Web)

| | |
|---|---|
| http://www.vmedia.com | Ventana Communications; check for online updates to this book |
| http://www.ktx.com | Kinetix |
| http://www.rhythm.com | Rhythm & Hues Studios |
| http://www.disney.com | Walt Disney Pictures |
| http://www.viewpoint.com | Viewpoint DataLabs |
| http://www.viewpoint.com/avalon/ | Viewpoint Datalabs: Avalon PD 3D site |
| http://www.bio-vision.com | BioVision (motion capture data) |
| http://www.digitaldirectory.com/animation.html | The Digital Directory |
| http://www.rga.com | R/GA Digital Studios |
| http://www.baraboo.com/3dcafe/ | 3D CAFE (3D Mesh Model Geometry and Graphical Imaging) |
| http://www.bergen.gov/AAST/ComputerAnimation/CompAn_TopPage.html | Computer Graphics and Animation Home Page |
| http://www.linder.com/newmedia.html | Pacific Interactive Media presents New Media Pioneers [Muybridge] |
| http://www.amazon.com | Amazon.com Books! Earth's Biggest Bookstore |
| http://www.cinesite.com | CineWebSite:Animation |
| http://www.cartoon-factory.com/wb_bc.html | Animation Art by Bob Clampett |

# Index

# Don't Miss Your Connection!

## Are you sure you have the latest software?
## Want to stay up-to-date but don't know how?

Ventana Online helps Net surfers link up to the latest Internet innovations and keep up with popular Internet tools.

- **Save money by ordering electronically** from our complete, annotated online library.

- **Explore Ventana's *Online Companions*™**—regularly updated "cybersupplements" to our books, offering hyperlinked listings and current versions of related free software, shareware and other resources.

- **Visit the hottest sites on the Web!** Ventana's "Nifty Site of the Week" features the newest, most interesting and most innovative online resources.

*So check in often to Ventana Online. We're just a URL away!*
## http://www.vmedia.com

# Power Publishing on the Web!

## Walking the World Wide Web, Second Edition

*$39.95, 800 pages, illustrated, part #: 298-4*

More than 30% new, this book now features 500 listings and an extensive index of servers, expanded and arranged by subject. This groundbreaking bestseller includes a CD-ROM enhanced with Ventana's exclusive PerpetuWAVE technology; updated online components that make it the richest resource available for Web travelers; Netscape Navigator; and a hypertext version of the book.

## The 10 Secrets for Web Success

*$19.95, 384 pages, illustrated, part #: 370-0*

Create a winning Web site—by discovering what the visionaries behind some of the hottest sites on the Web know instinctively. Meet the people behind Yahoo, IUMA, Word and more, and learn the 10 key principles that set their sites apart from the masses. Discover a whole new way of thinking that will inspire and enhance your own efforts as a Web publisher.

## The Windows NT Web Server Book

*$49.95, 680 pages, illustrated, part #: 342-5*

A complete toolkit for providing services on the Internet using the Windows NT operating system. This how-to guide includes adding the necessary World Wide Web server software, comparison of the major Windows NT server packages for the Web, becoming a global product provider and more! The CD-ROM features Alibaba™ Lite (a fully licensed Web server), support programs, scripts, forms, utilities and demos.

### Java Programming for the Internet

*$49.95, 800 pages, illustrated, part #: 355-7*

Create dynamic, interactive Internet applications with Java Programming for the Internet. Expand the scope of your online development with this comprehensive, step-by-step guide to creating Java applets. Includes four real-world, start-to-finish tutorials. The CD-ROM has all the programs, samples and applets from the book, plus shareware. Continual updates on Ventana's *Online Companion* will keep this information on the cutting edge.

### Official Netscape JavaScript Book

*$29.99, 400 pages, illustrated, part #: 465-0*

Add life to Web pages—animated logos, text-in-motion sequences, live updating and calculations—quickly and easily. Sample code and step-by-step instructions show how to put JavaScript to real-world, practical use.

### The Comprehensive Guide to VBScript

*$34.99, 408 pages, illustrated, part #: 470-7*

The only encyclopedic reference to VBScript and HTML commands and features. Complete with practical examples for plugging directly into programs. The companion CD-ROM features a hypertext version of the book, along with shareware, templates, utilities and more.

Books marked with this logo include a free Internet *Online Companion*™, featuring archives of free utilities plus a software archive and links to other Internet resources.

# Web Pages Enhanced

## Shockwave!

*$49.95, 400 pages, illustrated, part #: 441-3*

Breathe new life into your Web pages with Macromedia Shockwave. Ventana's *Shockwave!* teaches you how to enliven and animate your Web sites with online movies. Beginning with step-by-step exercises and examples, and ending with in-depth excursions into the use of Shockwave Lingo extensions, *Shockwave!* is a must-buy for both novices and experienced Director developers. Plus, tap into current Macromedia resources on the Internet with Ventana's *Online Companion*. The companion CD-ROM includes the Shockwave player plug-in, sample Director movies and tutorials, and much more!

## VRML Power Publishing With Caligari Pioneer Pro

*$49.95, 600 pages, illustrated, part #: 450-2*

Exploit the powers of the de facto interactive standard! Construct powerful virtual environments with this professional reference for programming, viewing and integrating 3D worlds into Web pages. The companion CD-ROM features sample worlds, clip objects for VRML, shareware and more.

## Exploring Moving Worlds

*$24.99, 288 pages, illustrated, part #: 467-7*

Moving Worlds—a newly accepted standard that uses Java and JavaScript for animating objects in three dimensions—is billed as the next-generation implementation of VRML. *Exploring Moving Worlds* includes an overview of the Moving Worlds standard, detailed specifications on design and architecture, and software examples to help advanced Web developers create live content, animation and full motion on the Web.

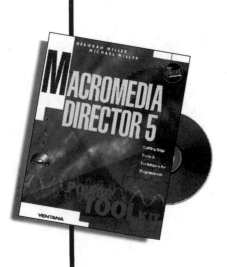

### Macromedia Director 5 Power Toolkit

*$49.95, 552 pages, illustrated, part #: 289-5*

*Macromedia Director 5 Power Toolkit* views the industry's hottest multimedia authoring environment from the inside out. Features tools, tips and professional tricks for producing power-packed projects for CD-ROM and Internet distribution. Dozens of exercises detail the principles behind successful multimedia presentations and the steps to achieve professional results. The companion CD-ROM includes utilities, sample presentations, animations, scripts and files.

### The Comprehensive Guide to Lingo

*$49.99, 700 pages, illustrated, part #: 463-4*

Master the Lingo of Macromedia Director's scripting language for adding interactivity to presentations. Covers beginning scripts to advanced techniques, including creating movies for the Web and problem solving. The companion CD-ROM features demo movies of all scripts in the book, plus numerous examples, a searchable database of problems and solutions, and much more!

Books marked with this logo include a free Internet *Online Companion*™, featuring archives of free utilities plus a software archive and links to other Internet resources.

# TO ORDER ANY VENTANA TITLE, COMPLETE THIS ORDER FORM AND MAIL OR FAX IT TO US, WITH PAYMENT, FOR QUICK SHIPMENT.

| TITLE | PART # | QTY | PRICE | TOTAL |
|-------|--------|-----|-------|-------|
|       |        |     |       |       |
|       |        |     |       |       |
|       |        |     |       |       |
|       |        |     |       |       |
|       |        |     |       |       |
|       |        |     |       |       |
|       |        |     |       |       |

## SHIPPING

For all standard orders, please ADD $4.50/first book, $1.35/each additional.
For "two-day air," ADD $8.25/first book, $2.25/each additional.
For orders to Canada, ADD $6.50/book.
For orders sent C.O.D., ADD $4.50 to your shipping rate.
North Carolina residents must ADD 6% sales tax.
International orders require additional shipping charges.

SUBTOTAL = $ _____

SHIPPING = $ _____

TOTAL = $ _____

**Or, save 15%–order online.
http://www.vmedia.com**

Name _____

E-mail _____ Daytime phone _____

Company _____

Address (No PO Box) _____

City_____ State_____ Zip_____

Payment enclosed ___VISA ___MC ___ Acc't # _____ Exp. date_____

Signature _____ Exact name on card _____

**Mail to: Ventana • PO Box 13964 • Research Triangle Park, NC 27709-3964  ☎ 800/743-5369 • Fax 919/544-9472**

Check your local bookstore or software retailer for these and other bestselling titles, or call toll free:

# 800/743-5369